THE STORY OF
MY LIFE

THE STORY OF MY LIFE

By

CLARENCE DARROW

New introduction by
ALAN M. DERSHOWITZ

DA CAPO PRESS

Library of Congress Cataloging in Publication Data
Darrow, Clarence, 1857–1938.
   The story of my life / by Clarence Darrow: new introd. by
Alan M. Dershowitz.
      p.   cm.
   Originally published: New York: 1932.
   ISBN 0-306-80738-6
   1. Darrow, Clarence, 1857–1938. 2. Lawyers—United States—
Biography. I. Dershowitz, Alan M.
KF373.D35A3   1996
340'.092—dc20
[B]   96-17195
                                                       CIP

First Da Capo Press edition 1996

This Da Capo Press paperback edition of *The Story of My Life*
is an unabridged republication of the edition first published in
New York in 1932, here supplemented with a new introduction
by Alan M. Dershowitz. It is reprinted by arrangement with the
Estate of Clarence Darrow.

Published by Da Capo Press, Inc.
A Member of the Perseus Books Group

INTRODUCTION

THE name of Clarence Darrow will always be associated
in the public mind with great advocacy on behalf of the
downtrodden, the unpopular, and the controversial. This
indeed was an important part of the public life of America's most celebrated 20th-century lawyer, but it was not
the only part. Darrow also represented the powerful, the
privileged, and the popular. He was a lawyer for all seasons
and a man who fully lived the passions of his time.

It is said that in England great criminal defense lawyers
are knighted, while in the United States they are indicted.
Darrow was twice indicted—for jury tampering in the infamous *Los Angeles Times* terrorism case. Although he was
acquitted on the first charge and had a hung jury on the
second, there is now persuasive evidence that he may, in
fact, have been guilty. In a recent account of the Darrow
jury-bribery case, Geoffrey Cowan puts the issue in its contemporary context:

> With considerable justification, and a bit of para-
> noia, Darrow felt that the judicial system was rigged
> against his clients. The prosecutors controlled the
> police and the grand jury, and they were backed by
> Burns' detectives, by the Erector's Association's
> money and by a generally hostile press led by a
> *Times* that was bent on revenge. His clients had
> been illegally kidnapped, dragged across state lines
> and forced to face criminal charges. Their friends
> were harassed, their witnesses intimidated. The
> judge was a member of the most elite club in the

v

city, and no one would be allowed on the jury who
did not own property and who was not acceptable
to the prosecution. The jurors all knew that they
would be rewarded for voting to convict the
McNamaras and punished if they voted for an acquittal. . . . The forces of capital bribed jurors too,
but the approach was a bit more subtle.

Cowan concludes that, in light of these realities and of
Darrow's strong belief in the cause of labor, "Darrow may
actually have believed that, under some circumstances, bribery was the right course, the moral course of action." Un-
derstandably, but unfortunately, Darrow does not devote
much of his autobiography to this painful episode in his
life.

If Darrow did indeed resort to bribery—regardless of the
perceived provocation—he disqualified himself as a role
model for lawyers. There is simply no justification for corrupting the legal system, even if it is done to level the playing field. Bribery and evidence tampering may be the tools
of revolutionaries and others who work outside the system,
and they may perhaps even be justified by a revolutionary
means-end calculus. But a lawyer who practices law cannot
employ such devices. The lawyer may rail against the corruption of his opponent; the lawyer may expose or condemn, and perhaps even be right to resign from the
practice of law to become a revolutionary, if the cause is
just and the provocation sufficient. But the lawyer may not
become part of the corruption in order to fight for justice.
If Darrow crossed that line, as Cowan argues he did, then
he does not deserve the mantle of honor he has proudly
borne over most of this century.

But even if Clarence Darrow no longer qualifies as a role
model, his remarkable career still deserves study by all citi-

zens who care about liberties and our legal system. Darrow's long career spanned the history of the first third of this century and his advocacy was instrumental in defending many of the most crucial cases of the day. His cases have become the stuff of legend, drama, and film. His defense of Leopold and Loeb against the death penalty inspired Alfred Hitchcock's *Rope* as well as numerous works of nonfiction and fiction. His defense of Tennessee schoolteacher John T. Scopes was docu-dramatized in the Broadway play *Inherit the Wind*, which was made into an Academy Award–winning film.

As with other legends, many liberties have been taken with Darrow's cases. Consider, for example, the way in which *Inherit The Wind* portrayed the great confrontation between Darrow and his nemesis William Jennings Bryan, who assisted the prosecution in the Scopes "monkey trial." In the most dramatic scene the Darrow character calls the Bryan character as an expert witness on the Bible. The attack is scathing and merciless, as the man of science destroys the man of religion before our very eyes. The questions are devastating: how could the early days of creation be measured before the creation of the sun? Were they really 24-hour days? How could Joshua order the sun to stop, when we all know that the earth moves around a fixed sun? The fictional answers are true to the caricature of know-nothing literalism manufactured by the author of *Inherit the Wind:* God knows how to measure time without a sun. Of course they were 24-hour days. God can make the sun move and stop.

As usual, the real story, as told in the trial transcript, was far more complex and far more interesting. The actual William Jennings Bryan was no simple-minded literalist. And he certainly was no bigot. He was a great populist, who cared deeply about equality and about the downtrodden.

Indeed, one of his reasons for becoming so deeply involved in the campaign against evolution was that Darwin's theories were being used—misused, it turns out—by racists, militarists, and nationalists to push some pretty horrible programs. The eugenics movement, which advocated sterilization of "unfit" and "inferior" stock, was at its zenith, and it took its impetus from Darwin's theory of natural selection. German militarism, which had just led to the disastrous World War, drew inspiration from Darwin's survival of the fittest. The anti-immigration movement, which had succeeded in closing American ports of entry to "inferior racial stock," was grounded in a mistaken belief that certain ethnic groups had evolved more fully than others. The "Jim Crow" laws, which manufactured racial segregation, were rationalized on the grounds of the racial inferiority of blacks.

The very book—Hunter's *Civic Biology*—from which John T. Scopes taught Darwin's theory of evolution to high school students in Dayton, Tennessee contained dangerous misapplications of that theory. The text explicitly accepted the naturalistic fallacy and repeatedly drew moral instruction from nature. Its very title, *Civic Biology*, made it clear that biology had direct political implications for society. In discussing the "five races" of man the text assured the all-white, legally segregated high school students taught by Scopes that "the highest type of all, the Caucasians, [are] represented by the civilized white inhabitants of Europe and America" (p. 126). The book, its avowed goal being the improvement of the future human race, then proposed certain eugenic remedies. After a discussion of the inheritability of crime and immorality the author proposed an analogy:

Just as certain animals or plants become parasitic on other plants or animals, these families become parasitic on society. They not only do harm to others by corrupting, stealing or spreading disease, but they are actually protected and cared for by the state out of public money. Largely for them the poorhouse and the asylum exist. They take from society but they give nothing in return. They are true parasites.

From the analogy flowed "the remedy":

If such people were lower animals, we would probably kill them off to prevent them from spreading. Humanity will not allow this, but we do have the remedy of separating the sexes in asylums or other places and in various ways preventing intermarriage and the possibilities of perpetuating such a low and degenerate race. Remedies of this sort have been tried successfully in Europe and are now meeting with success in this country.

These "remedies" involved involuntary sterilizations and eventually laid the foundation for forced "euthanasia" of the kind practiced in Nazi Germany.

Nor were these misapplications of Darwinian theory limited to high school textbooks. Eugenic views held sway at institutions of higher learning such as Harvard University under racist President Abbot Lawrence Lowell. Even so distinguished a Supreme Court Justice as Oliver Wendell Holmes upheld a mandatory sterilization law on the basis of pseudoscientific assumptions about inheritance and genetics. His widely quoted rational—that "three generations of imbeciles are enough"—was later cited by Nazi apologists for mass sterilization. Ironically, the journalist in the play and the movie was based on real-life reporter H. L. Mencken, whose newspaper paid some of the expenses for the defense. Mencken himself was a rabid racist as well as anti-religious bigot.

It should not be surprising, therefore, that William Jennings Bryan, a populist and egalitarian, would be outraged at what he believed was a direct attack on the morality and religion that had formed the basis of his entire political career. Nor was Bryan the know-nothing literalist of *Inherit the Wind*. For the most part, he actually seems to have gotten the better of Clarence Darrow in the argument over the Bible (though not in the argument over the teaching of evolution). To Darrow's question, "Do you think the earth was made in six days?," Bryan's actual answer was, "I do not think they were 24-hour-days." He then proceeded to suggest that these "days" were really "periods" and that the creation may have taken "6,000,000 years or . . . 600,000,000 years" (p. 302). When Darrow questioned Bryan about the biblical story of Joshua ordering the sun to stand still, he obviously expected Bryan to claim that sun orbited the earth, as the Bible implies. But Bryan disappointed him by testifying that "the earth goes around the sun." He explained that the divinely inspired author of the Joshua story "may have used language that could be understood at the time" (p. 286).

All in all, Bryan did quite well in defining his position, and Darrow came off as something of an anti-religious cynic. The law was on Darrow's side, although it took more than half a century for the Supreme Court to vindicate his position. But the primitive and misapplied evolution taught by John Scopes was neither good science nor good morality. The censorship dictated by Tennessee's anti-evolution law was not the proper response to the dangers of teaching high school students the kind of racist rubbish contained in the textbook used by Scopes. Religion does indeed have its proper role in constraining the misapplication of science, but not in the classrooms of public schools.

The case for which Darrow would probably like to be remembered is Leopold and Loeb. In that case he not only saved the lives of two young thrill killers, but proved that there is redemption and rehabilitation. Nathan Leopold lived a productive life both in prison and for the short time during which he was free. Darrow's eloquent plea for life has had a significant impact on the continuing debate about capital punishment. Most death penalty lawyers I know have read his masterful closing argument and many use parts of it in their pleas for life. If Darrow had done nothing else in his long and productive career, he would still deserve accolades for his brilliant and successful advocacy on behalf of the lives of two young men who were despised and hated.

Darrow repeats some legends in his life story, acknowledging that autobiographies are not history. But the stories are fascinating—an important piece of 20th-century Americana. There is also philosophy, criminology, labor economics, politics, religion, and even love. Whether legend, history, or a combination thereof, *The Story of My Life* is still must reading for any contemporary law student, lawyer, or citizen.

ALAN M. DERSHOWITZ
Harvard Law School
December 1995

CONTENTS

CONTENTS

CONTENTS

THE STORY OF MY LIFE

CHAPTER 1

BEFORE THE BEGINNING

IT may seem absurd that I should be sitting here trying to write about myself in an age when only a mystery story has any chance as a best-seller. I can think of nothing about myself to distort into any such popular fiction. If I tell anything it will be but a plain unvarnished account of how things really have happened, as nearly as I can possibly hold to the truth.

First of all, I have noticed that most autobiographers begin with ancestors. As a rule they start out with the purpose of linking themselves by blood and birth to some well-known family or personage. No doubt this is due to egotism, and the hazy, unscientific notions that people have about heredity. For my part, I seldom think about my ancestors; but I had them; plenty of them, of course. In fact, I could fill this book with their names if I knew them all, and deemed it of the least worth.

I have been told that I came of a very old family. A considerable number of people say that it runs back to Adam and Eve, although this, of course, is only hearsay, and I should not like to guarantee the title. Anyhow, very few pedigrees really go back any farther than mine. With reasonable certainty I could run it back to a little town in England that has the same name as mine, though the spelling is slightly altered. But this does not matter. I am sure that my forbears run a long, long way back of that, even—but what of it, anyhow?

The earliest ancestor of the Darrow family that I feel sure belonged to our branch was one of sixteen men who came to New England the century before the Revolutionary War. This Darrow, with fifteen other men, brought a grant from the King of England for the town of New London, Conn. He was an undertaker, so we are told, which shows that he had some appreciation of a good business, and so chose a profession where the demand for his services would be fairly steady. One could imagine a more pleasant means of livelihood, but, almost any trade is bearable if the customers are sure. This Darrow, or rather his descendants, seemed to forget the lavish gift of the King, and took up arms against England under George Washington. So far as having an ancestor in the Revolutionary War counts for anything, I would be eligible to a membership of the D. A. R., although I would not exactly fit this organization, for, amongst other handicaps, I am proud of my rebel ancestors, and would be glad to greet them on the street, should they chance my way.

But it is not for love of looking up my ancestry, or a desire to brag, that I am setting all this down, but for a much more personal reason. All of it had an important bearing upon me, and shows the many, many close calls I had when I was casting about for an ancestral line and yearning to be born. The farther back I go, the more unlikely it seems that I am really here, and I sometimes pinch myself to make sure that it is not a dream; but I assume that I am I, and that I really came all the way from Adam, with all the vicissitudes of time and tide that are so entwined with mortal life.

Did you, who read this, ever figure what a scant chance you had of getting here? If you did come from Adam, you must have had millions on millions of direct forbears, and, if one ancestor had failed to come into the combination, you would not be you, but would be some one else entirely, if any one at all. So I do not allow myself to worry about the long-lost trail, but am content with thinking over the slight chance my father and mother had to meet, and hence my own still lesser chance for life after I had jumped all the hurdles between Adam and my parents.

If a man really has charge of his destiny at all, he should have something to say about getting born; and I only came through by a hair's-breadth. What had I to do with this momentous first step? In the language of the lawyer, I was not even a party of the second part. Two generations back is not so very far away; the reader will not need to try to consider all the near-accidents since Adam, but I will illustrate the whole venture by one narrow escape I had seventy-five years before I was born.

It seems that my grandfathers from both sides came from Connecticut. They had never met in the East, and did not come at the same time. Both of them drove from New England, for there were no railroads in that day, much less automobiles. The journey was long, and more or less disagreeable. My father's parents came first, but, for some reason, stopped at the little town of Henrietta, near Rochester, N. Y. Why they stopped there, I cannot imagine. I was there once myself, but I did not stop. When I visualize the paternal grandfather Darrow driving off on a thousand-mile trip into a near-wilderness I can hardly refrain from shouting to tell him that he has left Grandfather Eddy behind. But later on my grandfather on my mother's side drove away into the unknown West as if in search of a mate for one of his unborn daughters, so that I could have a couple of parents after many years. He drove and drove for weeks and months into the West until he pitched his tent in the wilds that later were named Windsor, Ohio. No doubt they drove through Henrietta, for that was along the main road into the West, but they did not stop, even long enough to meet my future mother's parent. Some years later my father's father drove from Henrietta to western Ohio and stopped at the little hamlet of Kinsman, twenty-five miles from Windsor, the town where my mother was waiting to be born. Thus far, my chance for getting into the scheme was about zero. It was necessary for the boy and girl to meet before they could become my father and mother, and this chance seemed less than one in a million when the families lived in Connecticut.

Both grandfathers were poor and obscure, else they would have stayed where they were. But their children, as they grew up, were sent to school. About thirty-five miles from Windsor and sixty from Kinsman, was a little town called Amboy, in northern Ohio, near Oberlin. In Amboy was a well-known school. Emily Eddy and Amirus Darrow were destined to go to that school, and so they went. I can leave the rest to the reader's imagination. When I think of the chances that I was up against, even when so near the goal, it scares me to realize how easily I might have missed out. Of all the infinite accidents of fate farther back of that, I do not care or dare to think.

It is obvious that I had nothing to do with getting born. Had I known about life in advance and been given any choice in the matter, I most likely would have declined the adventure. At least, that is the way I think about it now. There are times when I feel otherwise, but on the whole I believe that life is not worth while. This does not mean that I am gloomy, or that this book will sadden the Tired Business Man, for I shall write only when I have the inclination to do so, and at such times I am generally almost unmindful of existence.

But as I write these words the sun is shining, the birds are making merry in the bright summer day, and I am asking why I sit and plague my brain to recall the dead and misty past while light and warmth and color are urging me to go outdoors and play.

Doubtless a certain vanity has its part in moving me to write about myself. I am quite sure that this is true, even though I am aware that neither I nor any one else has the slightest importance in time and space. I know that the earth where I have spent my life is only a speck of mud floating in the endless sky. I am quite sure that there are millions of other worlds in the universe whose size and importance are most likely greater than the tiny graveyard on which I ride. I know that at this time there are nearly two billion other human entities madly holding fast to this ball of dirt to which I cling. I know that since I began this page hundreds of these have loosened their grip and sunk to eternal sleep. I know that for half a million years men and women have lived and died and been mingled with the elements that combine to make our earth, and are known no more. I know that only the smallest fraction of my fellow castaways have even so much as heard my name, and that those who have will soon be a part of trees and plants and animal and clay. Still, here am I sitting down, with the mists already gathering about my head, to write about the people, desires, disappointments and despairs that have moved me in my brief stay on what we are pleased to call this earth.

Doubtless, too, the emotion to live makes most of us seek to project our personality a short distance beyond the waiting grave. But whatever the reason may be, I am doing what many, many men have done before, and will do again—talking and gossiping about the past. I am doing this as a boy plays baseball by the hour or dances through the night. I am doing it because all living things crave activity, and I am still alive. Whether the movement is a journey around the globe or an unsteady walk from the bedroom to the dining room and back, it is but a response to what is left of the emotions, appetites and energies that we call being.

The young man's reflections of unfolding life concern the future—the great, broad, tempestuous sea on whose hither shore he stands eagerly waiting to learn of other lands and climes. The reactions and recollections of the old concern the stormy journey drawing to a close; he no longer builds castles or plans conquests of the unknown; he recalls the tempests and tumults encountered on the way, and babbles of the passengers and crew that one by one dropped silently into the icy depths. No longer does the aging transient yearn for new adventures or unexplored highways. His greatest ambition is to find some snug harbor where he can doze and dream the fleeting days away. So, elderly men who speak or write turn to autobiography. This is all they have to tell, and they cannot sit idly in silence and wait for the night to come.

Autobiography is never entirely true. No one can get the right perspective on himself. Every fact is colored by imagination and dream. The young look forth across the sea to a mirage of fairylands filled with hidden treasures; the aged turn to the fading past, and through the mist and haze that veils once familiar scenes, bygone events assume weird and fanciful proportions. Almost forgotten men, women and children reappear along the far-off shore, and their shadows are reflected back in dimmed or magnified outlines in the softly setting sun. Then, too, all human egos, and perhaps other egos, place prime importance upon themselves; each is the centre of the great circle around which all else revolves; no one can see and feel in any other way. Although all intelligent people realize that they are as nothing in the procession that is ever moving on, yet we cannot but feel that when we are dead the parade will no longer move. So while we can still vibrate with tongue and pen and with every manifestation of our beings, we instinctively shout to the crowd to pause and for a little time turn their eyes and ears toward us. That is what I am doing now, and am doing it because I have nothing else to do. I am doing it because it helps to pass away the time that still remains. I know that life consists of the impressions made upon the puppet as it moves across the stage. I shall endeavor not to magnify the manikin. I am interested not in the way that I have fashioned the world, but in the way that the world has moulded me.

I hope that no one will turn from this book for fear it is sad and will make him unhappy. I am not an optimist in the ordinary sense of the word. I can tell of my life only as I see it, but I fancy that the story will not be unduly serious or tragic. I have never taken any one very seriously, and least of all myself. I am not trying to teach any moral or point any way. The billions on billions of humans that have come upon the stage, made their bow, and then retired beyond the scenes, have one and all played the same part. One and all they, for a time, have taken a distinctive form and name, and then disappeared forever. One and all, they have known joys and sorrows, and most of them are now lost in sleep and oblivion. My life has not been sad, and as the end approaches it brings no sorrow. When the evening hours have crept on I have always looked forward with satisfaction, if not pleasure, to the night of rest; a space of time with no consciousness to mar the peace and serenity of the void between the evening and the coming dawn. So, to-day, after a long life of work and play and joy and sorrow, I am fully aware of the friendly night that is stealing on apace. The inevitable destiny brings no fear or pain, so why should others be saddened by what I have to tell?

One cannot live through a long stretch of years without forming some philosophy of life. As one journeys along he gains experiences and even some ideas. Accumulated opinions and philosophy may be more important to others than the bare facts about how he lived, so my ambition is not so much to relate the occurrences as to record the ideas that life has forced me to accept; and, after all, thoughts, impressions and feelings are really life itself. I should like to think that these reflections might make existence a trifle easier for some of those who may chance to read this story.

As I have already said, my father's ancestors were rebels and traitors who took up arms against Great Britain in the War of the Revolution. It is easy for me to believe that my father came of rebel stock; at least he was always in rebellion against religious and political creeds of the narrow and smug community in which he dwelt. But ancestors do not mean so much. The rebel who succeeds generally makes it easier for the posterity that follows him; so these descendants are usually contented and smug and soft. Rebels are made from life, not ancestors.

My father, in his early life, was a religious man. He was born into the Methodist Church. This indicates that he came of plebeian stock, for there were also an Episcopalian and a Presbyterian Church in the little town. Either his parents were too humble for one of these aristocratic temples, or, perhaps my grandfather was converted at a Methodist revival, which was one of the affairs to go to, even after I was born. My father had a serious but kindly face. In his leisure hours he was always poring over books. I wish I knew more about his youth; it might furnish some interesting data as to the development of the family and the pranks of heredity and environment. He was one of seven children who came with their father to eastern Ohio, which was then almost a frontier land. The family must have been very poor, and their means of existence precarious in those early days, at the beginning of the nineteenth century. When a boy, I knew most of my uncles and aunts; they seemed fairly intelligent, but I cannot remember ever seeing a book in the house of any member of my father's family excepting in my father's home.

Not only were there no books in my grandfather's house, but there were practically none anywhere in the community. One of my earliest recollections is the books in our home. They were in bookcases, on tables, on chairs, and even on the floor. The house was small, the family large, the furnishings meagre, but there were books whichever way one turned. How my father managed to buy the books I cannot tell. Neither by nature nor by training had he any business ability or any faculty for getting money.

My mother's father was a fairly prosperous farmer. Neither

he nor any of his family were church attendants. Out of the five or six children, my mother alone cared especially for books. Her family were substantial people of fair intelligence, but were inclined to believe that a love of books was a distinct weakness, and likely to develop into a very bad habit. One who spent his time reading or studying when he might be at work was "shiftless" and improvident. Benjamin Franklin's Almanac, with its foolish lessons about industry and thrift, was the gospel of the family.

Aside from one uncle who seemed fairly well-informed, I do not remember that a single one of my mother's brothers and sisters cared at all for books. Of my father's children, seven of us grew to mature years, and all but one had a liking for reading and learning; most of us would leave almost any sort of work or amusement to spend our time with books. How did it come about that of my father's family he alone, out of seven or eight, had any thirst for learning? And why was it that of my mother's family she was the only one that cared for books? And why did it happen that of the children of my father and mother all but one always had an abiding love for reading?

Of the group interwoven with my father's early life, why had he alone that overwhelming desire for books?—a love so strong that it remained with him and solaced him to his dying day, at the age of eighty-six. Was it imparted to him through the seed from which he grew? Was heredity the cause? Apparently his father did not care for books, and certainly conveyed no fondness for learning to his other sons and daughters. My grandparents on both sides each reared one child who in the yearning for education seemed as strangers to the rest.

I know nothing of my great-grandparents, but they must have been still more obscure. Is there any reason for speculating upon some possible spark of life from some unknown and improbable outside source? In my parents' offspring, the case was reversed; but the problem is the same; one child cared nothing for the intellectual life, and all the others prized books. If I knew my father's and mother's childhood associates I might find that some companion or school teacher at the right time kindled the quenchless flame in their young minds; but of this I have no knowledge. It is clear that both my parents, who met at school, away from home, had already shown a bent for study; and this was doubtless nurtured by the school. They married, and their zest for books was a part of the new home life, and we children were brought up in an atmosphere of books, and were trained to love them. It is easier for me to believe that our taste for them came from our early environment than that it was carried down in the germ-plasm of which so little is really known. Why did one brother not care at all for books? Who can tell? He was older than I, and of course I did not know his closest friends or when some alien influence might have entered and moulded his life. It seems reasonable to believe that by some intervention at a critical period he was led into another direction that perhaps changed the whole tenor of his nature and his life.

Soon after the marriage of my father and mother they went to Meadville, Penna., for a time. My father chose Meadville on account of Allegheny College, a Methodist institution, located in the town. I know nothing of how they lived. I should have known, but, long before I ever thought of beguiling my last years with a story of my life, the lips which could have spoken were closed forever. It would be hopeless to search for the happenings and doings of an obscure man. My father must have undergone great privations. He graduated from the college, where my two sisters received diplomas later on. He was still religious. His religion was born from a sensitive nature that made him pity the sad and suffering, and which, first and last, tied him to every hopeless cause that came his way.

On one hill in Meadville stood Allegheny College, sponsored by the Methodist Church. On another elevation was a Unitarian seminary, and in the town was a Unitarian Church. Both my parents must have strayed to this church, for when my father's time had come to take a theological course he went to the Unitarian school in Meadville, on the other hill from the Methodist college, where he took his first degree. In due time he completed his theological course, but when he had finished his studies he found that he had lost his faith. Even the mild tenets of Unitarianism he could not accept. Unitarianism, then, was closer to Orthodoxy than it is to-day, or he might have been a clergyman and lived an easier life. In the Unitarian school he read Newman and Channing, but later went on to Emerson and Theodore Parker. His trend of mind was shown by the fact that his first son was Edward Everett. When it came my turn to be born and named, my parents had left the Unitarian faith behind and were sailing out on the open sea without a rudder or compass, and with no port in sight, and so I could not be named after any prominent Unitarian. Where they found the name to which I have answered so many years I never knew. Perhaps my mother read a story where a minor character was called Clarence, but I fancy I have not turned out to be anything like him. The one satisfaction I have had in connection with this cross was that the boys never could think up any nickname half so inane as the real one my parents adorned me with.

CHAPTER 2

MY CHILDHOOD IN KINSMAN

Some years before I was born my parents left Meadville and moved back to the little village of Kinsman, about twenty miles away. I have no idea why they made this change, unless because my father's sister lived in Kinsman. All life hangs on a thread, so long as it hangs; a little movement this way or that is all-controlling. So I cannot tell why I was born on the 18th of April in 1857, or why the obscure village of Kinsman was the first place in which I beheld the light of day. When I was born the village must have boasted some four or five hundred inhabitants, and its importance and vitality is evident because it has held its own for seventy-five years or more. If any one wants to see the place he must search for the town, for in spite of the fact that I was born there it has never been put on the map.

But in truth, Kinsman is a quiet, peaceful and picturesque spot. Almost any one living in its vicinity will inform the stranger that it is well worth visiting, if one happens to be near. The landscape is gently rolling, the soil is fertile, beautiful shade trees line the streets, and a lazy stream winds its way into what to us boys was the far-off unknown world. Years ago the deep places of the stream were used for swimming-holes, and the shores were favorite lounging-places for boys dangling their fishing-lines above the shaded waters. There I spent many a day expectantly waiting for a bite. I recall few fishes that ever rewarded my patience; but this never prevented my haunting the famous pools and watching where the line disappeared into the mysterious unfathomed depths.

The dominating building in Kinsman was the Presbyterian Church, which stood on a hill and towered high above all the rest. On Sunday the great bell clanged across the surrounding country calling all the people to come and worship under its sheltering roof. Loudly it tolled at the death of every one who died in the Lord. Its measured tones seemed cold and solemn while the funeral procession was moving up the hillside where the departed was to be forevermore protected under the shadow of the church.

If I had chosen to be born I probably should not have selected Kinsman, Ohio, for that honor; instead, I would have started in a hard and noisy city where the crowds surged back and forth as if they knew where they were going, and why. And yet my mind continuously returns to the old place, although not more than five or six that were once my schoolmates are still outside the churchyard gate. My mind goes back to Kinsman because I lived there in childhood, and to me it was once the centre of the world, and however far I have roamed since then it has never fully lost that place in the storehouse of miscellaneous memories gathered along the path of life.

I have never been able to visualize the early history of my parents. Not only had they no money, but no occupation; and under those conditions they began the accumulation of a family of children which ultimately totalled eight. These were born about two years apart. I was the fifth, but one before me died in infancy; it is evident that my parents knew nothing of birth-control, for they certainly could not afford so many doubtful luxuries. Perhaps my own existence, as fifth in a family, is one reason why I never have been especially enthusiastic about keeping others from being born; whenever I hear people discussing birth-control I always remember that I was the fifth.

All his life my father was a visionary and dreamer. Even when he sorely needed money he would neglect his work to read some book. My mother was more efficient and practical. She was the one who saved the family from dire want. Her industry and intelligence were evident in her household affairs and in my father's small business, too. In spite of this, she kept abreast of the thought of her day. She was an ardent woman's-rights advocate, as they called the advanced woman seventy years ago. Both she and my father were friends of all oppressed people, and every new and humane and despised cause and ism.

Neither of my parents held any orthodox religious views. They were both readers of Jefferson, Voltaire, and Paine; both looked at revealed religion as these masters thought. And still, we children not only went to Sunday school but were encouraged to attend. Almost every Sunday our mother took us to the church, and our pew was too near the minister to permit our slipping out while the service was going on. I wonder why children are taken to church? Or perhaps they are not, nowadays. I can never forget the horror and torture of listening to an endless sermon when I was a child. Of course I never understood a word of it, any more than did the preacher who harangued to his afflicted audiences.

At Sunday school I learned endless verses from the Testaments. I studied the lesson paper as though every word had a meaning and was true. I sang hymns that I remember to this day. Among these was one in which each child loudly shouted "I want to be an angel!—and with the angels stand; a crown upon my forehead, a harp within my hand!" Well do I remember that foolish hymn to this very day. As a boy I sang it often and earnestly, but in spite of my stout and steady insistence that I wanted to wear wings, here I am, at seventy-five, still fighting to stay on earth.

On religious and social questions our family early learned to stand alone. My father was the village infidel, and gradually came to glory in his reputation. Within a radius of five miles were other "infidels" as well, and these men formed a select group of their own. We were not denied association with the church members; the communicants of the smaller churches were our friends. For instance, there was a Catholic society that met at the home of one of its adherents once in two or three weeks, and between them and our family there grew up a sort of kinship. We were alike strangers in a more or less hostile land.

Although my father was a graduate of a theological seminary when he settled in Kinsman, he could not and would not preach. He must have been puzzled and perplexed at the growing brood that looked so trustingly to the parents for food and clothes. He must have wearily wondered which way to turn to be able to meet the demand. He undertook the manufacture and sale of furniture. His neighbors and the farmers round about were the customers with whom he dealt. Even now when I go back to Kinsman I am shown chairs and bedsteads that he made. He must have done honest work, for it has been more than fifty years since he laid down his tools. Now and then some old native shows me a bed or table or chair said to have been made by me in those distant days, but though I never contradict the statement, but rather encourage it instead, I am quite sure that the claim is more than doubtful.

Besides being a furniture maker, my father was the undertaker of the little town. I did not know it then, but I now suppose that the two pursuits went together in small settlements in those days. I know that the sale of a coffin meant much more to him and his family than any piece of furniture that he could make. My father was as kind and gentle as any one could possibly be, but I always realized his financial needs and even when very young used to wonder in a cynical way whether he felt more pain or pleasure over the death of a neighbor or friend. Any pain he felt must have been for himself, and the pleasure that he could not crowd aside must have come for the large family that looked to him for bread. I remember the coffins piled in one corner of the shop, and I always stayed as far away from them as possible, which I have done ever since. Neither did I ever want to visit the little shop after dark.

All of us boys had a weird idea about darkness, anyhow. The night was peopled with ghosts and the wandering spirits of those who were dead. Along two sides of the graveyard was a substantial fence between that and the road, and we always ran when we passed the white stones after dusk. No doubt early teaching is responsible for these foolish fears. Much of the terror of children would be avoided under sane and proper training, free of all fable and superstition.

My mother died when I was very young, and my remembrance of her is not very clear. It is sixty years since she laid down the hard burden that fate and fortune had placed upon her shoulders. Since that far-off day this loving, kindly, tireless and almost nameless mother has been slowly changed in Nature's laboratory into flowers and weeds and trees and dust. Her gravestone stands inside the white fence in the little country town where I was born, and beside her lies a brother who died in youth. I have been back to the old village and passed the yard where she rests forever, but only once have gone inside the gate since I left my old home so long ago. Somehow it is hard for me to lift the latch or go down the walk or stand at the marble slab which marks the spot where she was laid away. Still I know that in countless ways her work and teaching, her mastering personality, and her infinite kindness and sympathy have done much to shape my life.

My father died only twenty-five years ago. He is not buried in the churchyard at Kinsman. The same process of the reduction of the body to its elements has gone on with him as with my mother. But in her case it has come about through accumulating years; with him it was accomplished more quickly in the fiery furnace of the crematorium and his ashes were given to his children and were wafted to the winds.

Who am I—the man who has lived and retained this special form of personality for so many years? Aside from the strength or weakness of my structure, I am mainly the product of my mother, who helped to shape the wanton instincts of the child, and of the gentle, kindly, loving, human man whose presence was with me for so many years that I could not change, and did not want to change.

Since then a brother and sister, Everett and Mary, have passed into eternal sleep and have gone directly through the fiery furnace and their ashes are strewn upon the sands. I know that it can be but a short time until I shall go the way of all who live; I cannot honestly say that I want to be cremated, but I am sure that I prefer this method of losing my identity to any other I might choose.

The memory pictures of the first fifteen years of life that drift back to me now are a medley of all sorts of things, mainly play and school. Never was there a time when I did not like to go to school. I always welcomed the first day of the term and regretted the last. The school life brought together all the children of the town. These were in the main simple and democratic. The study hours, from nine to four, were broken by two recesses of fifteen minutes each and the "nooning" of one hour which provided an ideal chance to play. It seems to me that one unalloyed joy in life, whether in school or vacation time, was baseball. The noon time gave us a fairly good game each day. The long summer evenings were often utilized as well, but Saturday afternoon furnished the only perfect pleasure we ever knew. Whether we grew proficient in our studies or not, we enjoyed renown in our community for our skill in playing ball. Saturday afternoons permitted us to visit neighboring towns to play match games, and be visited by other teams in return.

I have snatched my share of joys from the grudging hand of Fate as I have jogged along, but never has life held for me anything quite so entrancing as baseball; and this, at least, I learned at district school. When we heard of the professional game in which men cared nothing whatever for patriotism but only for money—games in which rival towns would hire the best players from a natural enemy—we could scarcely believe the tale was true. No Kinsman boy would any more give aid and comfort to a rival town than would a loyal soldier open a gate in the wall to let an enemy march in.

We could not play when the snow was on the ground, but Kinsman had ponds and a river, and when the marvellous stream overran its banks it made fine skating in the winter months. Then there were the high hills; at any rate, they seemed high to me, and the spring was slower in coming than in these degenerate days, it seemed. To aid us in our sports there was a vast amount of snow and ice for the lofty, swift slides downhill, and few experiences have brought keener enjoyment, which easily repaid us for the tedious tug back to the top. I am not at all sure about the lessons that I learned in school, but I do know that we got a great deal of fun between the study hours, and I have always been glad that I took all the play I could as it came along.

But I am quite sure that I learned something, too. I know that I began at the primer and read over and over the McGuffey readers, up to the sixth, while at the district school. I have often wondered if there was such a man as Mr. McGuffey and what he looked like. To me his name suggested side-whiskers which, in Kinsman, meant distinction. I never could understand how he learned so much and how he could have been so good. I am sure that no set of books ever came from any press that was so packed with love and righteousness as were those readers. Their religious and ethical stories seem silly now, but at that time it never occurred to me that those tales were utterly impossible lies which average children should easily have seen through.

McGuffey furnished us many choice and generally poetical instructions on conduct and morals. And the same sort were found in other books, also. I remember one that I used to declaim, but I do not recall the book where it was found; this was an arraignment of the tobacco habit. It is not unlikely that this gem had something to do with the Methodist Church not permitting a man who smokes to be ordained as a preacher. Anyhow, I haven't heard of or seen this choice bit of literature and morals for sixty years, but here it is, as I remember it:

> " 'I'll never chew tobacco;
> No, it is a filthy weed.
> I'll never put it in my mouth,'
> Said little Robert Reed.
>
> Why, there was idle Jerry Jones,
> As dirty as a pig,
> Who smoked when only ten years old,
> And thought it made him big.
>
> He'd puff along the open streets
> As if he had no shame;
> He'd sit beside the tavern door
> And there he'd do the same."

The girls made their hatred of liquor just as clear, although I do not recall their words, but I do know the title of one recitation. The name carried a threat to all of us boys, declaring:

> "The lips that touch liquor
> Shall never touch mine."

From what I see and hear of the present generation I should guess that Doctor McGuffey and his ilk lived in vain.

I am inclined to think that I had the advantage of most of the boys and girls, for, as I have said, my home was well supplied with books, and my father was eager that all of us should learn. He watched our studies with the greatest care and diligently elaborated and supplemented whatever we absorbed in school. No one in town had an education anywhere near so thorough as his education that hard work and rigorous self-denial had afforded him.

I am never certain whether I have accomplished much or little. This depends entirely upon what comparisons I make. Judged with relation to my father, who reared so large a family and gave us all so good an education from the skimpy earnings of a little furniture store in a country town, I feel that my life has been unproductive indeed. How he did it I cannot understand. It must have been due largely to the work and management of my mother, who died before I was old enough to comprehend. But from the little that I remember, and from all that my older brothers and sisters and the neighbors have told me, I feel that it was her ability and devotion that kept us together, that made so little go so far, and did so much to give my father a chance for the study and contemplation that made up the real world in which he lived. In all the practical affairs of our life, my mother's hand and brain were the guiding force. Through my mother's good sense my father was able to give his children a glimpse into the realm of ideas and ideals in which he himself really lived.

But I must linger no longer at the threshold of life, which has such a magic hold on my conscious being.

In due time I finished my studies at the district school, and now, grown to feel myself almost a man, was given newer and larger clothes, and more books, along with which came a little larger vision; and I went to the academy on the hill, and timorously entered a new world.

My eldest brother, Everett, who was always the example for the younger children, was then, by what saving and stinting I cannot tell, pursuing his studies at the University of Michigan; and my oldest sister, Mary, was following close behind. I have not the faintest conception how my father and mother were able to accomplish these miracles, working and planning, saving and managing, to put us through.

Any one who desires to write a story of his ideas and philosophy should omit childhood, for this is sacred ground, and when the old man turns back to that fairyland he lingers until any other undertaking seems in vain.

But the first bell in the academy tower has stopped ringing and I must betake myself and my books up the hill.

CHAPTER 3

AT THE THRESHOLD OF LIFE

As I entered the academy I was at once aware that I had changed. I had stepped out of childhood, where we were controlled by commands, and had become a youth, where I had some rights. In all my years at the district school our teachers were women. Now we had a man. It took some time and trial to feel out just how far we dared to run counter to his will, or to act on our own. But we learned, in the true scientific manner, of trial and error, and trial and success.

We had left arithmetic behind and had algebra in its place. And instead of our English grammar we now made a bold effort at Latin. We took McGuffey's with us, for the sixth reader was not used in the primary grade. So we were still pursued by silly, fantastic stories teaching what McGuffey must have thought were moral precepts. But all this did not last long. Then, for the first time, we studied history. Not for any special purpose, or, seemingly, with any end in view, but it was necessary that we put in the time.

We still had baseball. We now were older and stronger and more fleet of foot, and took more pride in the way we played. Most of the games in the district school were far beneath our dignity at the academy, but baseball received all the former adoration, and even more. We began to be self-conscious about the girls, but this was quite easily and rapidly overcome.

As I look back at my days at the district school and the academy, I cannot avoid a feeling of the appalling waste of time. Never since those days have I had occasion to use much of the arithmetic that I learned. In fact, only the merest fraction has ever been brought into service. I am satisfied that this is the experience of almost all the boys and girls who went to school when I was young; and as near as I can tell this is true to-day. I began grammar in the grades, and continued it in the high school, but it was a total loss, not only to me but to all the rest. I would be the last to deny the value of a good understanding of some language, but the method of our public school was the poorest and the most expensive for getting that understanding. For my part, I never could learn grammar, at either the primary or the high school. I have used language extensively all my life, and no doubt have misused it, too; in a way, I have made a living from its use, but I am convinced that I was rather hindered than helped in this direction by the public schools. I am well aware of my own defects in the use of language and have always tried, and still try, to correct my shortcomings in this respect, but with only indifferent success.

Most of the rules for grammar and pronunciation are purely arbitrary. Any one who makes any pretense of observation and experience cannot fail to note the differences in the forms of speech and pronunciation in different countries and in various sections of each country. The correct use of words can only come from environment and habit, and all of this must be learned in childhood from the family or associates, otherwise it will not be known. Committing rules represents only feats of memory that have no effect on speech.

Memorizing history is likewise of no avail. We learned the names of presidents and kings, of the generals, of the chief wars, and those accidents that had been accepted as the great events of the world; but none of it had any relation to our lives. We studied Roman, Greek, and Egyptian histories, and then took English, French, and German, too, but all of the happenings had a dreary far-off setting that was no part of the world and time in which we lived. As well might Cæsar and Hannibal and Napoleon have inhabited Mars, so far as we students were concerned. To us they meant nothing but dry and musty dates and proper names. Even dates did not connect us with the events of their day. Ira Meacham, then the oldest citizen in Kinsman, seemed as far away in the past and as detached from us as Noah and his adventures with some kind of boat and cargo of animals and equally alien to our time and place. In youth, and probably in later life, everything back of our own existence seems weird and unreal and far removed from the life that we know. Attempting to store the brain with unrelated facts and matters entirely irrelevant to the present is worse than useless, for it confuses and distorts.

As I look back at the district school and the academy, I plainly see the boys and girls that gathered at the ringing of the bell. They were the children of the men and women of Kinsman and the territory just outside. Most of these families were farmers. Next in number were the small shop-keepers. There were two or three blacksmiths, a stone-cutter, a tinner, a carpenter, a few laborers, two doctors, two or three preachers, and a dentist. Few of these had ever been far from home, and all knew next to nothing of the outside world. Most of their children followed in their steps. Very few of these laughing, boasting boys and girls ever left the old village, and almost none were drawn into any broader or different fields than their parents knew before. None of them ever found any practical use for what they learned, or tried to learn at school beyond ordinary reading and writing. The exceptions who aspired to other avenues were moved by some inner or outer urge and specially prepared for their future course of life.

Schools probably became general and popular because parents did not want their children about the house all day. The school was a place to send them to get them out of the way. If, perchance, they could learn something it was so much to the good. Colleges followed the schools for the same reason. These took charge of the boy at a time when he could be of little or no use at home, and was only a burden and a care.

All established institutions are very slow to change. The defects of schools and colleges have been discussed for many years, and the lines of a rational and worth-while education have been developed to take their place, but still the old-time education with most of the ancient methods persists and flourishes yet.

It is worse than useless to try to make scholars of the great majority of boys and girls. In fact, scholarship as it is understood is not so necessary to life as people have been taught to believe. Man does not live by books alone. Indeed, they fill a very small part of the life of even those who know how to read.

Schools were not established to teach and encourage the pupil to think; beyond furnishing a place for keeping the children out of the way, their effort was to cement the minds of pupils according to certain moulds. The teachers were employed to teach the truth, and the most important truth concerned the salvation of their souls. From the first grade to the end of the college course they were taught not to think, and the instructor who dared to utter anything in conflict with ordinary beliefs and customs was promptly dismissed, if not destroyed. Even now there are very few schools that encourage the young or the old to think out questions for themselves. And yet, life is a continuous problem for the living, and first of all we should be equipped to think, if possible. Then, too, education should be adjusted to the needs of the pupil and his prospective future. Wise teachers and intelligent parents can tell at an early age the trend and probable capacity of the mind of the child. All learning should be adapted to making life easier to be lived.

After finishing at the academy, I went one year to Allegheny College, at Meadville, in the preparatory department. I still found baseball an important adjunct to school life. Here I continued my Latin and tried to add some Greek, with very poor success. I found geometry far easier, but no more useful. I did get something in zoology that remained with me; but I cannot to-day find the slightest excuse for studying either Latin or Greek; both are absolutely devoid of practical value. The college professor who gives his life to Latin cannot speak it as well as the street gamin who lived in Rome two thousand years ago; and all the treasures of learning that were buried in ancient languages have long since been better rendered into English and other languages than any modern student could ever hope to do. If perchance some untranslated manuscript should be unearthed, there is little need that all boys and girls should learn Latin so that it may be translated. There is no possible chance that the keys for translating languages will again be lost. To spend years in studying something that has nothing but what is called a cultural value is most absurd. All knowledge that is useful has a cultural value; the fact that it has some other value should make it more desirable instead of less.

Since I left Allegheny College I have never opened the lids of Virgil or any other Latin author, except in translation. Greek was even more useless and wasteful of time and effort than Latin. I never really attempted to do anything with either, excepting to "get by," and it is hard to understand the apologists for the dead languages of the dead. We live in a world full of unsolved mysteries. Their real study has been but begun. Every fresh fact that we master can add to the happiness of man, both by its use in life and by the cultural value that worth-while knowledge brings. I am inclined to believe that the age-long effort to keep the classics in schools and colleges has been an effort not to get knowledge but to preserve ignorance. The mythical soul really is not worth so much consideration.

I spent one year at Allegheny College. I came back a better ball player for my higher education. I learned to despise the study of Latin and Greek, although I never told my father so. He believed that there could be no education without Latin and Greek, and he had added Hebrew to the list. I did learn something of geology, and caught a glimpse of the wonders of natural science. Throughout my life I have been industriously enlarging my view of what some are pleased to call the "material" world, but what to me is the only world.

I went home for my summer vacation, intending to return to college the next autumn, but the panic of 1873 settled this matter for me. Although my father was anxious that I should go back, I was certain that I ought not to burden him longer. So I abandoned further school life and began my education.

My mother died before I went away to school. My memory of her is blurred and faded, although I was fourteen years old at the time. I know that she had a long illness, and for months calmly looked forward to swift and certain death. She had no religious beliefs. Her life was given fully and freely to her home and children, and she faced the future without hope or fear. On the day of her death I was away from home, so I did not see her in her last moments, though all the family were summoned. I never could tell whether I was sorry or relieved that I was not there, but I still remember the blank despair that settled over the home when we realized that her tireless energy and devoted love were lost forever.

After I left Allegheny College I was set to work in the factory and the little store. I was never fond of manual labor. I felt that I was made for better things. I fancy all boys and girls harbor the same delusion. I had no mechanical ability, and to this day have none. I could do rather well at a turning lathe, and could handle a paint brush, but I never bragged about it. But I still played baseball. I don't know just when I gave up the game, but I think that it forsook me when I was no longer valuable to my side.

During the winter I taught a district school in a country community. I remember even the salary, or wages, that I received. The pay was thirty dollars a month "and found"—the latter of which I collected by going from house to house one night after another, and then returning to my own home on Friday night. Boarding around was not so bad. I was "company" wherever I arrived, and only the best was set before me. I had pie and cake three times a day. I taught in the same school three winters, which completed that part of my career. I have been teaching more or less all my life, but confining my activities to those who did not want to learn. In this three years I had some fifty scholars, ranging from seven years old to a year or two above my own age. On the whole, it was a pleasant three years. I am not sure how much I taught the pupils, but I am certain that they taught me. In most district schools rods and switches were a part of the course. My school was large and had caused much trouble to the teachers before I came, but I determined that there should be no corporal punishment while I was there, and of this the pupils were early informed. I told them that I wanted no one to do anything through fear. I joined in their games and sports, including, of course, baseball when the snow was not on the ground. I lengthened the noon hours and recesses, which made a hit with the pupils but brought criticism from their parents. However, I managed to convince them that I was right, and am still quite sure that I was. Whether they learned much or little, they certainly enjoyed those winters. No matter when I go back to my old home I am sure to meet some of the thinning group whom I tried to make happy even if I could not make them wise. I feel sure that if the same effort could be given to making people happy that is devoted to making them get an education which could not be accomplished this world would be a much better home for the human race.

During my teaching days I began the study of law. I am not sure what influenced me to make this choice. I knew that I never intended to work with my hands, and no doubt I was attracted by the show of the legal profession. When I was still quite young the lawyers from the county seat always visited our town on all public occasions. On the Fourth of July and on Decoration Day, in political campaigns and on all holidays, they made speeches and were altogether the most conspicuous of the locality. Then, too, we lived across the street from a tin-shop, and the tinner was the justice of the peace, and I never missed a chance to go over to his shop when a case was on trial. I enjoyed the way the pettifoggers abused each other, and as I grew toward maturity I developed a desire to be a lawyer, too. Every Monday morning, as I started off to teach my school, I took a law book with me, and having a good deal of time improved it fairly well.

When my third term of teaching ended my eldest brother, Everett, was teaching in high school, and my sister, Mary, in a grade school. They were both as self-sacrificing and kind as any human beings I have ever known; they and my father insisted that I should go to Ann Arbor in the law department, which I did for one year. At that time the full course was two years. At the end of one year I was positive that I could make my preparation in another year in an office, which would cost much less money and give a chance to be admitted to the bar at twenty-one. So I went to work in a law office in Youngs-town, Ohio, until I was ready for examination for admission to the bar. In those days a committee of lawyers were chosen to examine applicants. They were all good fellows and wanted to help us through. The bar association of to-day lay down every conceivable condition; they require a longer preliminary study, and exact a college education and long courses in law schools, to keep new members out of the closed circle. The Lawyers' Union is about as anxious to encourage competition as the Plumbers' Union is, or the United States Steel Co., or the American Medical Association.

When I considered that I was ready for the test I presented myself, with some dozen other ambitious young men, for the examination. A committee of lawyers was appointed to try us out. That committee did not seem to take it as seriously as examiners do to-day. I was not made to feel that the safety of the government or the destiny of the universe was hanging on their verdict. As I remember it now, the whole class was passed, and I became a member of the Ohio Bar. Youngstown was then a promising manufacturing town and county seat. It was about twenty miles from the place of my birth. I would have been glad to open an office there, but it was a city of twenty thousand people, and I felt awed by its size and importance; so I went back home and reported my success to my father. He was delighted, and possibly surprised, at my good luck. Poor man, he was probably thinking what he could have done had Fortune been so kind to him. But, like most parents, the success of the son was his success. My neighbors and friends warmly congratulated me, but it was some time before they encouraged me with any employment. They could not conceive that a boy whom they knew, and who was brought up in their town, could possibly have the ability and learning that they thought was necessary to the practice of law.

CHAPTER 4

CALLED TO THE BAR

In the English expression, I had now been "called" to the bar. Lawyers are very fond of fiction; especially the English lawyers. Working a long time on obscure subjects, spending all your money, and as much of your family's as you can get, and finally passing examinations against the will and best efforts of the inquisitors, means getting "called to the bar." I now had a license to practice law, but no one had called me to practice on him. Perhaps I might digress on the brink of a new and untried world to take account of stock, as one might say.

I had no money and no influential friends. I had a rather meagre education. I had never been carefully and methodically trained, and I have felt the lack of it all my life. My law education came from a year's study at a good law school and from a year's reading under a lawyer's direction. I had never had any experience in court work or in the preparation of cases. I then knew, and have ever since been aware, that I needed specific training which I could not get. I was none too industrious, and I have never loved to work. In fact, strange as it may seem, I have never wanted to do the things that I did not want to do. These activities are what I call work. I liked to do certain things no matter how much exertion they required; I liked to play baseball, no matter how hot the day. I liked to read books that I liked to read. I liked debating in school and out of school. I liked to "speak pieces" and was always keen to make due preparation for that, no matter what the subject might be. I always preferred diversions to duties, and this strange taste has clung to me all through life. Again and again these tendencies have kept me from turning to things that my parents and teachers have felt that I should do. In this, the parents and teachers have doubtless often been right. Doing something that one ought to do means foregoing pleasure and enduring pain, or at least boredom, in the hope and belief that one will all the more enjoy a thing in the future by abstaining from it now. Undoubtedly often this is true.

I was strong and healthy. I seemed to have a good mind. I really had a rather good education. While this education was not detailed and explicit, still it was broad and comprehensive for one of my years. I had a strongly emotional nature which has caused me boundless joy and infinite pain. I had a vivid imagination. Not only could I put myself in the other person's place, but I could not avoid doing so. My sympathies always went out to the weak, the suffering, and the poor. Realizing their sorrows I tried to relieve them in order that I myself might be relieved. I had a thoroughly independent, perhaps individual, way of looking at things, and was never influenced by the views of others unless I could be convinced that they were nearly right. I had little respect for the opinion of the crowd. My instinct was to doubt the majority view. My father had directed my thought and reading. He had taught me to question rather than accept. He never thought that the fear of God was the beginning of wisdom. I have always felt that doubt was the beginning of wisdom, and the fear of God was the end of wisdom.

I took a little office in the village of Andover, ten miles from Kinsman, borrowed some money to buy some books, and flung my shingle to the breeze. I did not succeed at first. I am not certain that I ever did. In fact, I don't know the meaning of the word "success." To some—perhaps to most—it means "money." I never cared much for it nor tried to get much of it or ever had a great deal, but still most of my life I have had what I needed. To some, success means political preferment; this I never wanted. It is hard enough to maintain an independent stand and freely express one's self without being handicapped by the desire for office or money. Most people who follow a political career grow to be cowards and slaves; for that matter, so do men who sell prunes. In life one cannot eat his cake and have it, too; he must make his choice and then do the best he can to be content to go the way his judgment leads. Whether he really has anything to do with the making of a choice is still another question for which I have plenty of time and space later on.

Soon after I was twenty-one years old, while I was living in Ashtabula, Ohio, I married Miss Jessie Ohl, whose parents were neighbors and friends of our family. Of this marriage my son Paul was born. Later in life we were divorced—in 1897. This was done without contest or disagreement and without any bitterness on either side, and our son has always been attached to both of us, and she and I have always had full confidence and respect toward each other.

It would not have been possible to build up what lawyers call "a good practice" where my name was first posted on an office door. The part of Ohio where I lived and dreamed was of course a farming section, with farmers' ideas, if farmers can be said to have ideas. There were some things that they did not merely believe. These they knew. They knew that Protestantism was inspired and that all of its creeds, however conflicting, were true. They knew that the Republican party and all of its doctrines came as a divine revelation. They knew that the farmers were the backbone of the country and the most intelligent people in the world. They knew that all pleasure was sinful, and suffering was righteous; that the cities were evil and the country was good. Of course there were no saloons in the place.

The main industry of the farmers was the dairy business. This was carried on by taking milk to the cheese factories to be converted into butter and cheese; and then each farmer would receive his portion of the money coming from the sale of the output.

My business, as it slowly opened up, grew out of the horse trades, boundary lines, fraudulent representations, private quarrels and grudges, with which the world everywhere is rife. There were actions of debt, actions of replevin, cases of tort, and now and then a criminal complaint. Nearly all of the last mentioned grew out of the sale of liquor or watering milk before it was sent to the factory. The liquor prosecutions generally came from the villages, although here and there a farmer was fined for selling hard cider. The whole community was always against the defendant in the liquor cases, but not so in those pertaining to watering milk. Membership in a church in no way affected these cases of dilution. It was so easy to pour a bucketful of water into a milk can that many otherwise upright men could not resist.

In about two years of steady growth I was convinced that I was too big for that place, whereupon I moved to Ashtabula, twenty-five miles away, a town of about five thousand people and then the largest in that part of the country. Soon after my arrival I was elected city solicitor, with a salary of seventy-five dollars a month and the right to take cases on my own account, which salary and perquisites to me seemed all that I was worth.

Ashtabula furnished a somewhat broader field, but was not especially exciting. With me, as with most lawyers, a case became a personal matter, and my side was right. My feelings were always so strong that fees were a secondary matter.

The most important case I had in Ohio was an action of replevin for a harness worth fifteen dollars. There were other cases that involved more money, but this concerned the ownership of a harness which my client, a boy, had been given for attending a wealthy man in a case of illness. The suit was commenced before a justice of the peace ten miles away. I received five dollars for the first trial, but the jury disagreed. It was set for a second trial, but my client had no more five-dollar bills, so I tried it again at my own expense. My client lost the case, but I persuaded a friend of mine to sign a bond to appeal it to the Court of Common Pleas. By that time I had moved to Ashtabula, but went to the adjoining county to try the case, although after the first five-dollar bill I never got a cent, always paying my own expenses and those of my client, too. I won the case before the jury, but it was taken to the Court of Appeals, where the verdict was reversed. Again it was tried by the jury, who again decided in favor of my client. Once more it was carried to the Court of Appeals, which again reversed the case—the result hinged on a question of law. So I decided to appeal to the Supreme Court, although, in the meantime, I had moved to Chicago. I wrote the brief, argued the case, paid all expenses, and the court decided in my favor. It was seven or eight years from the time the case was commenced before it ended. I had spent money that I could not afford to spare, but I was determined to see it through.

This was long ago. There was no money involved, and not much principle, as I see it now, but then it seemed as if my life depended upon the result. Outside of the immediate jurisdiction it was not a famous case, but there are still living in Trumbull County, Ohio, a number of people who remember the case of "Jewell versus Brockway"—which involved the title to a harness.

A country law-business, in those days, had some interest and much excitement, although almost anything attracts attention in a little village. If a horse fell down on the street it drew a great audience. If a safe was lowered from the second story, the entire Main Street came to a standstill to watch it swung by ropes and pulleys to the sidewalk below. After that, we eagerly looked for something else to satisfy our curiosity and interest.

Fortunately, there was usually a poker game in progress somewhere, almost any time of the day or night. The limit was small, to be sure, as befitted a community of slender means, but none the less inspiring. After baseball, the next game to fascinate me was poker. With congenial companions, a deck of cards and a box of chips, and a little something to drink, I could forget the rest of the world until the last white bone had been tossed into the yawning jack pot. I don't know whether I would recommend the sport or not; I doubt if I would recommend anything if I thought my advice was to be followed. Everything depends on one's point of view of life. I am inclined to believe that the most satisfactory part of life is the time spent in sleep, when one is utterly oblivious to existence; next best is when one is so absorbed in activities that one is altogether unmindful of self. Poker is able to supply this for many, in all ranks of life; yet I would not advise any one to play, or not play, but do most emphatically advise them to keep the limit down.

But poker cannot be said to bear any kinship to the profession of law, excepting that in both games you are dealing with chances, which always helps somewhat to relieve one from the tedium and boredom of life. But law practice itself in a country town had its interesting sides. Necessarily, the cases were small; that is, the amount of cash involved was not great. But here, again, what is the difference whether one plays with a blue chip or a white one? The important thing is to play. And habit has much to do with the way one views the importance of the game. I am satisfied that no one with a moderate amount of intelligence can tolerate life, if he looks it squarely in the face, without welcoming whatever soothes and solaces, and makes one forget. Every one instinctively, automatically, seeks satisfaction from the annoyances and banalities of existence. Some resort to play, some to work, others to alcohol or opiates, and even to religion. But, whatever one takes, and quite regardless of relative values, we all seek something and accept something that gives rest and allays the tension of strenuous living.

Much of the business of the country lawyer in my day was the trial of cases before justices of the peace. These often seemed to be exciting events. And right now I am not so sure but that the old-time country lawyers fighting over the title to a cow were as clever, and sometimes as learned, as lawyers now whose cases involve millions of dollars, or human lives. The trials then were not so much a matter of rote. A lawsuit, then, before a justice of the peace, was filled with color and life and wits. Nor was the country lawsuit a dry and formal affair. Every one, for miles around, had heard of the case and taken sides between the contending parties or their lawyers. Neighborhoods, churches, lodges, and entire communities were divided as if in war. Often the cases were tried in the town halls, and audiences assembled from far and near. An old-time lawsuit was like a great tournament, as described by Walter Scott. The combatants on both sides were always seeking the weakest spots in the enemy's armor, and doing their utmost to unhorse him or to draw blood.

A country lawsuit not only gave the farmers and others not employed somewhere to go, but it left in its wake a chain of hatreds and scars that never healed.

In Ashtabula I was quite content, as I had been before in Andover. I had my friends and enemies, my cronies and critics; my arenas in which to fight, and my poker games at night. And, after all, even though now that life may appear small and superficial, and wasteful of time and opportunity— what does it matter? I am now so near the end of the trail that I can look back and contemplate and compare. Would it have

made the slightest difference whether I had remained in Ashtabula, or even in Andover, instead of coming to Chicago,
whether the stage was larger; or, whether I had been born at
all?

CHAPTER 5

I MAKE A HIT

CONSIDERING my age and the town, I was prospering in Ashtabula, and would doubtless be there now except for an important event for which I was no more responsible than I am for the course of the earth around the sun.

I was married when still a youth and was living there with my wife and son Paul, then four or five years old. I had been practicing law since I came of age, and was nearing my twenty-ninth birthday. Like most other young men I concluded to buy a home, and found one that I thought would do. I had five hundred dollars in the bank, and I bought the place for thirty-five hundred. The five hundred was to be paid down and the balance over a series of years. The owner was to deliver the deed to my office the next day. He appeared at the appointed time only to tell me that his wife refused to sign the document, so he could not sell the house. As I had made up my mind to buy this home I was peeved, to put it mildly, but managed to control my temper and answered bluntly, "All right, I don't believe I want your house because—because—I'm going to move away from here."

It is perfectly plain that the wish or whim of the woman shaped my whole future, and perhaps hers and her family's as well. Had I bought the house I would probably be in Ashtabula now trying to meet overdue payments. Perhaps I would be in the graveyard, perhaps in a little law office. No one can possibly guess. But certain it is, whether for better or worse, my life would have been a radically different one. It was easy enough to decide to leave Ashtabula when the woman refused to sign the deed, but where should I go? The world looked big and lonely, and my savings very small. My brother Everett was teaching in Chicago, and this doubtless had something to do with choosing that city for my new venture. Because of Everett's age and intelligence and kindliness all the family, including myself, always respected him and went to him for advice and assistance; and up to the time of his death, a few years ago, none of us ever looked to him in vain.

From my youth I was always interested in political questions. My father, like many others in northern Ohio, had early come under the spell of Horace Greeley, and, as far back as I can remember, the New York *Weekly Tribune* was the political and social Bible of our home. I was fifteen years old when Horace Greeley ran for the presidency. My father was an enthusiastic supporter of Greeley and I joined with him; and well do I remember the gloom and despair that clouded our home when we received the news of his defeat. From Greeley our family went to Tilden in 1876, but I was not old enough to vote. Of course most of the people in our neighborhood were for Hayes. In our town it was hard to tell which was the chief bulwark, Republicanism or religion. Both were sacred; but not to my family, who always lined up against the great majority. Our candidate, Samuel J. Tilden, was elected in 1876, but was not allowed to take his seat. The Civil War was not then so far in the background as it is now, and any sort of political larceny was justifiable to save the country from the party that had tried to destroy the *Union*. So, though Tilden was elected, Rutherford B. Hayes was inaugurated and served Tilden's term.

The Tilden campaign stimulated me to find out all I could about political questions, and I tried to carefully form an opinion on the issues of the day. My reading of history and political economy convinced me that states' rights and free trade were both sound doctrines. When the campaign between Blaine and Cleveland disturbed the political life of the Republic, I was for Cleveland.

As political questions have come and gone I have clung in my political allegiance to the doctrines of states' rights and free trade. To me they are as true and almost as important as they were in the historical campaign of 1884, when Cleveland was elected President of the United States. While I have always been interested in the political situation, I have never wanted a political career. The scheming and dickering and trading for political place never appealed to me, and I concluded early in life that if one entered a political course he must leave his independence behind, and this I could never abide. For a young man I took a considerable part in each of the three campaigns for Grover Cleveland, and then, and ever since, this President has been one of my idols. His courage, independence and honesty have always seemed far above those of most of the political figures of his time, or since his day.

Strange as it may seem, a banker in Ashtabula, Amos Hubbard, was the first man to give me some insight into radical political doctrines. He, like many others in that period, had been greatly influenced by Henry George's "Progress and Poverty." On his advice I read the book and felt that I had found a new political gospel that bade fair to bring about the social equality and opportunity that has always been the dream of the idealist. While Mr. Hubbard gave me a first insight into advanced political economy, Judge Richards, a police judge in Ashtabula, gave me my first sane idea of crime and criminals. He gave me a little book, "Our Penal Code and Its Victims," by Judge John P. Altgeld, of Chicago, which was a revelation to me. This book and the author came to have a marked influence upon me and my future.

I came to Chicago in 1888. Soon after my arrival I joined the Single Tax Club, and took part in the second Grover Cleveland campaign, then going on. This club met regularly every week for several years. In due time I realized that at every meeting the same faces appeared and reappeared, week after week, and that none of them cared to hear anything but a gospel which they all believed. It did not take long for Single Tax to become a religious doctrine necessary to salvation. But, the Single Tax Club furnished a forum for ambitious young lawyers to win a hearing in; and I generally participated in the debates, which led to my speaking at ward meetings and other public gatherings from time to time.

In those days I was rather oratorical. Like many other young men of that day, I did the best, or worst, I could to cover up such ideas as I had in a cloud of sounding metrical phrases. In later years nothing has disturbed my taste along that line more than being called an "orator," and I strive to use simpler words and shorter sentences, to make my statements plain and direct and, for me, at least, I find this the better manner of expression.

When I arrived in Chicago I rented a very modest apartment and took desk room in an office. I had no money to waste and never liked to borrow or be in debt, so I tried to live within my means, but in this I did not fully succeed in that first year in Chicago. I had few friends and acquaintances, and these did not have enough money to indulge in the extravagance of litigation. In that first year, all told, I did not receive in fees, or any other way, more than about three hundred dollars. I began to feel discouraged. From the very first a cloud of home-sickness always hung over me. There is no place so lonely to a young man as a great city where he has no intimates or companions. When I walked along the street I scanned every face I met to see if I could not perchance discover some one from Ohio. Sometimes I would stand on the corner of Madison and State Streets—"Chicago's busiest corner"—watching the passers-by for some familiar face; as well might I have hunted in the depths of the Brazilian forest. Had all my associates in Ohio suddenly come to Chicago en masse it would not have been possible to detect them there in the solid, surging sea of human units, each intent upon hurrying by and attending to his own small affairs.

At the Henry George Club I formed some congenial friendships and never missed one of their meetings; here I found a chance to talk so that I would not completely forget how to form sentences and feel at home on my feet. As the election of 1888 approached I was invited to make some speeches for the Democratic party in various halls throughout the city. When I appeared at a meeting it was with a long line of other ambitious young lawyers, each of us eager to make his voice heard in the general palaver; I was usually put down toward the end of the list, by which time I had little chance for attracting attention even if any one cared to listen. If by any luck I seemed to be getting the ear of the audience, I was soon interrupted by a string of candidates entering the hall anxious for their turn. The audience would rise and cheer and call for their favorite leaders, and the opportunity of the evening would be gone in the all-around din. Yet, in spite of all handicaps, I did make some acquaintances. Gradually it came to pass that some member of an audience would call for me, and I would respond without any pretense at reluctance. I knew that if I waited some other favorite would appropriate my chance. Now and then I was invited to make a talk at some civic meeting, but I did not seem to make a hit. Generally there were others whose faces were better known to the listeners. Then, my training had been neglected. My father had directed my reading, and had insisted that I study political economy, and speak only if I had something worth saving; at a political hubbub this was the worst thing one could do, and the last thing the audience expected or wished.

One night I was asked to speak at a West Side meeting, called to discuss some civic problem. The leading speaker was William B. Mason, who was at that time a State senator, and afterwards became a United States senator. I had long wanted the newspapers to notice my existence, but the reporters refused to even look at me. I entered the theatre through the back door and noted with joy that the place was packed. In front of the stage were a half-dozen or more newspaper reporters that gladdened my heart. Easily I sized up the situation and felt that my time had come. After a few preliminaries I was introduced amidst loud calls for Mason. I looked around and over at the audience, trying to gain their attention. The eyes can be very useful for quelling an audience or forcing people to focus on a speaker. I made my speech. I feel sure that it was not very bad. Probably not bad enough. I could see that the audience was waiting for William B. Mason, so I took no chances in delaying them too long. But the one thing that forcibly impressed me while I spoke was that not one of the newspaper men wrote a single line. They leaned back in their chairs and glanced at me with the complacent and sophisticated countenances of newspaper men. They knew why they were there, and whom their editors and the public would want to read about the next day. When I sat down there was slight applause. No speaker can get along without at least a little of that. Such approval as was manifested by the politest and kindliest there was drowned in the cries for "Mason!" They had come to hear him and were not interested in waiting. When he arose and stepped to the front of the platform, the entire audience stood up and wildly cheered; the newspaper men grabbed their books and pencils and began to write.

The next morning I hopefully looked over the newspapers. The front pages were covered with Senator Mason, but not a word about me. It was very discouraging for an energetic young man with the world before him. It began to look as though the world would always be before me. I had no envy for Mr. Mason, but what would I not have given for just a few lines of all that space devoted to him! After that evening I came to know Senator Mason very well, and never have I known a more kindly, humane and genial fellow. He, also, was an idealist, but not too far ahead of the crowd. He was a man of ability, filled with gentleness and good will toward all the world.

I was disappointed and discouraged, especially because the newspapers had made no mention of my speech. I did not know the press so well then as I do to-day. Since then they have given me more attention than I deserved, and often much more than I wanted. Through the first half of my life I was anxious to get into the papers; in the last half I have often been eager to keep out. In neither case have I had much success. Often I have felt that newspapers were unkind and unfair to me; and sometimes they have been. But, when I reflect that I have never been on the popular side of any issue, that I have always seemed to court opposition, that I have always stood with the minority against all popular causes and mass hysteria—that I have always voted "No" and been independent to the point of recklessness, I feel that I have gotten off easily. After all is said and done I am inclined to think that they have treated me very well. I always, really, have had many warm friends among newspaper men; a good many who were also minority men. Every large office has a number of this sort, and they have never failed to be as considerate as it was possible for them to be.

After the meeting at the West Side hall I was in gloom amounting almost to despair. If it had been possible I would have gone back to Ohio; but I didn't want to borrow the money, and I dreaded to confess defeat. I did not then know the ways of Fate. I did not know that Fortune comes like the day, sometimes filled with sunshine, sometimes hidden in gloom. I had not then learned that one must accept whatever comes along without regret; that he must not take either gratification or disappointment too seriously. I did not know, as Bret Harte put it, that the only sure thing about luck is that it will change. And luck can change as suddenly as daylight and darkness in a tropical land.

Soon after the blow in connection with the West Side meeting a "Free Trade Convention" was staged in Chicago. The closing session was held in Central Music Hall, at that time the most popular auditorium in the city; Henry George was to be the big drawing-card. Mr. George was then in the zenith of his power. I was invited to appear on the same programme. The great auditorium was packed, to my satisfaction. I looked out upon the audience with renewed hope. Every Single Taxer in Chicago seemed to be present, and a great throng besides. Mr. George was the first speaker, which looked ominous to me. I was afraid of either the first or last place; either one seemed fraught with peril. No one knew the tariff question better than Henry George. More than this, he was a strong idealist, and had the audience in his grasp from the first moment to the last. Every one but me was carried away with his able address. I was disappointed. I was sorry that it was so good. I twitched nervously in my chair until he had finished and the applause began to die away. I felt that after his wonderful address I would not be able to hold the audience. I realized that the crowd had come to hear him, and that but a few among them had ever heard of me.

When the applause subsided people began getting up and going away. The show was over. I said to the chairman, "For goodness sake get busy before every one leaves the house!" Quickly he introduced me, and my friends paused and did their best to give me a good reception. I had discovered enough about public speaking to sense that unless a speaker can interest his audience at once, his effort will be a failure. This was particularly true when following a speaker like Henry George, so I began with the most striking phrases that I could conjure from my harried, worried brain. The audience hesitated and began to sit down. They seemed willing to give me a chance.

I had at least one advantage; nothing was expected of me; if I could get their attention it would be easier than if too much was expected. Not one in twenty of the audience knew much about me. As a matter of fact, I had taken great pains to prepare my speech. The subject was one that had deeply interested me for many years, one that I really understood. In a short time I had the attention of the entire audience, to my surprise. Then came the full self-confidence which only a speaker can understand; that confidence that is felt as one visits by the fireside, when he can say what he pleases and as he pleases; when the speaker can, in fact, visit with the audience as with an old-time friend. I have no desire to elaborate on my talk, but I know that I had the people with me, and that I could sway those listeners as I wished.

But the crowning triumph had come as I warmed to my subject and waxed earnest in what I had to say, and became aware that the newspaper men down in front were listening, and were plying their pencils, recording my words, or seeming to record them, as fast as they shot past. When I finally finished, the audience was indeed generous and encouraging with its applause and appreciation. Henry George warmly grasped my hand. My friends and others came around me, and it was some time before I could leave the stage.

I have talked from platforms countless times since then, but never again have I felt that exquisite thrill of triumph after a speech. This was forty years ago, and even now I occasionally meet some one who tells me that he heard my speech at Central Music Hall the night I was there with Henry George. I know that at least a part of this enthusiasm came because I was unknown, and nothing was expected of me.

The next morning I was awake early and went out and bought all the papers. This time my name was all over the front page. The reporters had certainly done their best. I read them all carefully, and then I read them all over again. It was exceedingly pleasant to my senses. Since that day I have often seen my name prominently featured on the outsides and insides of newspapers; often I have refrained from reading what was said, and have felt that only by closing my eyes and steeling my heart could I go on with the work on which I had set my mind.

I went to my office earlier than usual the next morning. No customers were there. Soon some of my Single Tax friends and Socialist companions began coming in to congratulate me on my speech. This was pleasing but not profitable. Single Taxers and Socialists never come for business; they come to use your telephone and tell you how the world should be organized so that every one could have his own telephone. But of course I enjoyed their visit and appreciated their good will, and began to feel more hopeful.

The city did not look so big, nor feel so cold now. All through the day I received some real invitations to speak at good meetings in the campaign then in progress. DeWitt C. Cregier was running for mayor of Chicago on the Democratic ticket. I had been asked to speak at various meetings before, but never until then had I been invited to choose my hall and colleagues. This time I was asked to do both. I named my hall, but I took no chances, and said that I would speak alone. And I did.

CHAPTER 6

GETTING ON

In spite of my fond hopes, business did not come with a rush. Strange to say, the meeting did not bring clients, and these were what I needed most. A few weeks after Henry George and I had spoken at Central Music Hall, DeWitt C. Cregier was elected mayor of Chicago. Although I had taken part in his campaign I had never met him, and did not even try to make his acquaintance. I knew that almost every one who had voted for him would expect some favor in return, and I had no ambition to enter into that sort of contest.

It was perhaps two months after the election that I was wearily sitting in my office when a messenger brought me a letter. It was from DeWitt C. Cregier, asking me to come over and see him when I had time. The latter part of the sentence sounded like a joke. I had time right then. So I put the letter into my pocket and went to see the mayor. The hall and the offices were crowded with politicians looking for jobs. I sent in my name and was not kept waiting. After a little preliminary conversation Mr. Cregier asked me if I would take the position of special assessment attorney.

I had very little idea of the duties of a special assessment attorney. I was told that the salary was three thousand dollars for only a year's time, and this seemed to me a fabulous sum, so I told him that I would be glad to take it and do the best I could. He asked me when I could be ready to begin. I answered that I saw no reason why I should not begin right now. So I was placed on the pay roll before I left the office, and immediately and recklessly started in.

Very soon I grew familiar with the work. Of course many

questions came up for immediate answers which I did not fully understand, but I used the best judgment I had and always answered promptly. Seldom did I find that I had guessed wrong. I thought, then, that it was my natural judgment and wisdom that led me to always answer right. Since that time I have modified my opinion. I was working for the city of Chicago. I had all the strength of a large city behind my decision; few were able to contest my opinion, and even if they did, the tendency of the courts was always to decide for the city. All my experience in life has strengthened this conclusion. Every advantage in the world goes with power. The city, the State, the county, the nation can scarcely be wrong. Behind them is organized society, and the individual who is obliged to contest for his rights against these forces in either civil or criminal courts is fighting against dreadful odds.

When I had been special assessment attorney for about three months some political complication compelled the resignation of the assistant corporation counsel and I was given his place. My salary then became five thousand dollars a year. My duties were more strenuous and I gave them all my time and attention. This position kept me in court a great deal in contested cases. At the same time every alderman and city official had the right to ask my advice, which I learned to give as promptly as possible, often simply making the best guess I could, and almost invariably finding that my advice settled the whole controversy. For about ten months I remained in this office, and then the corporation counsel was stricken with an illness that compelled him to go south to a warmer climate, whereupon I became acting corporation counsel, and was the head of the law department of the city of Chicago. When luck began to change everything seemed rapidly to come my way. As acting corporation counsel I was in daily conference with the Mayor, and we came to be good friends. In one of my interviews I asked him how he happened to send for me and ask me to be special assessment attorney, never having met me before. He replied, "Don't you know? Why, I heard you make that speech that night with Henry George."

How much had I to do with all this? I had nothing whatever to do with my birth, which was a rather important event in the whole scheme. It seemed that in the infinite chances that bring forth life I was to be I. Nor had I the slightest thing to do with the sort of being that was spawned out with all the rest; nor the environment in which I found myself. Every turn of the development came from a cause that was controlling to me. Had I been able to deliberate, I could only have considered the arguments for and against each step, and my answer would necessarily have been in the way that seemed best to me in view of all circumstances, including my structure. Passing by an endless number of influences of equal import that determined my destiny, I had nothing to do with the woman refusing to sign the deed that drove me to Chicago. Had she signed that deed I should not have left Ashtabula, Ohio. I had nothing to do with being invited to speak at the Henry George meeting. I had nothing to do with a man being in the audience who afterward became mayor. I had nothing to do with being invited to become special assessment attorney. I had nothing to do with political differences that made me assistant corporation counsel. I had nothing to do with illness coming upon the corporation counsel, which placed me at the head of the department for the time. But, while I did not make the corporation counsel ill, I am afraid that I fully approved it. His sickness seemed to be what is generally called "an act of Providence." If it was such an act, it is plain that Providence was thinking of me and not of him.

For the following two years I was very busy with the affairs of the city of Chicago. Every man was my client; that is, every one who had any business with the city of Chicago. I found most of the officials, like the average office-holders, anxious to shirk responsibility. Nothing could be done without the advice of the Corporation Counsel's office. It was my business to assume the responsibility. I always took my share of the burden, and made no attempt to dodge. In cases of doubt I resolved the doubt in favor of the city, as all officials do, but I never let this rule prevent me from deciding in favor of the property holder and the citizen when I was satisfied that he was right.

In this place I made the acquaintance of all the aldermen and most of the politicians of Chicago. I never admired politicians, though they are generally kindly and genial, and often very intelligent; but seldom is there one with real courage. Their constituency is that mysterious entity known as "the people"—with all its ignorance, its prejudices, its selfishness, and, worst of all, its insincerity as to either men or principles. This is the despair of ever accomplishing anything of real value in the affairs of state. While I liked political questions, I did not like politicians, as such, and never wanted political office.

During these early years in Chicago I was very much interested in what passes under the name of "radicalism" and at one time was a pronounced disciple of Henry George. But as I read and pondered about the history of man, as I learned more about the motives that move individuals and communities, I became doubtful of his philosophy. I never believed that land should be reduced to private ownership, and I never felt that any important social readjustment could come while any one could claim the unconditional right to any part of the earth and "the fulness thereof." The error I found in the philosophy of Henry George was its cocksureness, its simplicity, and the small value that it placed upon the selfish motives of men. I grew weary of its everlasting talk of "natural rights." The doctrine was a hang-over from the seventeenth century in France, when the philosophers had given up the idea of God, but still thought that there must be some immovable basis for man's conduct and ideas. In this dilemma they evolved the theory of natural rights. If "natural rights" means anything it means that the individual rights are to be determined by the conduct of Nature. But Nature knows nothing about rights in the sense of human conception. Nothing is so cruel, so wanton, so unfeeling as Nature; she moves with the weight of a glacier carrying everything before her. In the eyes of Nature, neither man nor any of the other animals mean anything whatever. The rock-ribbed mountains, the tempestuous sea, the scorching desert, the myriad weeds and insects and wild beasts that infest the earth, and the noblest man, are all one. Each and all are helpless against the cruelty and immutability of the resistless processes of Nature.

Socialism seemed to me much more logical and profound; Socialism at least recognized that if man was to make a better world it must be through the mutual effort of human units; that it must be by some sort of co-operation that would include all the units of the state. Still, while I was in sympathy with its purposes, I could never find myself agreeing with its methods. I had too little faith in men to want to place myself entirely in the hands of the mass. And I never could convince myself that any theory of Socialism so far elaborated was consistent with individual liberty. To me liberty meant only power to do what one wished to do. Free will had nothing to do with the wanting. Man did not create the wishes; he simply struggled to carry them out. I never could imagine life being worth while without the opportunity to carry out individual desires. I always have had sympathy for the Socialistic view of life, and still have sympathy with it, but could never find myself working for the party.

Anarchism, as taught by Kropotkin, Recluse and Tolstoy, impressed me more, but it impressed me only as the vision of heaven held by the elect, a far-off dream that had no relation to life. So, without having any specific radical faith, I always was friendly toward its ideals and aims, and could feel and see the injustice of the present system, and generally found myself in conflict with it.

This is still my attitude on social and political questions. I believed in keeping society flexible and mobile, and embracing what seemed like opportunity to bring about a fairer distribution of this world's goods. Living in the North, and holding these views, I have always been driven to the support of the Democratic party, with few illusions as to what it meant.

Neither government nor political economy is an exact science. They concern the arrangement of human units. If it were possible to demonstrate what sort of an arrangement would be best for the individuals of the state, it would be of no avail. Humans cannot be controlled like inanimate objects, or even like the lower animals. Each human unit is in some regard an independent entity with his own ideas, his hopes and fears, loves and hates. These attitudes are constantly changing from day to day, and year to year. They are played upon by shrewd men, by influential newspapers, by all sorts of schemes and devices which make human government only trial and success, and trial and failure. Human organizations are simply collections of individuals always in motion and always seeking for easier and more harmonious adjustment, and never static.

I could see but one way toward any general betterment of social organization, and that was by teaching sympathy and tolerance. This in itself is so hopeless a task that every one despairs of any result worth the effort. Sympathy or its lack is so entirely due to the character of the physical organism that teaching is of little help. Sympathy is the child of imagination, and possibly this can be cultivated if the effort is begun in childhood. Imagination gives one power to put oneself in another's place. It does more; it compels him to rejoice and suffer with the joys and sorrows of those about him. Like almost everything else, it brings both pain and pleasure, and whether it adds to the happiness of the individual or increases his misery, cannot be told; of course it does both, but I know no way of finding out the net result.

In politics, political economy, and human institutions, men make the great mistake of thinking that any special adjustment of individual units is perfect or sacred. Probably no organization or any part of one is wholly either good or bad. Even if at some time it seemed to conduce to man's highest good it would not follow that it would have the same effect at all times or places. I could never be convinced that any institution was wholly good or wholly evil. This feeling has prevented me from obeying orders or being a bitter partisan on any question. Instinctively I lean toward the integrity of the individual unit, and am impatient with any interference with personal freedom. However, I know that society can not exist without recognizing the necessity of some control of the individual. If men could be taught to understand that the object sought should be to produce happiness, satisfaction, and general well-being for all, I believe the conditions of life could be made much easier and human beings made happier than they now are. This is a changing world, and still it must maintain a certain amount of consistency and stability or the individual units would separate, and chaos would make any co-operation impossible.

Naturally my connection with the city administration broadened my acquaintance and called me often to the discussion of social problems in all sorts of clubs and organizations. Every large city has many different cliques, societies and groups, and these are constantly on the lookout for new attractions to keep alive the interests of their members. Generally this becomes a burden to those who are more or less widely known; which is one reason why so few of the addresses are worth while. The speaker who talks at all sorts of meetings is apt to form hasty opinions, grow careless about what he says, and place too great an estimate upon his ideas and those picked up from others and passed along without proper consideration. One thing, however, is almost certain: clubs and societies are always looking for some one new, and just as surely they readily cast the old one out. This process gives the student a chance to test all opinions and explore fresh fields of thought. No writer or speaker should ever be satisfied that his view of things is sound. Only by constant trials and tests can one arrive at the truth, and there is no certainty that even these efforts will determine it.

CHAPTER 7

THE RAILROAD STRIKE

AFTER two or three years of service in the city law department, I resigned my position and became the general attorney of the Chicago and North-Western Railway Company. It was with a good deal of hesitation and consideration, and after all sorts of advice, that I undertook that position. I was aware that my general views of life were not such as fitted me for this kind of career. Every one connected with the offices of the company knew my opinions and attitudes, but gave me no cause for concern or uneasiness. I was treated with respect and all were most friendly.

This position with the company brought me into a new and varied field. All sorts of questions were submitted to me. I rendered opinions on the liability of the company, in cases of personal injuries, in claims for lost freight, in the construction of the statutes and ordinances, and all the numerous matters that affect the interests of railroads. I also tried a considerable number of cases, some of them involving my old employer, the city of Chicago. In spite of the kindness and consideration of all my associates, I knew that the position was one that I should never really like. It was hard for me to take the side of the railroad company against one who had been injured in their service or against a passenger. I was aware that I always wanted the company to help them, and in this my services were made easier by the general claim agent, Mr. Ralph C. Richards, whose sympathies were the same. I am sure that both he and I were able to help a great many people without serious cost to the road. Later, Mr. Richards practically gave up his position to inaugurate a great work for the prevention of accidents.

The policy that he brought about saved many lives and limbs, and has now been largely incorporated into the law.

It was during my services for the Chicago and North-Western Railroad Company that the strike of the American Railway Union occurred, in 1894. Neither before nor since has any such railroad strike happened in America. Mr. Eugene Debs was the head of that organization. He was an intelligent, alert, and fearless man. The strike grew out of a demand for better wages and conditions. The railroads refused to grant the demands. I had then been in my new position about two years, as I now recall it.

When I was sure that there was no chance to settle the difficulties, I realized my anomalous position. I really wanted the men to win, and believed that they should. This had for years been my attitude in cases of strike. I had no feeling that the members of labor unions were better than employers; I knew that like all other men they were often selfish and unreasonable, but I believed that the distribution of wealth was grossly unjust, and I sympathized with almost all efforts to get higher wages and to improve general conditions for the masses.

Still, my duty was to the road, and as the strike loomed it seemed sure that in some way I should be put in positions where one side or the other would doubt my loyalty. Within a few days I found that I had been placed on a committee of all the roads to assist in the management of the strike. I at once went to both the general counsel and the president of the railway company. Both were friends and had full confidence in me. I told them of the situation, and that I could not act on the committee. I made them understand my general feelings and my peculiar position. They recognized it and said that they would not insist upon my being on the committee, that they were perfectly willing to trust me to be neutral, and knew that I would be loyal. I felt then that I should resign my position, that the road had the right to men who were in full accord with their policy; but they urged me to stay, and, of course, their confidence and fairness made a strong appeal to me. So I told them that I would remain, and that if it ever came to a point where either they or I should feel any embarrassment we would take up the question again.

Day after day conditions grew more serious. There was a general interruption of railroad traffic from one end of the country to the other. In many of the great railroads the yards were crowded with idle freight cars. Deputy sheriffs and marshals were called out in all the large cities and many of the smaller ones. I watched the situation with anxiety. I preferred to stay with the North-Western Railway Company, but I could not avoid being in sympathy with the strikers. The Chicago and North-Western Railway Company was involved with all the rest of the roads, and all who came to the offices thought and talked of little else besides the strike. John P. Hopkins was then mayor of Chicago, and John P. Altgeld was governor of the State. These men were both Democrats, and the sheriff of the county was a Republican. Under the laws of the State it was the duty of the mayor in the city and the sheriff in the county to preserve peace. The governor had the right to call out the troops, but only on request of the sheriff or the mayor, when the legislature was not in session. Grover Cleveland was then President of the United States.

A great many cars were burned in the yards of Chicago and other cities. As in most cases, each side claimed that their enemies were responsible for the fires. One night I went to one of the railroad yards and saw many cars in flames. Crowds of people were gathered around to see the destruction; most of them were boys and young men. A number of them were deputies who had been sworn in to preserve the peace. The crowd was quiet and attempted no demonsration. They only stood and looked at the burning cars; and little, if any, effort was made to quench the flames. I presume that it was not possible to get much water so far from the city supply, but of this I am not certain.

I had no knowledge as to who started the fires, but I was satisfied that most of all those in the yards were sympathetic toward the strikers. They were working men and their families, who are always automatically on the side of the strikers, just as the wealthy are on the other side. I have no doubt that many of the deputies who were sworn in were friendly toward the strikers. I have observed many deputies and other officials in times of strikes, and also the militia, and have found that generally they were really in sympathy with the strikers. Most of them were poor, and so without taking any thought about the situation they sided with their class. This has been the case since man evolved. It was clearly the case in the French Revolution, and in all lesser political and social upheavals that ever came to my attention, either through experience or study.

Industrial contests take on all the attitudes and psychology of war, and both parties do many things that they should never dream of doing in times of peace. Whatever may be said, the fact is that all strikes and all resistance to strikes take on the psychology of warfare, and all parties in interest must be judged from that standpoint. As I stood on the prairie watching the burning cars I had no feeling of enmity toward either side. I was only sad to realize how little pressure man could stand before he reverted to the primitive. This I have thought many times since that eventful night.

The strike was hardly well under way before the railroads applied to the Federal Courts to get injunctions against the strikers. Neither then nor since have I ever believed in labor injunctions. Preserving peace is a part of the police power of the State, and men should be left free to strike or not, as they see fit. When violence occurs this is for the police department and not for a court of chancery. I had never been connected with a case involving strikes, but both by education and natural tendency I had a deep-rooted feeling for the men against whom injunctions were issued.

A short time before I had stood on the prairie watching the cars in a cloud of smoke, the railroads asked the Federal Court for injunctions. The General Managers' Association, including all the roads, had appointed Mr. Edwin Walker their attorney in these cases. Mr. Walker was a clever and very astute lawyer. For years he had been the general counsel for the Chicago, Milwaukee and St. Paul Railroad Company, and had also represented large interests in Chicago and other parts of the United States.

When the interference in train schedules became general there was, of course, delay in carrying the mails. The railroads put mail cars on every train where there was any possible chance of sending them out. The strike leaders were always advised by their lawyers to try to let mail trains through, but the general stoppage of work nevertheless caused delay.

The injunction cases were commenced by the United States Government. Mr. Edwin Walker was regularly appointed special attorney for the government in the prosecution of these cases. So, in this matter, Mr. Walker was general counsel for the Chicago, Milwaukee and St. Paul Railway Company, for the General Managers' Association, and a special attorney for the United States. I did not regard this as fair. The government might with as good grace have appointed the attorney for the American Railway Union to represent the United States. The A. R. U. had thus far been represented by their regular attorney from Indiana, and Mr. William Irwin, a well-known lawyer from Minneapolis. Soon after the injunctions were issued, Mr. Debs and a good many of my friends came to ask me to go into the case. I did not want to take it up, knowing about what would be involved. I knew that it would take all my time for a long period, with no compensation; but I was on their side, and when I saw poor men giving up their jobs for a cause, I could find no sufficient excuse, except my selfish interest, for refusing. So, again I went to the president of the company and told him that I felt that I should go into the case, although it would mean giving up my position; and I told him that I believed some one whose political views were more in keeping with their interests would be a much better man for the company. He was most cordial and attentive. He agreed that I must do whatever I considered right, but asked me to continue my connection with the road when I went into private practice and take such matters as we agreed upon, at about half the salary I had been receiving. This connection was thus kept up for a number of years. The president of the road was Mr. Marvin Hewitt. We remained the best of friends to the end of his life. He died about 1920, I believe.

And so I gave up my position and became one of the attorneys for Mr. Debs in the great strike of the American Railway Union. I did not want to take the position, and felt that I should not, but I had not been able to justify my strong convictions with a refusal to aid them in their contest. About the time of the issuing of the injunctions, and before I left the North-Western Company, Mr. Edwin Walker, as special government attorney, wired the President of the United States, Grover Cleveland, to send Federal troops to Chicago. He did this against the protest of the governor and the mayor, and clearly without legal rights. The Constitution of the United States provided that the President could send troops to a State on request of the legislature, or of the governor, when the legislature was not in session, but no one seemed to care for the Constitution, as no one does when an occasion seems important. I no longer get so excited over such acts as I once did. I know that when men are sufficiently aroused they ignore laws and customs and precedents, and try to get their way. The great World War demonstrates the impotency of human restraints and arrangements in the face of an overwhelming passion. Governor Altgeld asserted that there was no authority for sending the troops to Chicago; as clearly there was none. As a matter of fact, there was no need whatever of Federal troops, even had the President a legal right to send them. There was no rioting or uncontrollable disorder, no open defiance of the law. Here and there a few men might gather and some discussion might lead to a fight, but that is always a common occurrence in such cases.

It is true that a large number of cars in outlying districts were burned, but no military force could have averted that. This did not result from any uncontrollable disorder. The police at all times had the situation fully in their hands, and there was no sign or chance of disturbance. The Federal troops were really brought as a gesture, but an unfriendly one against the Constitution and the laws and the liberties of the people. When the troops arrived they stood around like the policemen and officers and citizens, until their presence was so obviously useless that they were recalled.

Mr. Debs and all the members of his board were enjoined—enjoined from what? Of course no one could tell. It depended upon how many inferences could be drawn from other inferences, and to what degree. But the injunction and the troops and the press made it impossible to win the strike. I do not mean to discuss the original merits of the strike. The men left the railroads en masse to keep their wages from being cut and working conditions lowered. The railroads resisted because to yield meant greater cost in the running of trains. Both sides were right, but I wanted to see the workers win. I knew of no way to determine what a workman should be paid; what he should have in a way is determined by what he can get, and, so far as we can see, every one's compensation is settled the same way.

In addition to the injunctions, Mr. Debs and all his executive board were indicted by the Federal grand jury for conspiracy.

Like all such indictments, these were framed in general terms, to cover anything that by fact or construction might justify a conviction.

If there are still any citizens interested in protecting human liberty, let them study the conspiracy laws of the United States. They have grown apace in the last forty years until to-day no one's liberty is safe. The conspiracy laws magnify misdemeanors into serious felonies. If a boy should steal a dime a small fine would cover the offense; he could not be sent to the penitentiary. But if two boys by agreement steal a dime then both of them could be sent to the penitentiary as conspirators. Not only could they be, but boys are constantly being sent under similar circumstances.

If A is indicted and a conspiracy is charged, or even if it is not charged, the state's attorney is allowed to prove what A said to B and what B said to C while the defendant was not present. Then he can prove what C said to D and what D said to E, and so on, to the end of the alphabet, and after the letters are used up the state's attorney can resort to figures for as long a stretch as he cares to continue. To make this hearsay or gossip competent, the state's attorney informs the court that later he will connect it up by showing that the defendant was informed of the various conversations, or that he otherwise had knowledge of them. Thereupon the complaisant judge holds that the evidence is admissible, but if it is not connected up it will be stricken out. A week or a month may pass by, and then a motion is made to strike it out. By that time it is of no consequence whether it is stricken out or not; it has entered the jurors' consciousness with a mass of other matter, and altogether it has made an impression on his mind. What particular thing made the impression, neither the juror nor any one else can know.

These conspiracy laws, made by the courts, have gone so far that they can never be changed except through a general

protest by liberty-loving men and women, if any such there
be, against the spirit of tyranny that has battered down the
ordinary safeguards that laws and institutions have made to
protect individual rights. In that event, any degree of freedom
cannot be established except by statutes of the Federal government and of the several States. In this event, these laws will
be chipped away by courts through sophistry and tyranny, as
they always have been destroyed. Liberty cannot prevail unless
the feeling is in the hearts of the people; and wealth, and the
hope of it, have taken this away.

CHAPTER 8

EUGENE V. DEBS

In due time, the strike ran its course, as strikes always do. The A. R. U. was destroyed. For many years its members were boycotted; they changed their names and wandered over the land looking for a chance to work. After the strike was over, the cases of Mr. Debs and his associates were called in court. Mr. S. S. Gregory consented to go into the trial of these cases with me. Mr. Gregory was one of the best lawyers I have ever known. He was emotional and sympathetic, he was devoted to the principles of liberty and always fought for the poor and oppressed. In spite of all this, he had a fine practice, and his ability and learning were thoroughly recognized. He at one time was president of the American Bar Association, and his legal attainments were everywhere acknowledged.

The criminal case was first put on trial. At the end of several weeks, and when the case was practically finished, the bailiff reported to the court that a juror was taken ill. The government asked for the dismissal of the jury and a mistrial. We offered to go on with eleven men; the government would not consent. When the jury was dismissed we were informed that they stood eleven to one for acquittal at the time of the discharge. We made several demands to have the case set for trial, but after fighting it off as long as possible the government finally dismissed it.

With exactly the same charge and the same evidence, Judge Woods, a Federal judge from Indianapolis, heard the injunction case. After taking a considerable time for deliberation he found Debs and his associates guilty of violating the injunction. In the whole case there was not one word of evidence connecting any of them with any violence or even the use of inflammatory language. Debs was sentenced to six months' imprisonment in jail and his associates to three months. We then took the case to the Supreme Court of the United States. For this hearing, Mr. Lyman Trumbull volunteered to argue it with us. He had been a judge of the Supreme Court of Illinois, and was for many years a United States senator. His vote in Andrew Johnson's impeachment trial went far to prevent his impeachment. He wrote the Fourteenth Amendment and was the author of much other important legislation of his day. He, like the rest of us, received nothing but expenses for his services. The treasury of the A. R. U. was exhausted before the litigation had really made a start, as it must always be in strike cases, or, at least, so it was twenty-five years ago.

The Supreme Court took the matter under consideration, and in due time decided against Mr. Debs. This opinion strengthened the arm of arbitrary power. It left the law so that, in cases involving strikes, at least, a man could be sent to prison for crime without trial by jury. The opinion of the Supreme Court was unanimous. Justice Holmes and Justice Brandeis were not then members.

So Eugene Debs was sent to jail in Woodstock, Ill., for trying to help his fellow man. He really got off easy. No other offense has ever been visited with such severe penalties as seeking to help the oppressed. When the idealist has tried hard enough and labored long enough it is always easy to lodge a specific charge against him.

A host of friends went to Woodstock jail with Mr. Debs. To be sure they were generally stopped at the door, although they would have wished nothing more than to remain there with him. During his residence in Woodstock the trains daily took visitors to his cell. No house in the town, and few in the land, were or ever had been so popular as the Woodstock jail. When the time for his release came a trainload of friends went from Chicago to Woodstock to welcome him. That night the great Convention Hall, Battery D, was jammed to overflowing with a wildly enthusiastic crowd of his admirers and supporters testifying their love and loyalty. The imprisonment of Eugene Victor Debs in the Woodstock jail made him a world-wide figure.

No one was so interested on either side as to know exactly what it was all about. Both sides swept away the chaff and technicalities. Both sides recognized that Debs had been sent to jail because he had led a great fight to benefit the toilers and the poor. It was purely a part of the world class-struggle for which no individual can be blamed.

In all this there was nothing weird or strange. It was an accident that displayed the workings of man's primal instincts and deep emotions. It was one of the experiences of life that bring hope and despair. Hope, to find that the world boasts some men and women whose idealism and devotion to sympathy for others makes them dare and suffer in a cause; despair, to learn that man is largely ruled by his feelings and emotions and will hate and punish as easily as he will love and approve. It is depressing, because one knows that the structure has not changed since he became a man, and that his very structure makes it impossible that he can ever change.

Eugene V. Debs has always been one of my heroes. And as he must figure further in this story I may as well complete what I have to say of " 'Gene" whether in the natural sequence or not. There may have lived some time, some where, a kindlier, gentler, more generous man than Eugene V. Debs, but I have never known him. Nor have I ever read or heard of another. Mr. Debs at once became the head of the Socialist party of America. I never followed him politically. I never could believe that man was so constructed as to make Socialism possible; but I watched him and his cause with great interest. He was not only all that I have said, but he was the bravest man I ever knew. He never felt fear. He had the courage of the babe who has no conception of the word or its meaning.

I differed with Mr. Debs again when America entered the World War. I felt that we should join with the allies, but Mr. Debs, who hated war in any form and for any cause, thought that we should stay out. I am quite sure that his sympathies were with the allies; at least he told me so ten days before he made the speech that was to send him to prison again.

During the war Mr. Debs said very little on the subject. I have always felt that he would have gone through the period without accident except that Rose Pastor Stokes was indicted for opposing the war. The case was ridiculous and flimsy, but the judge and jury were deeply prejudiced, as all of them were through that period, and Mrs. Stokes was convicted. Mr. Debs immediately protested in the strong and vigorous language that he knew how to use. But Mrs. Stokes did not go to prison; a higher court reversed the case, and she was never tried again.

I had nothing to do with the case of Mr. Debs. He knew my views on the war, as did all the others who opposed it, so that, with one or two exceptions, I was not even invited into those cases. While I was strongly for America entering the war, and did all I could to help, still I felt that the courts had gone mad and were heartless in their horrible sentences that would shame savages for their severity; perhaps I should have said: should shame civilized people.

Mr. Debs was tried and convicted. The case was very weak, but Mr. Debs insisted on arguing it to the jury. He told them that he was against the war from the beginning, that he had done all he could to impede it, and should continue to do so till the end. It would have been impossible for any jury to do otherwise under the circumstances, and I have no idea that Mr. Debs expected anything else than conviction. I am inclined to believe that he thought his place was in jail, beside the

thousands of others that the government pursued with relentless barbarity. We may admit that during the war it became
necessary to confine some men in prison. Most of these were as
honest and much higher-minded than most of the civilians
who were entrusted with the management of important details
connected with our part of the conflict. Every one knew that
most of these victims were upright, fine men and women, and
that they should have been subjected to no hardships or indignity, but all should have been pardoned at once as soon as
the war ended. In place of that, the ruling forces of industry
took advantage of the war. After it was over they caused an
espionage act to be passed in nearly every State in the Union
that was meant to strangle public and private criticism of public men and policies, in the sacred cause of Big Business. These
laws denied and defied every principle for which our forefathers fought to obtain freedom for the United States. The
treatment of the conscientious objectors, especially after the
war, was, to my mind, the worst blot on the intelligence and
idealism of Woodrow Wilson, for whom I always felt the
highest admiration and regard.

Mr. Debs, true to form, insisted that he had done nothing
but what he thought right, and refused to ask for pardon.
When he had been in prison for three years, and many efforts
had been made for his release, I went to Washington without
consulting Mr. Debs. I saw the attorney general, Mitchell
Palmer, who was supposed to be a Quaker; perhaps he is,
though any Quakerism that might have been in their family
probably mostly affected his ancestors. I told him my errand.
Mr. Palmer said he would like to help Mr. Debs, and asked if
I represented him. When I answered that I did not, he stated
that he did not like to discuss the matter with me unless I
could say that I represented Mr. Debs. I replied that if he insisted, I would go to Atlanta prison and talk with Mr. Debs
and return to Washington. It was in the middle of the sum-

mer and the ride was long and disagreeable. I landed in Atlanta early in the morning and went directly to the penitentiary and found the warden without any trouble. I had never seen him before, but he told me that for a long time he had been with Major McClowry, warden of the Illinois State Penitentiary, who was one of my friends.

I explained that I had come specially to see Mr. Debs, and would like to see him alone if possible, the reason for this request being that I had heard many reports of the bad treatment he was receiving in prison. I was doubtful of this, and wanted to know from Mr. Debs. The warden was more than willing, and invited me to use his private room if I wished, saying that he would take another for himself. In a few moments Debs entered and greeted me warmly. He and the warden seemed to be on the best of terms, so much so that I assured the warden that there was no need of his leaving the room. We three then discussed all sorts of subjects, from Socialism and Anarchism to prisons and punishments, and every other social question, until the forenoon had slipped away. I could not get a train for Washington until late at night, so I decided to wait in what was probably the most interesting place in Atlanta, if not in the United States.

The warden asked me to have luncheon with him at his house, and said how sorry he was that he could not take Mr. Debs, too. When we had finished the meal I said that I would like to visit Mr. Debs in his cell if it would be all right to do so. The request was at once granted and he took me there himself, and asked if I wanted him to stay or not. Of course I invited him to remain, and so he did.

Mr. Debs was in a very large cell, made for six persons. Just in front, with only the bars between, was a garden full of beautiful flowers. There was with him a mountaineer from the South, good-natured, simple and fine, who had done nothing but give Nature a chance to convert corn into whiskey; he could not imagine why he was there, any more than I can imagine why men who think themselves civilized build cells. There was also a business man from a Northern city who had been charged with a confidence game; though why his particular kind of confidence game should be singled out from all the rest I could not understand. There were two or three others in the cell, and there was the atmosphere of a happy family; and so it was, for the place was radiant with the sunshine and kindness and love of Eugene V. Debs.

We sat on boxes, on the beds, and the few chairs, the warden with the rest. We discussed with the frankness of friends our experiences, hopes and visions. A jail is a good place for these reflections; there is no business to be disturbed. In answer to my question, Mr. Debs said that he could not ask for anything from the administration, and could make no promises, but if I wanted to help him out he fully appreciated all that I was doing for him.

"Really," he said, "this place is not bad. I look at that garden of flowers. There are bars in front, I know—but I never see the bars."

Mr. Debs was loved and idealized by all the inmates. He did all in his power to help every one with whom he came in contact. He steadily refused to take easier jobs or receive any privileges that were not given to all, as Walt Whitman said, "on equal terms."

It was with reluctance that I bade Mr. Debs "good-by" and went home with the warden to dinner and then to the train. On my return to Washington I called on Mr. Palmer. I expected that Mr. Debs would be pardoned at once. But I was disappointed. It took more work and longer waiting. President Woodrow Wilson and Mitchell Palmer missed a great opportunity to show belated understanding of Mr. Debs and thousands of other honest men whose conscience and humanity had landed them in jail.

It was left for President Harding and Mr. Dougherty to pardon Debs. Although I was never a disciple or follower of either Mr. Harding or Mr. Dougherty, I always remember them with kindliness when I think of Gene. The truth is, no man is white and no man is black. We are all freckled.

Later, I formed the acquaintance of Mr. Harry Dougherty under very favorable circumstances. I told him that I could never forget that it was through his kindness that Mr. Debs was pardoned. He replied, "No, it was not. President Harding asked me to investigate the case and see if we could not let him out; so I sent for Mr. Debs, and asked him to come without guard to see me in Washington. He spent a large part of the day in my office, and I never met a man I liked better." He added, "Won't you please remember me to his wife and brother when you write to them?"

I had always admired Woodrow Wilson and distrusted Harding. Doubtless my opinions about both in relation to affairs of government were measurably correct; still, Mr. Wilson, a scholar and an idealist, and Mr. Palmer, a Quaker, kept Debs in prison; and Mr. Harding and Mr. Dougherty unlocked the door. I know at least two men who understood this: Lincoln Steffens and Fremont Older. So far as I am concerned, I never think of either Harding or Dougherty without saying to myself: "Well, they pardoned Debs!"

CHAPTER 9

HOW I FELL

In 1894 I opened an office and went into private practice. Neither then nor for any considerable time thereafter did I need to worry over business prospects. For many years my practice covered almost all sorts of litigation. When I began, it was with the intention of trying only civil cases. But no one controls his own destiny, and lawyers are no exception to that rule.

I was willing to undertake the injunction case brought by the railroad companies in behalf of the government against Mr. Debs and his associates, or, brought by the government in behalf of the railroad companies, whichever way one chooses to put it. How one puts it depends on how he views public questions. I had never had anything to do with criminal cases, and, like most other lawyers, did not want to take them. But Mr. Debs insisted that I should defend him, so I undertook the case. Naturally the trial attracted a great deal of attention throughout the country, and, as it resulted in victory for the accused, I was asked to enter other labor cases, and criminal cases as well.

Soon afterward I assumed the defense of Thomas I. Kidd, president of the National Association of Wood Workers, and others along with him, all charged with conspiracy, growing out of a strike in the large sash-and-door factories of Oshkosh, Wis. As in all places outside of big cities and industrial centres, the feeling was very bitter on both sides. The division was, as always, the rich of the community on one side and the workers on the other. The case was reported pretty closely by the newspapers of the Northwest, and the fight was intense and long drawn out. I shall not go into the details of this prosecution. It was one of the earliest conspiracy charges against working men growing out of strikes. The jury was drawn from people of all stations, but after short deliberation they returned a verdict of "Not guilty."

From then on I was very busy with all sorts of litigation: labor cases, strikes, condemnation, chancery, criminal cases, and many contests that were submitted to arbitration. I entered my first criminal case in the attitude of the "good" lawyer— the lawyer who attends all the Bar Association meetings and so gravitates as rapidly as he can to the defense of Big Business. The tragedies, the sorrow and despair that were present in the criminal court I knew nothing of, and did not want to know. A verdict of "Not guilty" or a disagreement had been viewed by me as by the general public as a miscarriage of justice and a reflection on the jury system. The jail was a place spoken of as we sometimes mention a leper colony.

Criminal cases receive the attention of the press. The cruel and disagreeable things of life are more apt to get the newspaper space than the pleasant ones. It must be that most people enjoy hearing of and reading about the troubles of others. Perhaps men unconsciously feel that they rise in the general level as others go down. By no effort of mine, more and more of the distressed and harassed and pursued came fleeing to my office door. What could I do to change the situation? I was not responsible for my peculiar organism. It was due to a certain arrangement of cells in which I had no choice that made it impossible to deny help to those in trouble and pain, if I could see or find a way to give them aid. It was really my lively imagination which put me in the other fellow's place and made me suffer with him; so I only relieved him to help myself.

Strange as it may seem, I grew to like to defend men and women charged with crime. It soon came to be something more than winning or losing a case. I sought to learn why one man goes one way and another takes an entirely different road. I became vitally interested in the causes of human conduct. This meant more than the quibbling with lawyers and juries, to get or keep money for a client so that I could take part of what I won or saved for him: I was dealing with life, with its hopes and fears, its aspirations and despairs. With me it was going to the foundation of motive and conduct and adjustments for human beings, instead of blindly talking of hatred and vengeance, and that subtle, indefinable quality that men call "justice" and of which nothing really is known.

I have read and studied and worked so much on this question of what men call "crime" that to fail to discuss it would be to omit the thoughts and feelings that concern me most, and have made up a large part of my activities in court. We know that man and his strivings and complainings represent a matter of small concern excepting to the individual during his brief consciousness here. Every one knows that the heavenly bodies move in certain paths in relation to each other with seeming consistency and regularity which we call law. If instead of the telescope we use the microscope, we find another world so small that the human eye cannot otherwise see it, but fully as wonderful as the one revealed by the telescope. No one attributes freewill or motive to the material world. Is the conduct of man or the other animals any more subject to whim or choice than the action of the planets?

It will be admitted that no one is responsible for his birth or early environment. No one is responsible for the sort of instruction that he receives in his childhood, or the absence of any, that might have shaped his religious, political, and general views of life.

As to all animals, excepting man, we now know that their actions are determined by causes such as heat and cold, hunger and thirst, and sex. We know that fishes and birds migrate thousands of miles in recurring seasons, probably moved by the instinctive desire to propagate their kind; and we know that all of these causes influence man the same as other animals that inhabit the earth. We know that man's every act is induced by motives that led or urged him here or there; that the sequence of cause and effect runs through the whole universe, and is nowhere more compelling than with man.

In ancient times the diseased were afflicted with devils, and to cure the ill these must be cast out. Jesus is said to have thus driven the devils out of an afflicted man, and the devils took possession of a drove of hogs that straightway jumped into the sea.

Magic was the origin of medicine as it was of religion. It was only when man began to recognize cause and effect that physicians learned something of disease and its causes, and studied means to prevent and cure. Now no intelligent physician would consider treating an ailment without trying to discover its cause. While cause and effect are not always easy to discover, our observations have been so general that we are warranted in the belief that every manifestation of matter, and what we call mind, is the result of some cause, or causes, most of them fairly obvious, but some of them still beyond the ken of man. That crime, so-called, stands out alone as an uncaused manifestation of human conduct is beyond the understanding of those who try to study and comprehend.

The truth is, the causes of crime are much better understood than the causes of insanity or many other ailments or diseases that afflict the unfortunate. There are few men to-day who can be called criminologists who do not recognize and fairly understand this fact.

In spite of the hatred, aversion and cruelty that attend the treatment of crime, we know a good deal about it now that may be called new.

Man has the innate instinct to satisfy his needs and desires that moves every form of animal life. In satisfying these instincts he often comes in conflict with obstacles forbidding their gratification in certain ways. The forbidden ways are not fixed and necessarily cannot be determined by any absolute rules or moral codes, which are always changing as new desires are developed and new methods devised for satisfying needs. The babe is born into the world without any thoughts or inhibitions on any subject. He is equipped with a human organism, and probably a few primitive natural instincts. He has no inherited consciousness that he should not gratify his wants in any way that he can find. The fox going through the woods in search of food happens upon a chicken; instinctively he grabs it and in spite of the chicken's cries kills and devours it to preserve his life. All lower animals pursue the same course, naturally. Instinct tells them what they want, and any possible means are resorted to for bringing about the result. The child is like any other animal; it sees what it wants and reaches out its hand to grasp it. He may like candy, and, as any other animal, takes what he wants where he can find it. Soon he observes that money will buy candy, so, he finds the money, takes it with him and buys candy. No instinctive feeling tells him that this is wrong. It is only through slow and patient teaching that he learns he can be permitted to get money in certain ways and not in others. He is not born with any natural inhibitions against taking it in these certain forbidden ways.

Only after special training does the child finally feel a reaction against taking things in the way called "doing wrong," and while he is being taught there is constantly the conflict between the desire to take things in natural ways and the inhibition that teaching has cultivated. He goes one direction or the other according to the relative strength of the needs and the influence of the created restraints. Nature has given him no sense that one is right and the other wrong.

No matter how fine the training, there are doubtless circumstances where any one will ignore restraints and follow his natural emotions. Any normal person would most likely steal before he would starve; certainly before he would let a member of his family suffer. Most people would steal far short of that line. With the majority there is always a question as to where that line should be drawn. It is determined by the control of the inhibitions and the strength of the need or the desire. It is obvious that no two human beings would draw the line at the same place. The criminal code is not content with certain limitations on conduct that seem perfectly plain. Most persons can see no distinction between stealing and cheating, except that to some cheating seems more cowardly. But what is cheating? If one scans the law books he will find endless conflicts in the opinions of courts. This is true in the nature of things, depending in the last analysis on how the particular sort of conduct appeals to certain judges. The law has always held that one had the right to "puff his wares," to represent that the thing he has to sell is worth much more than its real value, or is of much finer texture than it really is. He may publish broadcast cunningly worded ad's explicitly designed to make men and women of none-too-good mentality buy things that they do not need and cannot afford, in the belief that they are getting bargains. Essentially this is cheating, and published with the intent of getting people's money for nothing. How much moral difference is there between this and stealing outright?—or in burglarizing a home?

Some false representations contravene the law; some do not. The law does not pretend to punish everything that is dishonest. That would seriously interfere with business, and, besides, could not be done. The line between honesty and dishonesty is a narrow, shifting one and usually lets those get by that are the most subtle and already have more than they can use. The sensibilities of no two men are the same. Some would refuse to sell property without carefully explaining all about its merits and defects, and putting themselves in the purchasers' place and inquiring if he himself would buy under the circumstances. But such men never would be prosperous merchants.

Recalling that those found in prisons are practically always poor, it follows that their needs to get things must be great; and their desires being the same as those of others, the struggle between wants and inhibitions lands them outside the law, when under more fortunate circumstances they would conform. But whatever man does or does not do, he is bound to yield to the strongest motive. It must be remembered, too, that wants and needs are elastic words. In this day and generation, who is poor and who is rich? I can recall when it was scarcely believed possible to be a millionaire. But now, from the standpoint of many men and women, a millionaire is poor. Fortunes have grown so rapidly, their figures are so enormous, and the expenditures of the wealthy so lavish as to excite the envy and even hatred of the millions who toil and strive and save to satisfy the plainest and humblest needs. The new method that brings to some untold wealth adds to the desires of all classes of men and women. It brings new thoughts to the minds of men who know that they cannot play the game that others play. Some proportion, at least, is sure to find its inhibitions too weak to withstand the strain, or to ask what life is worth if one is to be condemned to endless slavery and self-denial.

Crimes such as larceny, burglary, and robbery are more numerous in hard times than in good seasons. They increase during strikes and lockouts. They flourish in panics and with closed shops and factories. They are more frequent in winter than in summer. They would well-nigh disappear if conditions of life came anywhere near being equable and fair and decent.

CHAPTER 10

CHILD TRAINING

PUNISHMENT as punishment is not admissible unless the offender has had the freewill to select his course. On this question biology has much to say. The beginning of individual existence is in the fertilized cell. When this is accomplished a great deal has happened to the growing life. A large and important part of the character of the child is formed before his birth. The potential strength or weakness of the structure is contained in the embryo. If the fertilized cell has the capacity of only a dwarf it can never produce a robust man instead. What is true of the body is true of the mind and its quality. The mind is the manifestation of the bodily activity. The same origin probably determines some of the larger instincts and tendencies. Surely the unborn has nothing to do with consciously controlling these. Sex is fixed before birth, and this has vital domination over the outcome of life. Color also is determined in the germ plasm, and the white man has an infinitely better chance than the black man.

No one chooses his parents or early environment in the first years which are all-determining after birth. Some are born to poverty, some wealth; some are born of wise parents, more of foolish ones. The early years of life are the most important in the development of the child; this is the special time for forming habits necessary in determining conduct. Education should begin at once, and should be in the hands of intelligent people who understand the nature and tendencies and building of the young. Nothing is truer than that "the child is father to the man." The child should be so carefully observed that parents and teachers are able to detect the trend of its mind and the best aptitudes of the youth. Training should always be with the view of equipping him for self-support, and should be manual as well as mental. No child should go forth from school or home without the best possible mental and physical development for facing its future in the world.

Our compulsory school laws, as administered, do not and cannot perform that function. To force a child into school when he has no capacity or trend for that sort of education is worse than useless. It does not educate, but fosters a spirit that grows rebellious and desperate. He sees others doing just what he cannot do and decides that he is therefore inferior to the rest. Children are naturally fairly adapted to some occupation. They may not care for books, but may like to make a chair, a table, or an automobile. Among rich and poor alike, comparatively few really care for books. Children like to play or work with their hands, which could easily be discovered by watchful, sensible parents and teachers, and if perchance children change their tastes and interests, the course of training should be changed accordingly. In modern cities we now have perhaps one manual school to ten of the other kind. It should be entirely the other way; there should be ten manual-training schools to one of those that teach reading, writing, arithmetic, grammar and the rest of the non-essentials that are taught in schools.

An announcement in a grammar school that any boy who wished could go to work in an automobile factory or an electric shop, or even at a carpenter's or bricklayer's job, and be given the same credits as if he remained in school, would at once disrupt the classes. Books and the education that goes with them is of very late origin. The fact is, even among the grown-ups, very few people now care for books. Let any one look at his neighbor's library, or even at his own, if he doubts it. It is perfectly plain that at birth any two children are equally good or bad, if one is so senseless as to use those words. No one is either good or bad; still, two boys may start apparently alike, and in a very few years one may be in the penitentiary and the other in Congress. What has caused this difference in results? There can be but two causes: one, natural equipment; the other, training and opportunity. If it is natural equipment, then surely no credit or blame should attach to the individual. If due to training, the individual is no more responsible for that. As a matter of fact, most of the individual comes from training and environment. There are but few, even among idiots, who cannot fairly well fill some useful position if rightly trained. Very rarely do clergymen or college professors or carpenters or steamfitters or other skilled workmen go to prison. Almost all the prisoners are persons who had no opportunities or advantages in childhood and early life. If this does not account for their position, something else will, and does.

The boy who lags in his class soon has an inferiority complex that is apt to follow him through all his life. To begin with, he does not want to go to school, which makes plain his deficiency. He plays truant; if forced back to books this increases his resentment. School, at best, is a hopeless bore to the average boy; each day, all through the term, he watches and waits for the playtime and for school to be dismissed at night. When he leaves the classroom he can find plenty of other boys with the same deficiencies that he feels in himself. These are the children of the poor; themselves untrained and incapable of directing improvement in their offspring. The rich can find other avenues for their children who cannot or will not learn; they can become stock brokers or follow some other kind of business and thus adjust themselves to life.

Practically all the inmates of prisons come from the homes of the poor, and have had no chance to become adjusted to conditions. Neither were they taught any occupation or trade to fit them for the stern realities of the world, when they are beyond the school age. The inmates of prisons are mostly the product of large cities, where as boys they had all sorts of companions; their playgrounds were the streets and the alleys, and such vacant spots as the poor of great cities can find. They enter unoccupied buildings and take out lead pipe which they sell to junk dealers. How else would such children get possession of a few coins for themselves? They do not know the meaning of an allowance. Their petty thefts furnish the excitement and emotion necessary to growing life which they can get in no other way. On account of playing ball on the streets, and slight delinquencies, they have already made the acquaintance of the policeman in their neighborhood. Soon they are on the blacklists and taken into the police stations and Juvenile Courts. They want the things that so many other boys get in some other way, but they do not have any other way. Their course is the straight and narrow path from the simplest misdeeds to the penitentiaries and electric chairs, and as inevitable as the course of the other boys who pass from grade schools to graduate from colleges. Who is to blame? To say that it is the fault of the one who goes the luckless way is a travesty upon logic, common sense, and the first elements of fair dealing.

This is not the history of an isolated case. It is the story of almost all of those who tread a dark and tangled maze which leads to disgrace, despair and, often, death in the electric chair. Every one who has the power to think and cares to investigate knows that this is true. And yet people who are discerning and humane can reason out no way to prevent crime excepting by inflicting untold misery, degradation, and dire vengeance upon the victims who are plainly the product of our boasted civilization. While these boys are training for prison they see the sons of the rich living in luxury such as their world has never known. They ask themselves many questions to which they are unable to find any reply.

Almost all convictions are for crimes against property. Aside from these, a growing list is furnished by the fanatical prohibitionists. These are fast piling up their victims under the Volstead Act. For all of this class of offenses, the blame really rests upon prohibition itself. The toll of these victims will continue to increase until Volsteadism is dead, or the public shall have lost the manhood to fight for and preserve their personal rights.

Some of the victims of chance languish long in prison; others are humanely fried to death by the State. Law makers are not students; they are politicians, and the common mass, that is clamoring for greater and more barbaric penalties, do not study or think; they only hate. In fact, there are no murders in the sense portrayed in stories and fables, and the dreadful present-day detective yarns, save for a few, so exceptional and so far apart that they cannot justly be cited as examples. We are turning our prisons into living tombs, inhabited by doomed men living in everlasting blank despair. The man thrust into one of these torture-chambers sees upon the menacing walls:

"All hope abandon ye who enter here!"

Small wonder that men kill to avoid arrest and the prospect of a prison existence. They know that in so doing they are facing almost certain death, but they take that chance rather than face a life of torment in prison.

The second largest number of killings occur between husbands and wives, lovers and sweethearts, men and women in the various sex relations. and most of them are the result of jealousy. For these no penitentiaries are of the least avail; neither men nor women who reach this pass care for consequences, and often seek to kill themselves without the aid of the law, and are frantically disappointed if they fail. Many of these cases could be prevented by sensible divorce laws, which would give easier rights to dissolve unhappy marriages.

People talk of criminals as though they were utterly different from "good" people; as though specially created in order that a large class of the community should have the pleasure of hating them. Those who enjoy the emotion of hating are much like the groups who sate their thirst for blood by hunting and hounding to death helpless animals as an outlet for their emotions. Property crimes, as I have stated before, come from the desire to get something, and the inhibition against getting it except in certain ways. The contrary ways are supposed to be evil because they have been forbidden by law, and all that are not forbidden are supposed to be honorable. Is the desire to get things in spite of all odds confined to criminals? Every instinct that is found in any man is in all men. The strength of the emotion may not be so overpowering, the barriers against possession not so insurmountable, the urge to accomplish the desire less keen. With some, inhibitions and urges may be neutralized by other tendencies. But with every being the primal emotions are there. All men have an emotion to kill; when they strongly dislike some one they involuntarily wish he was dead. I have never killed any one, but I have read some obituary notices with great satisfaction.

No one would steal without feeling that he wanted the property and could get it in no other fairly easy way. Machinery has made production easier and less costly; the population is steadily increasing; machines are doing so much of the work that there is constantly a large proportion of men who have no jobs; and even where men do have employment the great majority are so close to poverty that a shade of hard luck or loss of work reduces them to want. In a world of such abundance that we are constantly limiting production, most men live so near the life line that they are always worried for fear of still greater need. To get anything like a fair living men are forced to work longer and harder than there is any need to toil. Great as is the output of the United States to-day, it could doubtless be doubled if distribution were so general and equal, or nearly so, as to give all a chance for a decent living. If useful labor could get fair returns, the loafers, the idlers, the speculators, and even many professional and business men would go to work. Not half the men who are engaged in activities are *usefully* employed. If our great Captains of Industry, who have the wisdom and ideals, and who now understand organization, would give the same attention to the distribution of wealth as they do to its production, want and crime would disappear. Instead of that, our law makers and influential men think only of harsher laws and more terrorizing brutalities. Every seer, student, prophet, and scientist has taught that man cannot be controlled by fear. To employ that method is to admit defeat before even attempting a saner course.

No doubt there are some men and women who, from mental or physical defects, may always require isolation from their fellows, but this should not be accomplished in the spirit of retribution and revenge, but with an attitude of kindness and consideration. Saving criminals, in its last analysis, is only saving children. And if we save the criminal and the crime we will at the same time save the hypothetical victim.

It is indeed strange that with all the knowledge we have gained in the past hundred years we preserve and practice the methods of an ancient and barbarous world in our dealing with crime. So long as this is observed and exercised there can be no change except to heap more cruelties and more wretchedness upon those who are the victims of our foolish system.

To hold back what are called the evil forces by walls and dungeons and ropes is like an effort to keep back the flow of waters in a mighty river by damming up the stream; the water manages to seep through or work its way around, or mount high enough to sweep away the dam.

CHAPTER 11

I MEET MR. BRYAN

IT was at the national Democratic convention of 1896 that I first met William Jennings Bryan. He was then a young man thirty-six years old. At that time I was thirty-nine. For several years the country had, as usual, been suffering a financial depression, especially throughout the West and South. The two political parties were torn to pieces by new issues that were real. Up to that time the old question of slavery, secession and the Civil War was still powerful in the division of the two parties. But now both of them seemed to be dissolving as new questions forced themselves to the front. Throughout the West the low price of grain had given birth to the Granger movement. Its chief demand was for the free coinage of silver at the old ratio of 16 to 1.

The Western States and all their population were burdened with debt, and the price of land had slumped with all the products of the farm. Bonds and mortgages had been issued when both gold and silver were legal tender. The indebtedness of the West was held and controlled throughout the East. Every one then believed that the value of money was determined by the amount in circulation. It therefore followed that the demonetization of silver had increased the value of gold and correspondingly lowered the price of grain and farm and wages, and, in short, every commodity that was bought and sold in the market. Likewise the real value of bonds had substantially doubled because the obligations could no longer be paid in gold and silver, but must be paid in gold alone. It was one more great manifestation of the cleavage between the rich and poor. Many of the Western States that had continually been Republican, due to the issues growing out of the Civil War, were now in the political control of the Populist and Democratic parties.

When the forces were forming for the contest of 1896 it became clear that the lines were to be drawn on the restoration of the coinage of silver. The Republican convention met in St. Louis and nominated William McKinley for President. Up to this time McKinley had been an ardent advocate of the free coinage of silver. But he did not propose to let a question of this sort stand between him and the Presidency of the United States. The Republican party declared against the free coinage of silver, so McKinley at once advocated the single standard. Immediately upon the adoption of that platform in the Republican convention, the senators and congressmen of most of the States west of the Mississippi River bolted the convention and turned to the Democratic party. Grover Cleveland was then President of the United States, serving his second term. He was a Democrat, but from New York State, and was bitterly opposed to the free coinage of silver.

Not only had I been steadily aligned with the Democratic party, but my sympathies were with the common man. I was for the debtor rather than the creditor. John P. Altgeld, then governor of Illinois and running for a second term, headed the Illinois delegation.

Mr. Bryan had been twice elected to Congress from Nebraska. This in spite of the fact that Nebraska had long been a Republican State. Mr. Bryan was elected as a bimetallist, and although only thirty-two years old, had distinguished himself in Congress. In the convention of 1896, Governor Altgeld was probably the strongest man. Altgeld was never an easy or fluent speaker; yet he overcame his difficulties and spoke effectively. He was a good student, a good thinker, and an honest, fearless man. He was essentially a man of action, yet he wrote convincingly. He was the first person of any prominence that I had met after coming to Chicago, and after that he had always been my friend, and later was my partner for several months up to the time of his death.

Governor Altgeld made what was, in fact, the keynote speech of the convention. It was vigorous and straightforward. He not only was for the free coinage of silver, but for a political revolution. He declared strongly against the issuance of injunctions by the courts in labor cases, which he dubbed "government by injunction." Altgeld was always bold, aggressive, and radical. I had a seat on the platform near the speakers, where I could hear every word.

William Jennings Bryan entered the convention at the head of a contesting delegation from Nebraska. The gold forces, under the lead of J. Sterling Morton, had made a strong fight for the delegation. Mr. Morton was a man of fine intelligence, an independent mind, and a good student of economics. He had for years been connected with the Chicago, Burlington and Quincy Railroad, and was for a gold standard and free trade. Mr. Morton's faction had secured the credentials as the regular delegates from Nebraska. Whether they were elected I will not discuss, for I know nothing about that, and, like most of the delegates at that convention, I did not care. I was for the free-silver faction—not so much because I had any great confidence in its importance, but because it represented the disinherited, who had come to command my sympathy and my help.

When Mr. Bryan came to the Chicago convention in 1896 he was little known, outside Nebraska. He had gained some distinction in Congress, but was a young man and not a national figure. Without a doubt he came to the convention expecting to be nominated for President, but no one else thought of him as such a possibility.

The Committee on Credentials rejected the claim of Bryan and his delegation. He carried the contest to the convention, and took the platform to present his claim. In a few moments he had the attention of the great audience of twenty or twenty-five thousand that crowded the hall. He had a strong voice, well adapted to a large assemblage. He had complete control of himself and knew just what he wanted to say. Doubtless he had gone over it many times in his home on the prairies of Nebraska. Then, and always, he was a master of technique; he knew exactly how to hold an audience in the hollow of his hand, as it were. His voice, his personality, his knowledge of mob psychology, his aptness for forming rhythmical sentences left him without a rival in the field.

Platforms are not the proper forums for spreading doubts. The miscellaneous audience wants to listen to a man who *knows*. How he knows is of no concern to them. Such an audience wishes to be told, and especially wants to be told what it already believes. Mr. Bryan told the Democratic convention of 1896 in Chicago what he believed. Not only did he tell them that, but he told them what they believed, and what they wanted to believe, and wished to have come true. I have enjoyed a great many addresses, some of which I have delivered myself, but I never listened to one that affected and moved an audience as did that. Men and women cheered and laughed and cried. They listened with desires and hopes, and finally with absolute confidence and trust. Here was a political Messiah who was to lift the burdens that the oppressed had borne so long. When he had finished his speech, amidst the greatest ovation that I had ever witnessed, there was no longer any doubt as to the name of the nominee. Mr. Bryan was nominated for President; but he did not get the votes of the gold Democrats from the East, and he did not get the vote of the truest and bravest of them all, John P. Altgeld. This was not because he wanted the nomination himself; he was born in Germany, and was not eligible for the Presidency of the United States. I sat close to Mr. Altgeld while Mr. Bryan made his speech. He did not applaud, or shout, or throw his hat into the air. He listened to every word. His sad blue eyes seemed to look beyond the convention hall upon the cities and fields and prairies, and backwards through history that has recorded the vain struggles of man, and forward into the unopened book of the future, shut fast in the hands of Fate and shadowed with the cruelty, injustice, and tyranny of the past. The next day I was with him, and we discussed the convention, and Mr. Bryan's speech. He turned to me with his weary face and quizzical smile and said, "It takes more than speeches to win real victories. Applause lasts but a little while. The road to justice is not a path of glory; it is stony and long and lonely, filled with pain and martyrdom." He added, "I have been thinking over Bryan's speech. What did he say, anyhow?"

Governor Altgeld was then a candidate for governor for a second term; he was anxious for me to run for Congress, and I was offered the nomination. I reluctantly agreed to take it. The district was overwhelmingly Democratic, and I felt sure that with Bryan for President and Altgeld for governor there would be no doubt of my election. The Republican candidate was a clerk in a railroad office who had never taken any interest in politics and was not known outside his small circle of friends. I gave most of my time to speaking during the campaign, but gave no attention to my district; there I made no addresses and solicited no votes. I felt sure of my election; I knew that the whole ticket would follow the vote of Bryan and Altgeld, who, of course, were the leading figures in the Illinois campaign. As the weeks wore on, it became obvious that the Republicans were conspiring and using money as never before. But no one questioned my election. I knew that if I was not elected no other Democrat would be, in that section of Illinois.

In the last days of the campaign an enormous fund was raised and spent in the centres of population, including Chicago. Within two days many of the Democratic leaders were reached and the organization disrupted. As a consequence, Chicago and Illinois went overwhelmingly for McKinley. When the returns were counted I found that both Bryan and Altgeld had lost my district and the whole ticket was defeated. My opponent was elected by about one hundred votes. Even one day in my district amongst my friends would have assured my election, but I cared too little for the position and felt too sure. So I gave all of my time to what seemed doubtful States.

I really felt relief when I learned of my defeat. I did not want to be in political life. I realized what sacrifices of independence went with office-seeking, and in every way felt that I could not afford to go to Congress. So I turned my attention exclusively to law.

For the next few years I was constantly in court, trying all sorts of cases that fall to the general practitioner, including many labor cases, both civil and criminal, and representing the unions in a number of arbitrations, a line of work that appealed to my emotions and ideas, and that was full of interest and color. Governor Altgeld came back to Chicago, but for a time took no personal interest in political affairs.

I often wonder what would have happened to me had I gone to Congress. Perhaps I would have spent the rest of my life in the pursuit of political place and power, and would have surrendered my convictions for a political career. I never gave up my interest in the affairs of government, but always acted independently of party ties or affiliations. Through it all I have urged young men to pursue the same course, without being sure which way is best. This can be determined by only the strongest emotions that move the individual and by what, for lack of a better term, we call chance and fate, or fatality.

Mr. Bryan carried most of the States west of the Mississippi River, and the solid South. He received more votes than McKinley. He placed himself at the head of the Democratic party, and for many years thereafter wrote the political platform and dictated the candidate. The candidate was generally himself.

On the whole, during most of his career he remained true to the cause of the people, as he understood political and social questions. But his vision was narrow. He was much more certain of the correctness of his views than a student or scholar can possibly be. He never cared to read, much less study; he knew, without investigation or thought. To him, the most insignificant affairs of life were controlled by Providence, and he was sure that he had been chosen for a special work. No matter how often he was beaten, he had the same confidence that the Lord was on his side.

In the Spanish-American War, Bryan raised a regiment of soldiers in Nebraska, and, of course, placed himself at its head, received the title of Colonel, and marched blithely off to fight the Spaniards on the question of their dominion over Cuba. At the same time he jumped from Chautauqua to Chautauqua and lectured to immense audiences on "The Prince of Peace." Perhaps he saw no inconsistencies in these activities; but in this he was not unlike many others. I have never found any one who could not explain and justify conflicting attitudes, if he wanted to act in various ways.

In the meantime we defeated the Spaniards, and, incidentally, captured the Philippine Islands. In 1900 Bryan was again nominated for the Presidency, and made the campaign on the issue of giving the Philippines their independence. I thoroughly believed as he did, and gave my best endeavor to help him win; but he was defeated by a larger majority than before. In 1904 he was not nominated, but in 1908 he again turned the Democratic party to him. Evidently he had then determined to ignore dangerous problems, and applied his attention to a fight to require government guarantee of bank deposits, and the election of United States senators by direct vote of the people. His committee gave most of its time to handing out a little pamphlet containing his Chautauqua address, entitled "The Prince of Peace." This he considered was a strong document, especially in view of the fact that his opponent, Judge Taft, was a Unitarian.

Shortly before the campaign was opened Mr. Bryan came to Chicago. He asked me to meet him at his hotel, and, of course, I obeyed the summons. He said he hoped I would do some speaking for the ticket in the campaign. I asked him what he wanted me to talk about. He replied, "The guaranteeing of bank deposits by the government." I answered that my trouble had always been in getting money into the bank and not in checking it out. He then suggested, "The election of United States senators by direct vote," to which I replied that so long as we have senators it made little difference to me how they were elected.

That year I took a vacation instead of making campaign speeches. I felt that I had followed Bryan long enough. But it seemed to have been decreed that I was to see him once more, which came about in a rather strange manner in 1923.

CHAPTER 12

PARDONING THE ANARCHISTS

In Ashtabula, Ohio, Judge Richards had given me the little book, "Our Penal Code and Its Victims," by John P. Altgeld. I had never heard the name before, but had read the book because of the friend who put it into my hands; up to that time I had the conventional view of crime and criminals. In a vague way I believed that a criminal was somewhat different from other men. He was evil and malignant, because he deliberately chose that way of life. I never had reflected that his composition and environment had any share in his conduct.

This book, written by John P. Altgeld, then a Chicago judge, set forth how laws and their administration were largely responsible for the criminal. It made a deep impression on my mind, and on arriving in Chicago the first man that I deliberately sought was Judge Altgeld. He seemed surprised that a man in Ohio had read his book. He told me that he had published and circulated it at his own expense, and very few had ever heard of it. Naturally he was pleased that it had fallen into my hands, and that I had liked it. He asked me a great many questions about myself, and invited me to call again. So I saw him from time to time, and he seemed to take an interest in my affairs and expressed a wish to help me if the opportunity should occur. Later, I discovered that he had been very active in the election of DeWitt C. Cregier for mayor, and that he had urged him to appoint me as assistant corporation counsel, when the change of politics had forced the former incumbent out of office. This indicated that he had recognized me as one of his disciples and followers.

Judge Altgeld had come to America when about six years

96

of age. He was independent and aggressive, and believed in justice as he understood the word. He soon showed his sympathy for the labor movement, and through a fusion of trade-unionists and Democrats was elected to the bench. As a judge he was efficient and assertive and always in sympathy with the underdog. He was likewise a very ambitious man. He had good business sense and was always ready to take a chance. In the course of a few years he had accumulated about half a million dollars through dealings in real estate.

Judge Altgeld was on the bench in 1886 when the famous anarchist case was tried in Chicago. This case grew out of a movement for a general labor strike in May of 1886. A meeting was called for the night of May 4th by an anarchist group in the Haymarket Square, a wide area on the west side of Chicago. A permit was granted by the city, allowing the meeting to take place. When the 1st of May had passed, with many threats of disturbance, some of the citizens were fearing greater trouble, so the mayor, Carter Harrison, Sr., went to the square and listened to what the speakers said. The talks were made from a wagon brought to serve as a platform. The night was unpleasant, so only a small crowd assembled. It began to rain and more than half the audience left the street. Sam Fielding, an Englishman, once a Methodist revivalist, was speaking. The mayor told the policeman that the meeting was all right, and then he started for home.

No sooner had the mayor disappeared than a company of policemen marched up to the wagon and commanded the meeting to disperse. Fielding replied that they were about to go home anyhow. Thereupon a bomb was thrown from an alley into the Square, which landed in the midst of the policemen, killing seven and injuring about fifty. Immediately the city was aroused, and a man-hunt followed. Eight men were indicted for murder: Parsons, Spies, Fischer, Engel, Lingg, Fielding, Schwab, and Neebe. Previous to this meeting in the

Haymarket, a number of halls and assembly rooms had been raided and closed. There was evidence that three of the group, Fischer, Engel and Lingg, had agreed that if the police attempted to search halls or break up gatherings they would use force to defend their rights to assemble. Also there was evidence that Lingg had made the bomb that exploded at the Haymarket.

Fielding, Parsons, Schwab and Spies were scarcely acquainted with Engel, Fischer and Lingg. Spies was the editor of the *Arbeiter Zeitung,* a radical daily paper to which Parsons often contributed. Schwab was an editorial writer on the paper. Parsons was a printer on the Chicago *Daily News,* and a frequent speaker at radical meetings; and Neebe was connected with the circulating department of the *Arbeiter Zeitung;* the paper was an old-time German sheet, very radical in its tendencies, which had been published in Chicago for eleven years before, and even after, this event. Its editorial writers and contributors often printed inflammatory articles on general subjects, but were never interfered with by the postal authorities. It was not seriously claimed that Parsons, Spies, Fielding, Schwab, or Neebe knew anything whatever about any contemplated violence at the meeting in the Haymarket Square.

The court permitted files of the *Arbeiter Zeitung* and *The Alarm,* a paper published by Parsons, to be read in evidence, and allowed the speeches of Parsons in Chicago and various other cities in the United States to go into the record; and speeches by Fielding at different meetings, with the editorials of Schwab, were offered at the trial. The judge instructed the jury that if they believed, from the evidence, that these speeches and articles contributed toward the throwing of the bomb they were justified in finding the defendants guilty of murder.

At the time of the trial the country was aflame, and the jury was shamelessly packed to procure conviction. The jury returned a verdict sentencing Neebe to fifteen years in the penitentiary, and all the others to death. This sentence was affirmed by the Supreme Court of the State, and the day of execution was fixed. In the meantime thousands of citizens protested that the verdict was unjust. Among these were many members and ex-members of the bench, a number of the best-known lawyers, some of them representing railroad corporations and other great interests; and several bankers, including the president of the First National Bank of Chicago, Lyman J. Gage. Petitions for clemency poured in from all parts of the earth.

Richard J. Oglesby was then governor of Illinois. He was a former general in the Civil War and had been prominent in politics for many years. After giving consideration to all the petitions he commuted the sentences of Fielding and Schwab to imprisonment for life, but Parsons, Spies, Engel and Fischer were hanged; and Lingg, a boy about twenty-one, managed to get a percussion cap of some sort which he put into his mouth, exploded it, and thus tore his head to pieces.

While many judges of the sitting court petitioned and worked for clemency, Altgeld remained silent. He did quietly send money and clothing to the families of the men during their trial and their sojourn in jail.

The anarchists were executed November 11th, 1887. From the time of their death constant efforts were carried on for the pardon of those who were confined in prison. For some years William Penn Nixon, editor-in-chief of *The Chicago Inter-Ocean,* was chairman of the amnesty committee that carried on the campaign. These petitioners grew into the tens of thousands and included men of all classes of Chicago and the whole United States. It was but a very few years after the executions until the bar in general throughout the State, and elsewhere, came to believe that the conviction was brought about through malice and hatred, and that the trial was unfair and the judgment of the court unsound, and that the opinion of the court was a standing menace to the liberty of the citizen.

John P. Altgeld was elected governor in 1892. His friends and the public in general always considered him radical. He was a humane, kindly man, and no one doubted his courage. It was commonly believed, and often stated, that if he were elected he would pardon the anarchists. Most of those who had been working for their release thought that the pardon would be his first official act. I was one of that number and told him so. He replied that it would not be; that many affairs of state demanded his prior attention. He said that when he could spare the time he would go over the case and do what he thought was right, but he must take his own time in this matter.

Often after that I urged him to act, but he always eluded the suggestion. Finally I felt impatient and worried, and wondered if we could have been deceived in Altgeld. All of his friends realized that he had never held any anarchistic or even especially socialistic views. We knew that he was upright, liberal, honest, humane, and had thought that was enough, but I now believed that the time had come for a last talk with him about pardons in the anarchist case.

I went to him, confiding that his friends were growing doubtful and restless and disappointed, and that it should be done at once. I told him that every one expected it, that it had been generally asked for by all the people, that it would not even create hostility toward him, and that I and others could see no excuse for waiting. Mr. Altgeld turned to me deliberately and calmly said:

"Go tell your friends that when I am ready I will act. I don't know how I will act, but I will do what I think is right." Then turning to me he added: "We have been friends for a long time. You seem impatient; of course I know how you feel; I don't want to offend you or lose your friendship, but this responsibility is mine, and I shall shoulder it. I have not yet examined the record. I have no opinion about it. It is a big job. When I do examine it I will do what I believe to be right, no matter what that is. But don't deceive yourself: If I conclude to pardon those men it will not meet with the approval that you expect; let me tell you that from that day I will be a dead man."

I knew the governor's attitude toward me. He knew the depth of my devotion to him, and he knew how absolutely I believed in that pardon. I was sure that he would have told me his intention if he would have told it to any man. I was certain that he did not know then what he would do. I reported to my friends that it was useless to bother him again. All we could do was to wait.

About six weeks later the news came in the daily papers. It had been so long delayed that it came like a stroke of lightning, it seemed so abrupt and unexpected. He issued his pardon message. And what a message it was. It left no one in doubt as to how he felt. Immediately throughout the world a flood of vituperation and gall was poured out upon Altgeld's head. Of course very few knew anything about the facts, and fewer cared anything about them. Governor Altgeld was in the way of the forces that control the world, and he must be destroyed.

The main objection was launched against the part of the message that criticised the trial judge. This criticism was caustic and severe. The public thundered as though it were treason to censure a judge; but of course it is as admissible and necessary to criticise a judge as any other public servant, and it is largely criticism that has any tendency to keep officials interested in meeting situations. It should be done with the wish to be fair, but I have found a limited number who ever tried to be just where they have any personal feeling in a case. In the mountain of protest heaped on the devoted head of John P. Altgeld no one ever undertook to show that his reasons were not good or his judgment unsound. As it was, he had no power to grant clemency to the dead. He could not have pardoned Schwab and Fielding if Governor Richard J. Oglesby, a Republican and conservative, had not saved their lives. It is perfectly plain that he would not have saved them if he had not been satisfied that there was not sufficient evidence to connect them with the killing.

I have always felt sure that in the pardoning of the men Governor Altgeld would not have been true to his office and himself had he failed to act. But I feel that Governor Altgeld was wrong in laying all the blame to Judge Gary, the trial judge. Undoubtedly his rulings were biased and unfair, but where is the man who, under the lashing of the crowd, is not biased and unfair? If Judge Gary erred, the Supreme Court was still more to blame; it required one whole volume of the Supreme Court reports for explanations and excuses to justify the judgment of the trial court, and to palliate and excuse the verdict of the jury; and their decision came a year after the trial, and there were seven judges who might have divided the responsibility. To severely blame Judge Gary meant blaming a judge for not being one in ten thousand, and few men can be that and live.

If only Governor Altgeld had consulted some one I believe the great mass of the criticism directed against him would have been spared. He needed but to marshal the influential men from all ranks that had petitioned for the pardon; he needed but to point out that Governor Oglesby had saved their lives, and to call the attention of his censors to the fierce and bitter passions that reigned supreme at the time of the trial. But Altgeld never shirked responsibility. He accepted, and seemed almost to court the opposition of the world. I never ventured to tell him that he should have or might have performed his act in any other manner. And now he and all his family have long since passed to dust, and only his work and the memory remain. Many a time I have said that posterity would vindicate him. But it will not; a man's record, rightly or wrongly, is settled as he goes along. Posterity has affairs of its own to look after.

I went to the State Capitol as often as I could after the pardon was granted. The great building seemed lonely and abandoned. The governor's suite of rooms were barren and deserted. He was almost always alone. Still there was at least one man, brave and true, and understanding, who found no day too short and no night too dark to serve the man he loved. This was George A. Schilling, the secretary of labor. Mr. Schilling was about the first man I met when I came to Chicago, and he has been a close friend ever since. He is still living, at the age of eighty-one.

I used to go to the governor's quarter and sit and look at him in silence, just to be with him. He was never a great talker. Few really thoughtful people are voluble. Altgeld never gossiped; he never spoke of trifling things, and on the platform he almost never told a story. Yet, now and then, he would do that atrocious thing, but fortunately the stories never seemed to belong to the man or fit the time or place.

A speaker asks an audience to come and listen to his views, and they have done him the honor to come. Out of the whole span of life they have but an hour or two in which they can be together to consider the matter in hand. Life and such hours are too important and scarce to be wasted on the mere repetition of stories, most of which could be, and probably have been, read or heard before. Instead of yielding to idle conversation it might profit one to cultivate silence and contemplation. After all, every one virtually spends most of the time alone, or wishing he could be alone.

Altgeld was essentially a lonely man. And those were appallingly lonely days after the pardoning of the anarchists. The public let loose its vials of wrath and malice on his devoted head. But he did not wince and never complained. He could not tolerate sympathy. He felt that it was an assumption of superiority and the suggestion of defeat. The brave man goes straight ahead. He moves silently but with the force of the glacier or fate itself. His heart may be torn and bleeding, but it never shows in his face, and he is too proud to explain even when he knows that a word would make things right. Altgeld never moaned or cried in his agony, but went straight onward down his appointed path though he knew that it led to doom.

The second time Altgeld ran for office was some two years after the pardon message. By that time his friends were rallying around him, and even the time-server and hypocrite once more sat on his doorstep, asking for alms. The vote he received was not less than the rest of the ticket; in many places it was more. The newspapers, the profiteers, the money-mongers, and the pharisees, fought him bitterly; but in the humble dwelling-places of the poor, in the factories and mills, among the failures, the misfits and despised, he was worshipped almost as a god. For the maimed and beaten, the sightless and voiceless, he was eyes and ears, and a flaming tongue crying in the wilderness for kindness and humanity and understanding.

CHAPTER 13

JOHN P. ALTGELD

During his period of prosperity Altgeld had erected a building sixteen stories high; one of the most expensive and elaborate of the time. It was one of the first of the "sky-scrapers" within what is now "the Loop" in Chicago. He had put into this building all his assets, around six or seven hundred thousand dollars; and had encumbered it by a mortgage of two millions or more. He was always charitable and generous, and saw and did things in a big way. When he became governor and went to Springfield, Ill., the capital of the State, he was not able to give much time to his financial affairs. When he pardoned the anarchists many of his best tenants of the big "Unity" left the building, and it was refilled by young lawyers, radicals and idealists, many of whom could not pay their rent. Any one not able to pay office rent moved to the Unity Building. So Altgeld was obliged to default in his interest, and the bondholders showed him no mercy. In fact, they wanted him to fail. It would be a fine lesson in showing the punishment of evil and the triumph of virtue.

At that time Charles T. Yerkes was in control and practically the owner of the surface lines and one of the elevated roads of Chicago. He was formerly a resident of Philadelphia. He acquired the street-car property soon after reaching Chicago. Also he had succeeded in getting control of the city gas company, and was regarded with doubt and suspicion by the established financial men of Chicago. The laws of Illinois did not permit a street-car franchise to be issued for a longer term than thirty years. During Altgeld's administration, and after the pardoning of the anarchists, Mr. Yerkes applied to the legislature of the State for a law extending the franchises to fifty years, and permitting future grants for that length of time. All the newspapers of Chicago opposed him. It might not be amiss to remark that recently, in 1930, the same papers and interests that defeated Yerkes' fifty-year franchise voted the Traction Company a perpetual one. Thus the world moves forward. Mr. Yerkes was a man of iron will, and as bold as any buccaneer who ever sailed the financial seas. He and his family have long been dead, or I might not like to make these very moderate statements of fact. For all sentient organisms feel pain, and I always have tried to avoid causing it.

The State legislature was none too good. I have never known the representatives to be any different excepting at a time of some great moral crusade, and then they were always worse. They were worse, because the reformer is lacking in humaneness. He is cold and hard and self-righteous. He does not suffer and does not pity. Suffering for or with others means putting oneself in the place of the other fellow, and the reformer has not the imagination for this. Pity means an imagination so sensitive that one suffers what and when others suffer. You are cold when your fellow man is cold, and hungry when he is hungry, and you are inside the jail when the doors close on him.

Of course Mr. Yerkes had competent lawyers, as all rich people have. He employed the best and most skilful lobbyists to work for his bill. He managed to get control of the House and the Senate, the bills were passed, and up to the governor for veto or approval. Every one wondered what Altgeld would do. No one ever doubted his integrity, but his enemies hated him the more for that. Altgeld owed nothing to the forces that were against Mr. Yerkes. The campaign had made him virtually a bankrupt. The Unity Building, his pride, had been mortgaged for two million dollars, the interest was long in default, and, by the terms of the mortgage, the principal was due. All that was necessary was to file a bill of foreclosure and appoint a receiver, and then that part of the fruits of his labors and luck would vanish. Every one knew that Altgeld could easily get the money to pay the mortgage, or any other sum that he would be willing to take. He would not need to ask for it; only take it. He did not pass the bill; it was a legislative enactment; all that was required was to withhold a veto and let it become a law. I knew all of Altgeld's most trusted friends; we often discussed the matter among ourselves. So far as was known, he never asked advice of any one, and I, at least, never volunteered any.

The days went by and the suspense increased. Altgeld sat silent and pensive, gazing out beyond the petty affairs of men. He could even have vetoed the bill in a perfunctory way, and enough votes could have been gathered to pass it over his head. That would have done as well, and his record would have been consistent and clear. But Altgeld never did anything in a perfunctory way. At the last moment he sent his veto message to the legislature. It was a state document that could not be answered or avoided. No member of the Senate or the House could afterward support the bill without every one knowing the reason why.

After the veto was sent in an effort was made to pass it over his head, but this failed. In a short time the Unity Building passed out of Altgeld's control. He was about fifty-four years old at that time. In 1896, after his defeat for re-election for the governorship, he returned to Chicago. He seemed dazed and lifeless for a time. He said he was too old to begin a new career, that he had lived his life, and must stand by the record as it was. He once told me that he would be content to crawl under a sidewalk and die, if need be; all stricken animals have that desire. He did not want to go back to the bar to practice law; he had come to rather despise that profession; he felt that its strongest men sold themselves to destroy people, to perpetuate and intensify the poverty of the oppressed, and enlarge their burdens.

He sat in his office, day after day, receiving visits from the poor, the dreamers, the unadjusted and unadjustable, who were not only of Chicago but from all parts of the land. For several years the pathetic idealists, with their haunted and far-away gaze, came to his office, as the devout anchorite would visit a shrine. And it was a shrine. Hidden away in the consciousness of every man, whether he knows it or not, is some shrine where he burns incense and does homage.

We managed, at one time, to arouse Altgeld sufficiently to enter the race for mayor as an independent candidate. His petitions were circulated and he was placed on the ticket. He felt that the Democratic party was returning to its old idols and leaving the people in the lurch; for there is in every man and every organization a strong urge to leave the hard path of duty and self-sacrifice and return to the flesh-pots whose savory odor always lures with its promise of the pleasanter things in life.

"Altgeld for Mayor" was a slogan that gathered from the highways and byways the old guard that had frantically followed him and Bryan to defeat. Day after day his headquarters were crowded with weird-looking idealists and worshippers— the poorly clad, the ill-fed, the unemployed, the visionaries gazing off toward the rainbow espying something farther on than the very stars themselves. Governor Altgeld spoke at great meetings all over the city. Never were political quarters more crowded, never were audiences more enthusiastic. I remember one meeting in a large hall or armory that ran for twenty-four hours, and the "Amens" were as vigorous at the end as at the start.

Revealed religion is not the only magic that awakens zeal and devotion; or, perhaps our personal allegiance and political creed was a sort of religion of its own kind. Whatever one may think, it was a sort of zeal, the same sort of gazing into the future, the same sublimation of self into a strong emotion and a distant dream. But our great crowds were deceptive. For the same footsore and weary would travel from one end of the city to another and attend meetings night after night. The gospel was ever new each time the devoted heard it. Altgeld cared nothing for being mayor; he simply wanted to place the control of the city with the people; where he believed it belonged. He was too ethereal-minded to know that "the people" are also a myth, the figment of an illusion, a spectral cohort that only eyes of faith can see. When the votes were counted he was beaten. Altgeld was disappointed. He dwelt in the clouds; and this was some consolation for all the devotion that he wasted on an unwilling world.

After this he was often asked to give addresses in various cities. Wherever he went the auditoriums were crowded. The poor eagerly drank of his words of wisdom, and these are everywhere in great numbers. Aside from the poor, there was always a large proportion of students, lawyers, scientists, who appreciated what he had to say, and knew that he was right. He really belonged to the aristocracy of intellect. He wrote two fairly good books. His little volume, "Oratory," is the best that I have ever seen of its class. Usually a speaker is better off if he never reads books on this subject, especially one who has anything to say, for most speakers put the *manner* of talking above substance; and while the manner is of considerable importance the content is really of the first concern.

After Mr. Altgeld's property had disappeared I finally persuaded him to come into my office and resume the practice of l. w, although he felt that he could never be of any value in this field, either to clients or the cause that would always claim his allegiance. In spite of his fears he was able to take up that activity almost as if he had never been absent from the bar, and no doubt would have made a success of it if he had lived. But he died within six months after that last venture.

One new great emotion came into his life toward the end. This was the Boer War. All his friends were for the Boers. Although I had never been an enemy of England, I felt that this war waged by them was without excuse. Then, too, it presented the picture of a great nation trampling a small one into the earth. Both Altgeld and I held a large number of meetings for the purpose of awakening the sympathy of our country for the Boers.

On the 12th day of March, 1902, Governor Altgeld went down to Joliet, about forty miles from Chicago. For many years his heart had not been good. He had never seemed strong. Before going to Joliet he had been in court all day and was very tired that night; as I remember it, he had eaten no lunch; he went into the dining car and ate a hearty meal. He went directly from the train into a crowded hall and immediately began his plea for the Boers. He had gone but a little way when he was seized with an acute attack of indigestion. He fell and was removed from the stage; and for several hours his frail body was wracked with vomiting and pain. About midnight he was dead. I was called up, by long-distance, that night, and the next morning went to Joliet, attended to everything and brought him back in his casket.

He lay in state in the Public Library Building. All day long the people filed past and lavished their loving looks upon their great and brave champion, John P. Altgeld. It was the same throng that had so often hung upon his courageous words from many a forum; the same inarticulate mass for whose cause he had given his voice and his life. Men and women with sad faces and tearful eyes gazed into the now still white face of their friend as though all hope would be buried in his grave.

For the funeral, two invitations were sent to clergymen, supposed to be liberal-minded, asking them to conduct the farewell ceremony, but both found reasons for not being able to come. So Miss Jane Addams, of Hull House, a woman of rare ideals and intelligence, was asked to speak. Governor Altgeld had long admired Miss Addams, and was often a visitor at Hull House, and she had always understood and appreciated the fearlessness and unselfishness of the man. Her words were simple and sensible, such as she always uses. I also had the rare privilege of saying a few words of the many that welled from my heart, overflowing with admiration and affection and pain for a lost idol. Then we laid him in his grave.

His death was in keeping with his life. Had he been able to choose, he could not have made it more fitting to the man that he was. He died while speaking for the weak and oppressed who were struggling for liberty. He died as he had lived, fighting for freedom.

Whether it is good form or not, I have inserted in an appendix my heartfelt tribute to my dead friend, spoken at his grave, on March 14th, 1902.

CHAPTER 14

THE COAL STRIKE

THE great city was lonely and dreary after Altgeld's death. The radicals had lost their leader, and there was no one in sight that could take his place. The battles of Altgeld, the writings of Henry George, the Socialist campaign, and the general civic movements had combined to bring the question of municipal ownership to the front. This problem had been greatly aided by the persistent effort of Mr. Yerkes to get the fifty-year franchise through the legislature, and the veto by the beloved Altgeld. In order to accomplish municipal ownership it would be necessary to get a bill through the legislature, and coming so soon after the attempt of Mr. Yerkes to pass his extension act, the reformers supported the campaign authorizing municipal ownership.

However, the reformers and what was left of the Altgeld forces never could agree. There was a profound cleavage between us as to the meaning of the word "reform." To some it meant closing the theatres and saloons on Sunday. To us it meant nothing of that kind. Under the conditions, as they were, we organized a Voters' League and put up candidates for the legislature in various districts. The League insisted that I should run from my district, but I did not want the position. It meant a serious loss of business, which I could not afford. It also meant dickering and trading, anxiety and trouble, without substantial result. However, it was as hard for me to say "No" as it always has been, so I consented to run.

Our method of electing the members of the legislature in

Illinois requires three members from each district. As a rule, the majority party would nominate two, and the minority one. Under this arrangement each voter virtually casts three ballots. He can vote for three candidates, or cast two votes for one and cast the third for another, or, he can plump all three votes to one man. So long as I had promised to run I hoped to go about it an easier way. I had always been on good personal terms with the leaders of my district. My quarrels never were with men. So I assumed that the Democrats would put me on the ticket if I told them that I was willing to go. But by this time the friends of the corporations were aroused. I made the request to be placed on the ticket and was told that they were sorry, but I was too late. I told them that I thought I would go to the legislature anyhow; so I filed a petition to run as an independent, and organized a campaign committee, stating that I would pay for the halls in the campaign, but would use no more money nor make any promises. In all my talks I told the voters that I did not want the office; I told them why I was running, and that it was their fight just as much as mine. I notified them that if elected I would not ask for a job for any one or bestow any favors that I would not grant if I were not a member. As I recall it, I received more votes than all the others combined. At least I was elected by an overwhelming majority.

While I was carrying on the campaign, the anthracite coal strike was agitating the people of Pennsylvania, and, in fact, the whole country. The strike began in the spring or early summer of the year 1902. That section of the State furnished all the hard coal used by the United States. It is an immense industry, extending over a large territory and employing many thousands of miners. John Mitchell was then the president of the United Miners. He was a man of strong will, fine judgment, and great energy. The summer wore on with no signs of a truce. Both the mine owners and the strikers determined to fight to a finish.

At that time Theodore Roosevelt was President of the United States. Both sides made various appeals for his aid, but without success. The miners offered to arbitrate the case and let the President choose the board. The mine owners declined, declaring that it was no concern of the President's, which it probably was not. So the weeks went by. A coal famine was in sight, and the whole country, especially the East, was filled with fear. It seemed as if not only would people have no fuel for their homes, but, still more important, business would be seriously crippled, and, in many instances, bankruptcy would result. Once more the public and the press were calling upon the President to interfere. The mine owners were growing alarmed. They feared public opinion, which was rising fast. The miners, by that time, were not anxious for the President to take a hand; they felt that victory was in sight.

In this juncture President Roosevelt called both sides to come to the White House. He proposed arbitration, promising that if it was left to him to choose the board he would endeavor to have both sides fairly treated and every interest represented. But the miners were not anxious to arbitrate. They felt that the strike was won, as it doubtless was. But no one can overlook the great value of public opinion in one of these industrial contests. As a rule, the employers have much the best chance to get public opinion as they are generally closely linked with the press. But in the coal strike many influential papers were with the miners. However, Mr. Mitchell and his associates felt that they could not refuse arbitration. So it was agreed that the President should appoint the board, which he proceeded to do.

I had never in any way been connected with the United Mine Workers, but after the board was appointed Mr. Mitchell asked me to undertake the case, and I was very glad to be in this conflict. I had been in various arbitrations before; I had found arbitration more satisfactory than courts; there are seldom the same feelings of hatred that accompany a court proceeding at law. An arbitration is flexible and informal. Assuming that the board is fair, it is seeking to do justice and not looking to find violations of statutes. Then there are always some members on the board who know something about the matters involved, while a court is supposed not to know. In fact, a judge must not know, even if he does know. And then, in court every important issue may be thrown to the wind on account of the most senseless law or a crotchet of a judge.

The terms of the arbitration and the powers of the board were very broad. They were to have full leeway to find out the facts and make such orders as to them seemed right and fair. I had never had any relations with mining; I had not even dug coal. I proceeded at once to Wilkesbarre, where I was met by many of my clients and James Lanahan and the O'Neil brothers, who were associated with me in the case. These lawyers had once worked in the mines and were familiar with all the terminology as well as the method of the work, and were likewise well-equipped lawyers. I immediately got permission from one of the managers of one of the mines to make a thorough inspection, and then began the work.

Organizing the data for an arbitration of this importance is not an easy task, but in two or three weeks we felt that we were fairly prepared. Both sides had a corps of bookkeepers and expert accountants, and the board provided men of their own to see that no mistakes entered consciously or unconsciously into the situation. The mine owners were handicapped by too many lawyers. A large number of corporations and individuals were involved, and most of them came into court. Of course many of the lawyers were of the first rank, but few of them had ever had any experience in labor arbitrations, or knew much about the common man and his needs and desires.

The hearings were commenced in Scranton and then adjourned to Philadelphia. The case covered some two months of steady work. Almost every imaginable question arose. The matter concerned working conditions, living conditions, education, accidents, cost of food and clothing, rents, in fact, everything that enters into living and toiling. The lawyers seemed to vie with each other in courtesy and consideration. In the entire hearing there was scarcely an unkind word or sharp look by court or counsel. The arguments were closely followed by as many as could be packed into the court room in Philadelphia, and by the press generally throughout the country. Among the other matters considered was the question of making some permanent improved working conditions and methods of settling disputes to avoid strikes and lockouts.

The board took the time thoroughly to consider the case, delivered a lengthy opinion, and granted a substantial raise of wages, better conditions and shorter hours of labor, and found in favor of a plan offered for working conditions for the future. This plan was the outcome of discussion and consideration by both parties, and it was so well weighed and arranged that it kept peace in the anthracite regions for twenty-five years. I believe this was the first agreement reached for settling industrial disputes without resorting to brute force on both sides. Since then it has formed the basis for many other such agreements.

It was generally conceded that labor gained greatly by this arbitration. As soon as the method of the settlement under President Roosevelt had been arrived at the strike was called off and the mines were opened. It was agreed that when the decision was rendered the rate fixed by the board should cover all coal mined during the hearing. Under this decision the miners received several million dollars in back pay, besides gaining security, peace, better hours, and improved working conditions. The opinion scolded the miners for some acts of violence during the strike, but they did not much mind this so long as they won the main points for which they petitioned. Trade unionists are used to being scolded. All men know that a million people cannot live at the point of want without some acts of violence.

While I was still in the East I was visited by emissaries, friends and newspaper representatives from Chicago regarding the coming mayoralty campaign there. The old Altgeld forces were anxious for me to run. Many of the regular Democrats were for me and were certain that I would be given the nomination if I would consent to accept it. I did not want to run. I would not have wanted the position if it could have been had without a contest. I did not believe that any one could faithfully perform his duties as mayor and keep his friends. I had been in the City Hall connected with Mayor Cregier long enough to know and pity the hordes of hungry office-seekers clamoring for jobs. Some would go to the mayor's home in the morning before he could get away, and they were still arriving after he had left the office in the evening; and all day the rooms and halls outside the main office were crowded, all on the same errand, most of them with families at home, many of them in actual want. I knew that no one could run the business of Chicago as it should be run without closing his door and his heart at the same time to these appeals. I knew that the city was in debt, and spent at least twice as much for services as they were worth, and at the same time had to disappoint countless applicants.

This is the case with every city and State and national administration that I know anything about. This is politics. I believed that I could not help, and doubted if I could withstand the appeals of the needy who already looked on me as their friend. I knew that it is out of the question to have honest, economical government while a few are inordinately rich and the great mass of men are poor. In fact, it is to be doubted if anything really worth while can be done until there is a fairer distribution of wealth.

Then, too, I had just been elected to the legislature. It had been in session several weeks and I had not been able to take my seat on account of the miners' case, which I could not leave. It was hard to refuse my friends and supporters, but I was obliged to choose, and—I did not run. Many were grievously disappointed, but I could see it no other way.

CHAPTER 15

A FLIER IN POLITICS

The legislature had been in session two or three weeks when I arrived in Springfield to begin the duties that were new to me. I was acquainted with many of the members there, especially those from Chicago. It did not take long to learn how they worked; or, at least, did what they called work. Next to the courts, more time is fooled away at great expense in legislative bodies than anywhere else that I know anything about.

Every session was opened with prayer, and then a large part of the assembly proceeded to look around to find some one to hold up. This, also, is politics. There was the usual number of bills to unjustly tax railroads, telegraph companies, and other corporations. Many of the companies expected to see me supporting those bills, and many of the members believed that I would "fall for" them. But I knew that they were the usual bills introduced to make the corporations pay money for their defeat. I invariably fought them, and urged the corporations not to spend money for the tribute. I soon discovered that no independent man who fights for what he thinks is right can succeed in legislation. He can kill bad bills by a vigorous fight and publicity, but he can get nothing passed.

I tried to put through one bill. The law authorizing a recovery for deaths caused by negligence was old; it fixed a limit of recovery at five thousand dollars. This amount, considered in connection with the increased cost of living, was a travesty on justice. I introduced a bill to remove the limitation of the amount of recovery, leaving it in the hands of the jury. When I offered the bill the grafters came around me and pledged their support; but I knew better. I had never intended to leave the amount open. Soon I learned that members of the legislature had visited corporations to get money to defeat the bill; they had urged that I was dangerous, that I was against corporations, that there was a chance that the bill would pass. I waited until they had time to organize their opposition. I knew many lawyers and others connected with corporations, so I went to see some of these friends in the employ of the interests and told them what I knew about certain members' conduct in relation to the bill, and that if they wanted to spend the money to defeat it, well and good: I should make no investigation nor stir up any scandal, and believed that I could win anyhow. But still, I explained, I never believed in a bill that left the amount of recovery open. If through some negligence the wealthiest man in Chicago should be killed I was not interested in having his heirs get a million dollars on account of the loss of his service. I was only interested in employees and other workers, and even if the bill was unlimited the courts would not, and should not, permit a large verdict to stand where the financial loss to the family was not great. So, if they preferred to let my bill go unhampered I would be glad to amend it, fixing a limit of ten thousand dollars instead of five. They at once conceded that the present limit was too low; they agreed to call off the opposition. I amended the bill and got it through by a practically unanimous vote. Since then the cost of living has so greatly increased that the amount should again be raised, but no one has taken up the fight.

I was able to render a good deal of help in aid of the Municipal Ownership bill and the Child Labor law. But as the orthodox reformers were supporting both the bills they probably would have gone through without my help. I know I can safely say that in my service in the legislature I neither supported nor opposed any bill for political reasons or for any other reason excepting that I believed that a bill should or should not pass.

Often when I went down to the assembly room I would find an array of letters and telegrams on my desk. Looking at the grist I could say without opening them, "Now, here's another bill that I must help kill; I knew that no bill in behalf of the people could muster so many friends." Invariably I found that I was right. Frequently the member back of the bill had himself urged that these messages be sent. It is remarkable how many men will ask the legislature to do or not do certain things because of their personal interests or the interests of their class.

I remember one bill that all the politicians determined to defeat. The penitentiaries had been in the habit of leasing out the inmates to contractors, who, of course, exploited them in a cruel way. Finally a law was passed forbidding the leasing of the labor of prisoners. It was not long before it was observed that large numbers of men were lying idle in institutions, which required locking them into cells during the day. This was severe torture to the prisoners and a foolish waste of time. To cure this condition a bill was introduced providing for the manufacture of certain products in prisons. Immediately a lobby appeared on the floor largely made up of officials and members of the unions interested in the production of the goods that were to be made in the penitentiaries. It was not hard to get the aid of the politicians to support the request of the unions. They took it for granted that I would be with them without a request, but they finally asked me to assist in defeating the bill. I replied that as the bill then stood I felt that I should vote for it. Most of them were amazed. I set forth that the prisoners, for their own sakes, must have something to do, calling to their minds that practically no one but working people were in prisons and it was inhuman to keep them idle and locked in their cells during the day. I advised them to go back to Chicago and submit the question to the Chicago Federation of Labor, and if they would pick out the kind of work that should be undertaken in prisons I would stand for their bill if it was anything like a feasible proposition. Otherwise I should vote for the pending bill. They never were able to agree as to what sort of work should be done, so we were obliged to determine it ourselves.

Among the bills that I always tried to kill, and generally with good success, were laws increasing penalties and creating new crimes. Congress and every State legislature are always beset with this sort of legislation. Judges and State's attorneys constantly cudgel their brains to think of new things to punish, and severer penalties to inflict on others. Reform associations are likewise active in this regard. And many citizens who think that they have been unjustly dealt with, or have witnessed something that provoked their anger are always seeking to send some one to jail; so that I am satisfied that at least half the men in prison to-day are there for crimes that did not exist thirty years ago—violations of the Volstead Act, confidence games, conspiracy and offenses against many other statutes comparatively new.

The use of the conspiracy charge, in catching an endless number of victims and in creating penalties that have grown in number at a rapid rate, is increasing more and more each day. It took England more than a hundred years to abolish it, even after she began to agitate for its repeal. This crime began in the star chamber courts, where the defendant was not present in the trial, and was used to compass the death of some of the best and greatest men England ever had. It is a serious reflection on America that this worn-out piece of tyranny should find a home in our country.

Among the many new offenses that have found many victims is the confidence game. No one knows the meaning of "confidence game." It was fixed for transactions that were not quite honest but did not rise to the dignity of crime. Now this vague and flexible charge has its victims by the thousands in the prisons of the United States. No wonder that crime increases in America when men sit up nights contriving new accusations for sentencing others to jails. No matter how long the criminal code may be, it cannot apply to every dishonest act that may be committed.

I had the gratification of seldom failing to stop any proposed increase in the length of the criminal code or the terms of sentences for its victims. But my service in Springfield was a serious interference with my own business. Chicago and Springfield, the capital of the State, are two hundred miles apart, and if one attempts to attend to matters of the legislature as he should he might as well close his office and go there to live. Still, I have always been glad that I had the experience, and though I may not have accomplished much for the State, I have considered that the education I got was worth while to me.

In Springfield, and elsewhere, I have had the opportunity to observe the work of many reform organizations, and as a rule I have never liked them. All people are individually ambitious and anxious to be in the limelight and office, and one of the favorite methods is to join a reform organization. This brings prominence plus respectability. What I object to is the hardness that seems a part of reform. These bodies constantly seek to cause trouble for some one; many of their members are interested in Sunday laws, in fighting drink, in stopping the small gambling games that are the enjoyments of the poor, in regulating personal conduct, in their small, pestiferous, nagging manner that makes life a burden. Most of this class of people confound sin with pleasure; they think the world should be gloomy and sad, and pleasure should be postponed till kingdom come. This class of people do their utmost to bring about trouble and to kill joy. For my part, I agree with Omar Khayyam:

"O, take the cash, and let the credit go."

The Puritans were reformers when they hanged people for witchcraft and prohibited theatres, when in Congress they censured George Washington and LaFayette for taking part in a theatrical performance at Valley Forge, when they passed the Volstead Act, which crucifies millions of people for claiming the simple right to drink what they please. This class of Puritans are meddlesome and nosey and contemptible.

I am sure that there are many aldermen, members of the legislature, members of Congress, and others in places of power who take money contrary to law for doing things that they either should not have done or should have done without reward. Men of affairs in our big cities know scores of these men who grow wealthy in this way. All sorts of people who are interested have given them money for vacating streets and alleyways, for granting franchises, locating improvements, for all sorts of favors, for reducing taxes, for passing certain legislation, and much more. The one who does not know that this is true is ignorant of affairs. Most men who are well informed know the men and corporations who have passed out the money, and about how much was paid. They know that many of those who get the money grow immensely rich, and are members of the best clubs and the smartest social sets and churches. And very few seem to care. It has been the system of civilization in every age and land; it will continue to be the story so long as men love wealth above honor and their fellow men.

Even though this is true, as every man knows, I like the men who have taken the money and given it better than many of the reformers, and I believe that most people do; for they have not such an abiding belief in jails; they do not really enjoy

other peoples' sufferings; they do not gloat over hounding people with cruel laws; they are not strong for vengeance and
are not inherently vicious and hard; they are not sadists, who
delight in making others feel pain. But, I never liked either the
reformers or grafters, at that.

I have spent a large part of my life defending men charged
with crime. I have done this for those who paid me, and for
those who gave me nothing, and often have spent my own
money to provide for the defense. I have never let the lack of
money stand in the way of helping people in trouble. I am sure
that I have given at least half of my time and services to this
kind of work without any financial reward. I have had the
satisfaction of saving many from degradation and shame, and
have almost always found them worthy. My only regret is that
I have not been able to do more. It has often fallen to my lot to
try to get bail for unfortunates languishing in jail and waiting
for trial. I have never asked a reformer to sign a bond. I am
too intelligent even to try to induce him. I have preferred to go
to an alderman, an alderman that the reform organization op-
poses; or I would go to some one who has sympathy and feeling; some one who knows what trouble means; some one who
has had experience, if possible, and, if not, one who has vision
and some imagination.

As a rule the politician is a "good fellow" who is generous,
kind and liberal. Many a one is ready to help a constituent who
is in hard luck. It is not uncommon for any of them to feed the
hungry, clothe the poor, and bury the dead. In a world that
is none too generous at best these qualities are highly important and worth finding. Correct values are not easily arrived
at. In fact, there is no possible way to determine what values
are the most or the least worth while. I know the ones that
seem most desirable to me, but I do not expect all the world to
agree with my view.

My term in the legislature gave me an opportunity for reading, as I usually remained in Springfield all the week, and was not engaged in log-rolling; crossword puzzles had not then been invented. I never was bothered by fear of offending constituents. They had elected me. I had not asked them to vote for me; I had made no promises, and I did not want a second term. And I must say they respected my attitude. I conscientiously tried to serve all the people of my State, and from my standpoint I succeeded.

In 1903 I married Miss Ruby Hamerstrom. Since that time it has fallen to my lot to figure in a succession of rather unusual cases in various parts of the United States which have requited my concentrated efforts, so that she has accompanied me in all these out-of-town undertakings, as well as in all my travels in Europe, Egypt, Palestine, and elsewhere; and in recent years, during my debating and lecturing tours, my health and strength have been none too good, so that she has travelled with me most of that time, relieving me of all responsibility and exertion in arranging for everything in the way of transportation and hotel accommodations, baggage, communications, engagements, and the countless inevitable details. I really could not have made these journeys without her assistance and constant care.

CHAPTER 16

THE SKELETON IN THE FOREST

IN 1906 I was called upon by the Western Federation of Miners to defend Moyer, Haywood and Pettibone under an indictment charging them with the murder of ex-Governor Frank Steunenberg, of Idaho. This case had a most dramatic setting and attracted wide interest throughout America.

The Western Federation of Miners was one of the militant labor unions of the country. It included most of the metalliferous workers in the mines of the West. Their general offices were in Denver, Colo., which State was then one of the largest producers of gold and silver in the United States. The president of the organization was Charles H. Moyer, and the general secretary was William D. Haywood. Moyer was a man of great force of character, brave and determined. His life had been devoted to mining and the interests of the union. Mr. Haywood was a pronounced radical, an important member of the Socialist party at that time. He was a wide reader of books, especially on trades-unions and other economic subjects, and an excellent organizer. A strike had been called early in 1906, reaching into all the mines and smelters of the West. A great number of men were involved in the strike. In some sections the mine owners at once began filling the vacated places with non-union workers. It was the usual story which has been told so often in labor controversies the world over.

It is doubtful if there ever was a strike in America, unless in the anthracite region, where the feeling was so bitter as in this case. In Colorado, especially, the contest verged on civil war. Early in the strike Colorado was put under martial law, and

State and Federal troops were summoned and utilized by the owners of the mills and mines. These measures were then taken under the claim of the need to protect property and life, especially property.

It is not my purpose to enter the field of controversy, but only to sketch the background of the drama. The courts have often held that a strike in itself is violence, and that there never was a peaceful strike; probably this is an extreme statement, even in law, but most strikes have been accompanied by more or less violence, not alone by the strikers but also by agents, detectives, and other workers in the employ of the owners, and by outsiders whose sympathies were enlisted on one side or the other of these individual contests. In any settled community, with the easy and lurid publicity of our age, large masses of union men lose their jobs. These places are taken by non-union men who are almost universally called "scabs" by all the workers and their sympathizers. Often the substitutes are simply poor men who need the work and have a hard time to live. Many of them make this kind of labor their calling; and this class receive much more pay than the union men. They are usually strong, quarrelsome, reckless, and as a rule have no ties that restrain their conduct. They are called strike breakers. They have no ideals, and can always be had from detective offices which are engaged in connection with strikes. The strikers also often use violence.

Mirabeau said that you cannot make a revolution out of rosewater. Neither can you conduct a great strike by singing hymns. Women are often as active as the men, and even more interested. It is a serious matter for a workman to lay down his tools and join the ranks of the unemployed. It often means want and privation for himself and wife and children; perhaps a father and mother, too, are depending upon him. It sometimes means danger, and jail, and even death. It takes courage and devotion, and these are rare qualities in the world. It is strange that in these conflicts the whole community is divided, just as in war or religion. Those who are charged with violating the law in behalf of or against strikers are really not criminals. They are not working for merely selfish ends; whether on the right side or the wrong side, they are idealists working for a cause. All such crimes should be classed by any thinking people as political crimes. There is no more semblance to crime in matters involving industrial wars than in the hideous killings in the World War.

During the strike a railroad station near Victor, Colo., was dynamited, and some thirty men were killed. This happened about three o'clock in the morning, when the so-called "scabs" were leaving work. Other explosions occurred in different mines. Efforts were made to derail trains and to interfere with persons and property.

On the other hand, the mine owners and operators made full use of soldiers and private detectives. Many men were beaten; a considerable number were thrown into jail and denied bail or the right of habeas corpus. Moyer and Haywood were both among that number. The situation in the West was, as I have stated, virtually a case of civil war, on a somewhat modified scale. Colorado was not the only State involved. Utah, Nevada, Montana and Idaho had rich mines that came under the same class as Colorado. In addition to this, the smelter interests were very strong. Butte was the centre of this industry, and the United Mine Workers were in full control of their men.

Idaho had rich mines in the Cœur d'Alene district, and, in the beginning of the strike, Frank Steunenberg was governor of the State. He was elected as a trade-unionist. He was a printer, carried a union card, and got the union vote. When the strike came on he declared martial law; and thus the strikers viewed him as one who had received the votes of the union members and then deserted them and joined the enemy when they were fighting for their existence. Governor Steunenberg's term expired while the strike was on; he then left Boise City, the capital, and went back to his home in Caldwell, a small village about thirty miles from Boise.

One night about eight o'clock the little town of Caldwell was startled by a loud report that indicated an explosion of some sort. People ran from their houses into the street, and it was discovered that Governor Steunenberg had been killed by a bomb fixed at his gate in a manner that caused it to explode as he opened the gate; it was evidently placed and timed for his home-coming. A cordon was immediately thrown around the town, and no person was permitted to leave. Harry Orchard was later arrested. He had been staying at the hotel for several days, and seemed to have no business in the village. His room was searched. His valise contained some dynamite, some wire, and perhaps other things that indicated that possibly he might be the man that was wanted. He was traced back to Denver, and it appeared that he had been active in the strikes at Cripple Creek; sometimes on one side, apparently, and sometimes on the other. He had no visible means of support, and could give no reason for being in Idaho. He was locked up and subjected to the keeping of James McPartland, the manager of the Pinkerton Detective Agency in Denver. As the coils tightened around Orchard, he made a confession to Officer McPartland and the attorneys in charge of the case. He claimed that Moyer and Haywood had given him the money to come to Idaho and kill Steunenberg, and that George Pettibone was connected with the plot.

George Pettibone was not active in the union, though he had formerly worked in the mines in the Cœur d'Alene, and had been prominent in the organization. Years before, he had been connected with a strike in Idaho and had been blacklisted, for the owners had regarded him as one of the main men in the miners' organization. He was a man with a resourceful intellect, was something of a chemist, and seemed able to do almost anything that he set his mind to work at. He was witty, pleasant, and kindly; all his neighbors liked him, and all the children ran to him when he came in sight. For several years he had kept a little store in Denver. He had retired from the miners but was always interested in their affairs and was an enthusiastic supporter of the trades-union cause. He was well acquainted with Moyer and Haywood, he kept up a membership in the union and was always on that side.

In many ways Pettibone was a unique and interesting man. He was always jolly and friendly with every one he met. He never seemed serious. He could give information on almost any subject, and was ready to do a good turn for any one. He was supposed by the mine owners to be a desperate fellow. Everything that indicated special planning was believed to be his work. In one of the early lock-out difficulties in Cœur d'Alene he had been very active, and I used to hear some of his enemies tell of his exploits. The Cœur d'Alene is one of the most picturesque spots in America, and is situated in northern Idaho. It is deeply wooded with pine trees all over the region, the mountains rise abruptly, the valleys between are narrow and winding. A large smelter nestled in a pocket of this natural beauty, its power furnished by a stream that came from farther away and higher up and was carried down through a carefully constructed flume into and through the mill. When the strike came on, a high fence was built all round this property, and wires attached to batteries were arranged on the fence. The non-union workers kept inside the wall, and the place was closely guarded against the enemy outside. The miners not only worked under protection but boarded and slept there as well.

Some one evidently climbed the mountain and experimented with blocks of wood until he estimated just how long it took for a block to land in the mill. Some dynamite was placed in a block which was attached to a clock and put into the stream;

it seemed to land at the appointed time, and the top of the mill, as some of them reported, went up like an umbrella. I do not know anything about the casualties, but believe there was no loss of life. It occurred twenty years before Steunenberg was killed; but the detectives and agents always claimed that Pettibone made the contrivance, and in those days he was driven out of the region.

A policeman on the beat in Denver told me another story about Pettibone. He said that Pettibone came to see him about ten days before Thanksgiving and invited the policeman to come to his house to dinner, saying that he had a fine turkey in the cellar that he was fattening for "the feed." The day before it was to be served up for Thanksgiving, Pettibone again hunted up the policeman and asked him to come over and kill the turkey, as he positively could not do it himself. Could both of these stories be true? I think they could. The history of man shows his devotion to various causes. If he believes strongly enough that he is right, or that the cause is important to life or salvation, then he justifies the means in view of the end. No one marvels at this in time of war.

Kindly, honorable, and loving men doubtless blew up the *Lusitania* and committed unspeakable horrors on both sides in the Great War. John Calvin built a fire around Servetus and burned him to ashes for the crime of heresy, and the Christian men and women insist on poisoning liquor that is sent broadcast through the land so that any one who drinks it will die in agony. Only fanatics could do any of these things. When any one believes a thing too strongly the means are forgotten in reaching the end. But cruel as these actions seem to be, none have the semblance of crimes.

Moyer, Haywood, and Pettibone were indicted for the murder of Steunenberg, though Moyer and Haywood were in Colorado when the tragedy occurred, and therefore could not legally be taken to Idaho for trial, because they were not in

Idaho at that time, and were not fugitives from the State. Harry Orchard was also charged with the crime, and Jack Simpson, prominent member of the board of the United Mine Workers. But Jack Simpson had made his escape immediately upon the arrest of the others.

All the news in connection with the affair was kept strongly guarded so that no one should know the movements of the State officials. Late one night some strangers appeared unheralded in Denver. Certain persons were assigned to each one of the defendants, and promptly took them by force without legal process, each carrying out his part of the job. They all met near the depot, where a car was held in waiting. The prisoners were put aboard and the car taken rapidly away without stopping until far beyond the confines of Colorado. They were taken on to Idaho and locked in the jail.

The question of kidnapping was carried to the Supreme Court of the United States, which said that, while the taking was illegal, the defendants were in Idaho, and the court would not inquire into how they arrived in that jurisdiction.

I did not go to Idaho until after the case of kidnapping had been passed on by the Supreme Court of the United States. There was nothing to do then but fight the case in the Idaho courts. Associated in the case were Edmund Richardson, of Denver; Edgar Wilson and John Nugent, of Boise; and Fred Miller, of Spokane. Immediately we arrived in Boise we set to work at preparing the case. During this time many stories came of witnesses in Denver and Cripple Creek and other parts of Colorado who could give all sorts of valuable testimony. As the case was not to be reached too promptly, I took two weeks off, spending most of the time investigating rumors coming from Cripple Creek, Goldfield, and Victor. But the number of irresponsible stories that come to a lawyer in the preparation of a press-agented case is almost beyond belief. Men and women seek to tell marvellous tales by way of making themselves important. Many at once take sides. Then there are those who do not like some one who is on the other side of the trial. People are impelled by all sorts of motives and ambitions; most of their tales have no kind of foundation, and from among the dozens that were interviewed only two or three were finally taken to Idaho to give testimony in the case.

Soon after the arrest of Harry Orchard various people were sent for by the State, among them one Steve Adams, who was then living in Idaho. Adams was supposed to have a good deal of information concerning what had happened. He was brought in and quizzed, and finally made what was called a confession. We were not permitted to see Adams, as would have been allowed in many States, but we learned that he had been visited by an uncle who lived in Oregon. This uncle had been a farmer and a race-horse man, hailing from Kentucky, following these occupations in various parts of the West, and winding up on a large ranch in Oregon.

So we went to see this uncle, Mr. Lillard. He at once assured us that Steve had been frightened; that he had no money for defense, was afraid that he could get no counsel, and would be hanged; so he made the statement on the offer that his life should be saved. As soon as he made the confession he was taken to the penitentiary, where he and his wife were given a little house within the walls. The uncle told us that Steve had wanted to see us and that if we would defend him the uncle was sure that he would plead "not guilty," as, in fact, he knew nothing about the affair, anyhow. We told the uncle that if Steve should send for us, and tell us that he wanted us to defend him, we would do it as faithfully for him as for the rest.

Soon after this the State found out what Steve Adams intended to do. So they removed him from the penitentiary, at night, and took him to the Cœur d'Alene district in northern

Idaho. He was locked up in the city of Wallace, the county seat of that region. In Wallace he was indicted on the charge of having killed a young man named Tyler who was jumping the claim of a settler, a friend of Adams. This had happened six or seven years before and no one had known anything about how the unfortunate claim-jumper had met his death, or that Adams was in Idaho at the time, until the State found a witness after the indictment in the Steunenberg case. So they took an officer to a lonely grave in the forest, opened it and found human bones. There was no relative known except the victim's mother, who lived in a lonely spot in the woods. They took the contents of the grave to the mother, who identified some pieces of clothing which she said had been worn by her son.

In the meantime, Governor James H. Hawley, one of the attorneys prosecuting Moyer, Haywood, and Pettibone, came to Wallace, had his name entered for the prosecution, and had the case in Boise continued. It seemed evident to us that the State representatives were anxious to get a conviction of Steve Adams so that, in order to save his life, he would turn state's evidence and testify against Moyer, Haywood, and Pettibone. Thereupon, my associates and I entered our names as attorneys for the defense of Steve Adams in the case at Wallace, and at once began preparations for the trial.

We felt it necessary to take a long trip through the forest to investigate the scene of the alleged killing, and to find any witnesses who might know anything about the affair. It soon became clear that quite a number of homesteaders knew about the disappearance of the claim-jumper, but had never made it a topic of conversation in Idaho, and no officers or private citizens had made any investigation to learn what had become of the missing man. It was assumed by all the woodsmen that the dead man was a claim-jumper, and therefore an undesirable and unwelcome resident in a new section, and under those circumstances it was useless and unnecessary to search.

The trial was to take place in Wallace, the county seat of Shoshone County; we got together a number of investigators and hastily prepared as best we could for the approaching case. The purpose of the State was plain. They wanted Steve Adams to help them in the prosecution of Moyer, Haywood, and Pettibone, and they wanted to be able to offer him the highest inducement that could move a man—his life—in return for his services. And we, of course, were anxious to keep them from being able to make the offer.

The whole region of northern Idaho had a natural beauty and charm that one rarely finds wherever he may go.

Wallace, Idaho, is a town of about thirty-five hundred people. It lies in a basin surrounded by mountains, walled in on all sides with steep slopes of firs and flowers, and funiculars and flumes. Wallace is the hub of one of the richest mining territories in the world. Its mines produce mainly copper and zinc and lead. Twenty years earlier Wallace and its surroundings boasted large forests of fine timber, but it had been converted into lumber, and this, with its mines, had brought wealth to that section and its people; or, at any rate, to *some* of its people.

The little town took great interest in the trial of Steve Adams. They knew that it was merely a curtain-raiser to the real tragic drama of life about to follow at Boise. And it was one of the important scenes, at that. The country in which Wallace was located had been settled by homesteaders, the sort that, following Daniel Boone, had slowly made their way from Virginia through Tennessee and Kentucky on to the farthest limit of the unexplored world in Texas. The majority of them were men skilled in woodcraft and the handling of a gun.

The laws of the United States provided that one could file a claim for one hundred and sixty acres, and by building a shelter and living in it for three years the occupant became the owner of the land. All of the homesteaders were poor; many of them were obliged to go to work elsewhere through a portion of the year and bring back provisions enough to last through the deep snows of winter when they were pent up in their shacks.

As a rule, residence was never any too well established, but the government officers were apt to be considerate in helping the homesteader make his proof. On the heels of the homesteaders came the claim-jumpers, as is always the case in such sections. They would take possession of a hut and its little clearing when the original settler was away, and then file a contesting claim. These men in the human world are brothers of the cuckoo of the bird realm. Such interlopers are never popular in any part of the earth.

At about the time the killing occurred, Steve Adams had been spending several weeks with some of his friends in the big forests up in the mountains. He liked to hunt and fish, and this section was then one of the few remaining spots where game and fish were more plentiful than human beings.

As has been stated, in some way the attorneys or officers for the State found the lonely grave in the forest, and unearthed the bones and decayed clothing which they took to the dead man's mother. When she had examined some of these moldering rags, they carefully dressed the mother in widow's weeds and parked her in the courtroom day after day during the trial of the case. Probably never before had any one been convicted for killing a claim-jumper in that part of the State. Perhaps nowhere else. Jumping claims was an extra hazardous business in the dense forests of those coveted Cœur d'Alene of picturesque northern Idaho, and one entered this occupation at his own risk.

It was none too easy to get a jury. The natural instincts of the natives were for the homestead owner and against the claim-jumper. There was land enough up there for every man to file a claim of his own. All that could be gained by jumping another's claim was the cheap home and sparse clearing in the lonely woods.

On the side of the defense was added to our list of lawyers, Mr. John Wourms, who lived in Wallace and was an old-time member of the Miners' Union, and a fighter for their cause; though already far on the road toward respectability because of his able work for the mine owners, he became our friend and gave us his aid. There is neither time nor space for going into the details of the trial, but it was about as interesting and remarkable as any case in which I have figured. The great trackless wilderness where the scene was laid along the St. John River, the primitive, unlettered dwellers from the untrodden green woodlands, the claim-jumper trying to take the property of the pioneer, the courtroom filled every day with woodsmen and miners, with here and there a woman in her finery, made up a colorful scene. And amidst it all, the old mother brought out of the distant solitude dressed in her "weeds" eying the bones and tattered clothing of her resurrected son. Through it all were shadow pictures of Robin Hood and the greenwood tree, and Daniel Boone with his long rifle and buckskin jacket blazing the trail for a new civilization.

Except for the fact, which every one knew, that this fight was a skirmish staged by the prosecution to affect the case in Boise, the defense would have had an easy time in Wallace. But every one seemed to think of Steve Adams as a part of the Moyer, Haywood, and Pettibone case, and that fight was different. When the jury retired it soon became plain that they would not agree. After the men had been kept out two or three days, they reported to the court that they were hopelessly deadlocked, and the judge dismissed them from further service.

At Wallace, and later on at Boise, Steve's uncle was present at every session. He was one of those characters known as "a courtroom fan." He never missed a chance to hear a case, or listen to a well-known speaker. He also enjoyed the distinction of being the "next friend" of the defendant. All told, he got a great deal of pleasure out of it even though it gave him much concern.

After the disagreement in the Wallace case we were notified that the State would proceed with the trial at Boise. We sought to have Steve given bail, but the judge refused, as courts are prone to do. So we left Steve in jail in Wallace, under the careful protection of our friend, John Wourms, and set off for Boise.

After a time we learned that Steve had disappeared from the jail and we felt sure that the State knew where he was. Later he turned up in his hostelry in the penitentiary grounds at Boise.

CHAPTER 17

THE ATHENS OF THE SAGE-BRUSH

UNTIL entering this case I had never been in Boise. I had read of it, and knew that it was far away out West. I had pictured it to myself, but I never found an unfamiliar person or place that proved to be anything like my mental picture. Boise was approached from the east through hundreds of miles of dreary, dusty desert with no living thing in sight but gophers and sage-brush. During the trip one deliberates whether to keep the car-window tightly closed and die for want of air or raise it ever so little and be suffocated with the clouds of powdered alkali. I always did both, one after the other. Through the whole region of desert waste, a long strip of green wound and twisted its tortuous way in loops and zigzags across the desolate plain. This is the Snake River, named from the animal which Adam had in mind when he named Eve's tempter. As we neared Boise the scene changed. The fields were fresh and green, the orchards were luxuriant, the town resplendent with lawns and flowers, shrubs and trees; the houses were neat and up-to-date. The Snake River had been intersected with dikes, which irrigated the barren wilderness and made it a beautiful garden-spot. The landscape was most pleasing, and out beyond, a circle of mountains enclosed the little city; so that after the long, wearisome journey Boise seemed like a bright green gem in a setting of blue. It is the capital of the State, with attractive public and private buildings, and a good library. Except for the hard work, intense worry and suffering, and the bitter opposition, it was a pleasant place to visit. Boise had a pride in its town and people and culture, and could rightly be called the Athens of the sage-brush.

Getting back to the metropolis of Idaho was a great relief after the long stay in Wallace. Boise was much larger and the living conditions were better. And it was warmer, in the winter and early spring. I never did like cold weather, and therefore have spent most of my life where it has been hard to keep warm. Then, too, I was anxious to get to work on the main case. The "best people" were lined up on the other side and none too friendly toward the attorneys for the defense. But we had already become rather well acquainted with Mr. and Mrs. Edgar Wilson. Mr. Wilson was the first Congressman from Idaho, one of the earliest settlers of the State, and one of the most respected. Then, and afterward, the Wilsons were our loyal friends, and did a great deal to make life more tolerable in Idaho; and later on, in Los Angeles, they proved as staunch and devoted as any friends that ever came into our lives. Mr. Wilson has been dead for ten years, but Mrs. Wilson is the same kindly, attractive woman that she was at first sight.

The great mystery in the whole case was the coming testimony of Harry Orchard. When there is no way to get a line on the evidence of a hostile witness, one must assume that it will be even more damaging than can reasonably be imagined. We tried to get some inkling of what his story was to be, but could find no law that could give us any opening or relief. It was dangerous to meet the testimony of such a witness with no information about what his evidence would be, with the arena of the combat where the fight was to take place about fifteen hundred miles away from the main setting of the drama in Colorado. But, while we could not see him, an opportunity was soon furnished us to get his story.

A few days before the case came up for trial we picked up the paper, and there was Harry Orchard and his story all over the front page. It seemed that the various newspaper representatives from everywhere in the country had been called in to hear Harry Orchard tell his tale. The "news" was lurid enough to satisfy the cravings of any reader. This was sent broadcast and published in all the leading papers of the United States, at least. Immediately we detailed men to run down the events and incidents that he related, and by the time we had impanelled the jury we had fairly and carefully examined every statement made by him. Luckily for us, many of these claims were contradicted by the facts that we afterward adduced.

The document was a revelation of Harry Orchard's mind, and put him down as easily the greatest retail killer that the world had ever known. Then we looked for the motive that might have caused him to kill Steunenberg. We learned that Orchard had worked in the Cœur d'Alene mines in northern Idaho in the year 1899, and then, together with Ed Boyce, former president of the United Mine Workers, and Henry Day and his brother, and Al Hutton, a locomotive engineer, and one or two others, had located the Hercules mine, which at that time was merely a prospect. Orchard and some of the others had worked the mine while Hutton stuck to his locomotive engine and put his earnings into the prospect. The Day brothers and Ed Boyce worked in other capacities to earn money for developing the vein, and one or two of the Day sisters had taught school for a number of years and put their savings in the common pot.

As luck would have it, the Hercules turned out to be one of the richest deposits ever discovered, ultimately becoming worth many millions of dollars. Harry Orchard, as I remember it, had about a tenth interest in the property. He was actively interested in the strike of 1899 in the Cœur d'Alene—as those mountains and valleys were spoken of. Steunenberg was the governor, and called out the militia at the behest of the mine and smelter company. Orchard was obliged to dispose of his interest in the Hercules prospect and flee from the State. Of course, it was of little value at that time.

Incidentally, this case, as well as others, represents an illustration of fate and chance, and the futility of human plans. Had Orchard not been forced to flee from Idaho he would not have sacrificed his stock in the Hercules mine. Within a few years he would have been a multi-millionaire. He would, doubtless, have developed into a wealthy and respectable citizen, and a member of the Mine Owners Association. Orchard is a man of considerable natural ability, and, with opportunity, could have, and no doubt would have become, like all his associates of the Hercules mine, an outstanding figure in the affairs of the Northwest.

All the proceedings and events concerning the case were fully reported by the press, especially in Idaho, Washington, and Colorado, and had general publicity through the other newspapers of the land. The little city of Boise was not then very well equipped with hotels and lesser accommodations for the people streaming in. There were newspaper and magazine representatives, witnesses, tourists, laymen, and lawyers—people from all parts of the mining sections, and from hither and yon.

The siege in Wallace had been very wearing, living accommodations were poor, the climate rainy and cold. The worry and hard constant work with the rest of the discomforts began to affect my health. I was giving myself over to the work day and night as entirely and completely as the human system could admit. It was apparent that the cases in Boise were to be even more strenuous than the experience in Wallace.

Mrs. Darrow had come West with me, so we took a cottage on the edge of the town, where I was able to detach myself occasionally from the tension and congestion of people, and go back between spurts with new zeal to the responsibilities pressing upon me.

The prosecution was in charge of Owen M. Van Duyn, the district attorney, who was assisted by James Hawley, an old typical pioneer lawyer of the West, a man of ability, long a resident of the State, and had for many years been connected with most of the important litigation of Idaho. He had held various political offices, and soon after the trial was elected governor. Honorable William E. Borah was the third member of that staff. When I say that he was third, I do not mean in relation to importance. Mr. Borah had for twenty years been one of the leading lawyers of the State and, shortly before the trial commenced, was elected to the United States Senate, but did not take his seat until after the case was finished. Mr. Borah, then as now, was very popular throughout Idaho. He was a hard worker, astute, and in every respect an able adversary. He was always wary and cautious and thoroughly familiar with his case. As is generally true, most of the influential and wealthier members of the community were with the prosecution. The working class, the miners and the poor were for our side. The unknown quantity was the farmer, or rancher —the men of the pastures and plains out West, breeders and herders of animals, and producers of food for both animals and men. They were intelligent and independent, and altogether unlike the granger of the East. The Western ranchers are of the pioneer class, used to hardships, adaptable to life, alert to new ideas, more or less restless and discontented, and not always successful. Most of the jurors came from this element.

Before Orchard's statement we were not able to get much advance information concerning the side of the State. Our experience told us that no doubt the case would be tried on the lines of conspiracy—the modern and ancient drag-net for compassing the imprisonment and death of men whom the ruling class does not like. Sometimes, however, a member of this class gets caught in the net. We knew that conspiracy cases are not unlike the French procedure, where any one seems able to come forward and say what he thinks, express himself freely, and give his opinion on any subject that moves his mind. In case the attorney for the accused objects to any evidence on the ground that it is hearsay and the events and statements occurred outside the presence and hearing of the defendant, the prosecuting attorney rises and says that he will undertake to connect up the proof later in the trial. Thereupon the court promptly and mechanically and subserviently decides that the evidence may be admitted, and, unless later on it is connected up, it will be stricken out. Few judges are psychologists, or they would realize that nothing can be stricken out of a human consciousness after being once let in. Judges seem to be quite unaware that it is a hard task to put anything into the average mind, and, once in, an impossible one to take it out. The way the defendant is connected up later is to have the man who turns state's evidence swear that everything the witness claimed transpired with the knowledge, express or implied, of the defendant, or with somebody brought into the conspiracy through a chain back to the defendant. If, after days or weeks or months of taking testimony, the judge decides that some item was not connected up, he coolly tells the jury that they are to ignore this, that, and the other thing, probably without at all explaining his meaning of "ignore." The jury is so instructed, regardless of the fact that no one is able to know all the specific things that enter into his opinion, or take away, from an opinion already formed, any of the special facts, circumstances, guesses, or prejudices that go into its making.

An opinion is a state of mind arrived at from everything seen and heard during the trial. It is a composite thing; imagine a juror reaching into his mind and separating one item out of the mass and then seeing what is the state of his mind. This is one of the many ways in which individual freedom has been destroyed, by the favorite new method of conspiracy, supposed to have been abolished with the thumb-screws and the racks.

We did not believe that there was any direct evidence against any of the defendants, barring such statements as Harry

Orchard might make. And no opportunity had been granted the attorneys for the defense to see or examine Harry. He was confined and guarded in the penitentiary just outside Boise. He was kept as carefully under lock and key as if he had been the most precious jewel that ever decked a crown.

I have always been sorry for Harry Orchard. Believing, as I do, that human endeavors are as nothing in the presence of the eternal forces which move the universe and its every particle, I can see what Harry Orchard might have been instead of a convict sentenced to a life term in the prison in Idaho. Harry Orchard, like all other men, was the product of the forces that control everything that exists. It is idle to think that he had anything to do with the origin of himself and his destiny. To say that he was, or might have been, master of his fate is saying that he was, or should have been, stronger than the inevitable processes of the universe, which every one must know would be absurd as to Harry Orchard and every other mortal that has ever lived and toiled and suffered and died.

CHAPTER 18

THE HAYWOOD TRIAL

WHEN the case was called for trial at last, the courtroom was crowded with prospective jurors, witnesses, newspaper reporters, magazine representatives, and visitors, from all parts of the land, especially from the mining sections of the West. Empanelling the jury was a long and difficult process. Almost every one was familiar with the case; they had heard about it, read about it, talked about it, and of course generally had formed an opinion. Many were excused because they did not believe in capital punishment. Some were disqualified by artful questions of the prosecution in relation to circumstantial evidence.

Not only in that case but always in criminal cases, if the State does not want a juror he is asked if he believes in circumstantial evidence and if he would convict on that kind of evidence alone, if the evidence should be convincing. Lawyers ask the question, and judges permit it, although both know that the evidence is not wholly circumstantial, and the question has no relevancy to the case. In this the courts deliberately help the State to convict.

As is usual, there were many who did not want to serve, and also, as usual, there were many men called for jury service who did want to sit; some, no doubt because it was a well-known case, and others because they wanted to aid one side or the other. After several weeks a jury was finally accepted. Most of the members were ranchers, and, on the whole, they were rather outstanding, independent men. To be sure we had no members of the Miners' Union and no one who was a miner. The prosecution succeeded in qualifying one Mr. Robertson, with whom Steunenberg had made his home.

During the trial, which lasted for several months, the courthouse was filled with people, and the crowd extended into the corridors and adjoining rooms. The building stood in the middle of the square covered with grass and trees. There was always a line waiting to get inside, and an overflow scattered over the lawn hoping to hear or see something of interest in the celebrated case.

Every trial has its high spots and hours and days of special importance. There were many witnesses called for the State, and as many, or more, for the defense. In any long trial most of the testimony is soon forgotten, even by the lawyers, but there are always some witnesses who make a lasting impression on the listeners, as is the way in affairs in general through life.

Every one knew that the State's case largely depended upon Harry Orchard. Few had ever seen him, and every one wondered what sort of man he was. Most of those who attended the trial had read his story given to the press by the prosecution, which was repeated in Mr. Hawley's forcible opening statement to the jury. This served only to increase the curiosity to see and hear the man. Soon after the opening of the evidence there was an unusual commotion in the outside hall and along the aisle down the centre of the courthouse. We looked back and saw a line of deputy sheriffs making their way toward the judge's desk. In the midst of them was a short, stout man with a red face. At once we realized that this was Harry Orchard. He was brought into the courtroom under heavy guard and conducted to the witness box. A visible and audible sensation swept over the spectators. At last they were looking at the man who had seemed to boast of his many crimes.

Soon the room was hushed into silence, and under the questioning of Mr. Hawley, Harry Orchard began his story. And

what a story it was: He was a party to the blowing up of the
little railroad station at the Victor Mine in Colorado where
some thirty men were killed. He had also tried to dynamite the
mine while the men were at work. He had laid his plans and
made his preparations to dynamite the Idanha Hotel, the leading hostelry in Boise City, at a time when it was filled with
guests. He explained that he had prepared an infernal machine
which he intended to put under the bed of one of the inmates
at about midnight and then leave the hotel before the explosion; but some accident intervened that caused him to go out
of the hotel before he had a chance to place the machine.

He had gone to San Francisco to "bump off" a man once
connected with the mining interests who had been active in
fighting the miners in a former strike. He located his victim,
who lived in the top floor of an apartment house with his wife
and young child. He had made himself familiar with the
back stairway and found out what time the milkman left the
supply at the door in the early morning, and then planted the
machine so that it would explode when some member of the
family opened the door to take in the milk. The dynamite
exploded according to schedule. The building was practically
destroyed, although no lives were lost. The intended victim
owned the building and sued the gas company for causing the
destruction, receiving a large verdict, which was sustained by
the Supreme Court. Before the money had been delivered
Orchard had given testimony; the gas company sought to reopen the case, but the Supreme Court held against it, and the
money was paid.

Orchard told in detail of an attempt to kill the governor
of Colorado at his home in Denver, and how the attempt was
frustrated by the barking of a dog in the yard around the residence. Also he had fixed a bomb in a vacant lot in Denver
which a certain member of the Supreme Court was in the
habit of walking across every morning. But the judge chanced

to go around the other way that morning, so the bomb that had been left and arranged was set off by some one else who passed that way, and he was killed by the explosion.

Having lost his interest in the Hercules mine, Orchard went to Wallace, and while there visited Mr. Paulson, one of his former partners, now grown very wealthy. Paulson treated him kindly and invited him to a Christmas dinner. So Orchard bought a few toys for the Paulsons' little child and played with him on the floor, and while a guest in this happy home planned to kidnap the baby and hold it for a ransom; but this plan, too, somehow was defeated. Various other plans were made for killing other victims, some failing and some succeeding.

To close his testimony, Harry Orchard was asked by Mr. Hawley if the name he had used so long was his real name or an assumed one. He replied that it was not his real name, and, in answer to further questions, gave his real name, the place of his childhood, the name of his wife and his daughter, a girl then in her teens, both then living in a far-away place. It would serve no purpose to repeat the information here. In my closing address to the jury I made the most of this gratuitous statement of Orchard's to give credit to his story; I called attention to the countless men in prisons who live out their lives in blank despair and those who die on the scaffold refusing to reveal their names so that their disgrace shall not attach to fathers and mothers, wives and children and others who are left behind.

Orchard's story was long and detailed. Evidently it was carefully thought out and arranged. In his entire examination and cross-examination he was cool and deliberate, and held himself fully in hand. He was a man with little or no schooling, but gifted with a rather superior mind and a remarkably cool head. To be sure, he had been able to give many weeks of preparation to his story, and to consider every question that might be asked on cross-examination. Orchard claimed that during his exploits he spent a good deal of his time in Denver at Pettibone's home, and that he had many conversations with Haywood and some with Moyer.

Mr. Richardson undertook the cross-examination of Harry Orchard. He was thoroughly familiar with the case in all its details. He was a man of much force of character and full confidence in his own ability to accomplish whatever he set out to do. So, in a loud voice and antagonistic manner he re-examined Orchard for several days on every detail of his direct examination. Orchard remained perfectly cool and, like most witnesses, repeated on cross-examination the story already told. However, Mr. Richardson succeeded in laying the foundation for the impeachment of Orchard, by unbiased witnesses, regarding many statements made in direct examination. As a rule, it is futile to go over in cross-examination the testimony already given. But although Mr. Richardson was an able man, he was somewhat lacking in subtlety. From all the other witnesses called by the State there was no corroboration of any part of Orchard's story, excepting that he had been somewhat active in the strikes of the mine workers, and had been seen in the company of the defendants in Denver on several occasions during labor troubles. Orchard never was really very prominent in the union. He was friendly with a number of the agents and detectives in the service of the mine owners, and there were many doubts as to where he stood. But this condition, too, is not uncommon during strikes.

The whole trial was a vivid picture of industrial warfare such as was fairly common twenty-five years ago. In all these contests both sides put forth their best endeavors to win. Not only were the employers and miners in almost mortal combat, but all classes of society were divided into hostile camps. There were no disinterested people. There was no neutrality. Each side regarded a strike as warfare, and felt that every sort of means was justifiable in carrying it through. On the one side there was always a resort to courts, to the army and State militia, to the blacklist and boycott, to poverty and starvation, and strike breakers drilled for their calling with no respect for anything but to win. The closing of mines and mills often meant bankruptcy; much of the property was in lonely mountainous regions where it could not be preserved from depredation, disintegration, and waste. And the number of people involved in the unions and interested on the outside made it almost impossible to avoid violence. In industrial warfare the psychology is the same as in other warfare.

The trial of this case, like trials of all industrial conflicts, necessarily covered the widest possible field. There was practically no direct evidence against any of the defendants except the testimony of Harry Orchard. This was so tainted that the State attempted to bolster it up with evidence of every sort of conduct and violence, covering an area of six or seven States and more than two years of time. It was the task of the defense to rebut the evidence of the State and show that the defendants and the union were not responsible for the inevitable results that followed in such conflicts. It was also their task to show the efforts made by mine owners, detectives, allied organizations, scabs, and hostile citizens in the general disorder and social upheaval.

So this trial developed into a history of the strike, covering most of the mountainous sections of the West during that stretch of time. In this period nearly every person had the psychology toward his friends and his enemies that prevails in all other wars.

Mr. Haywood took the stand and flatly denied any connection with Orchard or knowledge of his movements. Orchard was simply one man of thousands in the strike, and was suspected of connections with the other side. His association with their agents and detectives gave a foundation for this opinion.

Most of the witnesses on both sides were not much shaken by cross-examination, and when the evidence was all in the jury-men were virtually compelled to act upon the evidence of Orchard, whose story, and powerful inducement to testify, made his evidence practically without value in the case.

I made the closing argument for the defense. This occupied about a day and a half, as court sessions go. The town was crowded with people from all quarters of the country. Only a small number of them could get into the courtroom, but it was summer time, and all the windows and doors were open, so that the crowds outside heard at least a part of what was said. The case covered a wide scope in time and space and events, as has been shown. Its setting was the great Rocky Mountain district of the West. Its actors were engaged in what was indeed a struggle for life. Society in general was divided into two conflicting camps. Every man and woman and every emotion entered into the combat. In all my experience I never had a better opportunity, and when I had finished I felt satis-fied with the effort I had made.

Mr. Borah followed me in the closing argument for the State. His presentation of that side was forcible and scholarly. It was worked out with care and understanding. Few men that I ever met in a courtroom contribute so much industry, learning, and natural ability to a cause as Mr. Borah.

There was a marked contrast between the audiences during his argument and mine. While I was speaking the courtroom was packed and the lawn swarming with working men, so-cialists and radicals, with idealists and dreamers, from every section of America. They devoured every word spoken. Each felt that in this case his personal cause had its day in court, and a spokesman who understood his life and sympathized with his needs.

Mr. Borah finished his argument in an evening session on a Saturday night. The courtroom was packed with the elite of

Boise and all the State. All of them were dressed as though attending a social event, which indeed it was. The common people had been given their opportunity in the afternoon. The courtroom had been thoroughly aired, if not fumigated, during the recess. The elect now had their turn. As I looked over the assembly I was reminded of Byron's description of the ball in Brussels on the eve of the battle of Waterloo:

> "There was a sound of revelry by night,
>   And Belgium's Capital had gathered then
>   Her beauty and her chivalry; and bright
>   The lamps shone o'er fair women and brave men."

The instructions of the court were lengthy, for the lawyers on both sides had asked for everything they could hope the judge would grant. The case was placed in the hands of the jury about ten o'clock that Saturday night, after a trial that had lasted nearly three months.

No lawyer interested in a case ever goes through a more trying period than the time when the jury is deliberating on the verdict. None of us expected that the jury would reach an early agreement. The case was one that lent itself to controversy. The trial had been long, and the feeling intense. Judge Fremont Wood, who tried the case, had been fair and judicial in his attitude, and the whole matter had been left to the jury, to determine the fate of Haywood.

After the instructions were read the defendant was taken back to jail, and we lawyers went to Mr. Edgar Wilson's office to wait. Finally Mr. Richardson announced that he would go home and go to bed. He said that he had performed his duty and could go to sleep as well as if he had never been in the case. But I could not sleep. With some of the other lawyers and a number of friends I walked up and down the streets. Everywhere little knots of men were standing at the corners discussing the case and prophesying what the jury would do.

Gradually the watchers drifted away and returned to their homes. I knew that I could not rest, so some of my companions and I walked about through the night. During all the hours a light was burning up in the jury room. The jurors asked for no further instructions, and made no request to be allowed to go to bed. They were apparently discussing and voting the whole night long.

About seven o'clock in the morning we were notified that the jury had agreed. The judge was sent for, the news spread over the town, and at once the streets began to show signs of life. At eight o'clock the judge arrived, the lawyers were in their places, the courtroom was packed, and people were crowding into the courthouse yard. The verdict was handed to the clerk, the room grew still as death. Haywood was perhaps the calmest one there. No one seemed to breathe until they heard the words "Not guilty." Then the crowd rushed out to the streets. The newspaper men hurried off to the telegraph office. Suddenly the streets were swarming with people. It was Sunday, and no one had to go to work. Up and down the streets they surged, some excited, some rejoicing and smiling, others frowning and downcast. All the forenoon, and all day, the townspeople and the strangers made such a solid mass of humanity that for hours and hours it was practically impossible to make headway in any direction in the business section of Boise. We lawyers wedged ourselves through and went over to the jail. Haywood and Pettibone were happy and could not conceal their joy, and did not try to. Moyer was shaving. He said a word or two, and kept on shaving. He was as calm and cool as a glacier. One could imagine him acting that way if the universe was falling around him. He had schooled himself to take life as it came along, a frame of mind almost impossible for most men to achieve.

For a few days the attorneys for the State did not seem sure what they should do. They had chosen their strongest case and were defeated. I arranged with them that I might go back to Chicago for a while, and would be notified in time to return. Mr. Richardson announced his withdrawal from the case.

The verdict made a profound impression throughout the country. On the one hand it was met with bitter disappointment; on the other there was unrestrained joy.

I had been in Chicago only a short time when my associates wired me to return.

CHAPTER 19

STILL RATTLING THE SKELETON

On my return to Boise I learned that the State had determined to make another effort to bring Steve Adams into their camp. They did not want to risk another trial in Wallace, so they took a change of venue to Rathdrum, Idaho, a small town near Spokane. They still hoped they might convict Adams before taking up the Moyer and Pettibone cases. Rathdrum is the county seat of a farming section. It had few miners or laboring men. We secured the services of the best-known lawyers there, Charles Heitman and Edwin McBee, old residents and men thoroughly acquainted with the country and every one in it; and of course we took along our good friend, John Wourms; of all the lawyers in that case, John Wourms and I are the only ones still alive.

The Haywood case had been a great tax on my strength and energy, and, to make my physical condition more precarious, I found myself suffering with the flu on my return to Boise. I had been back but a few days when I developed a violent pain in the left ear. The physician came to the opinion that I had received some infection and was in grave danger of its developing into a case of mastoiditis. I knew something of the treacherous nature of this trouble and endeavored to have the trial delayed, but without success. I realized that I was in no condition to go into the matter until I was sure of the nature of my malady. The pain rapidly grew intense. It became impossible to get any sleep without opiates. There was only one physician in Boise who made a specialty of the ear, Doctor Charles Hudgel. Unable to bear my agony I sent for him in the dead of night. I never met a finer man. He seemed like an anxious friend who was there to do his utmost, but nothing availed. I talked with him about an operation; he frankly said that the conditions must be carefully watched, and that I had better make ready to go suddenly, if necessary, to California or Chicago, for expert treatment, and that in the meantime I should not undertake another case.

I knew that he was right, but what could I do? Adams had turned his back on the State largely through his confidence in me. I had told him that I would try his case; it was set, and I could not leave him. If through my failure he should be put to death I could never forgive myself. I knew that I was seriously risking my own life to save his. No one but a lawyer can understand what a sense of responsibility one may feel toward a client. In this case I was daily warned of my danger, but I did not even consider leaving him, although there were other capable lawyers who had been in the case at Wallace. If Adams lost it meant his death, or his surrender to the State, which would further imperil the lives of Moyer and Pettibone.

Doctor Hudgel lanced the ear, hoping to drain it of any impurities that might be accumulating; but nothing appeared. It was decided to keep it from healing in case some relief might come from drainage, and the doctor regretfully helped me to go, furnishing me with an equipment for irrigating the open eardrum, with careful instructions to Mrs. Darrow about the detailed treatment and the sterilization of the instruments and the operation of the hypodermic outfit, still declaring that the symptoms were baffling.

In Rathdrum there was neither hospital nor nurse that could possibly be combined with the programme ahead. Thus we set off for Rathdrum, acquainting ourselves with our new cares and concerns, sterilizing and irrigating in the dining car at bedtime, and on a country-depot coal-stove the next day; and at last reached Spokane, where we hunted up a specialist, who made a thorough examination and gave the same opinion and advice as Doctor Hudgel—that it was not a case for an operation but should be watched and attended to immediately if it became definitely mastoiditis; and that from one to two weeks, or three at the outside, would determine the difficulty.

My nerves were very shaky from responsibility, hard work, pain and loss of sleep. The Spokane specialist said that I was risking my life by going into the case, that these infections generated fever, and, generally when not warded off with extreme care, proved fatal. I knew what was involved in risking life, and I felt that for Steve Adams above all others, under the circumstances, I must now take that chance with my own.

At Rathdrum I again tried to get a continuance, on an application to the court, but it was in vain. The judge thought that there were enough attorneys without me, which I could not deny.

We were in Rathdrum about two months. Two months of agony. In order to make ourselves as comfortable as possible we took accommodations with Mr. and Mrs. William Cleland in a one-story cottage near the courthouse. Mr. Cleland had the livery stable of the town. Our bedroom opened off the parlor. Over the door, as we entered, our eyes were arrested by a yarn motto in a carved rustic frame presenting in all the rose tints, "God Bless Our Home," and near the door stood an old-fashioned glowing base-burner that warmed both rooms; opposite us under an "enlargement" of the hostess was a flat-topped organ on which was a diamond-dust vase full of red paper carnations and a metronome glistening like gold. But brightest and best was the warm welcome and tender consideration extended by these people through all our travail in that little town. However long I live I shall never forget them.

I managed to keep my mind on the case during the day, but was completely exhausted by evening. There was scarcely a moment in court when I was not in pain. At night I would try to get some sleep with the aid of the hot rubber-bag which had to be reheated from hour to hour, and which was constantly and devotedly attended to by Mrs. Darrow. When the pain was unbearable, as it often was, we had to resort to the hypodermic, and in this way I got some rest. I could not possibly guess how many times Mrs. Darrow went to the kitchen with its coal stove to keep the kettle boiling, refill the bag, prepare the apparatus for injecting the codine, and then, irrigate the ear. When my memory roams over the West I try to skip Rathdrum. It was one continuous orgy of pain.

Much of the time the owners of the little home remained invisible, excepting at meals and as nods were exchanged in the kitchen, where they secreted themselves in order not to disturb me. But sometimes, when I seemed to be in less distress, the gentle mistress slipped into the parlor and practiced a "piece" that she was to play and sing at a special entertainment to be given by the ladies of The Eastern Star. It was a touching tale about a fair Indian maid whose lover had gone away and never returned. Over and over she sang the song to perfect a sort of wail over "sighing" and "dying" and a melancholy moan over "Red Wing—weeping her heart away." I am sure that if we had ever so slightly hinted that the mournful music or the motto or anything was not exactly as we wished, that devoted pair would never have forgiven themselves for overlooking any point in our favor. As I would doze off under the opiate I would hear "Red Wing, weeping her heart away" again, but when I opened my eyes a bit to see what it was all about and where we were, there would be no one but Mrs. Darrow, returning the bag at my neck and ear, but not a tear, apparently, excepting at the organ; so I would sink back to sleep, while the opiate soothed me, and on and on, through my restless slumbers I would be strangely aware of sobs and sighs softly poured into my aching ear, and would politely stifle the spasm because—there it was again, "Red Wing weeping—weeping her heart away—ay—y—" . . . alas——

It seems quite possible that in my last moments, as I am falling into that final sleep, I may sense again those same mourning sounds still haunting my ear, and shall know that—there again, close, close to me, is that luckless little "Red Wing—weeping her heart away" . . . poor girl!

But so anxious were these good friends to let me have all the quiet and rest possible, that only two of the neighbors ever dropped in for a little visit around the dining-room table after supper. These were the undertaker and his wife, over for a little chat about some funeral, discussing which families would want carriages, and about how many.

My infection was no better, but I was becoming used to the hypodermic so that now it took more and more to put me to sleep. I believe that Mrs. Darrow suffered as much as I did over that treatment, although she filed the needle-points to the slimness of hairs with finest emery-paper; the instrument had to be boiled, the needle, and the tablespoon that held the needle while it was being sterilized, as well as the liquid and codine; the outfit assembled with sterilized gauze so that no fresh infection would be added to whatever it was that I already had; meanwhile I waited for what I so needed, and hoped would be, some relief; each session seeming more than any one should have to endure, though accomplished as swiftly as fingers could fly. And yet, no symptoms to indicate the nature of the trouble, although the ear was kept open, and the weeks had lengthened into months.

But I did manage to try the case. Rathdrum was a farming centre, and even in the Northwest lawyers understood about the conservatism, the regularity and safety of a farmer jury when some one is perhaps to be hanged. We did not like the prospect. It was still hard to get a jury. Every one had read the papers, all about the Boise trial, and about the Wallace case as well. But, at last, we found twelve men, mostly farmers, who said that they had no opinion, and could render an impartial verdict, no matter what the facts might be. Then we went to trial.

Again the mother sat in her mourning clothes furnished by the State for the trials. Again the bones, including the broken skull with the bullet-hole, were turned out on the table. Once more the doctor lovingly handled the skull and, pointing to the fracture, gave it as his scientific opinion that the deceased had come to his death by a shot piercing the skull. Again lawyers wearily put on witnesses and examined them and cross-examined them by the hour. Over again the story was related to the jury, impressing upon the twelve men their evident intelligence, the importance of the trial in the affairs of the universe, and urging them to be fair and honest though the heavens fall. And as before, at last, the jury went out to deliberate. Again several days dragged by during the supposed deep thought; and again they reported that the jury could not agree, and thereupon, like the first, they were discharged.

It was beginning to look as though no jury was destined to agree. This is often the case where a political or religious or economic question is involved. Whatever the claims presented, jurors instinctively recognize that the real issue is a cause, and are definitely with one or the other side. The prosecution gave up the conviction of Steve Adams. They reached the conclusion that he probably would not help their side. So they took him back to Boise and again installed him in the house in the prison yard. We tried the best we could to have him admitted to bail, but the court refused. After the trial of Moyer, Haywood, and Pettibone was ended, an indictment was returned against Adams in Colorado, on some matter occurring during the strike, so he was taken back there; and there was acquitted of the charge.

At Rathdrum we were informed that the Pettibone case would next be placed on trial in Boise. I managed to coax the State to grant me a little time to attend to my infected ear. So we went to Portland for treatment with violet rays, which made no impression on my ailment. No specialist could tell whether I needed an operation, and none would risk the responsibility of guessing and acting, but would send me on to some one else. In Portland I was advised to go to Doctor Pischel, in San Francisco, a specialist of renown; so we repacked our equipment and took the train for the next experiment.

Doctor Pischel sent me to the St. Francis Hotel and put me under his observation and treatment for a week, at the end of which time he declared his inability to solve the mystery, but, like the rest, doubted that the mastoid was infected. And, like the rest, could only advise constant attention and watchfulness.

Then came a telegram that the Pettibone case was to be set for immediate trial. I sought by wire to get more time, but to no avail. Doctor Pischel thought it might be fatal to me if I went, but Pettibone thought it might be fatal to him if I stayed. So, despite the protests of the doctor and my wife, I boarded the train for the long ride to Boise. Mrs. Darrow spent the better part of the two days and nights going back and forth to the dining car for hot water and the application of the rubber bag, giving me hypodermics and irrigating the ear; and it seemed as if the journey would never end.

But in this world everything does end, no matter how long delayed. And so we did get to Boise at last, and I was taken to the St. Alphonsus Hospital there.

CHAPTER 20

IN SEARCH OF A GERM

In the hospital I was treated with the utmost consideration. All there combined with anxious interest in giving me all possible care, and most of the inmates proved sympathetic toward our side of the case. Again Doctor Hudgel was faithful in his attendance and desire to help me, but was as much in the dark as ever. All that he felt sure of was that I would die if I went into the trial. At this stage of my prolonged misery I did not much care whether I lived or died, so I did not even consider withdrawing from the case. I was having a few extra bad days which gave the press something to report.

One morning a turn for the better seemed to have come so that I was propped up among the pillows a while for a change, when the door opened silently and a face looking surprised appeared, followed by a man advancing with a genial "Good-morning, I just received a telegram from a Chicago paper that I'd better show you," handing me the yellow slip, which read: "Darrow reported dying. Interview him." I replied that I wasn't really ready for such an interview; I had not yet picked out my "famous last words" but now I would try to think up some because it would be too bad to disappoint his editor, who was all set for a scoop. I promised to let him know first, as soon as the grim reaper started his job in earnest.

My good friend, Judge K. I. Perky, came and insisted that I should go to his well-arranged home. So I left the St. Alphonsus, and was given all the comforts under his hospitable roof that a man could possibly have. Before this, we had concluded to take Judge Perky into the case with us, and with his assistance I managed to go to the court and pick the jury. This was difficult on account of the former trial and long publicity. I had suffered so much and eaten so little that I looked as though I could not go through with the fresh undertaking, but I determined to stick as long as possible.

When the jury was completed, the prosecution made an opening statement, and I reserved our statement until their case was in. I cross-examined most of the witnesses. Orchard told his story once again as he had told it in the first trial. I did not ask him to tell it over on cross-examination. I had heard it twice and read it once before and my curiosity was fully satisfied. I asked him to elaborate in more detail some of his most terrible deeds. I had him carefully describe Paulson's little boy and their playing together on the floor, and to relate in detail how he went into the Idanha Hotel with the bomb in his hand; I asked him if he knew how many people were in the place, and how many were women and children. I asked him if he knew that the man in San Francisco, living in the top flat, had a little child, and if he had ever seen it. As I went along one could see the jury drawing from him in horror and disgust. I took him back to his far-away home, asking if he had corresponded with his wife and daughter; if he knew whether the girl had married, if she had received word about her father's acts and if he had ever considered how it would affect her and her life. I did not undertake to contradict him. I treated him with what seemed kindness and consideration and pity, and, unlike his attitude in the former case, he kept his eyes downcast; he no longer looked at the jury, and they avoided him. I felt quite certain that every one of the jury looked upon him with distrust, hatred, and contempt.

After Orchard's testimony, the State rested the case, and I told the court that I did not feel able to go on, and requested a continuance until the next morning, which was granted. I went straight home, and, like Pepys, "so to bed." My strength was gone. I knew that I could not hold out. The doctor examined me and feared it meant certain death if I did not go at once to California, where the winter climate would be favorable, and submit to an operation. Pettibone, too, insisted that I should stay no longer. I called in the counsel, and at my bedside we held a consultation, and my associates all insisted that I should go. From the appearance of the jury, and with their knowledge of the outcome of the Haywood case, I felt sure that they would not convict, and probably would acquit. I went over the case fully with my associates, giving them my advice about what to do. Finally I agreed to go, but not until I had made the opening statement to the jury. I felt that I had prepared for this, and of course the others had not.

The next morning I was taken to the courtroom. I was not able to stand. The court permitted me to make my statement seated in a chair. I was told that I looked like a ghost. I suppose I did. I am sure that I felt as a decent ghost ought to feel. It was with the greatest difficulty that I went over what we expected to prove. I had already told the court that I would be compelled to leave the case, and I informed the jury that I was to remain no longer. I presume that the whole situation was impressive. It was certainly tense and painful. I could not raise my voice above a low conversational tone. The jury gave the strictest attention and bent forward to catch every word. Then we asked for an adjournment till morning, promising that the case would then go ahead without further delay. And thereupon I went back to my friend Mr. Perky's home.

The doctor and some of the lawyers came to see me and we discussed our favorite topics, the case and my health. I did not need to learn from the doctor how I was; I knew that there was small chance of lasting through the sixty-hour train-trip to Los Angeles. The doctor admitted that he could not possibly even guess what was the matter; that I had every symptom of mastoiditis excepting the most important ones, temperature and swelling, of which I had not a trace.

I ordered accommodations in the Pullman that was to be

taken out from Boise some time in the night for the long journey across the plains. The winter was coming on; I had always abominated cold weather, but never before so much as then, when my vitality was low. It seemed to me that I could not leave the case, but I knew that I could not go back to court even if I remained in Boise. Los Angeles looked beautiful from Boise. I had been there, and remembered its sunshine and warmth, its flowers and palms, and believed that there I might recover. Strange it is how mortals cling to life. I had few illusions or delusions left, and had no fear of death, but automatically wanted to hang onto life and worry and pain. I had been living for a long time and had formed the habit. It was what Schopenhauer called "the will to live."

Doctor Hudgel came for a final visit, to give us our instructions, to make sure that we were taking everything that might be needed on the way. This was more than twenty years ago. I did not see him for a long, long time. We exchanged holiday cards, and at long intervals letters passed between us, and I always hoped that something would bring my good friend to Chicago. Meantime, last year I was induced to engage in a series of debates that took me back over the Northwest and into some of the old haunts, including Boise City, as it was called when we were there. One of the gratifications of that trip was meeting a number of my former favorites, and among those who welcomed us to Boise were Doctor and Mrs. Charles Hudgel. The doctor, who had once been so good for a sick ear, was now decidedly "good for sore eyes," and we all reviewed our past, present, and future interests over dinner at the hotel there.

When I landed at Boise City, of Boise Basin, in the long ago, about the first person I met was William Cavenaugh. His face was as round as the full moon, and it beamed with a broad smile as he came toward me extending his hand. He was a stonecutter employed on a building that I was passing, and had thrown down his tools to come down and give me a warm handclasp and rejoice over my arrival in the town. He explained that he came from Chicago, and although we had never before met, he knew me well and was for me, which I considered flattering. In the succeeding months I grew to know him well and learned to love him.

"Billy"—as every one called him—did not care for the future or past. He lived only for the present. His chief urge seemed to be to scatter as much sunshine and brightness into the lives of his friends as he could contribute. From the time I arrived in Boise he seemed to be always doing all he possibly could for my entertainment and comfort, especially through my illness. He had a stone-cutter's large muscle, and would come to my room and give me alcohol rubs, and his merry laugh and cheerful smile often drove away the gloom and seemed to allay the pain.

We had been escorted by friends to the Pullman car that was waiting at the station for the through-train trip to the Coast, when suddenly Billy, all smiles, swung into sight with a huge valise that he was waving. When I asked him if he was going somewhere he answered that he was going to Los Angeles with me. This was a great surprise, and a pleasant one. He said he could not bear to have me miss my rub before trying to get to sleep, and—he hated to be left behind in Boise, away from me.

The trip was long and taxing, but with Billy's tireless efforts and Mrs. Darrow's irrigations in the ear and hypodermics in the arm I got to Los Angeles, and went directly to the huge California Hospital. There I was received by my friend, Doctor John Haynes, who had arranged to take charge of my case, and had assured me that he would find experts who would at once determine the ailment and proceed accordingly.

There was an immediate gathering of specialists, the most careful overhauling and testing and diagnosing, at the end of which they all, exactly like the others, declared themselves baffled and puzzled, and agreed that it would be necessary to further observe and experiment. Meantime, the agony had not lessened, and I got no rest excepting through artificial aid.

After a week spent in the hospital in this routine, with no signs of a solution, we moved to a small apartment on the hill, where the physicians continued watching the case for a number of weeks. There they announced that it might be a case of nerves—badly overwrought nerves—and that the pain might be largely imaginary. They explained that there were such cases. I knew that, and suggested that in such event I ought to send for a Christian Science healer. But they did not seem to favor the plan. I thought it all over carefully, and, as we were getting nowhere with the mystery, I getting no relief and the doctors unable to guess my malady anything but a nervous disorder, I saw no reason for further speculation and decided that I had better go home to Chicago. This they seemed to deem a suitable plan. No doubt they had wearied of hearing my moans and groans; so I had Billy take me to the railroad station and help me arrange for tickets and Pullman accommodations for eleven o'clock that night, and we went back up the hill into the sunshine. And Billy gave me a hot bath and another brisk alcohol rub; these, and his faith in my somehow recovering and his fine sympathy and ceaseless cheer, gave me a certain relief.

Also, by way of encouraging me to go on, I had received word from Boise that soon after my departure the jury had brought in a verdict finding Pettibone "not guilty." After I left, the attorneys for the defense concluded to offer no evidence and waive argument, which I am sure was the right move, because they won.

I had no more than returned from the ticket office than I felt a new sensation back of my ear, and certainly it was swelling, as the entire area back of my ear was visibly enlarging. So we at once telephoned the physicians, who declared that I must be taken to the hospital at once for an operation the first thing next morning. We were all apprehensive of what might be discovered, and of the result, because of my long illness and loss of strength, but there was nothing else to do.

The next day a really serious condition was discovered and removed. It was called a freak case of mastoiditis, having dragged through five to six months in reaching that stage where externally it could be recognized. But I made a splendid recovery, and it made life seem better worth while to be again free from pain.

This illness and recovery gave me another example of the controlling power of fate in the affairs of life. I had been suffering intensely for six months. A part of that time I had been so far away from medical attendance that if the infection had grown virulent I could not have reached aid in time to save my life. I went to Los Angeles, was there a month under observation, and then, believing that no crisis was near at hand, with the doctors' approval procured transportation for home and in three hours would have been on the way. Had the swelling begun after I had boarded the train it would have been three days before I could have reached my destination and medical attendance. Long before then the cyst would have broken and I would have been dead. I cannot know why fate has put off the end until a later day, or when that day will come, but I do know, in the language of the court, that I got "a continuance."

In the meantime, however, while in Los Angeles, Pettibone arrived at the hospital for treatment. He had occupied a cell into which the sun had never penetrated, and while waiting to be found "not guilty" had acquired the "stir disease"—the prison name for consumption—from which he had to die, soon after.

Meanwhile, the State of Idaho dismissed the case against Moyer, which had been saved for the last, because the evidence against him had always been considered very slight.

The whole period, from the time I left Chicago until my return, was about two years. The union had been put to such enormous expense that at the end of their trials their treasury was seriously impaired; indeed, the union was practically without funds. I was content to take much less than my contract entitled me to, although I knew that they would pay it all if I would let them. I felt that I should do what I could to help them regain their old strength and prestige, which they finally did under the leadership of Mr. Moyer, who is still their president.

I had travelled so much for my health, spent so much time and used so much money for hospitals, physicians, and all sorts of inevitable expenses, that when I reached home I not only had nothing left but was in debt. I was not able to pay all my bills. It was more than a year before these were liquidated, and my good friend, Doctor Haynes, waited until the very last.

CHAPTER 21

THE McNAMARA CASE

In the spring of 1911 the newspapers all over the country carried a startling story reporting that the Los Angeles *Times* Building had been dynamited and that twenty-one workmen in various capacities had perished in the ruins.

It was generally believed that the dynamiting resulted from the action of some one interested in the labor unions. The reason that the deed was laid at their door was because *The Times* newspaper was owned by Harrison Gray Otis, who had for many years been fighting the unions. And at the time of the catastrophe, the Los Angeles unions were engaged in a general strike to make that city a closed town, and *The Times* was leading the fight to continue the open shop. *The Times* was a non-union paper and none of its employees were connected with any labor organizations.

An investigation was immediately begun to find out the cause of the explosion, which soon disclosed a large hole in an alley that ran from the street into the building. One of the pressrooms was located under the alley. It soon became evident that the building had not been destroyed by an explosion, but that, in some way, a fire had been started and the inflammable material inside the alley and the building had been ignited, spreading the flames almost instantaneously through the plant. The unfortunate victims were found close to an iron door which had been used as an exit. This door, at the time, was so closed that it could not be opened. The nineteen men had reached the door and had suffocated in the effort to escape.

A catastrophe like this naturally aroused a deep wave of sorrow and also resentment against any person or persons who might be responsible for the act. At once a thorough search for its origin was set in motion. The non-union forces in southern California had for a long time been organized to fight the unions, who had not been able to organize Los Angeles. The investigation developed that a few days before the disaster three men had gone to a quarry near San Francisco where dynamite was used in blasting; they had sailed across the bay in a small boat, had taken some dynamite and gone away. Later on, dynamite was found in the vault of a building in Indianapolis, where some of the offices of the building were occupied by the headquarters of the Structural Iron-Workers, resulting in the discovery of the dynamite already referred to, stored in a safe-deposit box which had been taken out in the name of Joseph J. McNamara, the secretary of the organization. Very soon thereafter some dynamite was found in a barn in Indianapolis; this barn was owned, or rented, by a teamster named Jones, who had leased it to Joseph J. McNamara.

James B. McNamara, a brother, was a member of the Typographical Union. He had long been an ardent trade unionist, and an active member in his local. It was discovered that for several months he had been living in San Francisco. Soon after the arrests, Ortie McManigal turned state's evidence and made what purported to be a full confession in the case. The Structural Iron-Workers organization was affiliated with the American Federation of Labor, so the Federation undertook the defense of the case.

Mr. Gompers, with several other members of the executive board of the American Federation of Labor, came to see me and asked me to assume the defense. I urged them to get some one else. Of course I realized that the men should be defended, but I felt that I had done my share of fighting. It was not easy to combat the powerful forces of society in the courts, as I had been doing for many years, and I was now weary of battling against public opinion. I believed in trades-unionism, and knew the need of labor organizations. I believed that without them the industrial workmen were helpless. I fully comprehended that no single workman had any chance if he went alone to an employer to ask for higher wages or better conditions. He was at once told that if he did not like his job he should go somewhere else. One employee of a great railroad system or any controlling combination had no chance to bargain. The company offered the wages and terms that it saw fit, and told him to take it or go away. If a workman clamored for better wages or improved conditions he was discharged. This did not mean that industrial employers were not as good as other men, but only that in a contest every advantage was on their side; the employer could put the workmen out of business, but the workmen could not injure the company. But, if a union could go in a body, and collectively make demands of the employer, the situation was more nearly equalized. Then, if the employer or a company did not accept and act upon the demand, the workmen could quit work in a body; to have any independence, or any power to bargain, the workmen were forced to act together.

This question seems to be better understood to-day, but it took centuries of hardship and sacrifice and industrial war to bring this about. I have known many men on both sides, but cannot say that any in either faction, as individuals, are better or worse than the others; but, with an open shop, the employer has all the advantage, as every one knows. All this was plain to me; but I had fought through so many conflicts that I felt the need of rest from such strenuous work. Besides, it had been only three years since I came out of the Idaho cases, with their two years of strain and labor, together with all the anguish that I had endured and survived.

The very name of Los Angeles was associated with so much

misery and suffering that the thought of going back to that place and its painful memories seemed like forebodings that I could not quiet. So that, all told, the outlook was most uninviting. But the representatives of the Federation of Labor were so urgent that at last I could not refuse. How many times thereafter I wished that I had insisted upon some one younger and stronger and more anxious for the task. But I could not turn back. It seemed destined that I should take that path. It simply had to be. Hard as it was to give them my "Yes," it would have been harder to say "No."

And, even after counting all the cost of that tremendous experience, I am glad that I went. But it was with heavy hearts that Mrs. Darrow and I drove to the Chicago and Northwestern Railroad Station and boarded the train for Los Angeles.

On arriving in California I was met by more than the usual number of newspaper reporters, and men and women otherwise interested in the situation. I at once employed LeCompte Davis, one of the leading trial lawyers of Los Angeles, and Joseph Scott, an attorney of wide acquaintance and good standing. Job Harriman, a well-known Socialist of ability, was already interested in the case, and Judge Cyrus F. McNutt, a former member of the Supreme Court of Indiana, a man well learned in law, was also engaged. Judge McNutt was a man of unusual ability, and was thoroughly sympathetic toward the laboring class.

We rented a whole floor in one of the large office buildings, organized a force of investigators to go to all the different parts of the United States where it was claimed that dynamiting had occurred during building operations, and to gather evidence in relation to what happened in those cities, and what was its relation to *The Times* Building also. We hastily gathered a force for getting as full information as possible concerning political and religious affiliations and other points of view of those on the long list from which prospective jurors were to be drawn. In all these matters I was, to be sure, largely guided by the judgment and knowledge of the local counsel, who were familiar with the city and its people. The investigation of possible jurors was placed in the hands of Bert Franklin, a Los Angeles detective, who had at one time been connected with the city or county administration, and had done a good deal of work of this kind. I had brought with me from Chicago, John Harrington, long an investigator for the Chicago City Railway; he had spent years in arranging, sifting and marshalling facts in the damage suits of the surface lines of that city; and also I engaged Captain Tyrrell, an old-time detective, who had served in the preceding district attorney's office for many years. Each of these two managed his own department, and the money used and disbursed was given by me to each in charge for his separate handling, for service and expenses.

I went to the jail and for the first time met my clients. I found both men pleasant, prepossessing and, of course, glad to see me and the rest of the lawyers. All the preparation had to be done as rapidly as possible, for there was no time to lose; and so the work was left practically to those in charge, who made their reports to us, while we lawyers concentrated upon familiarizing ourselves with the law applicable in the case, especially the law of conspiracy. This always looms large in any labor case. Under the constant stretching of the conspiracy laws we could see that evidence showing any unlawful use of dynamite anywhere in the United States would be held competent under the statement of the prosecuting attorneys that they expected to connect it up with the defendants, or with some one else who would be linked up with the defendants.

I rented a very pleasant home close to the down-town district; so many people were clamoring to see me, bringing me all sorts of stories to be looked into, that there was little chance to be alone, day or night. It was but a brief time before the anxiety and tension began to tell on me. My health had been none too good since the departure from that city after the operation for mastoiditis.

Slowly we began to bring some order and system out of the chaos that overhung the case. I was conscious of the bitterness that always surrounds that kind of contest. Without any question, my clients were believers in a cause which, from their point of view, demanded all their efforts, and justified whatever sacrifice they could make. The employers also believed in a cause, and habitually resorted to boycotts that inflicted suffering on men, women and children; men who in the ordinary affairs of life were considerate and charitable were bitter partisans in matters pertaining to labor. I was aware that for more than a decade members now united in an organization for the protection of each other had looked with hatred and contempt at their fellow workmen who would not join the labor union. I was familiar with the old definition of "scab" that was announced many years ago in reply to President Eliot, of Harvard, and is as follows:

"The strike-breaker occupies in the industrial world a position precisely analogous to that of the renegade and traitor. He represents a type of man universally condemned in any other sphere of human activity. He sells himself for less than the thirty pieces of silver, but too often lacks the grace which caused Iscariot to go and hang himself. He commits the unpardonable sin of betraying his fellows. He purloins that to which he has no claim and is the one stumbling block in the path of the wage-earner. The attempt to make him respectable reflects discredit upon those engaged in it."

This is substantially the definition of the old English trades-unions, and has long been the attitude held toward non-union men by unions and their sympathizers.

I, for one, have never believed in violence, force or other cruelty. I hate pain and suffering for others as well as for myself. I had long been a non-resistant at heart, and had preached it as far as I could, but had learned that in the forces of life, clash and conflict were inevitable. My sympathy and experience had placed me on the side of those who had the hard tasks and the ill-conditions of life. Personally, I would go to any extent possible to prevent violence and disorder, but, when it came about, then I was for and with my side; for I sensed and learned the motives that moved men, and I believed that in the long sweep of time they were fighting for the amelioration and welfare of mankind. I knew that these endless conflicts had always been fraught with grief and distress, but Nature seems to provide no other way.

CHAPTER 22

LIGHTS AND SHADOWS

I HAD been in Los Angeles for more than three months, preparing the case, when the selecting of the jury began. This was, as usual, a difficult task. The case had been given such wide publicity, and feelings were so high on both sides, that it was practically impossible to find any one who had no opinion and seemed able to offer both sides a fair consideration of the case at hand.

Before I left Chicago I knew nothing about the facts. There were many rumors of dynamiting, and many others to the effect that the explosion was due to gas. The task for the lawyers of the defense was to see that the defendants were not condemned except on clear proof of guilt, and, if guilty at all, to get as small a penalty as possible—especially to save the lives of those on trial.

There were twenty-one separate indictments against each of the two defendants. The situation looked almost hopeless to me, for even though we might get a disagreement, or "Not guilty" in the first case, there were all the others, which would make endless trials possible. A strong feeling existed, not only in Los Angeles but throughout the rest of the country, and I knew that the State would never submit to defeat so long as there was any hope for them to win. Day after day men were brought into court to take a look at James B. McNamara, whose trial came first. It was apparent that this was for the purpose of identifying him as having been at various places where he had lived for several months, one of them in San Francisco, one where dynamite had been purchased, one in Los Angeles.

I have always hated capital punishment. To me it seems a cruel, brutal, useless barbarism. The killing of one individual by another always shows real or fancied excuse or reason. The cause, however poor, was enough to induce the act. But the killing of an individual by the State is deliberate, and is done without any personal grievance or feeling. It is the outcome of long premeditated hatred. It does not happen suddenly and without warning, without time for the emotions to cool and subside, but a day is fixed a long way ahead, and the victim is kept in continued, prolonged torture up to the moment of execution.

Oliver Wendell Holmes once said: "We are all sentenced to death for the crime of living." That is true, but we know nothing of the day or means of execution. The tragedy sometimes comes upon us with such swiftness that we do not even know what it is; or, it is the result of some illness which weakens the structure and gradually loosens the tendrils that hold us to life, and the doomed does not know that the end is at hand nor when it comes. It is over with before he realizes his danger or the approximate date of the operation.

For weeks I pondered how to save the lives of these clients, as did my associates in the case. The lawyer, if he has a deep sense of responsibility and warm sympathies, regards the human being in his hands in the same light that a physician views a patient in. Both try to relieve suffering, and no one would expect a physician to refuse to save the life of a patient, no matter who he might be. The lawyer's duty is just as binding; both try to allay pain and save life, although, in a sense, life cannot be saved, for the irrevocable doom hangs over us all from the time of birth; we can only put it off. And this is what I hoped to do in this case. The only way out that I could see was through a plea of guilty, with an agreement that the extreme penalty should be imprisonment for life. The question was, how to accomplish that hope. Publicity would have meant certain death.

I could not express my hopes and fears to many. To show the psychology of fear would be fatal to the case. A lawyer must walk hopefully with his client to almost certain doom, or he loses his last chance to save life. I first confided my feelings to LeCompte Davis and Lincoln Steffens. Both viewed the matter in the light in which it impressed me. But how to carry out my idea without letting our secret become common knowledge was important.

LeCompte Davis and John D. Fredericks, the State's attorney, were very good friends, and we felt that Davis might talk with Fredericks in perfect confidence, and that we might get one or two more opinions. Mr. Steffens and I went to San Diego and consulted Mr. E. W. Scripps, the well-known publisher of a large chain of newspapers. He was our friend, and a man of great ability. He felt as we did, that if a plea of guilty could be entered and the lives of the defendants be saved, it would be best for all concerned. Then I sent for Fremont Older, of San Francisco, strong, sturdy, intelligent, and gentle, and a wonderful friend; he was indeed like the shadow of a great rock in a weary land. Judge Cyrus McNutt, of Los Angeles, was consulted, and urged me to try to bring about an agreement. There were others who might have been trusted, but we dared not take many into our confidence for fear that in some way the plan would leak out.

Up to this time I had said nothing to my clients. The one reason that made me most anxious to save their lives was my belief that there was never any intention to kill any one. *The Times* Building was not blown up; it was burned down by a fire started by an explosion of dynamite, which was put in the alley that led to the building. In the statement that was made by J. B. McNamara, at the demand of the State's attorney before the plea was entered, he said that he had placed a package containing dynamite in the alley, arranged the contraption for explosion, and went away. This was done to scare the employees of *The Times* and others working in non-union shops; what is now too generally done by racketeers, and called a "pine apple." Had it been the intention to destroy the building, or human life, the amount of dynamite would have been much larger, and it would have been placed inside the building. Unfortunately, the dynamite was deposited near some barrels standing in the alley that happened to contain ink, which was immediately converted into vapor by the explosion, and was scattered through the building, carrying the fire in every direction. Directly under the sidewalk where the dynamite was placed was a large press in operation, and the explosion did not even stop the press, although it blew a hole in the sidewalk above it. No one really claimed that there was any intention to take human life.

My recollection is that our first conference about changing the plea was held in the jail. Judge McNutt, LeCompte Davis, Lincoln Steffens, Fremont Older and I being present. James B. McNamara, the younger of the brothers, strenuously objected, but his brother, Joseph J. McNamara, was inclined to accept the proposition, which called for a life-term for the younger man, and ten years in the penitentiary for the older brother, who was to plead guilty to being a party to placing dynamite at the Llewellyn Brothers' mill. We went over the case very fully at this conference.

We pointed out the impossibility of winning, or even trying the case, the number of indictments, the strong feeling, and the evidence in the hands of the State. We had no evidence of any importance that we could offer, and we could not put the younger brother on the stand, for he would not be able to sustain himself on cross-examination, even should he attempt to deny the evidence of the State. All we could possibly do was to save Joseph J. McNamara, and get a life-sentence for his young brother, James B. McNamara. Gradually "J. B." began to see that we were right.

When Mr. Davis interviewed Mr. Fredericks about the plan, he received the suggestion quite favorably, but could not act without consulting with some of the others interested, and that would require word from the Erectors Association of Indianapolis. The negotiations dragged on for a number of days. Then, Mr. Fredericks reported that Mr. Drew, of the Erectors Association, was willing to accept the proposition, and it looked favorable so far as the others were concerned. We urged haste, for we feared that publicity would be ruinous. Finally, J. B. decided to accept, and the agreement was made subject to the action of the judge, who was likewise reported in favor of the plan.

We purposely drew out the examination of jurors several days after the negotiations were complete. The procedure was, however, fully agreed upon two or three days before another complication set in. When all the parties of the two sides felt certain that the case was to be disposed of immediately, the man who had been placed in charge of the examination of jurors, Bert Franklin, was arrested on the charge that he had handed a prospective juror four thousand dollars on one of the main streets of Los Angeles, as the juror was on his way to the courthouse. Franklin was arrested on the spot and taken to jail. He then protested his innocence and asked us to furnish bail, and so we put up a cash bond, whereupon he was released. In spite of what had happened, the State carried out the agreement to accept a plea of guilty for J. B. McNamara with a life-sentence, and a plea in a separate case by J. J. McNamara with a ten-year sentence. But the judge insisted upon giving Joseph J. McNamara a fifteen-year sentence instead of the one that had been agreed to by the State.

The announcement of the plea of guilty caused a profound sensation over the country. I had never made any statement as to the guilt or innocence of either of the defendants. I had never prophesied about the outcome of the case. I was aware that one of the strongest motives that would appeal to those concerned with the prosecution was the contest for mayor then going on in Los Angeles. Job Harriman, one of the attorneys for the defense, was the candidate on the Socialist ticket and was holding meetings with large and enthusiastic audiences. Naturally, the business elements of the city were against him; the labor unions, the Socialists, and the poor were strongly with him. Any one could easily see that a plea of guilty would lessen the popularity of the Socialist ticket and make sure the election of the regular Republican.

To a certain extent, the mayoralty campaign and the case went together, and while I had never been a Socialist I was more or less in accord with that view, and thoroughly sympathetic with the aims of the party. On account of Mr. Harriman, I was sorry to have the plea of guilty entered, but, on the other hand, the lives of my clients were at stake, and I had no right or inclination to consider anything but them. I could not tell Mr. Harriman; it would place him in the position of either deserting his party or letting one client go to almost certain death, which we could not do.

I, together with the men who shared my confidence, felt obliged to face the situation. I did not hesitate for a moment to choose the welfare of my clients. I never had any question about it. My duty was perfectly plain. Perhaps there are some who can imagine my position in this dilemma, which was not really a dilemma—I knew just what to do. By every emotion of my life, by the rule of my profession, by every human instinct, I was bound to act as I did, and consider my clients only, and I am glad that I did not stop to think of consequences. I have no desire to invite compassion or sympathy. My life is made up, and must stand as it is. But I was in a terrible crisis that I faced almost alone.

Twenty years intervene between that fatal time of tumult and stress and the calm and serenity of to-day which softens the remembrance of it all; but if perchance I allow myself to slip back the bolt, with which all mortals seek to lock away some of the sad and unpleasant memories of the past, at once my mind goes straight to the courtroom in Los Angeles on the evening of the plea of "Guilty." The room was more than usually crowded. The silence was profound and ominous. I asked my associate, LeCompte Davis, to change the plea from "Not guilty" to "Guilty." For a moment the people sat stunned. Then there was a mad rush of the reporters to the wires. It was late in the afternoon. Slowly the great room emptied. The faithful followers of the defense were among the last to go. These came to the trial, filling the room, to give us their support. At last I went out with the rest. It was growing dark. A few street lights were turned on. Many of our most loyal friends tore the McNamara buttons from their lapels and threw them in the street. My old friend, Billy Cavenaugh, came to my side. He was then a policeman, and still my friend. He was alarmed at the attitude of the crowd, grabbed my arm and said, "Come with me." I was not brave, but I looked him in the face and answered, "No, Billy, I shall go down the street with the crowd. I have walked with them to the courthouse when they cheered me, and I shall go back the way I came." There were some sullen faces, and threatening gestures, a few hard and cruel words, but little did these matter, little did I care. I could see only one road to take, and I never asked myself whether it led to happiness or doom.

I never put myself in the position of prophesying or protesting the innocence of a client. When asked by reporters and others to be specific I have always answered them honestly if I could, and in case I could not give the exact information desired have always said frankly that I could not discuss the matter.

A case of such importance always creates intense interest and arouses bitter feelings and powerful propaganda on both sides. Many friends of the defendants without permission had made wild and foolish statements that I had done my best to prevent. Amongst these were outbursts of disappointment over the turn things had taken, some going so far as to charge me with betrayal and cowardice in letting the case come to an end.

A short time after Franklin was arrested he was taken in hand by the State's attorney, and then charged with attempting to bribe two jurors, and according to his story afterward in court he was promised immunity on condition that he should testify that I was connected with the attempt to bribe the jurors. Also, it was stipulated that if he knew anything against any one else connected with the defense he need not tell about it.

Immediately after the arrest of Franklin, when many people were anxious to believe that I was connected with that matter, Mr. Steffens hastened to me to talk over the whole situation. He had for years been a high-class well-known writer, intelligent, solicitous, and a good friend of mine. He understood the industrial question as well as any man I ever knew. He did not believe in violence any more than I believed in it, but he was in full sympathy with the workman's cause; he knew the motives of men, and could see the greater issues which so often were misconstrued and clouded by individuals. In fact, it was due to his intelligence and tact, and his acquaintance with people on both sides, that the settlement was brought about. Mr. Steffens knew all the strong men back of the prosecution, and was busy urging a general amnesty and a better feeling in all sections between capital and labor, with which many of them were in full accord.

It was after the arrest of Franklin that he came to tell me about what he was trying to do, and suggested that if I had been in any way connected with the attempt to bribe a juror to let him include me, and any one else who might have known, in the amnesty.

Plainly and unequivocably I assured him that under no circumstances would I permit any one to ask anything for me or for any one else in my employ; that I had never, in all my practice, considered my own financial or personal interest on any private or public matter except the interest of my client, and never would; and that under no circumstances should he ask anything for me. I told him that if any one thought I had done anything in connection with the jury or any other matter he should be left free to prosecute.

In short time Franklin was taken before the grand jury, whereupon I was indicted for conspiracy to corrupt a juror, in two separate cases. The intense strain on my mind and feelings was undermining my health, and I did not feel the strength and enthusiasm necessary for the fight.

Nevertheless, I summoned my courage and braced myself for the ordeal. I had many fine friends in Los Angeles, in spite of everything, and from everywhere they came to my support, and their aid and tender support smoothed the way, to some extent at least. And Billy Cavenaugh was still there, with the same smiling face, the same hearty cheer, the same buoyancy and optimism as in the old days when he came with us from Boise and tried to help me by giving me as many alcohol rubs as possible. And there was my friend of many years, James Griffes, better known as Luke North, who wrote beautiful things that did not pay but were a delight to read, whose devotion dated back to our youth in Chicago, and who found no day too long and no night too dreary to work in my behalf. There was Lincoln Steffens, clever and kindly and understanding, my brave and constant friend; and there was my friend of a life-time, Fay Lewis, of Rockford, Ill., who left his business and came to Los Angeles and stayed by my side through the endless experience. And at all times there was Fremont Older, of San Francisco. And, by degrees, those who had faltered came back and rallied to my assistance all the stronger for having seemingly hesitated at first.

I made no complaints. I gave out no statements. I did not criticise or censure. I mustered my courage and went my way. Mrs. Darrow and I took a small apartment and kept house. The rent was fifty dollars a month, and that, together with our meals, carfares for me, and all incidentals never quite amounted to a hundred dollars a month. Those were difficult days, but I settled down to wait and fight, and schooled myself to be fairly indifferent to it all, whatever the result was to be. At the first I was dazed. I had sat beside the accused for many, many years, giving them all my comfort and aid in their dire misfortunes. I had made their cause my own. I had worked with them and suffered with them, and rejoiced in their triumphs, and despaired with them in their defeats. Now I was no longer a lawyer pleading another's cause. I was a defendant, fighting against fearful odds.

I feel confident that no reader will blame me if I do not unduly dwell on this part of my story. As I write, the old ghosts creep out of the dimming past and dance around me as if in glee, and I am anxious to drive them back and lock them up where I cannot see their haunting faces or hear their mocking jeers.

I employed Earl Rogers, Harry Dehme, Horace Appel, and Jerry Giesler in the case, and looked after every detail myself. And the case was prosecuted by John D. Fredericks, Joseph Ford, Arthur Keetch, and Asa Keyes. The first trial was begun on May 12, 1912, and lasted nearly three months. I told my own story, denying any knowledge of or connection with an attempt to bribe any juror, and was cross-examined for four days. I had no more trouble about answering every question put to me than I would have had in reciting the multiplication table. The important points of Franklin's statement were overwhelmingly disputed by many other witnesses besides myself. I made the closing argument in the case. I felt as much at ease and as indifferent over my fate as I would have been standing comfortably at a harmless fireside surrounded by loving friends. My argument occupied a day and a half. It was a good argument. I have listened to great arguments and have made many arguments myself, and consider that my judgment on this subject is sound.

The jury retired and were not more than ten minutes arriving at a verdict of "Not guilty." The courtroom was crowded. I was kept for hours receiving congratulations, and then went with friends to a restaurant, where I was found and deluged with messages already pouring in from all quarters of the United States. Now that the news had gone out, I received telegrams from people who had been silent until then. Most of the communications, however, were from loyal friends and champions, many of whom would gladly have gone through the torture in my place, and for my sake, if possible.

The State had of course tried its strongest case first. No one supposed that they would ever try the other. But they waited three months and then put the second one on call. I did not consider it seriously, for everything possible had been brought out in the first trial. No one regarded the second as serious, so far as I could learn.

On the first day of the second trial, Earl Rogers, who had been my leading lawyer in the first trial, was taken suddenly ill. He left the courtroom and was not able to return during the trial. I wanted to go on, so took his place myself, but this was not easy to do. It is all very well to object to evidence and so-called evidence where some one else is concerned, but it looks bad if one is the defendant and has to rise up and protest against letting something in. It is not easy to know what to do in a situation so sensitive as that. And from the beginning I felt certain that some of the jurors were hostile. There is a large element of chance in picking a jury. In fact, the trial of a case abounds in chance, like almost every other experience in life. Again I made the closing argument, and consciously took the chance of saying something in defense of the McNamaras and their real motives, which I felt that I should say.

Then, too, just before the case was called, some twenty-five defendants were placed on trial in Indianapolis, charged with a conspiracy to destroy buildings and other property by the use of dynamite. These indictments included the McNamaras and all matters covered by the Los Angeles cases. Practically all of these were convicted of conspiracy in the use of dynamite. This case was fully played up in Los Angeles, and my second case followed soon after. Every lawyer knows that where two or more indictments are returned against one defendant, the strongest is called first. There was no reason why the Indianapolis situation should affect my case, but I knew that it would, and it did.

The jury in this second case remained out several days, and then reported a disagreement, and were discharged. I had then been in Los Angeles nearly two years. For about a year I had been fighting for myself. I had no money left, and had already borrowed about twenty thousand dollars from friends in various parts of the country, mainly Chicago. I felt discouraged and disheartened. That night I received a telegram which read as follows: "St. Louis, Missouri. Clarence Darrow, Los Angeles, California: I hear that you have spent most of your life defending men for nothing and that you are now broke and facing another trial. I will let you have all the money you need for the case. Am now sending draft for one thousand dollars. Frederick D. Gardner." The name was utterly unknown to me. This came from a total stranger. My eyes filled with tears.

This was twenty years ago, and as I recall this telegram and the signature the tears are in my eyes once more along with the rest of that agonizing past.

In a day or so a letter came containing the cheque for a thousand dollars from my unknown friend, Frederick D. Gardner, of St. Louis, and in the envelope was also a cheque from his wife for two hundred dollars. I used that money, but the case was soon afterward dismissed so that I did not need further help. There is a deep gulf between blank despair and the illusion of hope and comfort and confidence. Though the gulf between them is deep, often there is but a step across. I went home from the disagreement of the jury, sad and discouraged, but when I received the telegram from Mr. Gardner, and the letter, the sun shone bright again and the birds were singing in the trees.

CHAPTER 23

GEORGE BISSETT

SOME time in 1910 a woman came to me in Chicago to consult me about a case. She was old and poorly clad and had the look of grim despair that haunts so many faces of the unfortunate. She told me that her son was in the Chicago jail and had just been convicted of murder, and the jury had given him a life term in the penitentiary. She told me that her son had no money, and that the court had appointed a lawyer to defend him; later the judge had denied a new trial, and in the meantime the lawyer had died.

I said I did not see how I could possibly undertake the case, as the chances were that nothing could be done in the Supreme Court, no matter who handled it. I explained that if the Supreme Court should grant a new trial I would be obliged to try it in the lower court, that there was no chance to get any pay for my work, and some money would be needed for costs; much as I would like to help her, I could not afford to go into it, and I told her so.

She went on to say that she had a little home that could be sold and would bring me something and I could have that for the costs and my fee. I answered that I did not see how I could go into the matter under any circumstances, but that if I did I would not let her sell her home. It was really out of the question. She made no complaint, but went away with the look of despair that comes into the eyes of so many who have learned that for them life offers no hope. The face of this woman haunted me the rest of the day, and would hardly let me sleep that night. I began to regret that I had not taken the case.

But the next morning she was in my office again. I looked at her and knew that I could not resist. I asked if she had the testimony, written out by the court reporter. She had it at home. I told her to bring it to me, and if I could see any chance of getting a new trial I would go into the case. I assured her that I would not take her little home, either for myself or costs. Anyhow, the amount would not have been enough to do me any good, and would only have prevented my feeling of pride in taking the case without a fee. When I examined the record I was satisfied that there should have been no conviction, and that I probably could get the case reversed.

The next day I went to the Chicago jail to take a look at my client. He was a large man, about thirty years old. His countenance was not prepossessing, but I had lived long enough not to take countenances too seriously, especially if I met them inside a prison. He was a man without education. He had spent his life as a common laborer, but he had some ideals and a good deal of ambition. With all the rest, he was an intense Socialist, and was constantly talking about it and trying to make converts. I had learned from reading the testimony that he had once served a short term in the penitentiary, for an attempted burglary. One conviction is generally all the evidence that is needed to justify a second one, and I felt sure that this was really the cause of this conviction. I asked him why he tried to burglarize the house. He replied that he had wanted to start a Socialist paper, and as he had no education he could never get the necessary money by working.

The case for which he was now in jail grew out of a quarrel with two policemen in a saloon; none of them were drunk, but all had been drinking. The policemen were "plain clothes" men wearing no uniform, and were in the saloon when Bissett entered. Both officers knew of his former conviction which, according to their view, justified addressing him in any way they wished. They all drew revolvers and began to shoot. Bissett was hit by two or three bullets, all taking effect in the abdomen, puncturing the large intestine. He was taken to a hospital to die. Unfortunately, as I then thought, he recovered from the wounds. One of the policemen was killed by a bullet through the heart, and the other, though shot, had recovered.

Bissett's revolver was found on the floor with the requisite number of empty shells to match the policemen's wounds. Bissett denied shooting, when he took the stand in the first trial, but the empty holster of the revolver, and the empty shells, made it clear that his statement was not true. Two other eye-witnesses were unable to say who shot first, but testified that both policemen and the defendant used their guns.

It was plain that the case should have been tried as one of self-defense, but his lawyer had seen fit to believe his client's first story, and Bissett had sworn that he did not shoot. I asked him why he denied it, and he answered that he was afraid to admit that he had shot, fearing that an admission, taken with his first conviction, would be fatal. I pointed out that his only chance was in telling the story as it really happened—that he did shoot, and was afraid to admit it in the first trial. It was evident that he had no motive for killing the policemen excepting fear of being killed himself. The policemen made no attempt to arrest him; and no charge was pending against him.

In due time the case was argued in the Supreme Court and was reversed and sent back for a new trial. Then, of course, there was nothing left for me to do but defend it.

George Bissett is not brought into this book on account of that case. It is enough to say that on the second trial he was promptly acquitted, as he should have been at first. I had seen

George from time to time in the jail, and learned to understand
him quite well. It was not easy to talk to him on any subject
but Socialism. All the other prisoners had put him down as
a "bug" on account of his interest in Socialism. Socialists are
not often in jail except for believing in and practising free
speech, and then generally for only a short time. And although
George strongly insisted that if we had Socialism there would
be no need for jails, he found few converts, especially amongst
those who owned the jails.

When the trial was ended I took George over to my office
to talk with him about what he should do in the future. I did
not lecture him. I never believed that this did any good. I
mentioned that he had evidently become almost a professional
burglar, and asked him if he thought that it paid. I tried to
make him see that no one ever really made much at any such
trade, and I hoped he would find something else to work at.

He assured me that he did not expect to try anything of that
sort again, but he was as anxious as ever to have a Socialist
paper, and that he couldn't get a paper by working; that no
one ever did. He thanked me most earnestly for what I had
done for him, said he wanted to pay me, and would do it.
I told him not to bother about me; that I did not want him
to think about getting money to give to me, that the satisfaction of having freed him would be enough. I had learned
to rather like him, just as we all learn to like most people
when we really know them. And so he went away, and I did
not hear of him again for three or four years.

But George and his troubles, and his ambition, sometimes
came to my mind, and still he was only one more being in a
sordid world. He had professed great appreciation and gratitude for what I had done to help him, and had promised to
see me occasionally, to report how he was getting along. That
he had not returned caused me no surprise. Very few take so
much pains, and then, he might be dead, or in jail, or even

managing his Socialist paper at last. He drifted out of my thoughts, which were filled with other events.

But it was written that I was to see George Bissett again. He came to me in Los Angeles in 1912. I was waiting for the trial of the indictment that had been brought against me charging me with a conspiracy to bribe a juror, as told in the last chapter. It was one of a long series of days when I was very sad and when my friends looked good. I was sitting in my private office; the clerk came and told me that a man was outside who wanted to see me; he said the man looked dirty, like a tramp. I asked him to show the man in, which he promptly did. I saw before me my old client, George Bissett. I arose, shook his hand and said, "George, you are a long way from home; what are you doing here?" He said he had heard that I was in trouble and thought that he might help me. I asked how he got there. He said he had come from Chicago, riding on freight-cars and on the bumpers. I asked where he was staying, and he gave me the address of a cheap lodging house. I said, "George, it was fine of you to come all this distance to help me, and I appreciate it more than I know how to tell you, but what did you think you could possibly do?"

"Well," he answered, "I have been here about a week and have been getting a line on Franklin"—the Los Angeles detective previously spoken of. I asked George what he had found out about Franklin. He said he had found out where he lived, had watched what time he went away in the mornings, had some dynamite, and was going to kill Franklin the next day when leaving his home. All along through my life I have had many warm demonstrations of friendship, but this was the first time any man had offered to kill some one for me. I looked at George, and thought of this rough, unlettered man riding two thousand miles on car tops and bumpers and in seriousness offering to risk his life out of gratitude for what I had done for him.

I did my best to show my appreciation of this most astounding proffer. I said, "But, George, you have no idea what you are about to do. For two years this city has been deeply stirred. The cases and events have been published in the newspapers all over the world; the State's attorney's office has every means at hand for running down every clue that might have any bearing on any of the cases, directly or indirectly connected with the destruction of the Los Angeles *Times* Building. Here you propose to kill the chief witness for the State against me—in broad daylight. You must be crazy to think that you could do it without being hanged."

"Yes, I've thought of all that," he responded, "but I owe my life to you, and I'm here to take the chance. I want to do it for you."

I did not answer immediately. I pondered, wondering how to save him from almost certain death, and at the same time have him know how thoroughly I understood his motives, and how deeply I estimated his loyalty and devotion. Both of us sat in silence for a few moments, and when I turned to him I could hardly talk, but I managed to say, "George, I presume other men have run great risks for those they have wanted to help, but no such thing has ever before come to me. You have a deep affection for me on account of what I once did to save you; but let us look at this question as it is. Suppose you could kill Franklin, and suppose that by that means I could be acquitted, and suppose that your life was taken for my sake, should I ever again have a moment's peace or happiness? Could I accept your life to save myself? I think I have never consciously done a cruel act in my life; I hate killing in any way; could I let another man be killed—even Franklin—without trying to save him? I fancy few men have made such an offer of self-sacrifice, George; nothing like it has ever happened to me. But it must not be done!"

It flashed into my mind that I must somehow make sure of

it. I added, "But—I will give this a little more thought. I believe that I am in no danger here, really. I have reason to think that I shall have positive evidence within an hour that will make my acquittal a certainty. Let me have the name of the place where you are staying, and, if I am not assured very soon of the evidence that I expect, I will come and tell you. If I do not come, promise me that you will go back home. And, George—let me give you some money to pay your fare."

"No, no!" he insisted. "I will do what you say, and if I don't hear from you by to-night I'll go back, but I won't take any money of yours; I never pay railroad fare." There were tears in his eyes as I bade him good-by. My own feelings cannot be described.

For a time I sat motionless in my chair. I had known all sorts of men. I had so often found the good and the bad hopelessly mixed in almost all the people that I knew; I wondered if any human being really could pass judgment on another. I thought, too, of that verse I had so often used: "Greater love hath no man than this, that a man lay down his life for his friends."

Well, I did not need poor George's help, but it seemed to have been ordained that I should see him again, and this happened about five years later. This time I was sitting in my office in Chicago, as of old. The telephone rang; I picked up the receiver, and a harsh voice that had a familiar vibration asked if the caller was speaking to me. I said he was. He asked, "Do you know me?" I said I thought I knew, but was not sure. He said, "This is George." I knew, and asked, "Where are you?" He answered, "In the marshal's office in the Post Office Building." I said that I would be right over. It was my old friend, George Bissett. I shook his hand through the bars and asked the marshal to let him come outside for a talk with me, which he did. I said I was sorry to see him there, and asked him to tell me all about it. He informed me that he, with an-

other fellow, who had turned state's evidence, was indicted for
stealing some five hundred thousand dollars from a building
that he broke into; it was formerly the post office, but was now
used by the government as a storehouse. The building was in
Minneapolis, and the marshal was holding him, waiting for
requisition papers to take him back. I said, "I suppose they
have a good case against you." He answered that they wouldn't
have a case only they found the money in a trunk. I asked
where they found the trunk. He said, "In my house." I asked,
"Where were you?" He answered, drily, "Oh—I was there
asleep."

I reflected, and said, "Well—it looks suspicious, at the best.
I don't see anything ahead but a plea of 'Guilty.' Don't bother
them to get a requisition, George; just go back quietly, and I
will be there in a week or so and see what can be done." I expressed regret that he had gotten into this trouble. He answered, dolefully, "So'm I; I made a clean getaway, and was
going to start that paper."

In about a week I was able to go and see George, and found
him safe and sound in the jail. Before going to him I had
dropped in to see the district attorney who had charge of the
case. He was a high-minded, humane man whom I had known
for many years—Mr. Janquish, an able lawyer, who lives in
Duluth, who was appointed United States district attorney by
Woodrow Wilson. I told him the whole story, omitting nothing, not forgetting to tell that George had served a term in
the penitentiary. I explained that he had come back there
through my advice, and I wanted to make the best terms possible, within reason, and enter a plea of "Guilty." He asked if
the man had ever been in the penitentiary more than that one
time, and I replied that so far as I knew he never had, and if
there had been anything else it would have been brought to
light in Chicago; but he could take his time to look into it
if he wished. I inquired what was the lowest penalty the gov-

ernment allowed for burglary. He said, "Two years." Which
he felt would be pretty low for this case. I agreed that perhaps
it was, but that I never could judge how much or how little
punishment any one deserved, or if they deserved any. He
finally said that if I wanted to plead my client "Guilty" we
would go over and see the judge and I could tell him the story;
so we went right then.

The judge thought it a strange and interesting tale and asked
the district attorney what was the lowest penalty he could give
him; the district attorney replied, "Two years." The judge
reasoned that on account of George not making trouble about
extradition, and the money all having been recovered, he would
consent to giving him two years. As I wanted to go back home
that night, I asked the judge to have it disposed of that day
at two o'clock, which he arranged. I went to the jail with this
news. It was midsummer; the weather was hot; George was
sweltering. He was a large man with an enormous jaw, that
was none too good to look at. He was dressed like all the other
prisoners in that weather, without coat, vest or collar. His
shirt had done service for a long time, and the bosom was
mottled with tobacco juice. I explained our good luck and hurried away, saying I would see him later. He was delighted, as
might be expected.

At two o'clock I was in the courtroom. The judge and the
district attorney were there, and George was brought in. I
turned to speak to him. I was shocked. How could I have
neglected to instruct him to shave and put on his "Sunday
clothes"! He may not have had another suit, but I might have
bought him a clean shirt and collar. How could I have been
so stupid? A lawyer just out of school should have thought of
that. Would the sight of my client affect the judge as it affected me?

The case was called and I arose, and with very few words
plead my client "Guilty." I could see that the judge was in-

specting George, looking at his great size, at his heavy jaw, at the stubble on his face, the tobacco juice on his dirty shirt; poor, collarless, loyal, sweaty George! I had muffed it; I knew it, but was helpless. The judge looked him over again, asked him to stand up, voiced a few remarks about the case, then said, very slowly, and haltingly, "I sentence you to the penitentiary for two years—and—" (taking another look at George) "and —six months."

I went out with George and told him that I blamed myself for not telling him to dress properly for the occasion. He said, "Yes, I know; but I had no other shirt, and I couldn't get a razor, or get word to you," and he looked forlorn, but resigned.

Later in the afternoon I went back to see the judge. Neither of us could repress a smile. I assured him that I did not blame him. In one way I was glad, as I had always insisted that the length of time fixed for a prisoner depended as much on his appearance as upon the offense, and on how the judge felt about it, and this proved it. I told him that the only unfair element about it was that he should have given me the extra six months instead of my unfortunate client.

I left George at the courthouse door and took the train back to Chicago. Two or three years later I saw his name in a newspaper, in the nature of an obituary. He had been shot and killed in an early morning hour in the street in Detroit, in a quarrel over a woman. I don't know the details, but he seemed to have loved not wisely but too well.

Often I have thought of George Bissett; of what possibilities there were in his strong nature and his wonderful devotion. I have sighed over the motives and ideals, ambitions and limitations that determined his course, and I have felt that life had not been fair to him. He should have had his Socialist paper. I have felt about him as I have felt about thousands of others, about all of those who tread the dark road to doom—that under decent and helpful environment, and with a fair chance and some education, he would have travelled the regular route, the one called the straight path, where the pilgrim looks neither to the right nor left, but travels with the majority, on and on and on to a flower-covered grave in a respectable churchyard instead of under a layer of gravel in a potter's field.

CHAPTER 24

BACK TO CHICAGO

FINALLY Mrs. Darrow and I were once more in Chicago. By the calendar it had been but two years since we went away, but what a long time it was! It seemed a lifetime. So much had happened; so much of the stress and work and worry that time had been lost track of entirely; duration cannot be measured by the calendar or the clock.

I knew that I had many friends in Chicago, and I also realized that, while I had a few personal enemies, as all men have, still there were a great many people who had never approved of my position on important questions. It was natural to apprehend that some of these would feel satisfaction over my trouble, and would be pleased that my influence would perhaps be weakened. Much to my surprise I found friends where I did not expect them. One who has serious trouble always has two surprises: one over the friends who drop away, and another at the supposed strangers who stand by him in his hour of need. Perhaps this is due to the fact that we exalt our seeming friends, and do not justly estimate those who have looked askance, and whom we have not really known.

It is all well enough to say that a man is presumed innocent until he is proven guilty, but those who seriously make the statement know nothing about psychology. As a matter of fact, most persons who are accused are presumed guilty, and if a jury finds them not guilty it is thought a miscarriage of justice.

There was only one view that I was sure practically every one would agree on—that, whatever the facts might be, there had been no sordid or selfish motive connected with the affair. They would know that if the charge was true it was because of my devotion to a cause and my anxiety and concern over the fate of some one else. Most people did not remember or understand about the twenty-one indictments against each defendant, that to get a disagreement in each case, or even in ten, would be of no avail. People did not know the weakness of the State's testimony against me or the overwhelming contradictions of most of the important points in Franklin's statement. They did not know that Franklin was indicted; that they did not want any one but me. They did not realize that the effort to dispose of the McNamara case by a plea of guilty was admitted by the prosecution to have begun many days before the arrest of Franklin and that the agreement for the plan had been completed before that time.

Whatever my feelings, and whatever the attitude of the public, there was but one thing to do. I must go back to work. So I went to my office without delay. I made no statement, gave no explanations, I offered no excuse or extenuation. I said nothing about the matter unless some one asked me, and then I avoided their queries as much as I could. I went straight ahead as though nothing had interrupted my course, but I was conscious that something had taken place. I offered no occasion for snubbing me, if perchance any one might have been so inclined. If people wanted to see me, my door was open; if they did not care to come I never knew it. Every house has skeletons in its closets grinning and struggling to come out. It is doubtless better that they should be free and roaming in full light of day.

My prolonged absence from Chicago was enough in itself to destroy my business. I had to begin anew. But then, I was already known and had a wide acquaintance. I did not sit in my office only to wait for some one to bring me a good fee; any one who came inside my door was welcome; whether he had money or not was of small concern. Neither then nor at any other time in my life did I go after business. I simply took it as it came, and the criminal courts and the jails are always crowded with the poor.

The first case of any importance that came to me was an indictment of a negro named Isaac Bond. A professional nurse read an advertisement in a Chicago newspaper, asking for a nurse to go to a lonely village outside the city limits, and requested the applicant to call a certain telephone number for further information. A day or two after she answered the ad some one called at her home, and she left as quickly as possible to take charge of the case. She was next seen toward dusk walking along a country road with a tall negro. The following day she was found in a lonely spot in the country under a tree. Her body was almost naked and she was badly mutilated. Whoever killed her had evidently taken her watch. Her name was engraved on the inside. The day after the murder the watch was pawned at a shop in the negro district of the city. Strenuous efforts were then made to arrest a tall negro answering the description, and many suspects were brought in.

Several years before, Isaac Bond had been convicted of murder in southern Missouri, and had served a term of four years. During this time he was assigned to the governor's office, where he worked as a messenger most of the term. The killing occurred in a gambling house where Bond was an attendant. The victim was a white man, and Bond claimed that he shot to save his own life from an attack by the white man killed. When it is remembered that this happened in the South, the deceased being a white person, it is fairly evident that Bond shot in self-defense. While on a hunt for the slayer of the nurse, the bureau of detectives looked over all the pictures of ex-convicts in their files, and found Ike Bond. He was tall and black. The officers did not know where Ike was, so they gave the information to the press; his name, his picture and full description were published in the Sunday papers. At that time Bond was working in a saloon in Gary, a town about twenty-five miles from Chicago. His job was such as falls to the black people; he cleaned the spittoons and scrubbed the floors. Had he been the janitor of a church, the story might not have been the same, which should teach every man—but what's the use? I am not a moralizer, and it would do no good anyhow.

On Saturday night Ike Bond had come to Chicago and stopped at a boarding-house for colored folk, where he had been in the habit of staying whenever he came to the city. Before he left his bed that Sunday morning the landlady took the newspaper to him. Bond at once got up and dressed and went to the detective office, explaining that he had read the story and had come to give himself up if they wanted him. He told where he was that night in full detail. They locked him up, and some of his friends came to me. Of course he had no money. I personally went to Gary and interviewed the witnesses, who were such men as frequent a cheap saloon. Most of them were afraid to testify because they feared the police. Gary is in Indiana, and we could not force them to come. But a few did come, and testified that he was in the saloon that night, fixing the date by a political meeting and torchlight parade. Two men from the pawnshop testified as to the man that brought in the watch. They saw him for only a few moments, one of them thinking that Isaac Bond was the man, the other thinking that he was not. All there was to identify him as the fellow that was seen with the luckless girl was that he was tall and was a negro.

Most identifications are of little value unless a witness has been acquainted with the subject. It takes a close acquaintance when the meeting is casual, unless there is something specially noticeable about the person; if a man is black that is identification in itself, in most minds. But poor Ike was also tall. What more could one ask? Had the defendant been a white man under the same circumstances, the prosecutor would not have asked for a conviction on the evidence. The weirdness, the condition of the dead girl, the former conviction of Bond, served to give it considerable public attention. I made the best fight I could.

The jury argued all night, and in the early morning brought in a verdict giving Isaac Bond a life sentence. The killing of the nurse was so ghastly that nothing but the doubt saved his life.

Several years later I took his case to the pardon board, and am convinced that they thought I was right. One said that he was satisfied that I was, but they did not dare touch it unless the proof was complete as to who committed the act, because the killing was so brutal and revolting.

Ike came to be fully trusted around the penitentiary, and few, if any, who knew him believed him guilty. I felt sure that he had nothing to do with the killing of the unfortunate girl. Poor Ike lived in prison for almost ten years, always protesting his innocence to me and every one else he knew. Meantime, he contracted tuberculosis, and so he died of it.

It was not long before I again had enough to do, but it was four or five years before I could save enough from the simplest living to pay the staunch friends who had raised something over twenty thousand dollars to carry me through my long fight. Many, many times I have asked myself carefully if I regretted my Los Angeles experience, and I believe that I can honestly say that I do not. I feel that I had the courage and sense to make use of the long torture that I went through. What we are is the result of all the past which moulds and modifies the being. I know that the sad, hard experience made me kindlier and more understanding and less critical of all who live. I am sure that it gave me a point of view that nothing else could bring. Olive Schreiner somewhere tells the story of an artist whose wonderful colors of sunset and sunrise attracted the admiration of all who saw them. No one could imagine where he got his colors, which were the marvel of all who saw his work. When he died and they undressed him to put on his grave clothes, they found an old, deep, ragged wound just above his heart. And still they wondered where he got the color with which he mixed his paint.

What one eats does not so much matter as how one assimilates his food. The effect of our experiences depends mainly upon how we are able to fit them into our lives. I reasoned that if I had gone out into the street and a car had run over me and cut off a leg I would find a way to adjust myself to the new situation. This method I have sought to apply to every experience that has entered my life. No doubt some might have done it better, but I have done the best I could to adjust myself to the inevitables that have happened to be my lot. No one likes to hear hard-luck stories. There are those that we never can meet without having to hear a new batch of trouble and tribulation, as if no one else knows what sorrow is. Between the chronic retailer of personal ill-luck and the cheerful idiots, I have never found much to choose.

During my difficulties I used to wonder what the future would have in store this side of the grave. It did not look bright. I reflected upon what had been my following in Chicago. I recalled the night before I left for Los Angeles, when I was the speaker at a great meeting in the largest hall that could be procured in Chicago, the Auditorium. I was speaking for the candidacy of a man for mayor that I felt should be elected. The building was packed, and crowds were turned away, and I received an ovation such as men seldom get. I used to wonder if ever again such a throng would come to listen to what I might have to say. In a little more than two years after my return such an occasion came once more, in the same big Auditorium. This was during the war. The enthusiasm was more than enough. I always fear that I am playing a part, or catering, when the approval is too general and evident, because most people do not think and, as Ibsen said, "the majority is always wrong." Nothing is easier or more contemptible than stirring the masses with commonplace ideas and trite expressions.

Since the address in the Auditorium I have never been able to accept anywhere near all the invitations to speak that have been extended in Chicago, to say nothing of the world outside. Probably few men in America have ever spoken to so many people or over so long a stretch of time. I am satisfied that I like to speak in public, and although speaking often is a hardship, and in my case too often leads to unfriendly criticism—for I never could see things as others do—still I am sure that if I were not called upon I should feel sad and disappointed.

Soon after the return to Chicago we met Mr. and Mrs. Frederick D. Gardner of St. Louis. Mrs. Darrow and I were invited to their house over a week-end, and were of course delighted with the visit. Since that day we have met them at various times and places, and have come to value their friendship above that of most men and women that I know. Since our first meeting, Mr. Gardner has been twice elected governor of the State of Missouri. I have always hoped he might be elected President of the United States. This is not because I want an office, for that is entirely out of my line. I would hardly take any position unless it was very, very important and worth while—something like a prohibition agent, for instance.

CHAPTER 25

WAR

IT was in the summer of 1914, while visiting with my son and his family in Estes Park, Colorado, in the heart of the Rocky Mountains, that the sudden news of the war in Europe startled my senses and awakened my interest. Means of communication were none too good, but I eagerly sought and consumed every word I could get on the subject, carefully studying the dispatches sent back and forth in furious haste between European capitals and diplomats and other heads. It appeared plain to me that Germany wanted the war and that all the other nations, excepting possibly Austria, did everything in their power to avoid it. When, in violation of their express treaty, Germany sent her great army into Belgium, I at once felt that the whole world should help drive her back to her own land.

Up to this time I had believed in pacifism. Not only because I never wanted to fight, but because I considered it a sound philosophical doctrine that should rule men and states. For many years I had been an ardent reader of Tolstoy, and regarded myself as one of his disciples. When Germany invaded Belgium I recovered from my pacifism in the twinkling of an eye. It came to me through my emotions, and it left me the same way. I discovered that pacifism is probably a good doctrine in time of peace, but of no value in war time. The reasons became perfectly clear to me, and all my reading and thinking and observation since have thoroughly confirmed my view. The doctrine of pacifism involves a philosophy of the emotions that move men, and the relative importance and power of the emotions as against reason; and this, I am satisfied, hardly admits of argument.

In all situations the emotions are the moving forces among men, and through them, of states and all society. Reason has very little to do with human action. Reason is simply a method of comparing and appraising; it is always used to justify what the emotions demand. How far the reason of man can be used to inhibit emotions may be a subject of debate, but it can go but a little way. The structure of man determines his course under certain circumstances. An impression occurs, the emotion is carried by a nerve to the brain. This is automatic; just as automatic as the response of the organism to the signal. In stepping on a pin, the impression is conveyed to the brain by an afferent nerve, and immediately an efferent nerve running to the foot causes certain muscles to raise the foot. When sensations that come into the organism produce a reaction that we call rage, men will fight. Perhaps, to a small extent, these reactions can be modified by habits, but when the reaction is strong enough the response is certain.

When I read of the German army marching through Belgium I had exactly the same reaction that I would experience if a big dog should attack a little one. It was obvious that Germany had for years been preparing for war until she was really over-trained, which brought about her defeat; otherwise she would have taken Paris within six months after the beginning of the war.

Whatever the cause, or whether I was right or wrong, my sympathies were at once with France and England and Russia. This was not due to dislike of the Germans. As a matter of fact, I had found them in America more tolerant and liberty-loving than any other of our people, and as a consequence I had many friends among them, most of whom I hope I retained.

For one who felt so strongly, the early days of the war were gloomy and depressing. Through the Middle West, almost every newspaper was for Germany, and a large majority of people were anxious for her success.

For months I felt that President Woodrow Wilson seemed unconcerned, if not friendly to Germany. I am now inclined to believe that he had the right attitude, and it was my extreme feeling that misled me into doubting him. Before the United States entered the war there was little that I could do beyond expressing my opinions freely on every opportunity and occasion.

Eventually, to my gratification, Mr. Wilson spoke in no uncertain terms. Often have I heard him criticised by my old-time friends and by his political enemies because he was too slow, and because he should not have brought our country into the war at any time, but I could see no inconsistency in his procedure. It is true that he was elected the second time on the issue that he had kept us out of the war, but it was also true that Germany had then promised not to sink the ships of neutral countries, and it was after Mr. Wilson's second election that Germany withdrew her promise and gave out that she would sink the ships of neutral nations without giving any further notice, and without giving a chance to save the lives of passengers and seamen. Up to that time, at least, it was against accepted rules of war, and whatever Germany's needs might have been, President Wilson could not have avoided bringing America into the war at the time when he acted.

When we were once in the contest, I gave nearly all my time to making speeches throughout the United States. It was the first occasion when I had known of a war that I believed in. But the fact that our side so soon seemed to grow popular in America gave me misgivings, and very early I began to suspect that Big Business was unanimously enlisted on account of the vast financial interests involved; but even so, I could not see how England could possibly have kept out, and, with England in, I felt that our entry became inevitable.

At no time did I declare my adoration for my country after the manner of the professional patriot. I always distrust those who make a business of loving their country. I knew that many men and women did not believe in the war, and that as a rule they were moved by higher ideals than most of those who supported it. I felt then, and still think, that they were wrong. Over and over I went to the government offices in Chicago to save some one from imprisonment that I knew was not hostile to the United States, but who was accused of disloyalty. In most cases I succeeded because the authorities knew that I was for the war and they could trust my honesty in the matter. Luckily, as I felt, I was not invited into any of the cases of the conscientious objectors. Most of them, for the time, realized the gulf between us. I discredited the stories told of outrages by the Germans, suspecting them of being manufactured to create public opinion, and I never hesitated to say so. Later on, when I visited the warring countries at the height of the conflict, I was confident that they were not true.

Reading and experience have taught me that when governments prepare for war the first unit they mobilize is the liars' brigade. One celebrated Eastern divine went up and down the land exhibiting moving-pictures of German atrocities. He must have known that they were faked; the audience must have believed that the Germans, just before cutting off the Belgian children's hands, called in the photographers to witness and kodak the deeds. I did not tell these tales in my speeches. Reports of the presence of mutilated Belgian children then living in Chicago were constantly coming to my ears. I always offered a hundred dollars if the informant would bring one to my office or take me to see one. No one ever came back for the reward. Inevitably almost every German in America was regarded with suspicion, even when members of their families were fighting with the Allies.

As were others, I was invited to visit the seat and scene of the war, which happened to be but a short time before the massacre so suddenly ended. There I was repeatedly told gruesome yarns that my experiences in court taught me must be false.

On one occasion, on a train in France, a number of men were on their way to visit battle scenes. Most of these wore uniforms, but none of them fought. The conversation turned upon atrocities, which I promptly declared myself unable to believe. At once I was loudly taken to task for not joining with the chorus. But one man, rather large and wearing a uniform, spoke up and said that I was right. He stated that he had been working with the Y. M. C. A. and other organizations since early in the war, and had never seen nor been able to verify one single claim concerning German atrocities. This man was a clergyman from Montreal. He added that before he left home a story was told him with great care and detail about some Canadian nurses who were in a hospital that was captured by Germans, and the soldiers cut off their hands. He was so much interested in this that he began an investigation; when finally he ran it down he found that it had come from a letter written by a nurse in France stating that her hands were sore. This information ended the debate on the train. I feel especially prompted to relate the incident because the man was a clergyman.

When I returned to the United States in September they were raising another "Liberty Loan." I ventured to say that I could not see the need of asking men who needed their money to subscribe to the Liberty Loan at that time—that the war would be over before Christmas. Other speakers and various people thought that this should not be said; they had "got the habit" and enjoyed the excitement. It so happened that the war ended before the time I had set. I always was ultra-conservative.

Soon after the war was ended some of my German friends amongst the Turn Vereins asked me to speak to them about what I saw while abroad. I had resented the feeling that had grown in America against Germans. Not that I blamed any one in particular; I never believed that man was a rational being, anyhow. I knew how easy it is to fear, and how hate follows fear. And, always inevitably the great mass goes along with the crowd, particularly if appealed to with a popular slogan. I was very glad to do anything possible to generate better feeling and comprehension after the bitter hatred during the war, so I told them what I had heard and seen and knew about the German atrocities, and never missed a chance to tell it since.

When the war was over, and so many orators found themselves out of employment, I was urged to help form an organization of those patriots who, like myself, were safe in America making speeches with a view to inducing young boys to fight. It didn't appeal to me. I sensed that most of the members of the organization would be looking for office after they were all organized, and many of them did not wait that long.

Almost every day some of my friends came along parading the titles of "Colonel" and "Major" and so forth, who had been nowhere near the war, as every one knew. Thereupon I suggested that no American should have a war title if he had been anywhere east of Washington, D. C., during the struggle.

Somehow the whole thing did not look so good to me after the war was over. I began to ask myself many questions. I had been roundly denounced by many of my pacifist and radical friends. All of these were like most people; they were positive that they were right. The question did not even admit of reasoning; I soon saw not only the futility of it all but the cost of it all; I knew the effect, direct and indirect, of the torrent of malice and evil that had been let loose upon the world.

After all, was it so plain that Germany was all to blame? I wished to be right in my own opinion. I always want facts, and a chance to act on my own judgment. If I was right, how came it that the majority was on my side? Especially that large part of the majority who had never had any idealism or any gift for putting themselves in the other fellow's place; so I set to work to re-examine the whole case.

I had never been a professional patriot. I liked my own country best only because I was born here and most of my relatives and friends live here, and because I understand the language; but I never looked upon it as "God's Country." I assumed that if there was a God, and he was intelligent and humane, he should be an internationalist, so long as he was responsible for all countries equally. It must be that I always have had an internationalist's mind, although I never considered living in any other land.

On the best investigation that I could make, after I reopened the question, it seemed that Germany had wanted the war and brought it on. But was this enough to justify the conclusion that Germany was wrong? At the most, it only proved that the Allies were right, if indeed it proved that. France was invaded and forced to fight. England could not see Germany conquer France and get control of the entrance to the channel, with a seaport virtually on the Atlantic Ocean. If Germany started the war, why did she start it? Causation runs through all the acts of men. There is a cause for all things, and by the same logic there is a cause for every cause.

Germany was growing rapidly. She was an ambitious, virile, and prosperous nation. She had no chance to develop further inside her own domain. She wanted a place for her people to spread. There was plenty of vacant space on earth, but England held the vantage point on every sea on the globe. Germany could not grow unless England and France made a chance for her. Germany had tried and was trying to find outlets and colonies, and she had been balked in every effort. She could not expand without fighting. At least, that was the way Germany saw it, and that need was the cause that caused the war. But what was the cause of the cause of the cause? England wished to own the seas, because to control the seas meant to control the lands. It is useless to go further into causation, but it could be pursued to infinity with perfect logic.

What does it prove? It shows simply that all of it was inevitable. It shows what is true in even wider fields, that no one can be justly blamed. Men are here on this earth for a few brief moments of eternity. All men and all people are seeking power and place. From the ages of Egypt to the England of to-day, there has been a constant succession of rulers of the world. Inevitably England will one day lose her prestige. Then will come America, to grow and decay as others have risen and fallen. No one has anything to do or say about it all, for back of all is Destiny that holds the reins. What is Destiny? In Algebra we let x equal the unknown quantity. In human affairs we call x Destiny.

CHAPTER 26

THE AFTERMATH OF THE WAR

THE world could not pass through the welter of hate and destruction of life and property of the four years of war without bringing dire results. Indeed, the war well-nigh wiped out the best products of civilization. In America it brought an era of tyranny, brutality, and despotism that, for the time at least, undermined the foundations upon which our republic was laid.

No sooner had peace been declared than the same organization that had taken over the management of the war procured an Espionage Act, which forbade free discussion, either orally or in the press. This infamous law appeared almost simultaneously in Congress and in each of the several States of the Union. It was promptly passed under the name of Patriotism. The method of its appearance and the similarity of all its provisions in the various States showed its common origin. Men were arrested, indicted and convicted, and sent to prison, all over the United States, for daring to express their opinions by speech or press. Any so-called radicalism was unpatriotic because contrary to the views of the exploiting class.

Twelve members of the Communist party were indicted in Chicago, and I undertook to help carry on their defense. No act of any kind was proven against them. They had adopted a political platform which declared in favor of Communism. The case dragged out to a month. The State was allowed to bring into the evidence the Communist Manifesto of Russia. They were permitted to use evidence about riots in Seattle, Wash., and to present any act or event that had occurred in any part of the world that could be connected with any communistic movement, great or small. No intelligent man believes that old political structures die and new ones take their place without trouble, and often bloodshed. It took eight years of war to bring about the American Revolution. No new system is born without birth pains.

The twelve defendants may have been wise or foolish, but every one of them was an idealist who had committed no unlawful act. Every one was convicted. The case was appealed to the Supreme Court of Illinois, and that court affirmed the verdict. However, the chief justice of the court, Orrin Carter, wrote a vigorous dissenting opinion which breathed the spirit of the liberty of the individual. The governor, quoting from this opinion, then pardoned them before they spent a single day in prison. All over the country similar verdicts were rendered, and many men were sent to prison under this outrageous statute. In course of time it was repealed or died a natural death.

Wars always bring about a conservative reaction. They overwhelm and destroy patient and careful efforts to improve the condition of man. Nothing can be heard in the cannon's roar but the voice of might. All the safeguards laboriously built to preserve individual freedom and foster man's welfare are blown to pieces with shot and shell. In the presence of the wholesale slaughter of men the value of life is cheapened to the zero point. What is one life compared with the almost daily records of tens of thousands or more mowed down like so many blades of grass in a field? Building up a conception of the importance of life is a matter of slow growth and education; and the work of generations is shattered and laid waste by machine guns and gases on a larger scale than ever before. Great wars have been followed by an unusually large number of killings between private citizens and individuals. These killers have become accustomed to thinking in terms of slaying and death toward all opposition, and these have been followed in turn by the most outrageous legal penalties and a large increase in the number of executions by the state. It is perfectly clear that hate begets hate, force is met with force, and cruelty can become so common that its contemplation brings pleasure, when it should produce pain. This demoralization has never been more evident than in the United States since the end of the late war.

The main business of the world during the dark years of that monstrous conflict was the slaughtering of human beings. The next chief activity was money-making. Production was so necessary for the purpose of killing that it took into industry thousands who had never worked in ordinary times. It increased prices and wages beyond the wildest dreams. When the war was over, this movement was for a time kept in force by the momentum that it had gathered. Every sort of legislation was encouraged if it would raise prices or increase production or speculation. Every discussion of real problems or criticism of policies was frowned on, and even prosecuted by the worshippers of Mammon. With a few slight interruptions, business, or rather gambling, rode triumphantly over the land until the panic on the stock market in October and November of 1929. Then men and women who thought themselves wealthy saw their riches suddenly take flight.

This panic was much more than the collapse of the false and fictitious prices prevailing on the Stock Exchange. Since the beginning of the World War, which called into activity all the money power of the world, there was a constant increase of individual activity, especially in the United States. America indulged in a general orgy of selfishness and greed. Individuals forgot their old ideals and all the principles of political economy that had stood the test of years. A hundred and twenty million people of the richest and most prosperous nation in the world entered into a game of grab. The cry of efficiency drowned out the old American slogans of Liberty and Equality. The efficiency idea was coupled with progress, and both words were construed to mean the making of as many things as men and machines could possibly produce. With this went the effort of every one engaged in the crusade to raise the price of every article produced. The activity took no account of feeding, clothing and providing comfort for men and women, but only the nervous selfish interest of each one concerned in getting all he possibly could out of the general mass, and regardless of the public welfare. The result was the same as has been recorded in all lands and ages—enormous fortunes in the hands of the few, while the great majority were left dependent and poor and with no opportunity to protect themselves against disaster.

The enormous production and demonstration of wealth created a taste and desire for wealth among even men and women who were fairly content with their ways of life. These were seized with the prevailing disease. The stories of fabulous riches growing out of gambling in stocks, with the apparent increasing prices week after week and month after month, infected every one with the gambling madness. Even the poorest, who could possibly get any money, risked it in the market the same as they were wont to do in lotteries and other games of chance. The higher the prices soared the greater the number of stock transfers each day. Sober and conservative citizens practically gave up their small methods and means of earning a living in a wild attempt to get rich, as others had, without work.

The money lenders and usurers were busy. This was their harvest time. The banks of the country no longer loaned the money furnished by the government to business men at moderate rates. Instead of this, they sent it to New York to be loaned on the Stock Exchange at ten, twelve, and fifteen per cent.

It required no wizard or even genius to foresee the end. The collapse of the dream is now history. In spite of the fact that government officials tried everything in their power to lure the business men and the capitalists to risk their money, to stimulate circulation, and put new life into the dead, it was of no avail. When the pulmotor is taken to the sufferer it is almost invariably followed by the hearse. It was soon evident that the holdings and investments of the small and common man had been swept away. The effect on all business was practically automatic. It meant the loss and lack of employment, lower wages, less buying power, and general distress. The experience taught one lesson, that no one wants to learn: the ease of production, the folly of poverty in a world well able to furnish plenty for all, a world where abundance might and should prevail. But it has not taught the managers of industry, of business and politics, that the great problem of prosperity no longer depends on the production of wealth, but on its distribution. Without converting the world to any fantastic doctrines or distant dreams, a few men with the organizing ability of our Captains of Industry could easily and rapidly solve this problem if they could only be inspired with the desire to help their fellow man.

If any lesson is to be taught by the great war it should be the utter futility of that method of settling disputes. The loss of life and property was so enormous that it should seem that the first problem to be considered by the horrified world should be how to prevent future wars. This matter has had the attention of politicians for the last ten years, and men have hoped some scheme would be evolved to prevent nations from going to war. But all of these plans are based on the almost universal delusion that man is naturally a brute and that nothing but force can bring order. If man is so hopelessly brutal it would seem illogical to expect that one division of brutes should be trusted with keeping another mass of brutes in order. If the world learned anything from experience, it would have abandoned this plan long ago.

The truth is, that no section of the human race was ever entirely evil or wholly good; no part was ever all belligerent or absolutely peaceful. Man is not so constructed. Nations as well as individuals may be induced or trained toward war or peace.

There never was a war that was not preceded by a cause or causes, of course. If nations persist in treating each other as enemies instead of friends, they will always find causes for wars. In ancient times, when separate tribes rarely saw or knew about each other, a stranger meant an enemy and a cause for war. The peoples of modern nations are bound together by trade and commerce, by railroads and steamships, by political and religious beliefs and customs, creating acquaintance and friendship, and to a certain extent destroying the old barriers that once antagonized alien states.

All this should establish new attitudes and adjustments between the various countries of the world; but even with modern tendencies and advantages states are continually creating causes for enmity against foreign powers; nations develop and encourage super-patriotism, and their members are taught that their particular country is the wisest and worthiest of all on earth. Trade is regarded as an evil instead of a source of improvement and culture and co-operation, and these madmen vie with each other to put up tariff walls to bar out foreign products, at the same time individually needing foreign markets for their own goods; they seek vantage points in every sea and land that they may control the commerce of the world, and put up restrictions as to immigration and intercourse. All this leads to building forts and battleships and standing armies, and a general display of pomp and power. Everything is done to promote foreign enmities and jealousies instead of fostering and extending the friendship that makes for the preservation of family and community.

A large part of the wealth of every country is wasted in armaments on land and sea. The jingoist and super-patriot make a business of cultivating rivalry and hatred, and thus generating wars. Force cannot keep men from hating, and hate is the forerunner of war. Compelling nations not to fight would mean the establishing of a central organization strong enough to destroy any two or three countries indicating opposition, and such an organization would be a menace to the freedom of the world. The idea of the League of Nations was born out of the throes of the world conflict, when men deemed war the greatest evil in the world. But this is not so; tyranny is a greater evil and a worse menace than war. If the rulers of the world once come to think that there can be no resistance to their tyranny, civilization and liberty will go down in chaos and despair.

Patrick Henry's great sentence, "Give me Liberty or give me Death!" was full of courage, idealism, and truth. Never has America had more reason for cherishing this spirit than to-day. When the world shall courageously and systematically undertake to remove the inducing causes of war we shall know that a real peace-movement has been born. In this behalf, every nation should use all its endeavors to do away with armaments on land and sea. If nations are to prosper and maintain their rights only through a show of force, then the large nations will overcome the smaller states, of course. The more money and energy that one nation expends on war, the more the others are compelled to spend, so that the movement ends in universal waste without accomplishing any good.

If nations preserve their individuality by physical strength only, then, whether with or without preparedness, might will survive. If all nations should disarm and still have war they might as well begin with bare hands and pitchforks and clubs as to start with the modern equipment for killing.

However, it is a mistake to believe that the autonomy of a country depends upon power alone. If this were the case, not over five or six nations in the world could sustain themselves. What we know as moral forces are even more important than guns and battleships. These forces would constantly grow stronger if nations relied upon them and cultivated them instead of the munitions of warfare. It may be that the world will never be at peace, and that liberty will never be secure in any land. If liberty and "peace on earth, good will to men" shall ever prevail it will be after forts and arsenals and hatreds have disappeared.

CHAPTER 27

THE LOEB–LEOPOLD TRAGEDY

In the summer of 1924 I was called into the defense of the Loeb-Leopold case in Chicago. Few cases, if any, ever attracted such wide discussion and publicity; not only in America, but anywhere in the world. Two boys, named Richard Loeb, who was seventeen years old, and Nathan Leopold, eighteen years old, were indicted for murder. Both were sons of wealthy families, well known and highly respected in Chicago and elsewhere.

A young boy, named Robert Franks, fourteen years old, had disappeared on his way home from school. He did not return that night, and the parents were greatly alarmed over his absence. The next day the father received a letter saying that his son was safe and would be returned on the payment of a ransom of ten thousand dollars. The letter contained explicit directions as to how the money should be delivered. Mr. Franks was to put it in a package, stand on the rear platform of a certain train leaving Chicago about four o'clock that afternoon, and throw the money off at a lonely spot near a grain-elevator south of Englewood. Mr. Franks went to the bank for the money and was preparing to go to the train when the afternoon papers printed a story about the discovery of a dead boy lying naked in a culvert under a railroad crossing some twenty miles south of the city. Everything led to the belief that it was Robert Franks. The information was telephoned to the Franks home, and the father felt satisfied that the poor boy was his son, and he really was.

Before going to the place on the prairie where the money was to be delivered, both Loeb and Leopold saw the story in the papers, so, of course, they did not go after the money. The authorities immediately began an investigation. A number of suspects were brought in within a few days and put through strict grillings, as is usual in cases of murder. Two or three of these were seriously injured in their standing, and suffered notoriety and loss of positions from which they have never recovered, although wholly innocent of the charge.

In the inspection of the place and surroundings where the dead boy was discovered, a pair of eyeglasses was found. The oculist who sold them was traced, and he stated that he had never sold but two pairs just like that—one of these purchasers was now in Europe, so obviously he could not have been in any way connected with the crime; the other customer was a young man named Nathan Leopold. The Leopold home was near the Franks residence. These two families and the Loeb family had been neighbors and friends for years. Young Leopold was a graduate of the University of Chicago and was then in his second year of the law course in that university. He was to leave for Europe in a few days. This trip had been planned for some time. His father had given him the money for this summer vacation, and the tickets were purchased.

The eyeglasses having been sold to Nathan Leopold, the State's attorney sent for him and questioned him as to his whereabouts that night. Leopold answered everything that was asked, saying that on that night he and Loeb were automobiling in the parks and the country around Chicago, driving Leopold's car. No one in the State's attorney's office or anywhere else had the slightest idea that Leopold could possibly be involved in the case, but out of prudence it was thought best to hold him a short time for further investigation. The boy, after advising with his father and Mr. Benjamin Bachrach, consented to this, the two older men having not the faintest suspicion that young Leopold had anything whatever to do with the affair.

The next day the officers sent for Richard Loeb and asked him about that evening; he said he did not remember where he was, but thought that he and Leopold went driving, but could not tell where they went. It seemed to have been agreed that if anything happened and they were arrested within a week they should tell their pre-arranged story, as afterwards told by Leopold; but if arrested after that they were to say that they did not remember where they drove. As fate would have it, Nathan was arrested before the week was over, and Loeb after its expiration. Still, the officers did not lay any stress on the variance in their statements. Both boys were of wealthy families and always had plenty of money; no one could think of any possible motive for committing such a deed. It occurred to one of the officers, however, to send for Leopold's chauffeur and question him. The chauffeur said that Leopold's car was not used that night; that it was in the garage for repairs. This story was easily verified, and the boys were questioned further. In a day or two they broke down and confessed and told their story with all its ghastly details. The clothes were taken off the Franks boy so that identity might not be disclosed; some of them were placed in the lagoon in Jackson Park; some of them were buried; and some were burned. The boys were taken to all the places covered by their route, including the place where the clothes were buried, and their story was fully corroborated by what was found.

It seemed that Loeb had gotten it into his head that he could commit a perfect crime, which should involve kidnapping, murder, and ransom. He had unfolded his scheme to Leopold because he needed some one to help him plan and carry it out. For this plot Leopold had no liking whatever, but he had an exalted opinion of Loeb. Leopold was rather undersized; he could not excel in sports and games. Loeb was strong and athletic. He was good at baseball and football, and a general favorite with all who knew him. Both of them always had money.

Loeb had two thousand dollars in cash, a number of Liberty Bonds whose coupons had not been cashed, and a standing order to draw money whenever he wanted it by asking the cashier at his father's office.

Several times there was trouble between the boys about going on with their plan. At one time their correspondence, offered in evidence, and published by the press, revealed that they nearly reached the point of open breach, and extreme violence.

When their plans were actually completed they arranged to get a car from a renting office, and Leopold, under another name, was to refer to Loeb, also under another name, as reference for the expense and safe return of the car. Loeb's assumed name was given as that of a resident of the Hotel Morrison, where he had rented a room and deposited a valise in which there happened to be a book drawn by him from the University of Chicago Library.

Before this they had written the ransom letter. This was addressed "Dear Sir," as they had no idea whose boy would be taken and to whom the letter would be mailed.

Around four o'clock one afternoon they got into the car, drove within a few squares of Loeb's home, along one of the best residence districts of Chicago, over to a private school that Loeb had formerly attended, arriving there just as the afternoon session was over and the boys were coming out. One after another was surveyed by the boys in the car until poor Robert Franks came along. He was invited into the car for a ride; he got into the front seat with Leopold, who was driving; and within ten minutes he was hit on the head by a chisel in the hands of Loeb, was stunned by the blow, and soon bled to death. All this happened in a thickly populated section of Chicago and close to the homes of all three of the boys.

The car was then driven slowly for twenty miles through the main streets and parts of the south side of the city, solidly built up and congested with automobiles going in all directions. It was summertime; the afternoons were long and evenings late. Leopold was a botanist and a lover of birds. He had often been in that far section gathering flowers and catching birds; he had a rare collection and was creating a museum for himself; he had mounted the birds with great skill, and many of them were very valuable. During these excursions he had become thoroughly familiar with that out-of-the-way locality and remembered the culvert under the railroad tracks, which could be reached only by an unfrequented road. When they got into that vicinity the sun had not yet disappeared, so they drove for an hour or two waiting for the twilight to fade into deeper darkness. Then they placed the boy in the culvert and drove away.

When they got back to town they took out the ransom letter and addressed it to Mr. Jacob Franks, the father of the boy that they had left out in the country. They then went to a restaurant, ate a hearty meal, and drove to Leopold's home. This residence was in a well-settled block next door to a large apartment building. The boy was killed in the rented car and it was soaked with blood, not only inside but also on the outside. They left the car standing in the street in front of the house while they went up to Leopold's room and discussed the events of the day until a late hour, when Loeb went home.

In the morning after the killing Loeb came back to Leopold's home. They took the car into the garage and washed it as best they could, but did not remove all the stains, as the evidence brought out. When the car was dry, Leopold took it back to the agency where he had hired it.

Loeb is a good-natured, friendly boy. I realize that most people will not be able to understand this, and perhaps will not believe it. Some may remember Daniel Webster's address to a jury in a murder case. He pictured the accused: his low brow, his murderous eye, his every feature loudly proclaimed him a fiend incarnate. One would suppose from Daniel Webster's foolish argument that the defendant would be recognized as a murderer wherever he went. A part of this tirade was published in the old school-reader, and we used to "speak" it on the last day of the term. We youngsters wondered why the Lord needed to put a mark on Cain's brow, for after reading Daniel Webster's recipe we could go out on the street and pick out killers everywhere, for all seemed to be marked. But Daniel Webster was not a psychologist; he was a politician and an orator, and that was enough for one man.

"Dicky" Loeb was not only a kindly *looking* boy but he *was* and *is* a kindly boy. He was never too busy to personally do a favor for any one that he chanced to know. There was no reason why he should be put into prison for life excepting for the strange and unfortunate circumstances that might not occur again in a thousand years.

Leopold had not the slightest instinct toward what we are pleased to call crime. He had, and has, the most brilliant intellect that I ever met in a boy. At eighteen he had acquired nine or ten languages; he was an advanced botanist; he was an authority on birds; he enjoyed good books. He was often invited to lecture before clubs and other assemblages; he was genial, kindly, and likable. His father was wealthy, and this son was his great pride. Every one prophesied an uncommon career for this gifted lad. He is now in prison for life for the most foolish, most motiveless, act that was ever conceived in a diseased brain by his boon companion.

Leopold had scarcely seen Robert Franks before the fatal day. Loeb had played tennis with him and they were good friends. Why, then, did these two boys commit this rash and horrible deed? I presume they know less about the reason than others who have studied the case and the boys as well. There are many things that human beings cannot understand, and of all the fathomless questions that confront and confuse men, the most baffling is the human mind. No one can tell what will be the outcome of any life. To quote Oscar Wilde:

> "For none can tell to what Red Hell
> His sightless soul may stray."

The terrible deed had been committed. The two boys were in the shadow of the gallows; their confession had been made; their families were in the depths of despair, and they came to me to assist the lawyers already employed. My feelings were much upset; I wanted to lend a hand, and I wanted to stay out of the case. The act was a shocking and bizarre performance; the public and press were almost solidly against them.

In a terrible crisis there is only one element more helpless than the poor, and that is the rich. I knew then, and I know now, that except for the wealth of the families a plea of guilty and a life sentence would have been accepted without a contest. I knew this, and I dreaded the fight.

No client of mine had ever been put to death, and I felt that it would almost, if not quite, kill me if it should ever happen. I have never been able to read a story of an execution. I always left town if possible on the day of a hanging. I am strongly—call it morbidly, who will—against killing. I felt that I would get a fair fee if I went into the case, but money never influenced my stand one way or the other. I knew of no good reason for refusing, but I was sixty-eight years old, and very weary. I had grown tired of standing in the lean and lonely front line facing the greatest enemy that ever confronted man—public opinion.

But, I went in, to do what I could for sanity and humanity against the wave of hatred and malice that, as ever, was masquerading under its usual nom de plume: "Justice."

CHAPTER 28

THE LOEB–LEOPOLD TRIAL

We lawyers for Loeb and Leopold knew that it would be impossible to get much time for the preparation of the case. People who know nothing of Criminal Courts are always declaiming against the long delays. Truth is, when there is a public outcry against some defendant, all other business in the court is set aside for a criminal prosecution. The case must be tried at once while the haters are hating and hot on the trail.

Our attention is constantly called to the English and their way; but their newspapers are not permitted to publish details of crimes, or refer to the suspected authors, or otherwise to stir up the mob to anger against the defendant. In America, if the case is one of public interest, a campaign that reeks with venom is at once launched against the accused; columns of interviews and pictures are printed each day; what the defendant is alleged to have said is scattered in bold type all over the pages before the case is tried, and members of the family are followed about and forced to talk; all the neighbors and even casual acquaintances are interviewed, and the stories grow lurid and appalling. Newspaper sales shoot up beyond belief. Day by day efforts are made to get new versions so that the public will not by any means slacken their thoughts and feelings about the matter. Every prospective juror called into the box knows the case, and all its details, as presented by the press. He has all the bias of a partisan, and it is not possible for him to give the defendant a fair trial. Juror after juror is excused because of having an opinion. The lawyers for the defense are roundly criticised for the time they take, as though they should join the State and the mob and help get their clients hanged. Then the law must be changed; members of the legislature are politicians, and to them the voice of the people is the voice of God, so they must pass a new law authorizing a person to sit on a jury even if he already has an opinion but says he can set it aside.

Every one who thinks knows how common it is for men to set aside their views. Most men never have but one or two ideas, anyhow, and to these they hang like grim death. How often do people set aside their beliefs on politics, on religion, or any other question if in conflict with something they want to do? To set aside an opinion without evidence is not only psychologically impossible, but is physically absurd. Every man realizes that when he happens to be personally interested in some matter in court; whether the case be civil or criminal, on every question and point, he weighs what will be the attitude of the judge, and how it will affect the judge's mind. He feels the same about the jury. It is hard enough for the accused to get a fair hearing no matter how much caution is taken.

We knew that seldom had a case been handled like this one; and every one, far and near, had made up their minds what should be done. Naturally we wanted delay; all that we could possibly get. We needed it for preparing our case, but we needed it still more so that the passions of men might have a chance to cool. We were aware that there could be no defense except the mental condition of the boys. The statutes of Illinois provide that for murder in the first degree a sentence of death may be imposed, or one of imprisonment in the penitentiary for not less than fourteen years. And still, to this day the case is discussed as if the penalty was unheard of in the case of murder. From the beginning we never tried to do anything but save the lives of the two defendants; we did not even claim or try to prove that they were insane. We did believe and sought to show that their minds were not normal and never had been normal.

The statutes of Illinois provide that on a plea of guilty the court may hear evidence in mitigation or aggravation of the offense. I doubt if any judge anywhere in any civilized country ever failed to hear evidence or statements in mitigation or aggravation of an offense when he had to use his judgment as to the severity of the sentence to be imposed. With or without the statute, courts always find out what they can about the defendants before passing sentence.

Before any lawyer was employed the State had called into their counsel the best-known alienists in Chicago. This made it necessary for us to go outside the State of Illinois to find alienists to examine the defendants. About that time the National Association of Psychiatrists were holding their convention in Atlantic City. We at once delegated Mr. Walter Bachrach, one of the counsel for the defendants, to go to the convention and secure three or four of those of highest standing in their profession to come and make an investigation of the two boys. This was absolutely necessary. Thereupon we secured Doctor William Alanson White, Doctor William Healy and Doctor Bernard Gluck to come to make the examination.

Doctor White had for many years been superintendent of the United States Hospital for the Insane, in Washington, D. C., and had been long recognized as one of the leading authorities in the country. He has written more books on mental abnormalities, and the human mind in general, than any other man in America. Doctor William Healy was then, and is now, the psychiatrist of the Baker Foundation of Boston, organized by a judge with intelligence and a philanthropic spirit for the purpose of examining and reporting the delinquents that reached the Juvenile Court in Boston. Doctor Healy, years before, had helped in the establishing of the Juvenile Court in Chicago, and for a long time was in charge of the examination of the delinquents that were brought into its jurisdiction. He had written extensively on these subjects and was highly regarded and respected the world over. Doctor Bernard Gluck had for years been the alienist specialist appointed by the State of New York, having general charge and supervision of examining the inmates of prisons of the State. He was considered as unquestionably one of the most brilliant alienists in America.

These three physicians together with Doctor Bowen, of Boston, and Doctor Hurlburt, an able young alienist of Chicago, met in Chicago. Doctor Bowen was an expert whose business related to the careful and specific action of ductless glands, that now universally are believed to have so much of importance to do with human conduct. From the time of our entry into the case until the matter was called into court we were able to secure only a week's delay.

Two indictments were returned against each of the boys: one for murder and one for kidnapping. A few years before this a case of the kidnapping of a child in Illinois attracted a great deal of attention, indignation, and discussion, at which time, in obedience to the demand of the crowd, the legislature passed a law providing the same punishment for kidnapping as for murder. If they had used a grain of sense people would have foreseen that the statute would tend to the killing of every one kidnapped in order to destroy the evidence; murder could not add to the penalty if the offenders were caught. But the public and the legislature did not think so far.

Both the indictments against the boys were returned into court and were automatically placed on the docket of the chief justice, who, at the time, was the Honorable John Caverly. We spent considerable time deliberating as to what we should do. The feeling was so tense and the trial was so near that we felt we could not save the boys' lives with a jury. It seemed out of the question to find a single man who had not read all about the case and formed a definite opinion. Judge Caverly had formerly been a judge of the Municipal Court and had helped form the

Juvenile Court, and we believed that he was kindly and discerning in his views of life. After thorough consideration we concluded that the best chance was on a plea of guilty. Only a few knew what was to be done—the boys and their parents, two or three relatives, and the attorneys in the case. A large and expectant crowd was eagerly awaiting the opening of the court. I arose, and in very few words that we had most carefully prepared, spoke of our anxiety in the matter, and the difficulty of getting a fair trial, and said that under the circumstances we had decided to plead guilty in both cases.

Of course the State and every one else were taken by surprise. The pleas were accepted and entered without objection or delay. What we most feared was that if the State had any conception of our plan they would bring up only one case at a time, saving a chance, if given a life-sentence, to bring up the second case and, as it were, catch us on the rebound. We were conscious of the risk we were taking and determined to take one chance instead of facing two.

When the pleas were entered the reporters made a wild rush for the door to broadcast the news, but it took some time for the audience to comprehend what was happening, and the surprise was very great. Finally the astonishment in the courtroom subsided and the people sat quiet and waited for the next step. As the State had not been expecting our move, a continuance was granted until the next day.

Never did I have a more hectic life in an equal length of time than through the weeks that elapsed during the hearing of the case and the time used by the judge for consideration and preparation of his opinion. There was little rest by day and but little sleep at night. Of course, long accounts were run every day in the press. On the hearing of the case some forty newspaper reporters from all the main cities of America and all the press associations presented themselves. The proceedings became front-page matter in every hamlet of the country, and were closely followed in all parts of the world. I seldom went to my office in those troublous days, and rarely read any of the letters that came in stacks. These were usually abusive and brutal to the highest degree.

The public seemed to think that we were committing a crime in defending two boys, who probably needed it as much as any two defendants ever on trial for their lives. The most senseless and the most unreasonable criticism was indulged in against the defendants and their attorneys because of the lengthy hearing of the case. It was often asserted that no such proceedings could have been possible anywhere else, and yet the whole process was perfectly regular and would have been so in any State or country where the court had any power to fix the degree of punishment. To be sure the time allowed to lawyers and witnesses was more or less in the control of the court, but the procedure was fixed by the law, and was entirely regular and usual.

While the defense protested that the State should not be permitted to show the details of the killing on a plea of guilty, the State contended that they had the right to show it as bearing upon the condition of mind of the defendants, and the aggravation or mitigation of the penalty. Whatever undue length of time was consumed was caused by the State, as we offered no evidence of any kind on the subject. On the other hand, the State put in all the evidence of the killing with the greatest minuteness and detail. None of these witnesses were cross-examined.

Week after week the trial dragged along. The courtroom, the corridors, and the streets outside were always thronged with those curious to get glimpses of what was going on. The court and every one and everything connected with the affair were strictly guarded as we went back and forth. The days were hard and strenuous, the evenings and nights were given over to consultations and discussions.

When the representatives of the State had consumed all the time they wished, we put on ten to fifteen witnesses, mainly schoolmates of the two boys, who testified to their strange actions and their belief that neither of them was normal. In spite of our desires, some of them went so far as to express the opinion that they were insane. We then called our alienists, who told fully about the condition of the boys, as they understood them. Both boys were decidedly deficient in emotions, as shown by physical tests.

The emotions are most important in keeping both young and old from the commission of unusual acts. To one in possession of normal emotional structure, the thought of any act seriously forbidden by custom, law, or normal feelings is automatically immediately revolting. No such revulsion comes to one of a certain defective nervous system. These boys, especially Loeb, had carried the phantasies usual in children into later youth. Loeb had read and studied detective stories since he was very young and had experimented a great deal as an amateur detective since childhood. The detective was always the hero of the stories that he read, and he conceived the idea that a perfect crime could be accomplished that would baffle for all time the real detectives and police. He had lived with this dream for years. When the story of the killing of Robert Franks was published broadcast he went from place to place with the detectives, telling them how he thought it might have happened, and who might be responsible for the deed. His theories came close to the facts, as they were ultimately disclosed. He bought every edition of the newspapers as the story came out and talked of nothing else. He reminded the detectives that the first stories had spoken of a telephone message being sent from somewhere in Englewood the morning after the disappearance and asked why they did not go to every telephone booth in Englewood and thus probably get a clue. The detectives took his advice, and it transpired that he had done the telephoning himself. He talked incessantly to his family about the affair, unfolding his theories as to the way it all came about. Both he and Leopold were incipient paranoiacs. The whole case disclosed no motive that could induce a sane mind and normal person to commit such a deed.

The intelligence of the public is pretty well shown by their attitude toward the defense of insanity. When the populace clamors for a victim it wants no facts, theories, doctors, lawyers, or scientists to stand in the way. What we term "the public" knows just what it wants done. It also feels that "if 't is to be done, 't were well it were done quickly." There will be time enough to think it over when the turmoil of the trial is over and the victim is dead, and "better so"—for it is a common belief that it doesn't matter whether the one on trial is insane or not—he is of no use and it is just as well to have him put to death.

Perhaps there is truth in this flippant idea. No doubt that it could be said with a degree of reason about nine-tenths of the people of the world. Doubtless there are those who would say it if any one was submitted to them for their opinion. Is it at all necessary that a person should be of any value to the world? The justification for living is that you are alive and do not want to die. If one cannot justify life in that way, then it can not be justified. It would be very dangerous to be able to declare that a man could be executed because he was of no value to the world. If a trial of this sort should be fairly decided, most of the class who advocate such ideas would be found wanting, and therefore guilty.

Is insanity so rare that men should deride that condition as a defense in a criminal case? There are more people in our institutions for the insane than in our prisons. And besides the vast and growing colonies of insane inside asylums, there are large numbers who are kept by families and friends and their condition carefully concealed from the public; and a much larger class that are idiots, morons, and plain defectives, and upon any theory are entirely irresponsible for their acts. Any given individual is much more apt to be insane or mentally defective than he is to be a criminal. A large percentage of this class go through life without ever disclosing their real condition, and yet the smallest circumstance may reveal it at any time. Then, too, the criminal and the insane are very much alike. In all our large prisons, from time to time, many of the inmates are collected and sent to insane asylums on being expertly examined and found mentally unbalanced.

One of the most obvious proofs of mental defect is that there is no adequate consciousness of the relation between cause and effect in the conduct of the individual. In the case of these two boys every motive that moves ordinary mortals to action was absent. There was no malice or hatred, or even dislike against the unfortunate boy. There was no motive for getting money connected with the foolish plot. The whole performance was childish and silly, and proved of itself a decided abnormal mentality.

Aside from all of this, to have sentenced two boys of their age to death on a plea of guilty would have violated every precedent in Illinois in the one hundred and ten years that it has been a State. Only two of their age were ever put to death in Illinois, up to that time, and these were offered life sentences if they would plead guilty. On trial, the jury fixed the sentence at death, and the judge refused to interfere. Very few men, at any age, are sentenced to death on a plea of guilty. Only a small proportion of those who have been found guilty of murder in Illinois have ever been put to death, and the same is true of most States of the Union where the juries fix the punishment.

In view of these facts, to have executed two boys but seventeen and eighteen years old for the commission of a senseless, motiveless act, and on a plea of guilty, would have been without reason or excuse. Such a sentence would have been a direct response to the mob hysteria outside the court. Judge Caverly could have done nothing else but spare their lives without violating every precedent in the State; he could not have given such a sentence unless awed by fear to write a judgment without parallel in Illinois.

Never was the Criminal Court in Chicago so besieged for admission as during the closing days of this case. At times the crowd swept away officers and ran over each other in frantic efforts to get inside the trial room.

Manifestly, I cannot enter into any discussion of the closing arguments. For years I have been a fairly close student of psychology.

I endeavored in my address to make a plain, straightforward statement of the facts in the case, and I meant to apply such knowledge as we now have of the motives that move men. The argument took the largest part of two court days and was printed almost word for word in some of the Chicago papers, and very extensively by the press outside that city, so that people at the time were fairly familiar with the facts in the case, and certainly of the outcome. When I closed I had exhausted all the strength I could summon. From that day I have never gone through so protracted a strain, and could never do it again, even if I should try.

When the arguments were finished, Judge Caverly adjourned court to consider the case and prepare the opinion. At the end of three weeks he notified us all that he was ready. Every one connected with the defense went to the court under police protection. Judge Caverly was on the bench. The room, the corridors, stairs, streets were a solid jam of people clamoring to get somewhere near to the tragic situation inside. Judge Caverly evidently was deeply moved. The crowded room was deathly still, every one eager to hear. Until the closing words no one could predict what the end was to be. When the climax was reached, men and women rushed pell-mell for the doors. Those of us nearest to the ordeal waited until the building was cleared, then hastened to the street, got into our machines and quickly drove away. For us, the long suspense was over. The lives of Loeb and Leopold were saved. But there was nothing before them, to the end, but stark, blank stone walls.

CHAPTER 29

THE EVOLUTION CASE

IN less than a year after the ending of the Loeb-Leopold case, a most uncommon series of events brought me into even wider notice than any that had happened before. I cannot say that in this case I had nothing to do with the immediate cause of all this publicity. For the first, the last, the only time in my life, I volunteered my services in a case; it was in the Scopes case in Tennessee that I did this, because I really wanted to take part in it.

One can easily understand that lawyers are generally slow to offer their services; at best, it is a delicate step to take, for they might not be wanted, and that would be embarrassing.

For years I had been interested in the campaign that culminated in "the Dayton Case." An organization of men and women calling themselves "fundamentalists" had been very actively seeking to control the schools and universities of America. The members of this body claimed to believe that the various books that are bound together and are called "the Bible" are inspired in their every statement; that the whole of these books was virtually written by the Almighty and is in every part literally true. These books contain what is purported to be a story of the creation of the universe and man and what are regarded as the early activities on the earth.

The fundamentalists denied that these Bible stories are legends, opinions, poems, myths and guesses, and pronounced them history. It has not been long since all Christians held the same attitude toward the Bible. The books of the Old and New Testaments were written ages before the world had any knowledge of our science. To those old authors the world was flat, the sun was drawn across the horizon to light the day, and the moon to light the night. To lengthen the day it was only necessary to have the sun stand still. Man and every other animal were made mature and full-grown. Men believed that the stars were stuck into the firmament and that Jacob had a vision of angels going up and down on a ladder, which was the up-to-date mode of that day for that sort of a trip.

Finally men conceived the idea of taking a look at heaven, whereupon they started building a tower and got so near that it attracted the attention of the Lord who is said to have circumvented their bright idea by confounding the tongues of the workmen so that if one of them asked for mortar he would perhaps be given a pail of beer, and any one asking for more bricks might be handed water instead. This would make it impossible to proceed with the building. So they abandoned the project and it was called the Tower of Babel, and to this day the fundamentalists explain the many languages in the world as due to the confusing and befuddling the tongues of those workmen.

Between the periods of many presidential campaigns, and during the dearth of real issues, Mr. William Jennings Bryan placed himself at the head of this movement. Besides his interest in politics he was a theologian of note, and was wont to send weekly syndicated letters to many newspapers, discussing religious questions. The information was doubtless drawn mainly from "Clarke's Commentaries," which was almost universally read by right-minded people when I was a boy. This work was written a long time before Darwin, and of course is not much like "The Descent of Man." Among Mr. Bryan's lectures delivered to large Chautauqua audiences was one entitled "The Prince of Peace," which was circulated as his chief campaign document in the presidential race of 1908.

Soon after that campaign Mr. Bryan's attention was called to a book by Professor James H. Leuba, in which he stated that more than half of the instructors of modern institutions of learning are agnostics. This caused Mr. Bryan considerable anguish, so for several years he made a point of speaking in university towns and propounding a series of questions to professors and presidents of our schools of learning—questions concerning the origin of man, which could easily have been answered if the teachers had only looked at the first and second chapters of Genesis, by which Mr. Bryan marked the examination-papers of the instructors.

The more Mr. Bryan thought about this subject, the more excited he became. The children must be saved from the infidelity of the teachers and professors. Strange how anxious old folk are apt to be over "the children." The main reason for this is that children do not act like the old people. Mr. Bryan, being orthodox in his views, of course thought that the proper remedy in the premises was to "pass a law." This shows the psychology of a fundamentalist compared with the citizens of the effete monarchies of Europe, who have never even considered passing a law against teaching evolution.

Mr. Bryan travelled from town to town talking against evolution, and condemning the "infidel universities." Some years before that he had moved from Nebraska to Florida. During the hectic days when he was campaigning to "save the children" from getting an education, when he was translating "Clarke's Commentaries" into newspaper copy, he was working for the "Coral Gables Land Association" in Miami, Fla., making speeches at noon every day when the tourist crop was there, to induce investors to buy Florida real estate. These talks were addressed to those who had driven their Fords down South to escape the rigors and coal bills of our Northern winters.

But this was only a side-line. Mr. Bryan was a politician

and an organizer, and he had put his religious plans and purposes into action. So bills were prepared to forbid the teaching of evolution, or any doctrine in conflict with the Genesis story, in any school wholly or in part supported by public funds. These bills were presented to Southern legislators; and when the time drew near for putting it to a vote, Mr. Bryan appeared at the State House and made a revival speech to the members of the legislature and the assembled people of the State. Kentucky defeated the bill by one vote; it seemed to be too far north. Then came Tennessee and Mississippi, which were clearly within what Mr. Henry L. Mencken termed "the Bible belt." Both legislatures passed the bill by an almost unanimous vote. The governor of Tennessee wanted to veto it, but did not have the courage. So he contented himself by saying that he did not believe that it would amount to anything.

From any point of view, the law was silly and senseless. At the time of its passage, even in the States of Tennessee and Mississippi the schools were teaching that the earth was round instead of flat, and the day and night were due to the revolution of the earth on its axis and not from the sun and moon going around it, or being drawn across the horizon. This and many other things, taught in the public schools even down there, are flatly contrary to Genesis and, in fact, they refute the Bible account much more clearly than does the doctrine of evolution. I understand that the States of Tennessee and Mississippi both continue to teach that the earth is round and that the revolution on its axis brings the day and night, in spite of all opposition.

The little town of Dayton, Tenn., had never been heard of very far away from home. A boy, twenty-one years old, had come from Kentucky and applied for a position as teacher in the high school. His name was John T. Scopes. And he was destined to be famous. He was a modest, studious, conscientious lad. His father was a locomotive engineer and formerly a member of the American Railway Union. For his membership in this organization he had been placed on the blacklist, and after the strike he went to Kentucky to look for a job. He was a man of courage and independence, and brought up his family to have their own opinions and to stand by them.

John was a good teacher. He had the respect of the whole town of Dayton and the affection of his pupils. Among other subjects, he taught biology; the work furnished as a textbook was "Hunter's Biology." It seems strange that the Dayton school board did not adopt the first and second chapters of Genesis as a modern textbook on biology. Anyhow, Scopes told the little boys and girls that the origin of life was in the slime and ooze of the sea; that life developed from a germ, and gradually grew and changed until it reached the various forms of the life of to-day.

For this he was indicted for the crime of teaching the truth. John T. Scopes was not the first man indicted for this most heinous offense. So far as I know, he was the last, up to the present time.

I had been a close observer of Mr. Bryan's campaigns against knowledge, and I was somewhat acquainted with history and felt that I knew what it meant. I knew how the bill that Mr. Bryan and his organization sponsored was put through, and they had already announced that they would carry the campaign to every State in the Union.

When John T. Scopes was arrested he employed Mr. John H. Neal, a former law professor in the University of Tennessee, who, at the time, had established a law school at Knoxville. Mr. Neal is a man of ability, a good student, and has always supported progressive movements, but had not been active as a practitioner in his State. The Civil Liberties Union of New York City had furnished some aid to the defense, and was taking steps to finance the case.

I was in New York not long after the arrest of Mr. Scopes, and saw that Mr. Bryan had volunteered to go to Dayton to assist in the prosecution. At once I wanted to go. My object, and my only object, was to focus the attention of the country on the progamme of Mr. Bryan and the other fundamentalists in America. I knew that education was in danger from the source that has always hampered it—religious fanaticism. To me it was perfectly clear that the proceedings bore little semblance to a court case, but I realized that there was no limit to the mischief that might be accomplished unless the country was roused to the evil at hand. So I volunteered to go. With me went my friends, Dudley Field Malone and Arthur Garfield Hays. With Mr. Bryan volunteering on the one side, the matter soon attracted the interest of the entire country and the rest of the world.

Most of the newspapers treated the whole case as a farce instead of a tragedy, but they did give it no end of publicity. Not only was every paper of importance in America represented, but those of many foreign lands. Most of the local lawyers of Dayton were lined up on the side of the prosecution. We did have one local lawyer, but at the last minute he ran away from the case in fear and trepidation. The sentiment of the town and the State was more than he could face.

Mr. Bryan was the logical man to prosecute the case. He had not been inside a courtroom for forty years, but that made no difference, for he did not represent a real case; he represented religion, and in this he was the idol of all Morondom. His scientific attitude was epigrammatically stated in various speeches and interviews regarding what he did not know about science. He said that he was "not so much interested in the age of rocks as in the Rock of Ages." This left nothing more to be said by him to his credulous disciples who filled every hall and tent and crowded every grove when he appeared and defended The True Faith. A lecture advertisement by him on "The Prince of Peace" found men and boys clinging to the rafters when there were rafters, and to the limbs of trees when there were groves. Such a meeting in the countryside was an event. They were all there regardless of admission fees. As to science, his mind was an utter blank. He was willing to believe with Genesis that the earth was less than six thousand years old.

Mr. Bryan did not know that the monuments of Egypt, giving the genealogy of their kings and the dates of their reigns ran back more than seven thousand years. He closed his eyes to the ages between this day and the time of the primitive man. The endless centuries that rolled away while the lower animals fought and evolved and lived and perished ages before man arrived was a story of which he had never learned; neither did he know of the millions of ages when the earth sped in its path around the sun before it was fitted for any life, animal or vegetable. About all of this his mind was void. The solid rocks that were laid down millions of years ago meant not a thing to Mr. Bryan; their conflict with Genesis was settled with the sanctimonious sophomoric: "I am more interested in the Rock of Ages than in the age of rocks."

Mr. Bryan was like the traditional boy passing the graveyard at night—he was whistling to keep up his courage. His very attitude showed that he was frightened out of his wits lest, after all, the illusions of his life might be only dreams.

On the other hand, I had been reared by my father on books of science. Huxley's books had been household guests with us for years, and we had all of Darwin's as fast as they were published. Such books as Tyler's "Primitive Culture," Lysle's "Geology," Draper, Lecky, Winwood Reade, Buckle, Tyndall, and Spencer also were on my father's shelves, and later were on mine, and most of them I had read. They had long been my companions. For a lawyer, I was a fairly grounded scientist. Mr. Arthur G. Hays had also been educated in science and had an open and acute mind. I do not remember hearing Mr. Dudley F. Malone express an opinion as to whether he was convinced of the soundness of evolution. I presume he was never specially interested in the subject. He put his allegiance on a higher ground, as did we all. More than most men that one meets, Mr. Malone believes in freedom, in the right of every one to investigate for himself, and he resented the interference of the State in its effort to forbid or control the convictions and mental attitudes of men. Mr. John Neal had for years been a fighter for liberal causes, and must have been lonely indeed in these contests.

Associated with Mr. Bryan were his son, William, from Los Angeles (where he was assistant district attorney), the district attorney of that section of Tennessee, and four Dayton lawyers. When Mr. Bryan arrived in Dayton he was met by a throng of people. From the newspaper accounts one would judge the whole country was out to receive the defender of the faith. His reception proved that he was the ruler of "the Bible belt." The newspaper representatives flocked around him for crumbs of information, asking what he thought would be the outcome of the combat; and among other statements by him he said that this case was to be "a fight to the death."

The next morning I read Mr. Bryan's reply with some surprise. I had not realized that it was to be such a conflict. I arrived a day or two later. There was no torchlight parade to greet me as I stepped off the train. I did not miss it much, with the thermometer blazing away toward the hundred mark, where it remained nearly all the time that we were there. The sun did its best and worst to give us a hot time, if nothing else was had. Still, there were some people at the depot to meet me; I was received most kindly and courteously, at that. As a matter of fact, all through the event down there people treated us with extreme consideration in many ways, in spite of the fact that they must have been shocked by my position in the case. The banker of the town went off to the foothills for a family treat in order that we should have a cottage to ourselves in the village, which was so crowded that it became practically impossible to get accommodations of any sort, although every imaginable preparation was made for taking care of the multitude expected from near and far to bask before the master, Mr. Bryan.

All the farm products and dairy supplies and other provisions had been contracted for by the hotel and the little restaurants and boarding houses and the lunch counter in Robinson's drug store, so that any one wanting a bottle of milk or pound of butter had to skirmish about for some one willing to spare that much, or, more likely, tell of some farmer out in the real country who might have some to sell if one had a way of going out there to see. Worst of all, ice was well-nigh unattainable, so that one sweltering Sunday night, when we returned from a week-end absence of so-called rest, it was enough to make one almost believe in miracle-making when we opened our icebox and found it stocked with a slab of ice, milk and cream and butter, and even a choice cantaloupe for Monday breakfast.

Our next-door neighbor, Mr. Wilbur, and all the others on our short street, were always doing such things for us. And one day, when a message came from the family up in the hills inquiring if we were comfortable or if they could do anything to make us more so, we felt that we had tasted and would ever after recognize that far-famed "true Southern hospitality."

Most of the lawyers employed by the State were courteous and kindly and we all got along exceedingly well. But especially General Ben MacKenzie and his son, whom we took to be stolid Scotchmen, became most agreeable and even lovable, so that a strong affection developed between us which I am sure will continue so long as we live. After all, men in all lands and at all times have been found human and loving outside their religious attitudes.

When the reporters came to me to forecast what we should undertake, or what result we expected, I said very little. I can always tell more about such matters when they are over with. It is more or less embarrassing to have to take back what one has stated, and one really cannot tell a reporter that he may lose his case.

As I loitered along, getting into my clothes that first morning, trying to imagine how the venture would begin and end in that warped company that I was about to meet, my eyes caught sight of things glistening on the walls in the sunshine streaming in, and lo and behold, if they weren't strangely tinselled framed mottoes with assurances that "The Lord will provide," and "Jesus loves you," and "Put your trust in Him." How could I doubt myself after that?

The large red-brick courthouse stood in the middle of a square, such as one sees in much larger towns; the walks radiated from the building to the four corners of the square and were shaded by trees that one did not need to be religious to call a godsend. At the top of the grand staircase we entered the largest courtroom that I have ever seen, all freshly painted in glazed finish the same color as the glaring sun pouring in from all sides. With a population said to be about one thousand and five hundred, Dayton surprised us with a courtroom designed to accommodate at least one thousand of its townpeople, besides all the dwellers of all the hills roundabout, who were allowed to stand solidly jammed into the aisles and against the walls. Any case that had to be tried in a courtroom was an event to them, it seemed, and provision had been made for vast audiences at such times. And this was one of those times. In a crescent outside the huge rail were ranged over one hundred magazine and newspaper representatives from the four winds and beyond, one felt; one man was from

England, one was from Canada; each sat with poised pencil and eagle eye the entire sweep of the curve as we filed in, ready to record the feature story of his life.

The judge was a quiet and affable man. He had been elected on a fluke, due to some political mixup. The judge called a special grand jury to indict John T. Scopes. This indicates how seriously that part of Tennessee viewed the heinous offense of teaching evolution, which they all pronounced as though the word began with double EE. The special grand jury was not legal, as the regular grand jury was to convene in a few weeks and the statute provided that a special grand jury could not be called excepting as a certain length of time intervened before the regular jury would assemble and be available.

But even though the statute forbade the calling of the special jury, the crime was so terrible that the case could not be delayed. Then, too, there were other towns in the State that wanted the case, and the judge meant that Dayton should have the honor of prosecuting the boy for teaching science, and he himself would have the glory of defending The Faith. I might also mention that the judge's term would soon expire, and he wanted to run again. Of course, I do not know that this had anything to do with his illegally calling the special grand jury to stop the spread of infidelity in the shortest possible time. And if John T. Scopes was found guilty, the highest penalty that could be inflicted upon him would be a one-hundred-dollar fine. Still, the treason against religion was reason enough for ignoring the law and resorting to a special session to bar the teaching of "EEvolution" in Tennessee.

Tennessee seemed to understand the significance of the battle. Especially did Dayton. Fences, bridges, buildings, streets were placarded with giant signs, and mammoth banners swung from tree to tree in the courtyard that could be easily read a block away summoning the community to *"Come to Jesus,"* *"Prepare to meet thy Maker"*—and the slogan of all the section,

greeting one at every turn, was: *"Read your Bible daily."*
Certainly Tennessee can never be blamed if our souls were
not saved that hot summer, in that torrid land that might
have inspired one to beware of ever going to a hotter clime.

CHAPTER 30

SCIENCE VERSUS FUNDAMENTALISM

It was morning in Tennessee. And it was midsummer. Tennessee must be very close to the equator; or maybe the crust is very thin under this little sin-fearing section, or, where could such hellish heat come from?

The bailiff was calling the court to order, "Tennessee versus Scopes." The judge was sinking into his seat beneath a monster sign, saying, *"Read your Bible daily."* He had a palmleaf fan in one hand, and in the other the Bible and the statutes. As he laid these down on his desk I wondered why he thought he would need the statutes. To the end of the trial I did not know. Judge Raulston wriggled down into his high-backed chair and two tall policemen hopped forward close to his shoulder with Southern courtesy and big palm fans which they fluttered above and around his serious, shining brow. The policemen seemed to appreciate the arduous mental labor going on beneath the skull of the man under their wings.

Down below, at a long table, near the judge's bench, sat William Jennings Bryan, wearing as few clothes as possible. So few, indeed, that had he seen some girl so arrayed he would have considered her a bad sort, and straightway turned his head the other way. His shirt sleeves were rolled up as high as they would go, and his soft collar and shirt front were turned away from his neck and breast about as far as any one less modest would venture; not for the fray, but because of the weather. In his hand was the largest palmleaf fan that could be found, apparently, with which he fought off the heat waves —and flies.

Around Mr. Bryan sat several young men who were to be

his field marshals in this great Waterloo of science. We were facing another big banner dangling from the ceiling over the chairs inside the bar of justice, awaiting the jury, to remind them also to *"Read your Bible daily."* And in other places in the courtroom were other specimens of this. It looked as though there might have been a discount for ordering a wholesale lot.

This important battle between Revealed Religion and Infidelity had been likened to the Crusaders under Richard the Lion-Hearted, instead of Waterloo. Anyhow, there sat Bryan, fanning himself, looking limp and martyr-like between assaults upon the flies that found a choice roosting-place on his bald, expansive dome and bare, hairy arms. He slapped away at them with the big fan, constantly and industriously. Somehow, he did not look like a hero. Or even a Commoner. He looked like a commonplace fly-catcher. It is this picture of Bryan that abides with me. Of course, hair, or the lack of it, has nothing to do with intellect, and much less learning; but then, the day was hot, and sticky, and one cannot look like a hero unless he dresses and poses for the part. And, even then, he should be engaged in something more heroic than swishing flies.

I did not use a fan myself. I had something else to do and think about. Feeling as I did, I would have had to work the fan so fast that it would have made me still hotter. All over the ceiling and walls, from chandeliers and side-brackets, and extra sockets, swung electric wires that were attached to electric fans. It looked as though they might have bought fans wholesale, too. But only the backs of these were turned toward us! All those fans were set to cool the fevered feelings of the judge, the jury, the prosecution and the different distinguished natives invited from day to day to sit alongside "His Honor." And all their friends, the flower of Dayton, and Mr. Bryan and his friends sat in social state as cool and comfortable as possible over in the shady section, opposite our sun-scorched side. As Southern gentlemen, they must have been sorry that there were not enough fans to go around, nor one wee socket left for "the defense."

The lawyers, ranged around Mr. Bryan like a human halo, looked very glum, as though contemplating the safety of their souls, while at our table, in spite of the temperature, were signs of light-heartedness and even frivolity. We must have looked as though we were doomed, so far as being eligible for heaven was concerned, and so were getting the most we could out of Tennessee.

I try never to take things too seriously; if I did, I would have been wiped out long ago. As to the Dayton case, from the beginning it seemed to me a joke. And I was satisfied that it would be only that if we could get the world to see it in its right light, which we did.

The courtroom was packed, and still the people crowded together in the hallways, on the staircases; and the yard, too, was filling up. Spectators had come from near and far. "Hot dog" booths and fruit peddlers and ice-cream venders and sandwich sellers had sprung into existence like mushrooms on every corner and everywhere between, mingling with the rest, ready to feed the throng. Evangelist tents were propped up at vantage points around the town square, where every night one not knowing what was going on would have thought hordes of howling dervishes were holding forth. In reality, they were crying out against the wickedness of Darwin and the rest of us, and advocating as substitutes cool meadows and melodious harps in KINGDOM COME. There was no reason why they should not be prohibitionists, for they were so elated and intoxicated by their religious jags that they needed no other stimulants. Then, too, they had become so immunized to common liquor through their brand of "White Mule" that it required something else to give them any "kick," and religion was doing the trick for some of the most hard-soaked, or sun-baked sinners.

When the courtroom was packed just short of bursting apart, it seemed, the judge ordered the doors closed over the sweltering audience, and with great solemnity and all the dignity possible announced that Brother Twitchell would invoke the Divine blessing. This was new to me. I had practiced law for more than forty years, and had never before heard God called in to referee a court trial. I had likewise been to prize fights and horse races, and these were not opened with prayer. After adjournment we went to the judge and told him that in a case of this nature, especially, we did not consider it fair or suitable to play up their side by opening court proceedings with prayer; it was not a form of church service; it was a trial in a court; and at best it was an unfair weapon to introduce, particularly as the case had a religious aspect.

The lawyers for the prosecution seemed shocked that such an objection and request should be presented. Prayer surely could do no harm. But, of course, it is easy for a lawyer to seem shocked.

Before the opening of the next session I arose and stated what had happened in the matter, pointed out the character of the case, and made my objection to the court opening the proceedings with prayer. The judge overruled the motion, of course. The people assembled looked as though a thunderbolt had stunned them, and the wrath of the Almighty might be hurled down upon the heads of the defense. None of them had ever heard of any one objecting to any occasion being opened or closed or interspersed with prayer. That there should be no dearth of preachers, the court had appointed a committee of church members to keep us supplied, so that there would be a new one at every session of the trial.

I made a complete and aggressive opening of the case. I did this for the reason that we never at any stage intended to make any arguments in the case. We knew that Mr. Bryan was there to make a closing speech about "The Prince of Peace" and the importance of "The Rock of Ages" above the "age of rocks" and that the closing address he meant should thrill the world was doubtless prepared for the press in manifold copies before he left Florida, and that it would be for the consumption and instruction of those who knew nothing about either "The Rock of Ages" or "the age of rocks." We knew that such of the assembled multitudes as had the capacity to understand would refuse to learn. By not making a closing argument on our side we could cut him out.

We realized that a jury drawn from Dayton, Tenn., would not permit a man to commit such a heinous crime as Scopes had been guilty of and allow him to go scot-free. However, there were questions to be argued concerning the meaning of the statute, and what power the legislature had to make the teaching of science a criminal offense.

Then, too, we expected to introduce evidence by experts as to the meaning of the word "evolution" and whether it was inconsistent with "religion" under correct definition of both words. We had assembled many of the best scientists of America to cover these subjects, and Mr. Bryan had given out that he would offer proof that science was in conflict with religion. We knew the names of some of his witnesses, but at the last moment Mr. Bryan's witnesses did not appear, as we feared they would not.

The State brought in a number of bright little boys who were pupils of the school taught by Mr. John T. Scopes. They told how Mr. Scopes had tried to poison their young minds and imperil their souls by telling them that life began in the sea from a single cell that gradually developed into the different structures that are now scattered over the earth. The boys said, on cross-examination, that they did not see how this had done them any harm, but Mr. Bryan and the judge knew better. When court adjourned for luncheon I overheard one of the small boys saying to another, "Don't you think Mr.

Bryan is a little narrowminded?" Plainly, both of these boys had already been corrupted by Scopes. I am afraid their souls will be lost.

It was evident that Scopes was trying to do for Dayton, Tenn., what Socrates did for Athens. And so why should not Dayton, Tenn., do to Scopes what Athens did to Socrates? The State offered the first and second chapters of Genesis as published in the Oxford edition of the Bible, and thus the State's part of the case was finished. To be sure the case had been enlivened by a number of spirited arguments over various questions as we went along. In one of these arguments, Mr. Dudley Field Malone was particularly brilliant in his reply to his former superior officer, Mr. Bryan, in the State Department during the administration of Woodrow Wilson.

But the days of the trial were no more interesting than the night life of Dayton. Pop-corn merchants and sleight-of-hand artists vied with evangelists for the favor and custom of the swarms that surged back and forth along the few squares that were the centre of the community; speeches were bawled at street corners under the glare of trying artificial-lighting arrangements; the venders raised their voices to drown the evangelists who were the old-time sort who seemed to believe every word they said and were really interested in saving souls; and each worked his own side of the street, up and down.

Then over the river, under the trees, a band of Holy Rollers gathered every night. As they grew excited and shouted and sang and twitched and twirled, the people crowded closer around them in curiosity and wonder. Now and then some one would sidle forward from the dark woods and, seeming to be seized with some inspiration, would rush in amongst the other performers and dance and squirm and shout and stutter with such vigor and contortions that the regulars were put to shame for their mild form of worship. All sorts of weird cults were present in Dayton, all joining forces to put up a strong fight against Satan and his cohorts. It was really another Armageddon. Some of the performers were doubtless half-wits and they seemed to more definitely represent sincerity and the will of a supreme force controlling their actions. These increased the value of the services and demonstrations.

On Sundays, and sometimes evenings, Mr. Bryan spoke in the churches. With fifteen hundred inhabitants, Dayton boasted eleven churches. It must have taken some system on the part of the preachers to keep its little population divided into so many congregations. But during the Scopes case Mr. Bryan must have helped a lot to lure listeners in to hear about "The Prince of Peace" and "The Rock of Ages." Bryan's voice would boom out above all other sounds and the audience would be as silent and awed as the other denizens of the wilds were when the lion was abroad at night proclaiming himself king of the jungle realm.

The judge was much impressed with Mr. Bryan as a leader of the faith, and when some question would be raised and argued he would adjourn court for a day or two to consider it and then come in and automatically decide in favor of the mouthpiece of the fundamentalists. Only a small percentage of the people could crowd into the courthouse at any session. The congestion added to the suffocating temperature, and the two policemen were kept busy offsetting the tropical atmosphere around the judge's sanctified spot. One policeman solaced his own stifled feelings with a wad of tobacco that swiftly melted away into a cuspidor at his feet, and the other worked off his pent-up patience on a gob of gum that had the advantage of being of an indestructible brand, so far as could be guessed. Whether he chewed the same flavor as the judge fished out of his mouth and pasted on the underside of his desk every noon after lunch I had no way of knowing. The judge was always a little late coming in, partly because newspaper photographers waylaid him as well as others, and

His Honor was a particularly obliging subject. One noon when he already had called court to order, a camera man, a bit bolder than the rest, took a chance and slipped up to the judge's side, whispering something, whereupon the judge interrupted himself, explaining to the audience that he had been requested to pose for a picture to be hastened East in the afternoon mail, which would take but a few minutes. Instantly the whole body of picture men sprang to their tripods begging leave to snap him at the same time, which he smilingly granted, placing his right hand inside the front of his coat and the left one under the back of it in true statesmanlike fashion, thus accommodating "the boys"—and soon we were back to where we had left off when beginning the afternoon programme. After that, just before court, he would call out in a loud pitch, not unlike an auctioneer sing-songing his "going, going—once, twice,—are there any more bids?—*Gone!*"—that if any one wanted any pictures to please step forward before court convened.

And so it came to pass that there were groups showing Judge Raulston hugging the Bible and the statutes with one arm while being fanned by the two policemen and directing a preacher to invoke the Divine wisdom in settling the momentous question between Charles Darwin and W. J. Bryan; of the judge and the author of "The Prince of Peace" shaking hands for the Sunday Supplement Syndicate, and, at recess one day the august judge let the press have a carefully posed and timed likeness of himself in the act of bringing down the mallet on his desk as though calling some one to order; which I am mentioning because it was said to be the favorite one and best liked by himself as well as by his friends. All in all, that was a summer for the gods!

Even the preachers must have revelled in their master effort; they came forward from the hills to their hallowed duty in Dayton, and with voices hushed or howling and gestures static and ecstatic, trying to seem unconscious of their nice, new clothes, beseeched *Him on high* to pay attention to the "EEvolution" case, confidently and intimately intoning and cajoling up to God about as a snake-charmer or voodoo-conjurer would handle the job, not forgetting to also bless the Associated and the United Press boys.

The trial wore on, the sun waxed hotter and the palm-leaf fans grew in size and number as at each session, by magic, a few more, and still more, people were wedged in, and the crowd in the yard thickened and multiplied. Rumors began to go the round to the effect that there was danger of the floor in the courtroom giving way. The exact origin of this report was never quite made known, but together with that came another pretty generally credited to the judge, suggesting that a platform should be built down on the ground and the case continued outdoors. The crowd readily seconded the motion, and no one blamed the judge, for it was his first, and, as it turned out, his last real appearance, excepting for a few vagrant lectures that he attempted on or against "EEvolution" after the trial was over. So we moved down to the courthouse lawn.

So far the jury had been excluded from the courtroom, until the judge could write his opinion on various questions of law. The jurors had spent their time circulating with the throng, acquaintances and friends and strangers; but on the afternoon of this historic day the stage seemed cleared for action; the workmen had put up a platform, had erected a throne for "the court" and set apart a space for the lawyers. The jury was given front seats, and right before them was a great sign flaunting letters two feet high, where every one could see the magic words: "READ YOUR BIBLE DAILY." As for the improved accommodations for the audience—well, there were now acres of audience, branching off into the surrounding streets, waiting for the curtain to rise.

I began the proceedings by calling attention to the flaming instructions to the populace and the jury to *"Read your Bible daily"* and made a motion, for the sake of getting it into the record, pointing out the very evident purpose of influencing the jury, and asked to have the banner removed. Every one paused in awe at the audacity, but it was not a rainy day so that I was taking no chance with lightning. The judge and all the rest of the prosecution expressed great astonishment at any such motion; Mr. Bryan's voice rose above all the others. However, we stood our ground until the attorneys for the prosecution rather thought that we might be right about its being "a bit thick" and consented to the removal of the blessed banner.

The judge had admitted one of our witnesses to give testimony as to the meaning of the word "evolution" and to describe the process of it as taught. This was Doctor Metcalf, of Oberlin College, a man whose attainments were everywhere recognized. Then I called Mr. W. J. Bryan as an expert on the meaning of the word "religion." At once every lawyer for the prosecution was on his feet objecting to the proceeding. The judge asked me if I considered it important. I reminded him that the statute was based on a conflict between evolution and religion, and that we were entitled to prove the meaning of the words so that the jury could determine whether there was any conflict. Mr. Bryan relieved the situation by saying that he was perfectly willing to take the stand, that he was ready to defend religion anywhere against any infidel. He said that he wanted to go on the stand on condition that I would go. I said that they could put me on at any time they wished and I would try to answer their questions. And of course this left the judge with nothing to decide.

CHAPTER 31

THE BRYAN FOUNDATION

When Mr. Bryan took the stand, I began by asking him concerning his qualifications to define religion, and especially fundamentalism, which was the State religion of Tennessee. In response to my questions he said that he had been a student of religion all his life, that he was familiar with a great deal of the literature concerning Christianity and the Bible; that he had lectured on religious subjects at religious meetings and Chautauqua gatherings for years; that for a long time he had been conducting a Bible class at Miami on Sundays during the winter season, and that for a number of years he had written weekly syndicate letters for various publications extending over the country; that he had spoken on evolution in many college towns in the North and had been active in getting the Tennessee statute through the legislature and in urging similar statutes in various other States.

Then I proceeded with questions that brought out points illustrating the fundamentalists' ideas of the Bible and religion. These questions were practically the same that I had prepared and had published in a Chicago paper two years earlier. These questions were prepared because Mr. Bryan had submitted a list of questions through the press to the President of Wisconsin University, which appeared in the Chicago *Tribune* in July, 1923. My questions were presented in the same month, in reply to Mr. Bryan's. Needless to say, when I ventured those questions two years before I got no answer. *The Tribune* had him interviewed at Winona Lake, Ind., where he was attending a religious convention, and he replied that he had not read my questions; that Mr. Darrow was an agnostic, and that he had no quarrel with agnostics, that his controversy was with men who pretended to be Christians but were not Christians. Even had he read the questions propounded two years before he would have been compelled to choose between his crude beliefs and the common intelligence of modern times.

Now Bryan twisted and dodged and floundered, to the disgust of the thinking element, and even his own people. That night an amount of copy was sent out that the reporters claimed was unprecedented in court trials. My questions and Bryan's answers were printed in full, and the story seems to have reached the whole world.

When court adjourned it became evident that the audience had been thinking, and perhaps felt that they had heard something worth while. Much to my surprise, the great gathering began to surge toward me. They seemed to have changed sides in a single afternoon. A friendly crowd followed me toward my home. Mr. Bryan left the grounds practically alone. The people seemed to feel that he had failed and deserted his cause and his followers when he admitted that the first six days might have been periods of millions of ages long. Mr. Bryan had made himself ridiculous and had contradicted his own faith. I was truly sorry for Mr. Bryan. But I consoled myself by thinking of the years through which he had busied himself tormenting intelligent professors with impudent questions about their faith, and seeking to arouse the ignoramuses and bigots to drive them out of their positions. It is a terrible transgression to intimidate and awe teachers with fear of want.

The next morning I reached court prepared to continue the examination all that day. The judge convened court down in the yard, and another preacher asked the blessing and guidance of the Almighty. After allowing time for taking pictures, the judge arose, rested one hand on the statutes and the other on the Oxford Bible, and said that he had been thinking over the proceedings of the day before AND—in spite of Mr. Bryan's willingness again to take the stand—he believed that the testimony was not relevant, and he had decided to refuse to permit any further examination of Mr. Bryan and should strike the whole of his testimony from the record. Mr. Bryan and his associates forgot to look surprised. It needed no lawyer to grasp that the attorneys for the prosecution could see the effect Mr. Bryan's answers were having on their case and the public in general, and had concluded that something must be done; so it was arranged that the judge should be there in the morning to relieve them of their distress in court. The ruling of the court was by that time extended to forbid the testimony of our scientists as to the meaning of evolution.

The court held that the jury had the statute before them and had heard the testimony of the witnesses proving that Scopes had told his pupils that life began in the sea and had gradually evolved to the various forms of life, including man, that now live upon the earth. The State had offered in evidence the first and second chapters of Genesis, and the jury could judge whether these were in conflict with the teaching of Scopes.

We all agreed that the ruling of the court had made it impossible to introduce any evidence, and useless to make any arguments. The attorneys for Mr. Scopes were satisfied that what we had undertaken, the awakening of the country to what was going on, had succeeded beyond our fondest hopes. Every one had been informed that a body of men and women were seeking to make the schools the servants of the church, and to place bigotry and ignorance on the throne. It was some satisfaction to know that in this organization were very few scholars or men of intelligence, and that the great mass of their following was mostly the illiterate.

We knew that it was hopeless to fight again for a verdict in Tennessee so long as the State remained in its present stage of civilization. All that was left was to take the case to the Supreme Court of Tennessee, and, in the event of defeat, to carry it to the Supreme Court of the United States, if the Fourteenth Amendment was broad enough to give the Federal Court jurisdiction.

The State opened the case with a short address, whereupon we waived our argument and submitted it to the jury. This made it impossible for Mr. Bryan to deliver the speech already prepared so long in advance. This was really a pity, because of all the copies thus withheld from the press. In a short time the jury reported a verdict which was delivered by the foreman, who was by all odds the best looking and most carefully dressed of any member of the twelve, or, for that matter, of any one else in the room. The verdict of course found Scopes "Guilty." It might be mentioned that the next autumn the foreman ran for a county office on the strength of his loyal service to the State of Tennessee and Genesis and his good looks. The court then entered the verdict and fined Mr. Scopes one hundred dollars, and, as Bret Harte once wrote, in relation to a fist fight in Virgin City, Nev., over a dispute on religion: "The cause of infidelity was beaten on that day."

We made the necessary motions for an appeal to the Supreme Court of Tennessee and asked the court to permit John T. Scopes to be released on bond, which was promptly furnished by the Baltimore *Sun*. And then the court adjourned.

The next day was Saturday, and I went to the Big Smoky Mountains in search of a breeze. On Sunday, at sunset, as I was turning back from the walk we had taken to the top, I was met by a reporter with the news of Mr. Bryan's death. The newspapers, next morning, carried the announcement that he was to have spoken on the Sunday afternoon and evening in some town outside Dayton, and had eaten an unusually heavy Sunday dinner and had gone to his bedroom for a nap, and when the family went to call him they found him dead. The irony of fate—a man who for years had fought excessive drinking lay dead from indigestion caused by over-eating.

When he came to Dayton his health was much impaired. He had been cautioned by physicians against over-eating, and no doubt he was somewhat weakened by the extreme heat; and his anxieties and efforts in the case, which perhaps were all the greater because he was not familiar with court proceedings, must have told on him. The too generous meal, with the thermometer around a hundred degrees, brought on his death. Right after the trial, Mr. Bryan had delivered to the newspaper representatives copies of the address that he had meant to make to the jury, but they had declined to carry it. However, after his death, some of them did publish it. It was loaded with the religious aphorisms that he had revelled in for so many years.

It developed that he had long desired that when the time came he should be buried in Arlington, in the government cemetery. He had raised a company of soldiers in Nebraska for the Cuban War and was made colonel of the regiment. While the company never got beyond Florida, this activity gave the basis for a burial in Arlington. Perhaps no man is really ever consistent, but it seems passing strange that after years of talks on "The Prince of Peace," and resignation from Woodrow Wilson's Cabinet because of his disapproval of our entrance into the World War, he should, at his own request, at last lie buried in Arlington.

Judge Raulston, not easily daunted, achieved some further glory through speech-making in fundamentalist churches on the evolution question as he saw it. He was eminently qualified; he had never read a line on the subject, and very little on any other, and had held that to teach evolution was a criminal offense in Tennessee and therefore presumably wicked everywhere. But there was no great rush at the box office to attend his lectures, so he went back to his home town in

Tennessee, and when his term expired he ran for re-election, but was defeated for nomination. Later he tried to get the nomination for governor of the State as honor and glory for having served the Lord, but was beaten in that lofty ambition. So it was "back to the mines," and he resumed trying replevin cases and collecting bills for the town merchants.

The county superintendent of schools who had employed Mr. Scopes also ran for an office in the autumn after the case was tried. He circulated his cards through the State, which bore the glorious emblem "Prosecutor of John T. Scopes." But Tennessee once more proved itself ungrateful; he was not nominated. Dayton and Tennessee had been given all the notoriety out of the case that it deserved. So the county superintendent, whose name I believe was White, though it might have been Smith or Jones, or even Black, also returned "to the mines," although I believe that he was a carpenter, or perhaps a plumber.

Mr. Bryan lost his hold in Tennessee when he testified in court, but his tragic end, which came so soon after, restored him to their hearts. Great throngs of people visited the little house in Dayton to take a last look at their hero. All the people of that section seemed to be at the funeral. Then he was taken by a special car to Arlington. The train stopped at all the towns on the route. It took a long time to make the journey, for everywhere a large concourse of mourning friends stood waiting, sometimes for hours, with wreaths and furled flags, in sorrowful remembrance of their lost leader. This out-turning of admirers ended only when they laid him in his grave. I am sincere in saying that I am sorry that he could not have seen all this devotion that followed him to his resting-place.

Mr. Bryan's friends afterwards formed an organization to build a great monument in Washington, in testimony of his labors. It was to be provided with a number of bells which should chime over the city every hour. On the committee were governors of States, senators, congressmen, preachers, and devoted friends and politicians anxious to preserve his name and fame and the causes for which he fought. Secretary Josephus Daniels, of North Carolina, was chairman. But the money was never raised, and the building and tower never adorned Washington, and the chimes never disturbed the sleep of the just who live in Washington.

Another organization was formed to build a university in Dayton, to be named for him. Mr. Robinson, in whose now-famous drug store occurred the argument that led to the evolution case, was, and probably is, treasurer of the enterprise. Agents and representatives of this undertaking are scattered over the country. Wide-awake land owners in Dayton donated some forty acres for the site. This is located on a hillside overlooking a very beautiful valley stretching off to the Blue Ridge Mountains beyond. The land donated, however, has no value except for a fundamentalist college and for scenery, and a broad vista of the Bible belt. Somehow, the memorial does not prosper. Dayton has had her day in the sun. In the summer of 1928 I drove through that lovely valley across the old battle-ground, and was warmly received by many gracious friends who gave me a dinner in the Aqua Hotel, a name more suitable for an oasis in a desert than a hotel in that arid place. My hosts drove me to the grounds of the Bryan University that was to be, a really sightly spot. Here they had dug a deep hole, perhaps a hundred feet wide and two hundred feet long and ten or fifteen feet deep. And this was what there was of the Bryan University. The patrons of fundamentalism had somehow not come through. The trustees were hoping to get something from the Bryan estate, but had been disappointed. The family was slow about tendering the money, but was to donate his library; but it is safe to guess that Bryan's books would be a total loss for any real university. And then, that kind of a school would need only the Oxford Bible. My latest information is that the hole is still there on the lovely hillside, wide enough, long enough and deep enough for a fitting grave for the monster project. Bigotry and opposition to learning are not a good foundation for any university in these modern times.

Eventually I went to Nashville, the capital of Tennessee, to argue the evolution case before the Supreme Court of the State. In addition to the force of lawyers of the Dayton trial, two of the ablest lawyers of Tennessee joined us in the argument. The court extended the time to double the length given by the rules. The State also had new recruits; two of the most important lawyers of Nashville having allied themselves with the prosecution.

Ascending the slope toward the State House, I found the streets full of people, the State House grounds teeming with men and women who wanted to hear the arguments of both sides. As in Dayton, the courthouse and grounds were packed beyond capacity. The court consisted of pleasant, dignified men who did their best to have every one well treated and given as much consideration as was possible with such a throng. The distinguished gentleman who made the closing argument for the prosecution spoke of the importance of the case to the people of Tennessee, and about how God-fearing fathers and mothers would feel when their children came home from school infected by this dangerous heresy. He is really an able man, and made a good argument for his side. Perhaps the crowded courtroom filled with his neighbors and friends and admirers inspired him in his closing remarks; at any rate, when he finished there was a general burst of applause through the building, even in the halls and adjoining offices, as might have been expected in Tennessee. But the court, like the rest of us, were no doubt taken by surprise, so let it pass, as it seemed and doubtless was best.

I was selected to close the case, and was given plenty of time.

The court and every one else paid the closest possible attention, as I aimed to put the matter plainly and simply without flourishes of any sort. I sympathized with my opponent about the sorrow of fathers and mothers when they found that the children were leaving them behind, but, that was the way of life, and the old have no right to stand in the way of the young. I made no effort at effect, but when I closed I was amazed that the whole room and adjoining offices broke forth in spontaneous applause far greater than had rewarded my opponent, and the court made no sign to check it; the previous outbursts having been allowed to go unnoticed and unremarked, this received the same right.

A year went by before the court handed down a decision. Five judges heard the argument of the case. In the meantime one had died. The opinion was rendered by four. They unanimously decided that the case should be reversed because the court instead of the jury had fixed the fine. Also, they said that there was no reason why Tennessee should be further burdened with the case, and they ordered the attorney general to dismiss it. However, each judge wrote an opinion as to how he construed the anti-evolution law. Two of them said that the law was constitutional; one of them held that it was unconstitutional; and one held that it was constitutional but had no application to the Scopes case; that it was only meant to forbid the teaching of materialism. But all the opinions were no part of the decision of the case, being what is in law called *obiter dicta,* as the case was reversed and dismissed.

A few months later the National Association for the Advancement of Science met in Nashville. The chief justice referred to the Scopes case in a jocular vein, and told the scientists that they need have no fear over expressing their views on evolution openly in that State.

Tennessee never deserved all the unfavorable notoriety that the fundamentalists brought to it. The legislature that passed the foolish law was not elected for that purpose. No campaign was made on the issue. Very few of the members knew anything about evolution. All they had heard on the subject had come from their local ministers. What they said, of course, did not add to knowledge. The question was suddenly sprung on them while Mr. Bryan was making his campaign against education. No one met the challenge and it went through by default. I met a great many intelligent people in Tennessee who did not believe in the law. There are a great many bright young men and women in the State who are graduates of universities, most of them evolutionists. In fact, there is no other theory to teach regarding the origin of the various animal species, including man. Evolution is absolutely a necessary theory for the physician, or any one who inquires or desires a liberal education.

Tennessee is a Southern State and, like all the South, was almost destroyed by the Civil War and reconstruction, and like the rest of the South, has never recovered from the scourge. The great movements in science and general progress that remade the North passed by the South, that was then trying to raise itself out of the ruin and desolation of the war. Tennessee was a border State who sent its quota to both North and South. She was riven with internal discord as well as with war. But, Tennessee is nevertheless farther north than most of the other Southern States. She is rich in natural resources, is very productive, and is already beginning to feel the pulsations of a new life. In natural beauty no State surpasses her. A large proportion of her people live in good-sized towns and cities. There are four really large cities in that State, and these cities contain a large fraction of the residents of Tennessee. Cities always lead the thought and trend and enterprise of the world; but, due to a foolish law, Tennessee is classed all over the world as a backward community. Yet Tennessee cannot much longer be led by the ignorant country preachers, the Holy Rollers, and the other weird sects that flourish in the fastnesses of the lonely mountains and the poverty and undevelopment and mental vacuity that goes with wide distances and deadly isolation. I prophesy that it will be only a few years before the senseless statute will be wiped from her books either by repeal or the decision of a final court.

During the trial of this bizarre case I felt that the attorneys for the defense were sadly misunderstood; in only a limited number of the papers did we get the credit we deserved. We entered this case solely to induce the public to stop, look and listen, lest our public schools should be imperilled with a fanaticism founded on ignorance. We believed that unless the public could be awakened soon it would be too late. Whether history will ever give us credit for accomplishing it I do not care. It can do me no personal good at my time of life, but I feel sure that what we did was right. There is reason now for feeling confident that no more States will permit their fanatics to place them in the position of Tennessee without any pecuniary reward; and in spite of an unpleasant notoriety we accomplished this result.

It is true that many people did not appreciate the peril that confronted the freedom of education, although the sharpshooters of bigotry were picking off its victims in our schools and colleges day after day. I used to sit in the courthouse and note how exactly Mr. Bryan represented the spirit of intolerance that he sat fanning into flame. He had greatly changed in recent years. The one-time sense of humor that softened his nature had been driven out by disappointments and vain ambitions. In his last days he had the appearance of one who felt the injustice of many defeats and welcomed the chance to get even with an alien world. He did not grow old gracefully. Instead of disarming the enemy with a smile and a joke as once was his wont, he now snarled and scolded when any one stood in the way of his dreams.

I see him now as he sat in Dayton in that country courtroom in those blazing July days. Where was the pleasing smile of his youth which had so often lighted his face and his path? The merry twinkle had vanished from his eyes, his head was entirely bald save for two tufts of bristles back of the ears, his thin lips set in a long straight line across his face, his huge jaw pushed forward, stern and cruel and forbidding, immobile and unyielding as an iron vise. His speculations had ripened into unchangeable convictions. He did not think. He knew. His eyes plainly revealed mental disintegration. He had always been inordinately conceited and self-confident, but he had not been cruel or malignant. But his whole makeup had evidently changed, and now he was a wild animal at bay. I sat watching him. I had known him well in our early years. I told my associates that I could see the rapid decay that had come upon him. He had reached a stage of hallucination that would impel him to commit any cruelty that he believed would help his cause. History is replete with men of this type, and they have added sorrow and desolation to the world.

And yet no right-thinking person can blame them, but can only be sorry for their plight, and combat the spirit of fanaticism and cocksureness that has brought them to such a state. I truly felt sorry for Mr. Bryan. I had to a certain extent followed him through his career, had recognized his idealism and zeal and force, and it was a shock to me to see this concentrated energy and power turned to wormwood and gall through failure and despair and bigotry.

None of the attorneys on our side asked for or wanted any compensation. We raised the money to pay the expenses of the case, and I think each of us paid his own. For myself, I took my household to Tennessee and lived as nearly as I could in the way I did in Chicago. Besides this, I made three trips to New York City and two to Tennessee. I was out not less than two thousand dollars, but I believed that the cause was worth while, and was always glad that I helped.

It was gratifying to find that even though the case was not taken seriously by the public, still, the able scientists who were with us at Dayton, Tennessee, did realize the worth and importance of our labors. These well-known scientists gratuitously sent me a copy of a letter that was addressed to Doctor Pupin, of Columbia College, New York City, who was president of their organization, which reads as follows:

Dayton, Tennessee, July 17, 1925.

Dear Doctor Pupin:

In addition to the letter enclosed, you may be interested to know that different ones of our scientific group here, I believe all of them, have expressed to Clarence Darrow personally their genuine respect for his ability, high purposes, integrity, moral sensitiveness and idealism, and their warm personal regard. He has been really the controlling counsel and doubtless will be in the further proceedings. I am sending this letter for your personal information, after showing it to all of these men, and they cordially approve it.

Faithfully yours,

(Signed) MAYNARD M. METCALF.

Endorsed: H. H. Newman, Fay Cooper Cole, W. C. Curtis, Jacob Lipman, Watson Davis, Frank E. A. Thorne, Wilson A. Nelson, Wm. A. Kepner.

CHAPTER 32

A "DRY" AMERICA

A SENSATIONAL case is always followed by a great influx of mail. During the Loeb-Leopold case I made no effort to read the letters from all parts of the country; most of these were from cranks. The Scopes case brought even more mail and more outbursts still more fanatical; and as usual I could not, and would not, try to examine them, but at intervals gathered a number of persons around a table who opened and read, or partially read, some of the most important or personal letters. But many contained foolish criticisms, threats, advice, and sometimes intelligent suggestions. Answering them was out of the question.

The number of people on the borderline of insanity in a big country is simply appalling, and these seem especially addicted to believing themselves saviors and prophets. It takes only a slight stimulus to throw them entirely off their balance. Perhaps nothing so contributes to this as a religious controversy. Men's opinions on this subject are so carefully instilled that it seems to them a personal affront not to believe in their creeds. Now and then devout Christians wrote me kindly, anxious letters begging me to come into the fold before it would be too late, and some told of prayer circles organized to implore the Lord to make me see the light, and countless well-meaning ones have written me through the years about offering up their prayers for me at certain hours of the evening and morning, and have dedicated to me little compositions of their own, meant to be little hymns and designed to make me want to meet them in heaven.

One woman came to me in Dayton, Tenn., introducing herself as one of an organization who were daily praying for me, reporting that she had asked Mr. Bryan what he thought of the plan, and he had replied that the Lord might possibly aid them in their effort, but he thought it highly improbable. I treated all these efforts with friendliness when they came to my attention, but this, too, was dangerous and annoying, for zealots need but little encouragement to lead them to redouble their attempts.

Even after I had returned to Chicago many of these soul-savers were still in pursuit with the evident mission of saving me from self-destruction. If I answered them kindly I would receive longer and more irrational discourses, until finally I would be forced to consign them all to the waste basket unopened. One ambitious Southern preacher wrote me urgently to embrace religion. He hoped that I could be prevailed upon to profess faith and be baptized. He said he was a young man with a small country congregation; that if I would consent to it he would come to Chicago to do the baptizing, and it would do him a lot of good and greatly help his standing with his church down South. I sent him a line saying that as I was feeling at that time it looked as though I should die without ever being baptized, but that if I changed my mind I would let him know. But as I forgot to save his address, I could not be baptized by him if I wished to. So I shall probably get along without it.

The inundation of letters continued for months, and even years, but gradually they have grown fewer, although they still come, and probably always will. I have so long been interested in psychiatry that I rather easily gauge the mind and personality of a letter-writer. In fact, there is nothing this side of real mania that is so sure a key to a disordered brain as letters. The most pronounced cases of insanity can generally be detected from the address on the envelope. I seldom miss a guess from this alone, and strangely, or not, most of them are from women who, if not wholly mentally irresponsible, are at least victims of hallucinations and hysteria.

The senseless criticism against the defense of insanity seems to impress the public. Newspapers and individuals constantly belittle this defense, and still, given any general test, it is more apt to indicate insanity than criminality. It is constantly being claimed that there is an increase of criminals, while the fact is that insanity is very much more rapidly increasing throughout the world. Most of the unbalanced minds go through life without being detected or recognized as such. These do the hard work and disagreeable tasks, and are really most important to the community. When some unusual strain is placed upon them they are swung off their equilibrium, and as life grows more strenuous and complex and exacting the cases of overtaxed minds and nerves multiply accordingly. Most of these cases could get by under fairly primitive conditions, but they crack easily in an automobile or airplane or stock-market age. The number of men who even try to understand the workings of the human mind are very few. When one seriously undertakes to discover the motive forces that determine conduct he finds a new field opening before him. If this does not make him wiser, it at least makes him more kindly and considerate in his judgment of men.

For many years I have been in the habit of speaking at all sorts of gatherings. I presume this is because I have an urge to fight injustice. Never at any time would I speak for any cause in which I did not believe. From time to time I have changed and modified my beliefs, but whenever I have spoken the audience was sure of getting my real attitude at the time. Frequently I have come to the conclusion that some view I once held was not sound, and have often felt that I have magnified some special idea far beyond its value; if one is interested in the truth, he should constantly examine and re-examine his own convictions from all possible points of view, both old and new. I am inclined to think that every one is a propagandist by nature. When one has an idea, he feels it his duty to share it with his fellow man. People want every one to believe as they believe, to see as they see, regardless of whether the new viewpoint would make them happy or not. And in this I have always been like the rest. I have sought to convert people when I knew that I could not do it, and when I was not sure that it would help them if they exchanged their views for those that I held. And all my life I have observed that others do exactly the same thing.

Our Christian brethren raise money and send their missionaries to foreign lands in the endeavor to get the natives to accept a new religion in place of the ones that they and their forefathers have long believed. These same people are forever asking me why I try to make others unhappy by robbing them of their religion. The disciples of other countries in turn come to us to point out the truth and utility of their creeds. Very few ever make a careful examination of any faith to determine whether it is true or false; they assume the verity of the one they have adopted. The majority of people accept the views of those around them, in religion, politics, and social conduct. But somehow I seemed not to be of that majority, but with the minority. Indeed, the fact that the majority believed a thing always made me doubt its worth. So, when I have spoken, as I have for so many years, it has been for the minority people and the minority views.

When I came back from the Scopes case I wanted to give up the law. I had practiced almost fifty years, and for a long time had wanted to stop. But it is not easy to follow one's inclinations. It is not easy to establish a law business, and it is just as hard to give it up. After a lifetime of law or medicine there are

Made by Velona, during the
murder trial of three Italians
in New York City.

From *The World*, 1924.

TO MR. DARROW
WITH KINDEST
REGARDS FROM
DON WOOTTON
CLEVELAND PLAIN DEALER
1926

DON WOOTTON

A cartoon by Don Wootton, made during a lecture in Cleveland, 1926.

always some who feel that no one else can save them if they are troubled or ill, and it is not easy to resist their pleadings, even when one is convinced that it is wrong to yield.

After the Scopes case there came an avalanche of invitations to speak, and these were from every section of the country. Lecture bureaus made alluring offers, none of which I accepted, for I did not like the sort of publicity and advertising that seem necessary for carrying on their work. All sorts of associations asked me to talk about the subjects that interested them, and so thought them important. Inclination led me in the direction of speaking, however, and for months my publicity got me crowded houses wherever I went, and often a great number were turned away. This, too, was very wearing, especially as I no longer had the strength of earlier years. Still, I often filled engagements in different parts of the country, at inconvenience, and through this activity and absence I was able to gradually begin my withdrawal from the practice of law. New questions are always arising to divide the people, all of which creates discussion. One that has most vitally provoked me of late is prohibition.

Ideas have come and gone, but I have always been a champion of the individual as against the majority and the State. I advocate the fullest liberty of self-expression, and long before prohibition became the policy of the United States I had fought for the right of the individual to choose his own life. By that I mean, doing the things that he wants to do.

Of all the political leaders of the past, Thomas Jefferson made the strongest appeal to me. Personally, I never cared much for intoxicating liquor. I never drank to excess. I have occasionally taken wine or whiskey, but never regularly or in any way that could possibly be called a habit. So far as I personally was concerned, the use of liquor in any form would never have influenced or affected me, but in prohibition I saw a grievous and far-reaching menace to the right of the individual. I knew it was supported by all the forces that were hostile to human freedom. I foresaw that it meant a fanaticism and intolerance that would hesitate at nothing to force its wishes and ways of life upon the world. The line between what should be the rights of the individual and the power of the state has never been clearly drawn; in fact, no one can set down a hard and fast rule for settling the limitations with any certainty. Still, broadly speaking, humans are divided into two classes; one of these is always urging more laws and stricter rules for each and all; the other faction is ever doubtful and distrustful of authority, and does not believe in the wisdom of the mob. These thoughtful, inquiring ones fear the majority. They know how tyrannical and unscrupulous the majority has always been; they know the conceit of the ignorant, the intolerance of the bigot, and they instinctively fight for the rights of the individual against the crowd. In this contest I am, and always have been, with the individual battling for the right to express himself in his own life regardless of the mob. Essentially, the problem of prohibition, like many another, is a question of attitudes.

Long before the adoption of the Eighteenth Amendment and the Volstead Act, I did everything in my power with addresses in public and articles in periodicals to protest against the rising danger. For seventy-five or a hundred years most of the evangelical churches of America have been the meeting places for all sorts of restrictive measures. Beginning in the early colonies, especially in Massachusetts, capital punishment was inflicted for the practice of witchcraft. Under those statutes old women were hanged for an offense that never had any existence. The criminal code was one of the bloodiest that the world has ever known. If a child struck its parent it could be put to death, but the parent could strike the child with impunity. It was a crime to take a journey on Sunday. All sorts of work and play on the Sabbath were forbidden by the severest penalties. Many of these statutes are still in operation in the United States, and an organized society of fanatics send out their moronic literature and constantly appear before legislative bodies to urge penalties against any one who works or plays on the day they hold sacred, and to forbid all amusements and diversions of all sorts on Sunday except going to church. This is done on the theory that if there is no other place open on Sunday many people will feel compelled to go to church. Theatres were forbidden in New England not only on Sunday but on every day of the week. Even to-day the Methodist Association for Temperance Prohibition and Public Morals send out their literature denouncing the theatres.

This association, from its convenient vantage-ground, across the street from our National Capitol, keep men on guard to watch if perchance any one may smile on Sunday, or may have any real pleasure at any time. And then they browbeat and intimidate weak-kneed and weak-minded legislators to pass their absurd and outrageous laws. Their leaflets, that they send out by the million, urge all sorts of Sunday legislation. They condemn all dancing. They oppose all theatre-going. They propose legislation against the use of tobacco in every form, and card-playing is frowned upon. A world made over by this organization would banish all real enjoyment and entertainment from the earth.

The rural districts of America have always been overwhelmingly Protestant. Up to forty or fifty years ago the great majority of our people lived in villages and outlying sections. Such organizations as I have mentioned, together with the old-time temperance society, furnished the social life of the natives of a bygone period. The early emigrants from the country to the city carried with them the customs, habits, religion, and stern views of life that go with new communities. They were people who were converted by the old-time revivalists and were nourished upon the old prohibition speeches of men like

Gough and Murphy, who were wont to go up and down the land inoculating their hearers with the religious and social bigotries that always prevail in the isolated passes and unfrequented stretches of a new nation. Literature, art and learning were slow in reaching the waste and unready areas. The Protestant churches and lonely schoolhouses in the vast unsettled prairies were the centres of social exchange, and there was little incentive for original liberal ideas.

Cheap land, abundant natural resources, and hard work brought prosperity to the early settlers who drifted to America. This degree of wealth had been entirely unknown to their native life. Their good fortune gave them plenty to eat, and, when a peasant people first get plenty of food they eat too much; some of them also enjoyed getting something to drink, and it was not the beer and light wines they had known at home, but was the stronger liquors which are indigenous to sparse populations. They not only ate too much but they drank too much. Moderation in eating and drinking comes only with civilization and culture. No one paid any attention to over-eating, but over-drinking furnished a spectacular and colorful example to the propagandists. There were always more graves filled from over-eating than over-drinking, but the gluttons quietly groaned their lives away without exhibiting any hilarity or undue emotion in the process, and so were unmolested. On the contrary, the drunkards boisterously and riotously, and, to all appearances, with great glee reeled into their drunkards' graves.

Puritanism has always associated pleasure with sin. To the real Puritan, life is a grim, depressing duty; this earth is nothing but a preparatory school for entering heaven. And to be happy in heaven, one must be unhappy here. So the old revivalist and temperance reformer had no difficulty in holding up the drunkard as a horrible example: Just see how happy and carefree and unmeddlesome he was; always so satisfied with his lot in life and willing that every one else should do as he liked; naturally there was something wrong with such a method of living. The glutton dragged himself to the meeting and shouted "Amen!" in the right places, a friend to heartburn but not to hiccough. It was not difficult to teach the people that all the evil of this world came from *rum*.

The temperance societies, like The Good Templars, superintended the social gatherings. Their speeches were about *The Demon Rum*. Their songs were moving exhortations against rum and its dangers and downfalls; some of their favorite "recitations" were "Father, dear father, come home with me now," and "Lips that touch liquor shall never touch mine," which poetical classics, from generation to generation, would be followed with warnings about the first drop being the fatal one; after that there was small chance of saving the soul from everlasting damnation, so all the young men there must not wait another minute but come forward at once and sign the pledge and never go anywhere without the little white ribbon in the coat lapel to scare off the tempter.

Going to the theatre was forbidden, but the town halls and schools were permitted to present "Ten Nights in a Barroom," and this touching "mellow" drama furnished the old and young with all the histrionic art that was good for them. It was in vain that these primitive folk were told that few people of intelligence and culture ever lived who did not drink. It was in vain that the old classics mentioned the taking and enjoying of liquor as freely as the temperance preachers spoke of corned beef and cabbage and fried chicken with their savory flavors and odors.

Devouring all the food that one could hold was praiseworthy. But drinking liquor, even one mouthful, was damnable. No one talked temperance in eating, nor drinking—only total abstinence from *rum*. They read their Bibles, calmly forgetting the statement of Solomon, God's wisest man: "Give strong drink unto him that is ready to perish, and wine unto those that be of heavy heart. Let him drink and forget his poverty, and remember his misery no more."

They had church suppers on all the established religious holidays and anniversaries, and on as many local and special ones as they could invent and afford, these celebrations being chiefly competitions among the women to furnish the greatest possible amount of the richest, most palatable and irresistible, but wickedly indigestible and injurious, dishes, with each family donating a share of "refreshments" feeling insulted and hurt if any one declined to "taste it" and brag about it, and even take a second helping. Only when it became "impossible to swallow another mouthful," were they allowed to stop stuffing themselves with chicken, pork-and-beans, apple dumplings, cottage cheese, sausage and buckwheat cakes, corn muffins, noodles, cider and grapejuice, onions, waffles and honey, catsup, fried fish, sourkraut, headcheese, hot bread, jellies, soda biscuits, pigs' feet, sardines, coffee and doughnuts, crumpets, rich gravies, rice, and cream "that you could cut with a knife" and preserves and pickles and cucumber "delight" and homemade pepper-sauce and banana-fritters and horseradish and maple syrup, and root beer and cocoa and lemonade, and milk, and cold meats on the side, and salmon, and smoked raw ham and things like that for the first course; after that came mince pie, caramel custard, more coffee (of course), tarts, cocoanut kisses, seed cookies, floating island, combination salad with much mayonnaise, and no stint of whipped cream, and devil's food and angel's food and layer cakes, and ice cream and hot chocolate and suet-pudding and candy and raisins and nuts, until none of them could down another crumb that day. But each family carefully collected whatever was left over to take home and consume the next day before it could spoil, while the men and those who were not needed to help clear off the tables ranged themselves in the assembly hall and listened sanctimoniously to the sinfulness of even a sip of liquor and how such an act would forever disgrace the guilty one, and all his immediate family and even distant relatives. Every man should show his strength of character by totally abstaining from strong drink and come to church and gorge himself like a gentleman with the respectable people who are so much better off attending oyster festivals than rum debauches, because it is a crime to spend father's savings for too much *drink* instead of buying shoes with it for little Willie.

Then they unanimously offered a hearty vote of thanks for the good uplifting "remarks" and said that wine and real beer were the invention of Satan himself; once more they signed the pledge and solemnly vowed never to take a drink, and coaxed others to come forward and put their names down, too. Then, a soulful prayer asking that they might never weaken but stick to their pledge, and although they could hardly waddle they made their way home, where they managed to amble around long enough to concoct doses for indigestion and gas pains, mixing mustard plasters for the outside, while they couldn't understand why they should have gout, and were afraid the new doctor was not all that he should be because the pills he gave hadn't yet stopped the rheumatism that seemed to be coming on again. And with all the self-love of their kind they would have a last little chat about the excellent progress being made by the workers in saving people from too much liquor, and would absorb a few spoonfuls of sulphur-and-molasses because they thought they looked a little florid and their blood might be out of order. The next morning they would tell about not having slept well, and read advertisements to find out if possibly they might have liver complaint, on account of having a strange dizzy feeling every time they woke up in the night. They did not even know that a glass of rum would have helped digestion.

It was on this popular foundation that prohibitionists organized their forces and waged the campaign to destroy the liberties of American citizens. It was on this foundation that they foisted upon the United States a reign of terror, intimidation, violence, and bigotry unprecedented in the modern world.

CHAPTER 33

THE EIGHTEENTH AMENDMENT

LIKE many other evils, prohibition was adopted under the cloak of the great World War. It was brought about under the guise of a bill for the conservation of food. The men who were responsible for it were much more anxious to prohibit the use of liquor than they were to win the war. The story has been told in a very naïve way by Doctor Irving Fisher in his book entitled "Prohibition at Its Worst." The committee that had charge of food conservation in the conduct of the war was deliberately packed by Wayne Wheeler, Doctor Irving Fisher, and others, so that the food bill should forbid the use of any intoxicating liquor during the war. It was intended that no one opposed to the plot should have any notice of what was going on. Unfortunately, one man out of several hundreds who were trusted with the secret revealed it just in time to prevent the bill passing as the conspirators had designed. Doctor Fisher, for his services in the matter, earned the enduring fame of receiving from Wayne Wheeler the compliment that he had done more for prohibition than any man in America wearing shoe leather. Wayne Wheeler and the rest of the fanatical drys did their best to tie up the whole bill for food conservation unless President Woodrow Wilson would consent to the prohibition clause. As between their fanaticism for making the country dry or winning the war, there was no question as to the stand maintained by Mr. Wheeler and his supporters.

Under the preparations for war, the Eighteenth Amendment was submitted to the States by Congress and vetoed by President Wilson; and then passed over his head by two-thirds majority, and finally was submitted to the States. Its ratification was a foregone conclusion.

There was one legal purpose, and only one, for passing the Eighteenth Amendment, and that was in order to give Congress concurrent jurisdiction with the States to prohibit the manufacture and sale of intoxicating liquor as a beverage. This could have been done by an amendment to the Constitution, authorizing the Federal government to legislate as well as the States. Instead of that, so long as the war had placed the power with *the drys,* they prohibited the sale of intoxicating liquor in the Constitution, intending thereby to make it impossible ever to permit the sale of intoxicating liquor in the United States. The principles of our government, as laid down in the Constitution, were simple and admit of no argument. The individual States were the units of the government; these contained the police power necessary for political action. The United States was a federation of sovereign States. This left the individual units to enjoy local self-government meant to fit the various States. What they needed could be determined by the character of the inhabitants of each State, the manners, customs and methods of living in the separate territories of a land too large and heterogeneous to adopt uniform laws. So the American Constitution provided for local self-government.

The Constitution was designed for the protection of the citizen; instead of this, the prohibitionist used it to destroy personal liberty, and to prevent its return except through the laborious and almost impossible method of once more amending the Federal Constitution. The prohibitionists loudly talk of the impossibility of getting rid of prohibition without changing the Constitution. Every one knows that to get a majority of two-thirds of Congress to submit the repeal of the Eighteenth Amendment to the States, and have this ratified by three-fourths of the States of the Union, is almost impossible. It would not come about unless at least nine-tenths of the people of the United States were in favor of such legislation. I say nine-tenths as an estimate. Most of the needed States have long

been dry; a movement that would make them wet would require almost a unanimous vote in the centres of population.

The prohibitionists laugh at any attempt to change the
law. They say that the Constitution is sacred, and it were better that tyranny and despotism should reign than that the Constitution should be ignored. Men have made an instrument so
strong that it cannot be changed, and the document is more
important than the citizen. The creature has destroyed the
creator.

At one period in English history the Great Seal was thrown
into the Thames, and it was seriously claimed that the government could no longer function without the seal. That the
people of America cannot act without a majority of nine-tenths
is a sillier superstition than the taboos of the primitive savage.

There cannot be the least doubt about the difference between
the Constitution and the Volstead Act and the relation of each
to prohibition. The last clause of the amendment, like the final
clauses of all Constitutional amendments, declares that Congress shall pass laws to carry the provision of the Constitution
into effect. A Constitutional provision cannot enforce itself. No
one is indicted for violating the Constitution, but for violating
the Volstead Act. As a matter of fact, the Volstead Act violates
the Eighteenth Amendment; the amendment refers to intoxicating liquors; the Volstead Act makes it criminal to sell,
transport, etc., any liquid containing more than one-half of
one per cent alcohol by volume. This means about a teaspoon-
ful to a quart of liquid. Every one knows that this is not intoxicating. However, the courts have held that Congress had the
right to fix the amount of alcohol to be allowed. They could
have fixed it at one-tenth of one per cent or nine-tenths of one
hundred per cent. The courts cannot take judicial notice of
what per cent of alcohol constitutes intoxicating liquor.

We are continuously informed that if Congress should amend
the Volstead Act by making twenty-five per cent alcohol in-

toxicating it would be unconstitutional because the sale of intoxicating liquor is forbidden by the Constitution. If any court did declare such an act unconstitutional it would simply mean that there was no Federal law in reference to the sale of liquor, and the subject would automatically be relegated to the several States.

Senators and representatives are charged with the responsibility for the statutes that they pass. If they have due regard for their own importance in the government of the country they will not be coerced by the Methodist Association for Temperance and Public Morals, the Anti-Saloon League, the W. C. T. U., or any other organization. That they have been coerced is beyond doubting. If senators and representatives had voted as they drank, no such legislation would ever have disgraced America.

Congress certainly now has the power to define the percentage of alcohol that makes intoxicating liquor. If they may say that a mixture is intoxicating which is not intoxicating, then they may likewise say that a mixture is not intoxicating when in fact it is. Unless Congress can define it, then whether a concoction is or is not intoxicating is a question of fact for the jury to determine.

Quite aside from the legal question, it is absurd to suppose that a great country like America can ever consent to have a body of fanatics tell its people what they may or may not eat or drink. If a man cannot choose his own beverage to suit himself, then what can he do for himself? Drinking is one of the primitive desires and needs, and the individual who would seek to control another in this prime instinct would stop at nothing that he chose to regulate.

Many statutes and constitutional provisions are enacted that never really become the laws of the land. Before they can be so classified they must have that sort of general approval that makes them a part of the customs and habits of the people. No such general approval has ever been given to prohibition. Criminal statutes are very different from civil regulations. Punishment is inflicted on the theory that the thing done is so obviously evil that a right-thinking person could not commit the act without a feeling of guilt. No such feeling has ever been experienced with the taking of a drink of intoxicating liquor. It is not sufficient that a mere majority shall approve a criminal statute; before such a statute can be generally obeyed or enforced it must have behind it practically the unanimous support of the people.

Most men and women readily approve the great mass of the laws that are passed by the legislative bodies. In fact, they are entirely too ready to let others tell them what they must or must not do. A small minority cannot nullify a law, but where a statute is considered tyrannical and unjust it always meets with protest. Refusal to be bound by it is such a protest. If protest is so great as to interfere with its enforcement by ordinary methods, it is plain that it has no place in the law of the land. Since men began making laws, the favorite form of repeal is by non-observance. It was in this way that Christianity conquered the Roman Empire. If Christians had obeyed the laws of Rome their religion would have died in its birth. It was this procedure that modified the brutal laws of England that punished with death some two hundred so-called crimes, not more than a hundred and fifty years ago. It was by this same method that the laws against witchcraft were destroyed. It was by non-obedience that the horrible persecutions of heresy no longer terrified the earth. Even in America juries refused to convict for witchcraft before the laws could be wiped out. And witchcraft and heresy have put to death more victims than all the other criminal statutes men ever passed.

Men were as sure that it was just to condemn heresy and witchcraft by death as their lineal descendants are sure of the righteousness of spreading poison broadcast to-day in the interest of the "Noble Experiment" of prohibition. The whole series of Blue Laws in America have been repealed by their defiance by intelligent men. Some of these disgrace the statute books of backwoods States like Massachusetts and South Carolina to this day, but they are rapidly dying a natural death.

Emerson long ago said that a good citizen should not be too obedient of the law. Men came before laws, and will be here after laws are in limbo. Nothing is so loved by tyrants as obedient subjects. Nothing so soon destroys freedom as cowardly and servile acquiescence. Men will never have any more liberty than they demand and are ready to fight to take and preserve.

If the prohibition law had been treated like any other act of Congress or State legislation it would have died long ago. No other statute is openly enforced with guns and revolvers. For no other minor offense can officers with impunity shoot down a human being in seeking to make an arrest. The people of the world have suffered all sorts of torture in the dark ages of the past; they have been chained and fettered in dungeons, they have been broken on the rack, they have been crucified, they have been starved and beaten and maimed by the bigoted and unmerciful who paid no heed to the misery or wants of those they had learned to hate; but in spite of all the cruelties of the past, it has been left for the prohibitionist to commit the final outrage against justice and humanity. So far as I know, no organization of human beings heretofore has coldly and deliberately advocated poisoning any one who might run counter to their will. The prohibitionists insist that alcohol sold for mechanical purposes and shipped broadcast over all America shall contain deadly poison. They advocate this, knowing that much of it is redistilled and used as a beverage, that many people might and do get it through accident and without any design to take intoxicants; and that, at best, or worst, to drink it is only a mild offense; yet men and women, who in ordinary life are kind and humane, are so obsessed by their delusions and so sure of their convictions, and so resentful of those who do not follow their dictates, that they are willing to condemn to blindness and death thousands of people, without arrest or indictment or trial, by putting poison into their drink. Heretofore such measures have not been resorted to against anything but rats and vermin, and many humane persons hesitate to do this.

The prohibition law never has been and never can be enforced. An attempt to make it a law of the land, after the lessons that we have learned, is not an attempt to enforce law; it is a wicked attempt to awe the American people, to tyrannize over a land that once was free, to destroy the resistance, the devotion and the independence of a great nation with bullying and threatening with blindness, imprisonment and death, calmly sacrificing the young and the innocent, along with all others.

For more than ten years tens of millions of people have refused to be coerced by this fanatical law. More money has been spent in an effort to enforce it than all other Federal criminal statutes. As many men and women have been sent to prison by our Federal courts for the violation of this statute as for all other offenses put together, excepting selling dope. More lives have been recklessly and wantonly taken in the mad effort to make the United States dry than by the efforts in behalf of all the rest of the criminal code. This law has developed more snooping, sneaking, informing, prying, and entrapping than all the other acts of Congress. Men have submitted to enormous taxation through these twelve abnormal years that the fanatics should have their way, and now, after ten years of a merciless crusade, the protest against the bigotry that stands back of this legislation is stronger than ever before. This protest is growing so insistent that it threatens the peace and security of the country.

The prohibitionists care nothing about the nature of man,

the theories of government, or the lessons of history. They could take a leaf from the story of the alien and sedition laws that were passed under the first President Adams and his officials; the press and the citizens defied the odious laws. Back of opposition were the giant figure and vigorous intellect of Thomas Jefferson, who was chosen President of the United States. He did not call the alien and sedition laws "a noble experiment." He did not say that the laws should be enforced though the heavens fall and the people perish. He knew that the laws were despotic and violated all human rights, so he demanded that instead of enforcing the laws Congress should repeal them, which it promptly did. The statesman knows that laws should be like clothes, made to fit the citizens that make up the State. He knows that when a protest is long and persistent, the law should be repealed.

The tyrant believes that if the laws do not fit the people then the people must be bent to fit the laws and forced to obey. He would insist that if a tailor should make a pair of trousers that were too short for the man, then the man must have his legs cut off to fit the trousers. There is no question as to the duty of the statesman to seek to alter laws that do not meet the general approval of the citizen. The Volstead Act in effect brands every one who takes a drink as a criminal, as a felon. It does this in spite of the fact that the greatest men of the world have always taken intoxicating drinks. If we were to discard all the literature produced by men who drank, all the great classics of the world would be consigned to flames. There would be no literature, no art, no music, no statesmanship if we relied on the prohibitionist for works of genius.

Even were it proven that the use of alcohol in moderation was harmful to the individual, that would furnish no excuse for sending men to jail for making it and selling it and drinking it. Many people believe that because a thing is injurious a statute should be passed making it criminal, but there is no foundation or justification for it; most people who can afford it eat too much, drink too much, and play to excess. All people violate many of the rules of health and no doubt shorten their lives. Teaching temperance in all things is a task for the educators, the schools, the press, the public itself. No matter how thoughtful men may be of their health or welfare, they will always do some things in excess, or will unduly abstain. It is not given to human judgment to find the exact line, or to hold to it without becoming mechanized. Men and women who spent all their time seeking this line, and trying to follow it, would die for lack of emotions and friends.

A world made up of such people would be like a sailing vessel lying in the doldrums. Life at best is a venture. No one can prophesy the time and means whereby the curtain shall be rung down. The individual may die in peace or agony. He may die in youth or old age. He may die from over-drinking or from lard on the liver. He may possibly die from delirium tremens, but, much more likely, from dyspepsia, gout, or cancer. No one ever wants to know all that is before him; he prefers the venture. No one would wish to be told in advance on what day or by what means he is to be taken away. It would be the same as a death sentence, leaving each sojourner checking off the days with terror. All of us are living under a death sentence, but we do not know the day or method of execution. It is only the vitality and hope and joy as one goes along that keeps the mind from dwelling upon the day of dissolution. It is only the adventure that kindles us to close our eyes and quicken our steps and feel that the moment of consciousness is life, and that we should make the most of what we have, and, as nearly as possible, in the way that we shall choose to live.

CHAPTER 34

THE NEGRO IN THE NORTH

AFTER nearly fifty years of practicing law it was really a relief to give so much of myself for a time to the questions that interested me most. I never missed a chance to speak or write against prohibition. It was a matter of fighting for the liberty of the individual. I had no delusions about mankind in general. I knew his origin and the method by which he received his ideas and opinions. I knew the weakness of his intelligence, his narrow experiences, his misinformation on all questions pertaining to life, the depth of his prejudice, and his inordinate conceit; and yet I liked him. Never did I blame him, but I always feared him. In the hands of the powerful and crafty he is like clay in the grasp of the potter. Under the leadership of the tyrant he is dangerous to the peace of the world.

I enjoyed talking on social, political, and religious problems particularly. I wanted to make converts. I wished to make every one reasonable and tolerant. To be sure I realized that what really drew me to these endeavors was the self-satisfaction that I got out of it all, and so I am aware that it has not been a desire to help my fellows nearly so much as to gratify certain feelings of my own.

I had determined not to get into any more cases that required hard work and brought me into conflict with the crowd. I had fought for the minority long enough. I wanted to rest, but to rest would be something new. But I could not rest. I get tired of resting. And something always comes along to disturb my restful contemplations, anyhow, so—I was in New York, and a committee of negroes came to see me. I knew they were negroes because they told me so. In color and intelligence they were like many of the most intelligent white men that I know. The committee came in behalf of the National Association for the Advancement of Colored People, an organization of negroes with headquarters in New York City. Doctor J. E. Spingarn is its president; and Mr. James Welden Johnson, at that time, was its secretary; and Walter White, the present secretary, was then assistant secretary. Each member of the committee was a man of attainments in the realm of arts and letters. Their great individual intelligence cannot be due to their white blood, because so many of my Southern friends assure me that persons of mixed blood take on the worst characteristics of both strains. Personally, I do not know, because I have never known any one who was not of mixed blood. And neither have I ever known what-all it was mixed with in its long journey from the sea urchin to man.

This committee wanted to engage my services to defend eleven negroes in Detroit, on the charge of murder. I made the usual excuses that I was tired, and growing old, and was not physically or mentally fit. I knew that I would go when I was making the excuses. I had always been interested in the colored people. I had lived in America because I wanted to. Many others came here from choice to better their conditions. The ancestors of the negroes came here because they were captured in Africa and brought to America in slave ships, and had been obliged to toil for three hundred years without reward. When they were finally freed from slavery they were lynched in court and out of court, burned at the stake, and driven into mean, squalid outskirts and shanties because they were black, or had a drop of negro blood in their bodies somewhere. I realized that defending negroes, even in the North, was no boy's job, although boys usually were given that responsibility. I was the more easily persuaded because my good friend, Arthur Garfield Hays, was willing to go with me.

On my way home from New York I stopped in Detroit to find out what I could about the case. I found my clients all in jail, excepting one, the wife of one of the defendants, who had been admitted to bail; the rest were men and boys.

The facts were simple. Up to the beginning of the war, Detroit had some twelve thousand negroes. There, as everywhere, they were packed into the lowliest and the dirtiest quarters. When the war in Europe broke out, the people of America saw their opportunity to serve humanity and get rich. Detroit enjoyed an unprecedented demand for automobiles. So, the manufacturers sent south for negro labor. Most of these men and their families remained in Detroit after the World War was over and we were freed from Germany.

At the time that my clients were arrested, the negro population in Detroit had increased from twelve thousand to sixty-four thousand; it was attempted to pack these into a space that had been overpopulated by its former lesser number. The negro workmen could stay in the automobile factories in the daytime, but they had no place to stay at night, so they expanded the negro section, and some of them moved out to what was called the white districts. Many of the negroes in Detroit were old-time citizens. Even before the Civil War the runaway slaves would come to Detroit, for this city was in sight of the Union Jack which was flying beyond the river, in Windsor, Canada. To the footsore slave fleeing from his master, the Union Jack was the emblem of freedom, just as to-day it is for the thirsty. By degrees the negroes became citizens of Detroit, and amongst them are doctors, lawyers, and many others of marked mentality. In the early days, Detroit and other Northern cities were friendly to negroes; but that was a long time ago.

The negroes were not the only people who came from the South to the North during the war. White workmen as well as colored ones came up to all our industrial centres. The whites brought with them their deep racial prejudices, and they also brought with them the *Ku Klux Klan*, which was very powerful for a time at least in every northern city, except perhaps New York and Boston. In Detroit the Klan was strong. A number of colored families bought homes just outside what was called the negro section, among them a doctor, Ossian Sweet, and his wife. More than one of these families of colored people had been driven from their new homes with guns and clubs, and in two or three instances the houses had been pulled down over the heads of their owners. Most of these homes had to be abandoned after that, of course. In various parts of Detroit where the Klan was the strongest, the body had openly led the fight. Sometimes the Klan factions organized under other names, like "The Improvement Club" and the "Neighborhood Association."

Doctor Ossian Sweet, the main defendant in the case I was undertaking, was a man of strong character. He began his career in Detroit as a bell-hop on the lake boats plying between that city and Cleveland, after which he took all sorts of odd jobs such as fall to the man whose face is black. By a hard struggle he worked his way through college, and then through the medical school at Ann Arbor. After that he managed to get the money for taking a post-graduate course in Europe. When he had completed his years of study, he opened an office in Detroit. In the meantime he had married, and had a child about two years old at the time that he was arrested for murder.

It is always hard for a colored man to find a decent living-place in America, North or South. We have a colored banker in Chicago whose home has been bombed nine times, obviously by good people who want to drive him away. The home of Oscar DePriest, a colored congressman of Chicago, has been bombed a number of times. In none of these cases is any one ever arrested, much less sweated and beaten and maltreated, as is growing to be the usual treatment for any one suspected of crime.

Doctor Sweet had been living in congested quarters with his wife's family, and for some time had been looking for a place that he could buy. Finally he selected one in a middle-class neighborhood at the corner of two streets, Charlevoix and Garland. Diagonally across from his home is a large school-house. Between the time he bought the house and the time he moved into it, several negroes had been driven from their homes, so, the doctor waited, hoping that the feeling would subside. But as soon as the neighborhood found out that Doctor Sweet, the owner, was a colored man, they proceeded to band together into what they called an "Improvement Association," of which practically every one in that locality became a member, and a meeting was held in a schoolhouse, at which the speakers made dire threats as to what would happen if a negro should settle in their street.

Soon after that public meeting, Doctor Sweet notified the police department that he would move in on a certain day, whereupon a number of officers were sent to protect him and his family and their belongings when they moved. But the furniture was not all that he took with him. Among other things, there was a long package of gunnysacking hiding a number of guns, and there was a valise well supplied with cartridges. Along with the load of goods went the doctor and his wife, a thoroughly resolute and intelligent woman, and also their small child, with a brother of Doctor Sweet, who was about to go to a university in Ohio for the graduation year. Later in the day, another brother, a dentist, and six other men, friends of Doctor Sweet, came to their house.

The house was located close to both streets, had two floors, and an unusually large number of windows. In front was a porch with steps down to the sidewalk. Two bright, colored girls, interior decorators, came late in the afternoon to plan the furnishing and arranging of the house. Toward night the guns were distributed and the different men placed themselves at certain windows and were instructed not to shoot until word should be given. As dusk came on, people began gathering on the street and in the schoolhouse grounds across the way. The two girls were afraid to go outdoors, so they stayed all night. No lights were turned on inside the house, fearing that it would only attract trouble, for a crowd of white people surged up and down the streets and around the house all night. No one inside went to bed. The next day the two girls went away. The others remained at the house.

Again night came on; again the throng gathered around the house, increasing in number and restlessness. As near as could be estimated from the evidence, the streets and the schoolhouse yard were crowded. In the early evening people came out and sat on the porches of all the houses in the neighborhood, and toward eleven o'clock the crowd grew boisterous. Some eight to ten policemen were stationed around the place, but it seemed that they were mainly ornamental. The colored men were standing watch at the various windows with guns in hand, as the mob came swarming toward the place. A volley of stones was thrown toward the house, and two of the windows were broken. Thereupon shots were fired from inside the windows, and the crowd moved back; at once the policemen entered the house, and took all the inmates to the police station. It soon transpired that one man had been killed and another wounded by the fusillade.

As might be expected, the feeling in Detroit was strong against the accused. Few colored men in America charged with killing white persons have ever lived to tell the tale; they have been lucky if they survived long enough to be tried in court under the forms of law and legally slaughtered.

When I went to court to arrange for the trial, I found a judge who not only seemed human, but who proved to be the kindliest and most understanding man I have ever happened to meet on the bench, Judge Frank Murphy; since then he has become the mayor of Detroit.

Somehow, it is supposed that a judge must be stern and devoid of human feelings. This is the right attitude for one who is to judge his fellow man and try to tell with absolute accuracy what sort of sentence a culprit must receive. It takes a mighty intelligent mind to determine with absolute justice whether another man shall live or die, or how long he should be kept behind prison bars. To do this with fairness and wisdom, a judge must be endowed with omniscient discernment, and must be self-righteous as well.

A man who practices law in the criminal courts should be able to tell something about a man by looking at his face. A large part of his work is sizing up judges, jurors, and witnesses at the first glance. At any rate, I did not take a change of venue from Judge Frank Murphy, and an extended and rather close association with him convinced me that I was not mistaken in him.

It was not easy to get a jury. As expected, almost every one had an opinion, and it was obvious that these opinions were not favorable to my clients. Eleven colored men were on trial, and although nearly a tenth of the population of Detroit were negroes, it was certain that none of them would be jurors in the case. I kept wondering what a white man would think of his chances for getting a fair trial in Africa if he had killed a negro and was placed on trial before twelve men with black faces. After considerable time we managed to get twelve men who said they could be fair, but of course they knew nothing about that. No one knows so little about a man's ability to be fair as the man himself. To a man himself all his opinions, attitudes and prejudices are fair or he would not hold them. But no one ever wanted a fair juror; at least, no lawyer ever did. The State wants a juror who has grown cold, serious, unimaginative, and, a Presbyterian, if possible. The lawyers for the defense want a man who is alert, witty, emotional, and who is a Catholic, or without any religious faith whatever. No one ever *judges* any one else without finding him guilty, no one ever *understands* another without being in sympathy with him. A person who can understand can comprehend why, and that leaves no field for condemning.

It was a pathetic case. The courtroom was always filled, and a crowd outside waited for admission. As everywhere, the white people were served first, although I insisted that a certain proportion of colored people should be admitted; and they were, as the State's attorney did not object. But the colored folk all sat in the big part of the courtroom behind the railing. As the case progressed, fewer whites and more colored sat beyond the rail, and before the close, no white persons sat back there; it was completely crowded by the negroes. Of course, white people do not like to sit beside colored people because they are smelly and not clean, but this in no way incapacitates them from cooking, waiting on the table, and suckling the babies of the whites. It operates only in regard to sitting together when neither are working.

There was no question of the facts in the case, yet fifty or seventy-five white persons came into court and deliberately testified that there was practically no one along the street corner that night, in spite of the proof that the streets were roped off for two blocks, and ten or twelve policemen were posted at and near the house. On Sunday afternoon I went over to the place where it all occurred and managed to get into conversation with a boy about ten years old. By encouraging him a little he told me all about it. He was standing in the front room of his home when the guns were fired. He said that the crowd immediately ran past his place and there were so many running that the street was blocked. The boy's mother who was standing beside him had already testified that no one was in the street. It was easy to show by cross-examination that the witnesses for the State were not telling the truth; as fast as they came on the stand they began contradicting each other, and even themselves, demonstrating that they were lying about the whole affair.

And yet, these people were almost all members of churches, and in the ordinary matters of life were truthful and kind. Their fear that their property would be injured, together with their racial feeling, justified them in their testimony. Invariably one meets these experiences in court, where prejudices show up very marked and deep. I could realize how seriously some of them must have feared the loss of their property, and neither then nor since have I judged them.

Of all the people on the street through that event, we were able to get not over five white men and women to testify for us, and it was difficult to keep some of these in line. I am sure that every one knew that the whole neighborhood had joined an association to keep Doctor Sweet from moving into his house, and that they all had combined to drive him out. The crowd that assembled that fatal night included men from all sections of Detroit. The mayor had taken a firm stand for the protection of the negroes, but few leading citizens, and no newspapers, had used any effort to defend them, in their clear legal right to occupy their home. Although a number of white clergymen had come to me and warmly expressed their sympathy for our side, not one said a word from a pulpit to prevent or denounce the outrage.

The trial revealed a marked contrast between the Klansmen and other witnesses for the State, and the colored defendants and their friends, who testified for our side. Practically all the negroes who came upon the stand were men and women of culture and refinement, many college graduates, and in every way the superiors of the witnesses for the prosecution. The courtroom during the closing arguments presented a pitiful and tragic picture. The whole of the space beyond the railing was packed with negroes. With strained and anxious faces they made a powerful mute appeal to the white men who seemed to be holding in their keeping the fate of an outraged and downtrodden race. Through it all the judge was calm, kind and impartial, and his instructions to the jury were clear and forcible, and scarcely left a chance for them to do anything but acquit. The jury deliberated for more than twelve hours, and finally reported that they could not agree. The next day the judge admitted the defendants to bail and they were released.

About a month later, the case was again put on the calendar for re-trial. Under the law we had a right to demand separate trials for each defendant, which we concluded to do. The State then chose to put Henry Sweet, the doctor's brother, on trial. Henry was about twenty years old, and had just completed his junior year in the Wilberforce College, in Ohio. The evidence was plain that he had shot out of the front window in the direction of the deceased. Henry was very fond of his elder brother, the doctor, who had helped him while attending school. He was really a member of the family, and what he had done was naturally in defense of his brother and kinsfolk, and his race. Even though he might have been hasty in shooting, he was justified in doing so if he believed that the home and the inmates were in danger. Henry made an excellent appearance in the witness chair. He was frank and open-mannered and made no attempt to conceal his part in the tragedy.

Between the first and second trial a serious effort was made to burn Doctor Sweet's house. And although policemen were in possession and on guard, and saw some one running from the premises after the fire was started, no one was even arrested for the deed. The second trial revealed nothing new. There is always a large chance in every case. Little things often have a vital bearing on the result. On the whole, the case seemed to run more smoothly in the second trial. The same eager crowds haunted the courthouse. The same tense faces watched every move in what to them represented a part of the tragedy of the whole race. I am sure that their silent, appealing looks were more eloquent than any words that I could offer. This, in spite of the character of the case, the inherent justice of our cause. My long sympathy for the colored people conspired to help me make one of the strongest and most satisfactory arguments that I ever delivered. The jury was not long in returning a verdict of acquittal. The verdict meant simply that the doctrine that a man's house is his castle applied to the black man as well as to the white man. If not the first time that a white jury had vindicated this principle, it was the first that ever came to my notice.

After this verdict, the State's attorney dismissed the other cases. Doctor Sweet was never again molested. Soon after the trial his little child died, and after a vain fight against tuberculosis his wife also died. It is only fair to state that the Honorable Robert Toms, who prosecuted the case, was one of the fairest and most humane prosecutors that I ever met. And this despite the fact that he was quite zealous, as most lawyers are. A year later I had the pleasure of meeting both him and his able assistant, Lester Moll, and they both told me that they had come to think that the verdict was just and did a great deal of good in Detroit.

The defense of this case gave me about as much gratification as any that I have undertaken. While I was certain that my clients were right and that they were grievously wronged, I never had any sense of resentment against the community. The people who sought to drive that colored family from their home were only a part of the product of the bitterness bred through race prejudice, for which they were not responsible. So long as this feeling lives, tragedies will result.

CHAPTER 35

A YEAR IN EUROPE

NOT long after the Detroit case, I was prevailed upon to assist in the defense of a case in New York. For several years I had been promising myself that I would retire from the practice of the law. Each case was to be my last, but like most other men I was always letting myself be persuaded to do one more.

Two Italians were charged with killing two Fascists, who were trying to board a train in the Bronx, on their way to join a body of Fascists about to parade in their national regalia along with the American soldiers on Decoration Day. This incensed the Anti-Fascists, who protested against allowing this to occur. After considerable effort by the police, two Anti-Fascists, Donato Carrillo and Calegoro Grecco, were indicted for the killing. Both men had been very active in Anti-Fascist campaigning, and were known to be hostile to the Fascist group. A committee, headed by Norman Thomas, undertook to raise the funds to pay the expenses for the actual defense of the case. Neither Arthur G. Hays nor I asked or received any payment for our services. The case hinged around the identification and proof of an alibi, and was colorful and interesting to a rare degree. The mother of Grecco was a fine type, like one who had stepped out of an old Italian landscape by some master. When she had told her story, she turned to the judge and asked with motherly affection and womanly dignity, "Please, may I embrace my son?" Grecco had shown no emotion until then; suddenly he burst into tears, and there were few eyes in that court-room that were not equally affected.

The jury was out but a short time, when they returned a verdict of "Not guilty" in both cases.

In 1928 I had been in the law for fifty years, which surely is long enough to follow one occupation. While I was practicing I felt that I had other interests and inclinations that I wished to gratify, and the time was growing short. There was no reason why I should abandon the practice of law in 1928 instead of 1927 or 1926 or 1930 or 1931, but, automatically we take account of time; the first of the year, or first of the month, or Christmas or a birthday is supposed to be the best time to begin something new or stop doing something that has long been a habit. This custom, like most others, is not based on logic. So far as Nature is concerned, time is continuous. It has no breaks. It goes on and on, and we can imagine neither a beginning nor an end.

So I determined finally to retire in 1928, after fifty years of what men are pleased to call service, which of course means serving one's own inclinations and purposes. I planned to go to Europe for a year, and then I could break the chain. But I could not get away in 1928; at least, I thought I could not go; so I waited until the spring of 1929 to begin a new life. But this I did not do; although I went to Europe; and I am convinced that no one ever begins a new life, and I am sure that I shall not, although the old one will come to an end without much delay.

A few years ago I would doubtless have thought that a visit to Europe could easily be the subject of many chapters. And so it could; but Mark Twain and many others have done that job so much better than I would be able to do it that I shall not make the attempt. And then, too, a trip to Europe is nothing to talk about now, unless made in an airplane, at least. And even then it is no distinction to have visited Europe, but it is rather a condescension to tell about it, for it carries the assumption that the reader has not been there. Otherwise, the comeback might be a languid, "oh, yeah?—I hadn't heard that you were away, because I myself just got back from a spin around the world."

Not that a visit to Europe was new to me. I had taken it many times before, and really did not need to go. Still, the absence for nearly a year was worth while. I figured that many people who had been in the habit of thinking that they could not get along without coming to me for advice might discover that they could consult some one else; but, at that, I couldn't feel sure that they would. In a sense I felt sorry for them, for being deserted by me in that way. But to my surprise, people were not cluttering up the dock, impatiently awaiting my return; I seemed to be pretty well forgotten at the end of my holiday! I also have found that a good many of my old companions had died during the absence of a year, and I am still getting returns of further permanent departures of those who I supposed were still here on earth.

I have noticed that most autobiographies contain lists of names that are important at home and abroad of men and women who were intimate friends of the author, especially of the great ones met abroad. Of course I did meet many people that year in Europe, but most of them were Americans. Often I met them at Simpson's in the Strand, and frequently in Lyon's, though one shouldn't mention Lyon's Corner House any more than one does Childs', on account of the prices being so low, despite the excellence of the food. And in Paris the Duval's cafés suggest home-cooking, they are so American-looking. Unless you have a villa on the Hudson, and summer in Newport and winter at Palm Beach when at home, it is almost safe to say that one's American friends can be easily located around meal-time at any of these popular places. I would not set this down excepting that I have never read any tales of travels wherein the writers emphasize having patronized or preferred these places, nor heard any Americans boast of going to them; but they take special pains to mention having dined at the Ritz in London once, and having one day lunched at Ciro's in Paris.

It is always interesting to go to London, no matter how often one has been there before. I found the four lions still guarding Lord Nelson, who was as usual standing on the tall monument in Trafalgar Square; they had not budged an inch from their post since the last time I looked at them. The Parliament Building had not changed, nor Westminster Abbey, save to add a new name-plate in its floor for Thomas Hardy. Which reminds me that I did meet a few whom I could mention in a book, but I shall not, for some of the meetings were too casual, or complimentary, and would not interest any one but myself, anyhow.

England is rather famous for its well-dressed men. The best-dressed man I saw in London was standing in front of the Metropole Hotel. I noticed that he greeted the distinguished-looking taxi-patrons as they came and went, at the doorstep, and he gave the impression of great wealth and importance, his clothes were so resplendent. I had lived at the hotel several weeks before I dared to nod to him, but much to my surprise there was nothing "stuck-up" about him after all, for he talked to me as cordially and kindly as though I belonged to his class; and on second thought, I shouldn't wonder if I did. But even more resplendent and important-looking were the two horsemen who sit booted and spurred in front of Buckingham Palace. Of course I did not presume to speak to them; they might run me through with a spear, or shoot me on the spot. I have seen these men, or some that resembled them, several times. This is also a very likely place to meet Americans.

However, I believe I should mention a few well-known Britons that Mrs. Darrow and I saw day after day. One was the Irish-English statesman, T. P. O'Connor. I met him first in America during the war, and it happened that we crossed the Atlantic together; and after that I saw him every time I was in Europe. T. P. O'Connor was a real statesman, the oldest member of Parliament at the time of his death. He was a kindly, lovable man, with a sense of humor that infected all who had the luck to come into his presence. He was ill when we were in London that last time we met, and almost every evening we were at his home in Morpeth Mansions; for weeks before the end he was having dinner-parties, inviting as many as could be accommodated. Doubtless he felt the shadow hanging over his head, and wanted to see us as often as possible.

He loved his friends and was a wonderful host, sipping a few drops from his champagne-glass, toasting us all to our long lives and happiness, never admitting that he was really ill, until gradually he grew weaker and it was evident that he could not recover. We were there early on the very evening before his death. He always talked affectionately of America, and regretted that he should not see it again. No man in Great Britain was more deeply loved and honored than this great human Irishman, T. P. O'Connor.

Another citizen of London that I sometimes met was John A. Hobson, one of the foremost economists of England. He has long been a contributor to progressive papers and magazines on both sides of the Atlantic, and is the author of several well-known books in his field. And now and then I had a day with Henry S. Salt, at Brighton, whom I have known for many years. This gentle, kindly man has devoted his life to humanitarian causes, especially the protection of the dumber animals against the cruelties of "God's noblest work," Homo Sapiens; also, he is an essayist and poet of high order.

Oftener still, we were with Mrs. Byles, whom we first met in America years ago, the widow of Sir William Byles, who had been a member of Parliament, so that I should call her Lady Byles, as she is known over there, but, somehow, I could not. I never took to titles as most Americans do; but it did not matter to her; she was one of the really great women of England, a liberal, and deeply interested in every just cause. When last we were with her she was well past eighty years of age, but her mind was alert and keen to a remarkable extent. Then there was Miss Eva McLaren, an unusually clever and charming young woman hailing from England but travelling continuously, who considerably added to our enjoyment of the Riviera by being in Cannes when we were there.

Of course we met and knew many other interesting people, but, why brag about it here?

The stay in Cannes, and an excursion through England, Scotland, Wales, and the Isle of Wight on a motor-trip, registering over four thousand miles in England alone, were the most interesting and profitable experiences of our European holiday. In all that trip we had but one day of rain, which was a remarkable feature of such a jaunt; we were told that it was the driest summer Great Britain had known for fifty-two years.

It chanced that we met an old-time friend of mine, William R. Kellogg, from Jamestown, North Dakota, who had taken a car to Europe; he proposed the trip, inviting us to share it with him. Of course we lost no time in accepting. So far as I have seen the world, I have found no landscape that compares with England. To be sure, it has no mountains, but its villages, its trees, its winding rivers, green fields, and hillsides are beautiful and picturesque. Certainly America has no rural beauty that can compare with the English landscape. As there is no spot in England that is more than sixty-five miles from the sea, it would seem impossible to be able to drive all those thousands of miles without running into the ocean. But we did.

There is nothing new to say about English landscape, for Americans, from Washington Irving down, have used this land for practicing the art of description. But I want to speak of one place, not because of its beauty alone, but because of the psychology that it illustrated. It is the Doone Valley, in western England—a really delightful spot.

The Doone Valley is famous all over the English-speaking world. It lies hidden behind and below huge hills that curve and fork into ranges that lead away from the thoroughfare so that it is rather hard to discover. The gorgeous golden gorse envelops entire mounds high and low so far as the eye can reach, and the miles of miniature mountains covered with purple heather surpass anything of the kind to be found elsewhere in Great Britain. We were told that a thousand visitors arriving in automobiles had been there that one day, and that this was about the usual number of tourists any day in the height of the season. But they did not go there because of the fine scenery. They were there because of Blackmore's story of "Lorna Doone."

A large rambling farm-house has been converted into an inn, where we found the most surprising assortment of old-fashioned cooking and baking which guests were invited to help themselves to without limit to portions; the charge was small, and was so much a person, so that no one went away hungry or in any other way dissatisfied. Ponies are furnished for going to the various points of interest, fabled and real. Thatched huts and shelters are shown as having been the homes and haunts of John Ridd and Lorna Doone, where she was wooed and, of course, won; and one thatched cottage in particular, the largest there, is said to be the one that she occupied as a bride. Lovely lanes lead through shadowy stretches to the brook that ripples along the roots of the trees that bend low over the stones by which Lorna tripped across the narrow stream to meet her lover on the other side. This place is called "The Tryst." From the barnyard one turns another direction into a cleft between two small hills that take one to the farm-house of John Ridd's parents. Post-cards are sold showing the sweethearts "before and after taking" as it were, in the farmyard, crossing the stream, at the church, and a beguiling pamphlet is to be had for fifteen cents telling all as it occurred. Yet, there was no Lorna Doone; no John Ridd; no wedding; nothing but a story that was all woven from the brain of a clever preacher who knew what the people liked to read. And this romance was written only about fifty years ago. One of these days Lorna Doone will be canonized as a saint, and miracles will then be wrought in her name. There is nothing so eagerly believed as the things that are not so.

Before going to England we spent two months in Switzerland. I seldom go to any part of Europe without swinging into Switzerland. Cities are much alike in all the civilized world, now that they all have plumbing and elevators, gas and electricity, pavements, policemen, taxicabs, and department stores. But in the country the scenery is not all the same. I have seen most of America and Europe, I have been to northern Africa and Asia Minor. I have been to Jerusalem and other parts of the Holy Land, and something tells me that I shall never again go there, either in this life or the next; if perchance there be a next. If one loves scenery, the most beautiful countries by far, in Europe, are Switzerland and Italy.

The main trouble with travel is that it keeps one going—going away from sights and attractions that should be lingered over until they become a part of one's being. I would stay as long as possible in the most picturesque spot to be found, if I can ever find it. I never tire of viewing a beautiful landscape, a lofty mountain, or a lovely lake. All of them are everywhere in Switzerland. Not only are they there, but they are huddled close together, as if for the benefit of the tourist. On this most recent trip we went to Montreaux, one of the chain of villages delightfully situated on the southern side of Lake Geneva. The Castle of Chillon, an outstanding part of the panorama, about a mile away, is an interesting bit of architecture made famous by Lord Byron over an event that never happened. As a matter of fact, most of the famous events never really happened, or, if they did, they happened in some other way. The truth is never so fascinating as fiction. Hence, most writers, even historians, write fiction.

Montreaux, on the willow-bordered, rose-banked shore of Lac Léman, the other name of Lake Geneva, seemed too beautiful to be true. On the opposite side the Alps rise almost directly from the water, their tops seven or eight thousand feet above us, and loftier ones still rise farther beyond, some white with snow, some green, the sky and the lake reflecting their various hues. Great white swans glide gracefully below the spreading, overhanging branches, in the upper limbs inky rooks sway and flutter, and all along the promenade stroll humans in their kind of "plumage" more costly but not so picturesque.

Back of the little town are high hills which furnish splendid observation points for revelling in the vast view all about. There I sat for days, for weeks, on the balcony veranda looking across the big blue lake, at the majestic mountains rising to the sky, and there I began these memoirs which should be much more entertaining considering the advantage I had. Here, at the same hotel, the Beau Rivage, was my old-time friend, Charles Edward Russell, with his wife, and never shall we forget the evenings we four spent together on our balconies, watching the changing colors of the waters, the mountains, the trees, and skies as the sun went down, all of the beauty heightened and mellowed by wonderful wines of that little land; and later, glorious highballs for night-caps, if we wished them. Everything was beautiful and inspiring. Not an ugly spot or blot or prohibitionist marred the summer nights. Here, under these benign skies, I found myself in the mood to begin this book. Mrs. Darrow rented a machine and typed and revised as I spun my reveries into form, with the clicking of the portable in the wing across the garden to inspire and awe and goad me on as the scholarly and industrious Charles and Theresa Russell daily fitted together facts and translations toward what now is "The Life of Charlemagne," by Mr. Russell.

We did not like to leave Montreaux, nor the Russells, but the autumn was coming on, and I never liked the cold, so we reluctantly broke camp, and in due time resorted to the Riviera for the winter with our other good travelling-companion, Mr. Kellogg. This was one place that I had missed visiting, although I had twice sailed across the Mediterranean Sea.

So, after the sojourn through the British Isles, finished off with a trip to Ireland, we reached Paris by train, where we remained over one night only. This is not a reflection on our appreciation of Paris; we had been there many times before; over and over I had seen Napoleon's Tomb, the Eiffel Tower, the Bon Marché, the Louvre, the Place de la Concorde, the Bois de Boulogne, the American Express Office, Notre Dame, and The Morgue. All had given me much pleasure, excepting the Morgue, and even that had been a rare experience. But I knew when I had enough. It had all grown as familiar as Marshall Field's store, Lincoln Park, the Masonic Temple, the Stock-Yards, and Potter Palmer's Palace. But I had not been to the Riviera, and I had heard that it was warm.

The railroad journey to the Mediterranean is rather long and hard for one who is not well, and doubted if he would ever be any better, though he might at any time be worse. The promise of a mild winter cheered me along. But the Riviera failed me in one important particular. It was not warm; at least not what I call warm. Still, the Riviera is a wonderful combination of natural beauty in every direction, with its wooded hills and towering mountain peaks, flowery gardens up the steeps toward the villas of the wealthy, the wide walk for miles and miles along the beautiful Mediterranean filled with all sorts of craft from all parts of the world, while along the banks and out in boats the fishermen are hauling in their nets. I used to watch them pulling in these nets but never saw a fish worth speaking of. So they were what fishermen always have been: very poor, stupid, ignorant, superstitious, grossly trusting creatures, or they would not have expected better luck. Generally four of the barefooted peasants dragged in the net; they walked back and forth with a regular plodding step, their faces betraying no emotion or feeling of any sort, not even hope, as the great webs swung near. No wonder that wherever a fisherman is referred to in the literature of the world it is "a poor fisherman."

In front of the hotel the great promenade was alive at all hours with men and women, jauntily, gaily dressed, as befits the South and the life of leisure. They were everlastingly walking back and forth, it seemed. Most of the women were exercising little and large dogs at all sorts of intervals during the day; the larger the woman, the tinier the dog. Cannes seemed to be a paradise for dogs, in fact. They over-run all the walks everywhere one turns, and are allowed to make themselves perfectly at home, which they do, indeed.

At the back, above the parade, rose marvellous hotels shaded by immense palms and other tropical trees and shrubs. Perpendicular heights were covered with masses of flaming foliage and suspended vines, and winding stairs led upward and around curves and corners and were lost in a wilderness of gardening. At the centre of the great bend around the harbor was the Grand Casino, which every one frequented, and where gambling was as openly enjoyed as on the American Stock Exchange. I used to watch the players now and then; none of them seemed happy; they all wore a serious expression; it was not pleasure, it was business. I was told that from time to time an unfortunate would throw his last franc onto the table and lose, and then go out and put a bullet through his brain. Still, that is what they do on the Stock Exchange, and, in fact, in all business affairs when faced with failure. No other trouble

seems to affect one so much as the loss of money. No doubt this
is because money is so inevitably necessary to real life.

The entire Riviera is much the same. The sunshine lures the
Briton, the German, and the American from the icy north to
where life goes along under sunnier skies through the winter,
and where in every other respect life is as easy and restful as a
pleasant dream. Men who buy and sell stocks at home can buy
and sell chips in the luxurious wide-open gambling houses
abroad. To be sure, there is a percentage in favor of the house
just as there is a commission collected on the purchases and
sales of stocks and wheat and corn in other parts of the world.
Success means the same in both games, and failure leads down
the trail to the same end.

Indoors and outdoors, in Cannes, "I loafed and invited my
soul," without detecting where, or that, it lies hidden within
my body. The margin of the Mediterranean forms a huge
horseshoe between a long slanting cape, off to the left, and the
Alps to the right softly slope down into the blue sea, where we
found an ideal anchorage. The highest ridges were often show-
ered with snow, and then the air was far too chilly for sitting
on the balcony of The Majestic to see the sun set between four
and four-thirty in the afternoon. In this atmosphere of beauty
and majesty and serenity it was easy to muse and continue my
memoirs. Again Mrs. Darrow rented a typewriter and kept the
manuscripts corrected, revised, and in other respects set to rights,
which may not have been as simple as it sounds, for often my
thoughts come faster than any pencil can spin, and in racing
over the paper many words abbreviate themselves into a kind
of shorthand of their own brand which sometimes even I can
not figure out afterward; but with care and patience it has been
unravelled until not a syllable is missing; in spite of which to
us this book represents an interesting experience, whether or
not any one else will find it worth his while.

In Cannes, I met my old-time friend, Brand Whitlock, of

Toledo, Ohio. Whitlock was one of the warm friends of Altgeld during the latter's term as Governor of Illinois, and, in fact, all through his career. He was appointed Ambassador to Belgium by President Woodrow Wilson, and thereby gained distinction through his intelligence in handling a prolonged and delicate situation during the World War. This involved the distribution of the food sent by America to Belgium. Since the war, Mr. Whitlock has virtually remained abroad. He finds more freedom in Continental Europe than in his native land, with its bigotry and intolerance. He is one of the few who really care for freedom, both in theory and in fact. He feels like thousands of other cultured Americans, that the prohibition fanaticism, with its espionage, meddling and violating of personal rights, is rapidly converting America into a den of spies, informers and self-righteous dictators, preventing those who still respect individual initiative from living here if they can go elsewhere. So, Mr. Whitlock gravitates between Belgium in the summer and the Riviera in the winter, writing, travelling, leisurely enjoying the day and the morrow as they pass by.

We often took long, lazy strolls along the beach of the historic sea that we both love so well, and out to the far points of one or another of the numerous capes that stretch far out into the Mediterranean, and talked and dreamed of the civilizations old and new that have basked beside those blue waves beneath those blue skies, at the gateway of the gorgeous Alps.

Here I met H. G. Wells, who works and plays through the winter months in the beauty and sunshine that has for so many seasons lured the countless generations. It takes but a very short acquaintance for discovering how richly stored is his marvellous mind. The enormous work that he has accomplished arouses one's amazement if not envy. And in spite of it all, he is much more modest and unassuming than most men who have spent their lives dawdling and dreaming and getting ready to begin to commence to do something worth while, perhaps. He is a splendid host, a good fellow, an unusually comfortable and comforting man to be with.

Between Nice and Monte Carlo, in another "mansion 'neath the skies," lives W. Somerset Maugham, in a wonderful old place perched on a pinnacle of the lower Alps, where, with Jo Davidson, we had the honor and pleasure of a visit one day; and later on Mrs. Darrow and I were guests over a midday meal, with a better opportunity to appreciate the rare treasures from other parts of the world, and gaze out over the Mediterranean from the terraced garden sloping off to the brink of the clouds, it seemed. Mr. Maugham radiates a quiet, dignified geniality which sends one away realizing that any visit with him would be too short. These joys were added to other ever-remembered days of that year over there.

From our windows we looked out upon the parade of people and dogs, the carnival, the regatta, flower floats, French uniforms, and always the Casino, where not alone expensive gambling goes on, but the most extravagant entertainments are furnished for the beguiling of visitors; and once inside, there are magnificently equipped restaurants, private rooms for gay and elaborate functions, and immense ballrooms; a high-priced jazz-artist leads a large orchestra through all sorts of trick performances; in all directions are countless tables where the choicest and most costly liquors are served day and night. But the real, the exclusive, the most wealthy gambling set paused not nor so much as glanced at the public tables but were admitted at an elegant side-entrance of a wing occupied by its club members only. All along the Riviera are other Casinos at the adjoining resorts, each a centre of successful and unsuccessful life, extreme elation and utter despair, along the margin of the matchless Mediterranean.

As a rule, I am not given to sentiment over inanimate things or historical events. But, somehow, I could never think of the Mediterranean Sea, much less look at it, without being profoundly moved by its remarkable story. The earliest, and even the latest civilization has closely hugged her shores. The first knowledge we have of man's origin and development clings to its blue waters. The first ships of which we have record sailed those beautiful waves. One after another, nations and civilizations have risen and vanished around the Mediterranean Sea. Egypt, Asia Minor, Arabia, Syria, Greece, and the Roman world; Spain, Italy, France, all have been washed by this sea. The Pharaohs, Cæsar, Pompey, Hannibal, Anthony and Cleopatra, too, made the Mediterranean immortal in history, song and story. Even now it lies in the heart of the civilization of the world. Most of the history of the Western world has been written there, and no other body of water of anywhere near its size has the same importance in the world.

CHAPTER 36

LEARNING TO LOAF

Most Americans, as well as Europeans, and all other people, write of the deep and holy emotions that well up from their hearts as they reach their native shore. Well, I had emotions, too. I was surprised that the Goddess of Liberty was still standing in the harbor. I visited lands where every one seemed to enjoy joy; where pleasure carried with it no suggestion of wickedness; lands of color and sunshine and eating and drinking; lands where no one was employed by the Government to say "No!" and where you can gamble without pretending that you are "doing business." Places where you could drink when you were not thirsty, and even when you knew that you already had too much; just as Americans usually only commence to eat when they have already had more than enough.

In Europe no one is afraid to enjoy life in his own way. There the people have never heard of Benjamin Franklin and his tribe. Here we have been taught that "early to bed, and early to rise, makes a man healthy, wealthy and wise." Neither does Europe seem to have imbibed Henry Ford's idea of efficiency. I saw no working men sitting alongside a moving platform with their eyes vacantly staring ahead to note when a nut or a screw or a spoke or a rod would pass their way. These neither went to bed early nor began work early. All of them had their noon-day meals with plenty of time to eat and drink them; for in most parts of Europe all stores and activities take a two-hour recess for luncheon, and in England there is in every office and shop time for tea. On the Continent, not only are the shop-doors closed and locked, at noon but the handles are taken away so no one can try to break in and spend his money. No body of working men in Continental Europe are so poor that they cannot sit on the sidewalks with bread and cheese and a bottle of wine, and eat and drink and visit and laugh and talk the time away. And strange to say, no one gets drunk. Their nights, too, are bright and gay. No one tells them what to do, or what not to do. And still they come and go and conduct themselves like the rest of us.

As we sailed into the harbor of New York, every one was on the deck, surging to and fro, or in the dining-salon, or in the "American Bar," or in their cabins taking rounds of farewell drinks. The Goddess was still standing there looking toward the land that we had just left, with her back turned on puritanical, efficient America. The Rotarians who might or might not have belonged to the organization looked eagerly at the shore; they seemed pleased and even happy, and cudgelled their brains for some wise remark to confide to their neighbors. Generally they expressed the same gem of wisdom, "Well, America is good enough for me!" And thereupon they seemed to have a sense of patriotism and originality.

Many authors have described their rapture over coming into view of their native land after a long absence, and all alike have translated this emotion into proof of the worth of America. Even observation does not teach them. All people on the earth feel glad over coming home after a long absence. They give no thought to the relative intelligence or opportunity of their own country and a foreign land. They have made no comparison of their respective laws or institutions. They are glad to see their home-land, and to the patriot this proves that the home-land is the best. As a matter of fact, they neither know nor care which is best. It isn't America that they want to see, but Mary Jane, and sister Lou, and Susie and the corner policeman or a school-chum and a host of other people who are so much a part of their daily lives that they miss them when away. Every man and woman and dog and cat and house and street have been made to fit into their tastes and habits. Then, too, they have a sense of relief because they are hearing their own language, eating their favorite food, and resuming the way of living and doing that has come to be what fits them best. I never saw a cargo of people disembark on any land but that their eyes brightened, their talk grew vivacious and extravagant, while their steps quickened and they were glad.

I feel sure that if any one could intelligently, honestly, and carefully compare the advantages and disadvantages of Europe and America, most of them would give the preference to Europe. The landscape is much more beautiful and diversified. There the places of amusement are more numerous. Its cities are more attractive, and as a rule its climate is more agreeable. Through long experience and great care the European has learned the art of living. He has developed more forms and varieties of entertainment, many of them simple, and a talent for enjoying them, however simple. In America the opportunities for the poor have always been better because the country is newer, land is more accessible and cheaper, and, along with this, wages are higher. But this advantage is rapidly passing away, if it is not entirely gone. And no one can settle the relative advantages of two localities by the way he feels in the one or the other. These emotions are too personal, and under other circumstances would have been attached to any other land.

I approached New York as I have done before with mixed feelings of depression and exaltation. I had been away for a long time, and much might have happened while I was gone. In this instance an unheard-of panic had stricken America. Many of my friends had lost all they had. I myself had suffered severely. This might interfere with my plans to give up the practice of law. At any rate, I was apprehensive of the news I should receive on landing, even though it might be both good and bad. As Bret Harte said: "The only thing sure about luck is that it will change." I never believed that man had any control over his destiny. To me life has been a series of optimistic and pessimistic emotions and outlets. On the whole I have deemed it wise to prepare for the worst. In the words of the exquisite poet, A. E. Housman:

> "Therefore, since the world has still
> Much good, but much less good than ill,
> And while the sun and moon endure
> Luck's a chance, but trouble's sure;
> I'd face it as a wise man should,
> And train for ill and not for good."

On landing at the wharf and on the way to the hotel I am always wondering and doubting and fearing as to the sort of news that I shall find. But the letters were about the same as usual, the customary greetings, the regular proportion of tales of trouble with requests for help; the pleasant and the unpleasant; the good and the bad; the onset of familiar obligations and sensations that at once makes one feel as if he has not been away and makes him wish that he had not come back. While in New York, however, I met many old friends and managed to so blend and balance the good and the ill that it seemed possible to still get some satisfaction out of the years yet unlived. Thereupon I definitely determined no longer to practice law, but to follow a less strenuous course and try to realize a few more long-cherished dreams.

Like most lawyers, who dare to think about their profession, I had for a number of years viewed it with doubt and distrust. The lawyer always sees the seamy side of life. He deals with troubles, misfortunes, fraud, deceit, and all sorts of misunderstandings. On the civil side, his clients are ever seeking to get and keep an advantage; they are trying to get the best of every situation. The lawyer's business is to help his client get all he can and pay the least possible. Every rule involved and every argument conceived is to get more and give less. Cases are long delayed, and carried from court to court, and often, after travelling their weary course to the last resort, come back once more to go over the same wasteful road. The delays of the law are proverbial. Lawyers and judges take their profession seriously, but if business men dawdled and talked and quibbled and dodged and evaded as do lawyers and attachés of courts they would never accomplish anything of worth and importance. Tempers are lost, dispositions ruined, and fortunes squandered in the courts. Instinctively business men seek to avoid lawyers, judges, and any building that is decorated with a blind woman holding a set of scales in one hand. If they sell goods on credit, they insure their bills and let some one else quarrel over litigation whose trade it is to live in the courts. Their automobiles are insured against accidents as their bills are insured against default. In drawing contracts they more and more provide for arbitration of differences. More and more the well-managed business is leaving the courts, and newer and more economical methods are devised for settling disputes. Although men of affairs have a feeling that courts add to the safety of society, they always distrust them and, in fact, view the whole system with doubt and dread. With them, courts are always associated with bankruptcy, waste, heart-burning, irritation, and delay.

It seems to the layman that no case is ever ready for trial, that lawyers and courts conspire to get the client into their net and then never let him out. The time of courts and juries and witnesses is consumed by endless questions, speeches, delays, and postponements. There is never such a thing as a direct approach to any question if an intricate, winding way can be found or created. In the endless palaver the substance is lost in technicalities, reason is subverted by quibbles, courts convene only to announce a recess for the noon or to adjourn for the day. Corporations who live from litigation are organized to keep men out of court for an agreed price and to take the risk themselves. The ordinary man considers a lawsuit about as he would a fire where no insurance is carried, or a death in the family, or some other calamity. It is extraordinary that a system hoary with age, extravagant and wasteful to the greatest degree, should not be supplanted by some method of getting at facts directly, and having them passed on by men who understand the controversies that they seek to solve. Every strongly contested case is replete with long arguments, interminable interruptions, and appalling waste.

When it comes to the criminal court, the process is still more archaic. Instead of squandering fortunes, lives are sacrificed and hopes are destroyed. The methods of criminal courts are hundreds of years old, and their conceptions a thousand years older than that. They were born of a time when an animal, a stone, or a block of wood that hurt some one was accused and at least morally condemned. They were born of a time when every kind of conduct was moral or immoral, and every human act was right or wrong, and every wrong act should be punished by some sort of torture. Sane ideas of human conduct are not much over fifty years old, and the last thirty years have done more for the understanding of man than any five hundred that preceded them. We now know something about the causes of human behavior, whatever that behavior may be, but the courts still take little account of such causes, and administer the law under the theories of a thousand years ago. There is no more excuse to-day for indicting and trying a person in a criminal court than there is for hanging him for being ill or insane. A criminal court presents a trained set of lawyers seeking to send a derelict to prison or to death. These are moved by a public lashed to insanity over a perfectly understandable human psychology. The prisoner is poor and dazed and helpless, and has little chance against the fearful odds that he meets. Every criminal trial is a man-hunt where the object of the pack is to get the prey. The purpose of the defense is to effect his escape. It is a game where the dice are loaded, and the victim is almost sure to lose.

I had stood with the hunted for many years. I had fought against hatred, passion, and vengeance to save liberty and life, and I was weary, and timorous of the crowd. It was hard to longer brace myself for the fray. I wanted to rest and play, and not be harassed and worried in the few years left through which I might cling to life. I did not want longer to fight in a court-house all day and study and contrive far into the night, and be back in the court-room at ten in the morning after a troublous sleep. I wanted to get up when I wished and stay at home all day if I wished, and read some of the books in my library that I had always intended to enjoy but could not, and work cross-word puzzles whenever tired or bored.

So I determined to close my office door and call it my day's work. Or a life work. Loafing and dreaming looked calm and restful and alluring to my tired nerves and mind. I was seventy-two years old, and it was high time that I should begin to stroll peacefully and pleasantly toward the end of the trail, which, at best, must be but a little way beyond.

CHAPTER 37

THE CAMPAIGN AGAINST CRIME

On my return from Europe I was deeply grieved and some-what surprised to see the cruel results of the steady and un-scientific campaign against crime. This was well under way before I left America. The whole movement was directly in conflict with modern psychology and, in fact, with all the teachings of science. No doubt the Great War was responsible for the beginning of this reaction.

It takes long effort and training to make any progress in teaching kindness and mutual help. These qualities come from the development of the imagination, which is of slow growth. A few years of war seem to undo the patient work of a cen-tury. During this period all the world taught hatred and cruelty as the chief virtues in life. For five years the world was con-triving new and more terrible ways to kill and maim. No other human activity approaches the brutality of war. And never in the history of the world had it been developed to any such extent as in the recent conflict.

In times of peace the old and young are taught the value of human life. The best scientists are engaged in finding ways to lengthen it and make it free from pain. The preservation of life is the first concern of the State. All this was changed in a flash. Science and wealth and energy were everywhere called into the service of taking life and destroying property. When day after day the world read of the deliberate slaying of one thousand, ten thousand, or twenty thousand men or more, kill-ing soon became one of the commonplace events in every-day life. Slaying lost its terror to millions of people. Four or five years of this psychology produced a direful effect upon the minds of men. After the great conflict, in every warring nation the homicide rate rapidly increased. From the returned soldiers came a large percentage of the slayers. Killing was no new sight or sensation to them. They had been thoroughly trained to hate and destroy, and to glory in it. As time went on the war faded away, and in most countries the homicide rate declined.

In America another condition brought about a psychology that led to all sorts of violence. While the soldiers were fighting in Europe the United States adopted its drastic, absurd prohibition law, which was resented by substantially half the population of the land. In a short time the partial enforcement of this law filled our prisons to overflowing, and many defenseless men and women were shot down on mere suspicion. The result of all this has been what any student of human nature or machinery of government might have foreseen. From the time of the passage of the Eighteenth Amendment and the Volstead Act the citizenry has waged almost open warfare. Of course men did not stop drinking. Neither did they cease to buy and sell. Necessarily the laws led to illicit manufacture and importation of intoxicating liquor. This logically led to the organization of a new industry. So long as the business was outside the law the dealers were obliged to make laws of their own. Customers who bought illicit liquor did not hesitate to censure and condemn those who sold it. The law itself, with the hypocrisy that goes with that sort of legislation, made it a crime to sell, but left it perfectly legal to buy and to drink.

The open violence, the crowded prisons, the state of anarchy that prohibition has brought about led to a mad and senseless crusade against crime. New penal statutes were passed, prison terms were lengthened, courts and juries, in obedience to the mania, convicted defendants almost indiscriminately. Many innocent persons were sent to prison and executed in this carnival of hate. Such infamous acts as the Baumes Law—providing that a fourth offender should be sent to prison for life—were passed in most of the States. One woman in Michigan was sent to prison for life for selling a half-pint of whiskey. Many others, whose first offenses were committed when mere children, were sent to the penitentiaries for life for an act that carried with it no feeling of wrongdoing. To be sure, in this madness mistakes were made. Men and women who were guilty of no crime often suffered the severest penalties. Judges meted out the most outrageous sentences. New statutes created new crimes, increased the penalties, and destroyed age-long safeguards for freedom. Boards of parole and pardon ceased to function. The unfortunates in prisons felt that there was no chance for regaining liberty once the prison doors closed upon them. This hopelessness kindled prison revolts, which led to fearful slaughter, to the destruction of all that the years of earnest work had done to modify conditions by building up humane prisons, caring for juvenile offenders, and giving even the condemned hope or opportunity once more to be free.

For myself, I always worked against capital punishment, and all severe penalties. I had always believed in clemency to first offenders, and believed, as do most men of science, that every kind of human conduct comes from causes, and in order to change conduct the causes that bring it about must be altered or removed. One needs only to read a sketch of the treatment of what we are pleased to call criminals in the past to know something of the depth of the ignorance and brutality of the old-time statutes. It is less than two hundred years since animals were tried and solemnly executed for crime. Children of seven and eight years of age were once upon a time put to death by the State. For slight offenses men were banished to penal colonies to die a pitiless death by disease, or be torn to pieces by wild beasts. In former years, banishment meant death in the most hideous way. As a rule, it means the same to-day.

In the olden times the criminal and the insane were tortured and chained indiscriminately, and, for that matter, they are to-day. There is no way of determining who is sane or who is insane, or who is good or who is bad, but one thing is certain: in the treatment of criminals a great change has come over the world in a hundred and fifty years. This change has been toward humanity, tolerance, and understanding. Most of this important work has been brought about in the last fifty years, for it is only a short time since scientists have even tried to find out the causes of human conduct. Amongst the scientific men who deal with the problem of the human mind there has been an almost universal agreement about the cause and treatment of crime. But ideas are very slow in affecting the mass of mankind. They are held back by prejudice, by ignorance, by common conception until long after the intelligent specialist has thoroughly proved conditions and discovered remedies.

I can hardly remember the time when I was not sorry for the inmates of prisons. I have no doubt that this feeling made me more readily undertake their defense in courts. To be sure I sympathized with them long before I made any study of the subject called crime. After I began the defense of men charged with crime I often visited these unfortunates in jail, of course. They were in no respect like the idea I had formed from the general conception of criminals. I found that they had the same likes and dislikes as other men, that they acted from the same motives and impulses as those outside the jails. They loved their mothers, were devoted to their children, and loved their wives and their friends. All of them could explain the reasons for their special deeds. I soon began to see that they could not possibly have done any other way. I discovered that their conduct, like the conduct of every man, followed cause and effect. Not only did they generally love their families, but they were loved in return. Fathers and mothers would tell of the generous acts and decencies of their sons; wives would sacrifice everything they had to help them in their trouble; little children would reach their hands through the bars to greet their fathers in jail. These fathers and mothers and wives and children had seen the prisoners in a different light from those who judged and hated and condemned them without trying to understand. Outside of the family there was always a circle of loyal friends, many of whom would face death for the man that the world condemned. All of this impelled me to try to understand these men as I have tried to know others. With the right psychology they were not difficult to fathom.

I soon discovered that very few of the inmates of prisons have any schooling. Very few had ever learned a trade or had any of the regular means of earning a living. Seldom was there any one who had any money. Almost all of them had begun their career in their youth. As a rule, the inmates of prisons do not grade high intellectually; now and then one is found with a fair mentality; but even these usually have weird ideas, and do not interpret the world as others do. Often they are sent from the prison to an institution for the insane; a very large proportion of them are on the border-line between sanity and insanity.

Of course, each different offender had a distinct and different psychology. In controversies between capital and labor they all have the same psychology; whatever is done is an act of war, just as opposing armies would be guilty of the most atrocious deeds if their acts were not committed in the name of some cause. This psychology is well known to every man, but still men do not think or reason when their feelings are involved.

It is very seldom that any one is in prison for an ordinary crime unless early in life he entered a path that almost invariably led to the prison gate. Most of the inmates are the children of the poor. In many instances they are either orphans or half-orphans; their homes were the streets and byways of big cities, and their paths naturally and inevitably took them to their final fate.

The first instinct of life is to keep on living, and every organism seeks it in the easiest way. The best scheme for the well-born and the well-to-do is in one direction; the easiest way for the poor and the outcast is in another. The great virtue that society attaches to learning lies in the advantage the educated man has to adjust himself to life. No right-minded person could ever think of leaving his child in ignorance to thus make his way through the world the best he could. All parents ask what would be the result if their own children were left to find their way through life without education, guidance, and protection. Whether education should be of the brain or hands, or both, no child should reach the age for making a living without being equipped with some means for earning it. Ignorance and poverty almost certainly lead to crime. Should it be argued that if all children were trained there would not be work enough to go around, this would only prove that we have not learned how to distribute wealth. It is an ignorant, or a very sordid world where people are poor because there is too much; and yet this is true to-day. Sometime, perhaps, our captains of industry who have already solved the problem of production will take up the problem of distribution. When this is done, and all children are taught to do something useful, we can close our prison doors, but not before.

The first instinct of all animal life is to satisfy its wants. A well-known idealistic representative of our "upper class"—Daniel Willard, president of the Baltimore and Ohio Railroad—in a public speech before the Wharton School of Finance and Commerce, stated that if he found himself unable to get work, rather than let those dependent on him for support face starvation, and rather than starve himself, he would steal. This remark should not have caused any alarm or wonder. Every man would do the same. In effect, what we now do is to leave perhaps a quarter of our children without the means of making a living. We fill the prisons with the victims of a civilization that we do not understand, and cannot control. The man or woman who believes that we can deny so many of our boys and girls a chance to live, and then control them through the fear of terrible punishments, needs educating, to say the least; that is, assuming that educating such people is possible.

More than three-fifths of the inmates of our state prisons are confined for getting property by unlawful means, or for offenses like killing which grew directly from burglary, robbery, and the like. A large part of the rest of the inmates are there for sales of liquor, opium and other dope. The hundreds of other provisions of the criminal code furnish comparatively few victims. It is safe to say that almost none of these would have gone to prison except for poverty. It is now so easy to create wealth that men and governments use every endeavor to prevent its production. This is done to bring about a scarcity that will permit the owners of property to charge prices that they otherwise would not get.

The boundless and senseless belief in the virture of punishment is one of the anomalies of the human animal. Society in general has the idea that only fear keeps human beings from cutting each other's throats and pillaging their homes. As a matter of fact, very few, if any, have such tastes or tendencies. If fear had been the mainspring of human behavior the race would have perished long ago. The doctrine that fear and punishment tend to order and system and justice is denied by practically every religious scheme of the world, and by the ethical ideas of mankind. Fear is not the strongest motive; it is one of the lesser emotions that move men. Pride, charity, love and pity are much more controlling. Nor does the State punish because of the need of self-protection. The State punishes, that is, inflicts pain, because it gives men pleasure to know that others suffer. No one can inflict suffering on another unless it gives him gratification to cause it. There is a mixture of sadism in every human being that makes him enjoy another's misery.

Endless reasons have been given for punishing people. It is a common assertion that the evil-doer is punished in order to help him. But every one knows better. Humiliating men, degrading them, dressing them in stripes or any other brand of prison uniform, substituting numbers for names, shaving their heads and depriving them of everything that a human being desires does not help them but only destroys them. Every one familiar with prisons knows that this is true. The spectacle of the State doing everything in its power to degrade, debase, and destroy a human being, and then seeking to help him to recover from the effects of his punishments is a fine example of the idiocy of man. No one was ever helped by punishment. If perchance some weak person has been made so to suffer that he does not dare repeat the act, it only means that he has been weakened to that extent by the treatment he received. To punish men because they have done wrong without heeding whether any good can come from the pain inflicted is pure vengeance.

When all is said and done, the last excuse given for punishment is that it is administered for the protection of society. There is no evidence, and from the nature of things there can be none, that punishing an individual in any manner aids society. If A is to be punished to make B safe, then even though it might help B it is an unforgivable indignity and hurt to have made A endure pain for the sake of B. Assume that A knows that he will suffer pain for doing a certain act; what is the effect on A? This knowledge does not stifle the desire to do the act; if it has any effect, it makes him cautious in accomplishing the deed. No one who commits an act that he thinks might bring him misery ever expects to be caught. Plans are always made for escaping arrest, and they generally succeed.

It is one thing to rear a child so he will not want to do a certain act; it is quite another to prevent him through fear. Even should he be restrained from the specific act through fear, have we made him stronger or weaker, better or worse? Of all the enemies that pursue and haunt man, fear is the greatest. When man conquers fear, most of his suffering will vanish. There is no logic, and no kind of evidence that justifies any kind of punishment. By punishment I do not necessarily mean restraint. We have built institutions for the insane and placed them under control. But no man of humane instincts hates the mentally unbalanced. These unfortunates are not confined because of hatred. Every means known to science is employed to restore their reason, and when they have recovered they are gladly released. The smallpox patient is likewise isolated to prevent spreading the disease, but he is treated with kindness, and is released when the danger of infection is over.

The whole question rests on the attitude of society and the law toward the unfortunate. If crimes were considered as a manifestation of life due to cause and effect, and not due to the wicked will of the offender, it should be, and then would be, treated like any other conduct. If it is a misfortune, the cause should be found, and the remedy discovered if possible. If a cure is effected, either through treatment or some other process, the unfortunate one should be released. If he is not safe to be at large he should be kept confined with all the kindness and consideration that are given to other diseased and defective men and women. It is the public and private attitude that is held against the criminal that has made his lot the hardest and the most unfortunate of all mankind. The odium and cruelty come from the illogical and pitiless attitude; when this is changed, all else will adjust itself.

CHAPTER 38

CAUSE AND EFFECT

So far as the individual offender is responsible for crime, the question, like most others of its kind, goes back to the child. The whole idea of education emphasizes the importance of training the young. Common observation shows how hard it is to uproot habits and convictions that have been long imbedded in the youth. The new-born child comes into the world with no ideas of any sort; he has an organism ready to receive such impressions as are made upon him by those nearest to his life. Instinctively he seeks to satisfy his needs. If he is hungry, he gets his food in the easiest way; if he sees something that he wants, he reaches out his hand to take it. He did not bring into the world the elaborate code of morals that are meant to protect him, and the still more complicated code of laws that the wise and foolish have conspired to create for him to observe and obey.

The child soon learns to protect himself from dangers in simple ways. For instance, when he begins to try to walk, he clutches a chair to keep from falling. He instinctively learns to tell lies when he finds that some one will hurt him if he tells the truth. Gradually he learns to love, to hate, to fear; the child, like the other animals, seeks only to enjoy himself and to protect himself.

Our laws of life and business are so complex that the child cannot go far in a simple way. His imagination cannot be so cultivated that he can put himself in another's place and instinctively feel that he must treat that other as he himself would wish to be treated. If all men did this it would be the destruction of the most sacred thing in the world: Big Business.

What society and commerce mean to teach is that the strong and cunning may and should overreach the weak and profligate, but they must only take their victims' money in certain standardized ways. The rules and exceptions are too long and two many for any child, or even grown person, to master. And, aside from this difficulty, the rules are constantly changing. The child can learn to do things, and the rules of right and wrong, in a big way, but never can master the code. As he grows in years he reads ads, and if he is at all bright he knows that these are, in effect, lies, written to deceive unwary customers; and by degrees he discovers that, even so, they are not so bold as to go against the law. As the child grows up he finds that he himself is often swindled in this way. As a matter of fact, no other literature pays as well as the writing of ads, and the artist who can fool the most people into buying what they don't want, and paying for it much more than it is worth, is the one who succeeds above his fellow artists, and his services yield an exorbitant price. Every effort may be taken, and is taken, to sell inferior goods, fake stocks, houses and lots that have no value, in fact or prospect. All sorts of art productions are claimed to be "originals" and a new vast field of "used" and "rebuilt" contrivances now are guaranteed (?) to be "good as new." Aside from this, large interests conspire to control products, markets and prices, and keep the wealth of the world forever flowing into great pools, leaving the rest of the land famished.

The number of homeless men and women, ruined fortunes, idle workmen, broken banks, and abject despair, in a land that should be one of abundance and plenty for all, is evidence of the ease with which adroit men can defraud and cheat and transfer the property of the world into the hands of the few.

It is sheer nonsense to think that the laws have much to do with conduct or virtue, or that they are made to be generally enforced, or that they are always right or just, or that they are ever equal. Long ago Blackstone said that the man who bases his conduct on the law is neither an honest man nor a good citizen.

Life and human institutions are always in flux. No sooner have we learned to use one machine than we are given a new one. No sooner have we mastered one rule of human conduct than we must learn the exceptions, and each change brings its new victims. It sometimes seems scarcely worth while to learn a trade, for new inventions and substitutions soon make it of no value.

When I was a boy every young man wanted a horse. Life seemed hardly bearable without a horse and buggy. This desire led to horse stealing, and societies were organized to catch horse thieves. I well remember the great joy that came to the organization when a horse was stolen; after sending men in every direction, and riding fast and furiously, a horse thief was brought into camp. Almost invariably he was a weak, helpless, underfed half-wit who had the psychology of the common people, and wanted a horse and buggy. The day of the horse is gone. The automobile has driven him from the roads. The boys and men and women of this generation must have automobiles. Those who manufacture them and sell them have made fortunes unknown in any former age. Every automobile costs more to sell than to make. No one can even guess at the cost of this new invention to the country or the change that it has brought to life. New roads have been built at great expense so men may ride quickly to some point so they can ride back more quickly if possible. Finance companies have helped the poor to get further into debt; an automobile complex demanding haste, change, and going and coming, has taken possession of mankind. With all the rest, it has furnished an extra harvest of unfortunates for our prisons.

Men and women, boys and girls, who were adjusted to the life of the past cannot stand the new environment. These machines have been used to make a quick trip to the doctor to save human life, to make a long trip to a bank or store in the night to aid in a burglary, all in order to keep up with the progress and process of a moving world. The automobile symbolizes both good and evil. The organism of man is not so adjustable and changeable as his inventions. It will take him a long time to accustom himself to the automobile age. Before that time comes the airplane most likely will have taken the place of the "horseless wagon," and the human system will have accustomed itself to fresh demands accordingly.

To mete out justice, the judge must understand the prisoner. This he does not do, and cannot do. Every one judges his fellow man from his own standpoint and equipment and circumstances. The judge who may get fifteen or twenty thousand dollars a year for short hours and pleasant surroundings cannot appreciate the life of the casual workman, pressed by debts and harassed with ambitions that he cannot satisfy. Without this understanding he cannot decide aright. No one has or can have this ability. To know life, one must have lived. The only approach to understanding is through imagination, and this gift is bestowed on few. Those who have it seldom use it. For to know all is to understand all, and this leaves no room for judgment and condemnation.

Every one who has observed human conduct, even his own, could understand the effect of punishment if he would give it the slightest thought. Punishing the child does not change its conduct; it only teaches it to deceive or conceal what he is doing by lying to his accusers. As a rule, there is little love and less understanding between parent and child. The ordinary parent approaches his offspring as if he were endowed with infallible wisdom and knew what is right and wrong, and invariably does right himself. If the child does wrong he is to be punished, or at least humiliated and made miserable. The parent seldom sees the act from the standpoint of the child, and of course cannot brook opposition or even argument. The parent, too, is so much older than the child that it is difficult to comprehend the emotions that moved the child, and he seldom tries to. Often the child chooses some one else rather than the parent in whom to confide. To many parents the idea of a child's disobedience is as terrible as the disobedience of Adam and Eve seemed to God, when they ate an apple. Obedience is taught to the child as one of the chief virtues:

> "Theirs not to question why,
> Theirs not to make reply;
> Theirs but to do and die,"

is the almost universal rule. If there is anything that the child needs in its training it is love and perfect confidence, and those cannot be received unless given. There is no reason why a child should not have its own ideas of right and wrong. What is wrong for the parent may not be wrong for the child. Right and wrong consist largely of intent, and there is a great gulf in both years and experience between the parent and the little one. If people are to have children they should be willing to take the responsibility that belongs with their rearing.

How often does one hear some stupid, blundering man or woman cry out that the children of to-day are spoiled by overindulgence, and how much better they were because their parents whipped them! Generally the good is not apparent; the old folks' method did not improve their offspring so much as the braggarts claim. There is nothing within the range of his nature that cannot be taught to a child if the parent or teacher is wise enough to know how. The prisons are not filled with the children of parents who were too kind. They are crowded with those who never had parental teaching and co-operation and discernment and help needed by the very young. Often the father or mother died while still young, bequeathing neither property nor the education needful to the living. In such cases the children are forced into the only avenues left for the utterly poor. Disaster and defeat are the result. When the smug and comfortable are rejoicing over the execution of a murderer, it is almost always a case of this sort that make them glad. Even if it is some other kind of a lad gone wrong it is just as easy to find the real reasons in his case as in the other, for nothing happens without a cause.

The boy of to-day wants an automobile just as his father wanted a horse. Very likely he has not the ability or the training to earn the money to buy one. The inhibitions against taking one are not strong enough to overcome the desire, so he takes the machine without buying it. Listen to the story of any one who has gone to prison, and see if he ever had a chance to go anywhere else.

Once in a long time a rich man goes to prison. He may have been a banker. He may have been a swindler. But none of these deserve to be condemned for having an inordinate greed for money, for our social system breeds that, too. It is not enough to be rich; one must be very rich; and this also involves risk. I have known a number of bankers who were sent to prison because of the failure of their banks, but, with one or two exceptions, they were not to blame. I am writing this in June and July of 1931, in the midst of crashing banks, where it is rarer to succeed than to fail. A few of the present disasters were due to wild plunging by those who had caught the universal obsession of the times, the hunger to get rich without delay, but most of them found their securities made valueless by an unexampled panic and period of depression, caused by the captains of industry who built up a machine that they could not control or even understand. Most of these bankers sacrificed all they had and went down in ruin. The laws are not all just to the banker. He is obliged to have the depositors' money on hand, and he cannot furnish it unless he loans it to the public. It often happens that he cannot produce the money at once to pay the loans. He does not dare to close his bank, for then all is lost. He generally holds on in the face of the danger of prison, to save the property of his depositors. Punishing the banker does no good. He is less averse to prison than he is to having his depositors lose their cash.

The idea that men keep to a certain path because they are afraid of prison is a gross superstition without any basis either in logic or experience. Let us take a simple example: Here is a burglar who has no other trade. Probably he has a family, and loves his children just as other men do. Burglary is his business in life. He could not be a lawyer, or a preacher, or a banker, or learn any other, better trade. He works in the night time. At about midnight he goes out on his professional errands. He goes to visit a house. He puts a gun into his pocket, though the last thing he wants to do is to kill. He may take fifteen minutes to turn a doorknob, he is so careful not to disturb any one's sleep; he takes off his shoes before entering the house, and every movement is calculated with exactness so as not to awaken any one in the place. If no one hears or stirs, he finishes his job and quietly leaves the house; but, if his victim is aroused and shows fight, he shoots to kill. He knows that if he is caught in the act of burglary he will stay in prison for about five years; if he kills and is convicted he will probably die; yet to avoid being arrested he takes the chance of being put to death. The truth is, that what is called crime is not prevented by fear of punishment. It has never been influenced that way. This is due to causes that are not always clear and distinct and readily understood. No amount of cruelty and threatening can affect the cause. To prevent burglary the cause must be removed; it can never be done in any other way.

CHAPTER 39

THE BLIND LEADING THE BLIND

For half a century I almost lived in court. Like everything else, this institution has an atmosphere of its own. In the criminal court I studied the prisoner, the judge, the witnesses, the jury, and the curious crowd that is always drawn by an unusual or strange case.

A murder that seemed especially brutal, as all killings do; a case growing out of sex relations; the weird, the salacious, the painful, the seemingly mysterious—all especially appeal to the crowd, and, more than the rest, the family of the accused are the centre of attraction and are woefully appealing. In spite of the clamor outside the doors, in spite of the savage stories carried by the newspapers, in spite of the hatred and venom so thick that you not only see it in the faces and hear it in the air, but you even feel it to your very bones; in spite of them all, the child, the father and mother, brother and sister and close friends never waver in their allegiance. They ask no questions, they sit stolid and unmoved as though their nerves were dead and their hopes were gone. Whatever is said of the accused man they love makes no difference in their devotion. They may not know every act of the defendant's life, but they know him, the composite man constructed from their experience, the man who to them, after all, is the real person, rather than the one who may or may not have performed a certain act.

The cause of the act is so obscure that no man can trace or solve it. It may go back to his youth. It may precede that, on back to when he was sleeping in his mother's womb waiting to be born. Or, perhaps, it may reach back to remote ancestors and have come to him through subterranean caverns affecting the brain or nerves or other parts of the structure. More likely it was born of the events of his life, his struggles and efforts, and utter despair. The scientist simply knows that if he committed the act there somewhere lurked an all-sufficient cause which most likely he cannot fathom. Often one recalls Omar Khayyam, who ranged human beings before him as pieces of moulded clay, and soliloquizes:

> "After a momentary silence spake
> Some vessel of a more ungainly make:
> 'They sneer at me for leaning all awry;
> 'What!—did the hand then of the Potter shake?'"

But few acts result from a simple cause. Perhaps a defective structure together with an infinite number of incidents before the occurrence of the event conspired to cause the man's undoing. Every one is more or less capable of most things that others have done, but some of the inducing causes are absent among some of us and we are spared. The poor men who have gone to their death on the gallows are not the only murderers. Killing may be in the hands or head, or both, and doubtless every one has some of this feeling in the mind at times.

As a rule judges are stolid and unemotional, and their knowledge is purely conventional. Like Roosevelt, "They know that right is right and wrong is wrong." This is a superficial statement, based on the letter of the law, but a far wiser man than Roosevelt saw deeper. St. Paul said, "The letter killeth, but the spirit giveth life." Most judges have neither the experience nor the imagination to comprehend life, and of course they are not scientists, and few of them know much about the operation of the human organism or the causes that produce actions. The jury, like the judge and every one else, including the lawyers, believes that the defendant is guilty or he would not be there. They also thoroughly understand the meaning of the word "guilt" and the prosecutors assume that the accused is guilty, as do the officers who have collected the evidence by giving the victim the third degree, and who are ready to testify that they did no such thing.

A prosecutor hopes and expects to be judge, and after that he will aspire to be governor, then senator, and President, in their regular turn. To accomplish this noble ambition he must in each position give the people what they want, and more; and there are no rungs in the ladder of fame upon which lawyers can plant their feet like the dead bodies of their victims.

Each incident and procedure in the courtroom may be of the greatest importance in determining the verdict, and no one can tell why certain matters carried certain weight. Even those who were influenced do not know. If the case is important, there is always the same morbid audience absorbing the details. You can find them, or their likes, at coroners' inquests, at the morgue or any place that savors of the mysterious, the tragic, and the grewsome. The lawyers on both sides strive to get in the evidence that they want, and keep out what they do not want the jury to know. All courtroom proceedings seem more like a prize-ring combat than a calm, dignified effort to find out the truth. All judges and lawyers know this. None seem to see any way to change it, except with added tyranny and greater cruelties. It is not easy to figure out the way to improve their method. Men are continually jumping from the frying-pan into the fire, and back again. People believe in jury trials, when behind closed doors star-chamber courts convict innocent men for treason and other crimes. Then they consider a jury a sacred institution. Then they get the right of trial by jury imbedded in constitutions and laws, and after that judges and powerful interests seek to take it away. This they do by urging that juries are not competent to weigh evidence and that they acquit the guilty through sympathy and feeling. In my rather extensive experiences I never knew any one who did not want sympathy for himself; neither do I know any justice that is not entwined with sympathy. No man is looking for justice, and, in fact, no one knows what the word means. The word "justice" has become associated with fear and foreboding, and is in tune with horrifying words like "stern," "impartial," and "deserve." Real justice can be neither stern nor forbidding in its attitude, but must radiate mercy and charity, and cannot be measured alike to all.

A courtroom is a hard place for a man or woman of inferior ability, little schooling, timid and embarrassed, as most people are in new and hampered surroundings. Neither the method nor the make-up is calculated to determine facts; it is too formal; and its rules are entirely too strict. Sometimes they are right and sometimes wrong, and no one ever knows until the last appeal is taken; then they are sure only because they can go no farther.

Still in history and science, and philosophy, justice and charity and mercy are always overruling courts of last resort, and preserving the finer and rarer qualities that, in spite of rules and precedents and judgments, still inhere in man. It is strange how men are obsessed with words; they talk of justice as though they could comprehend it and everything that goes with its determination. They laugh at pity and mercy as if they had no proper place in the emotions of man. And yet no one wants justice or can understand what it is. But every one wants mercy, and knows exactly what that means.

If the jury finds the defendant guilty he is turned over to the tender mercies of the judge. All that any one can predict about the term of the sentence is that it will be given in accordance with the decimal system. If the offense is a misdemeanor and very slight, but still in the judge's wisdom deserves more than a fine, he may give him ten days in jail. If he reflects on the matter and thinks this is not enough he does not give the man eleven or twelve days but jumps to twenty; if this does not seem enough he skids to thirty. If he doubts that in the balancing between offense and penalty thirty is not sufficient, he goes not to forty, or even fifty, but makes it sixty. After that he considers nothing below ninety, and if he passes that he skips to one hundred and twenty, and from there goes to six months; twelve is the next; then two years; next, five; then ten years, and so on up in regular numbers, as the impartial court may elect. A jump from two years to five or six, and ten, makes easy work for the judge and court; but with the prisoner each hour moves with leaden feet.

It is perfectly obvious that no court has any idea just what punishment any sort of act deserves. So far as the victim is concerned, the act depends upon his origin, his make-up, his opportunities, the strength of the inducement to do the thing measured against the intrinsic power of the individual and his experiences in life; and upon what he knows, and does not know, and what he feels and does not feel; upon all the circumstances of his life. These can never be accurately known or weighed, and yet courts and juries and the public are constantly destroying hopes and ambitions and individual lives and entire families on what every thinking person knows are the wildest guesses.

What, then, can we do about those whom some are pleased to call criminals without comprehending the meaning of the word? Those whom others call the anti-social, without in the least trying to learn who are the anti-social, which I suppose would mean those with whom the community could not well live, with safety to their lives and property. Still, an important discussion could be staged whether or not the anti-social are those who take small amounts by stealth or force, or those who amass great fortunes by applying their peculiar kind of wits to the monopolization of the world's resources of life. This

I shall not discuss. Let us take the common idea of the criminal: the ignorant, the poor, the unfortunate, the dispossessed, the wretched who make up the great mass of victims of all the courts, the jails, the prisons, insane asylums, poorhouses, and death chambers all over the world. What can we do with them? What can we do for them, to make living easier and safer for the rest of us who are good? I am willing to admit that something should and must be done; something less critical and guarded, more human, more helpful, more permanent, more certain than the present worn-out, idiotic, unavailing and merciless measures we take to determine who shall languish in prison and who stay out.

That this class of unfortunates is rapidly increasing in number in far greater proportion than the population I think is true. Probably the cause may be broadly stated as the impossibility of the human organism to adjust itself in pace with the ever-changing requirements of our so-called civilization, and the rapid increase of criminal statutes, which means more and smoother roads to doom.

There should be no trials, no lawyers, no judges to pass upon moral guilt. All of those who for any reason cannot or do not adjust themselves to important rules should be examined by experts to find out why it is and what can be done; if need be they should be kept under proper and sufficient inspection. They should be helped in every way possible. Regardless of what they have done they should be released when it seems safe; meantime they should be kept under supervision in kindness and sympathy instead of harshness. It is entirely possible that a person guilty of homicide could safely be set free in a short time, and that a sneak-thief or a beggar could never be changed or cured or released. Each individual should be considered by himself. To subject every inmate of prisons to the same treatment is like giving every hospital patient the same doses of medicine, or the same surgical operation, and, of course, however absurd this might seem to those who do not think, the time will come when something like this will take the place of the archaic, costly, and pernicious system that has long since been outworn.

Even in the present state of intelligence this idea is not fantastic. Nearly every city of any importance has established juvenile courts. We have evidently abandoned the hanging of children. Even during the present terror it has not been necessary to give the people an emotion by putting a small child to death. We have discarded the regular and time-honored method of dealing with children in the way we treat full-grown men and women. To be sure, we have not reached a degree of intelligence where "full-grown" refers to anything but the body. But in all States where science and humanity have penetrated, separate laws have been made for the delinquencies of children under eighteen years of age, and in some States for those under twenty-one. In these courts they are not sent to prisons, but are at least theoretically in the hands and control of the State, to be educated and cared for as they could not have been at home.

However, in passing, I must say that I never knew a child of a well-to-do family being taken in charge under this statute. This is doubtless because their parents can procure for them better care than the State could give; and then, children of wealthy families don't have to steal. In juvenile courts, these provisions, which are constantly being enlarged, simply mean that the child is not responsible for his acts. Of course there are many children under eighteen years of age who are more understanding than some men and women are at fifty, or even seventy-five. Age is only one way of fixing intelligence, and what some people call self-control.

Aside from all this, most cities have a psychopathic department to which they send all people charged with crime, if there is any doubt about their mental condition. Both the juvenile courts and the psychopathic clinics recognize, what the whole scientific world knew long ago, that cause and effect operate in every part of the universe, and therefore determine all human action. It is too late in the scheme of things to treat man as though he is the "master of his fate" and "the captain of his soul." Unless some great catastrophe comes upon the world, it will not be long before all men will place all human behavior on the same basis as all other manifestations of nature.

Those who wonder and doubt and refuse to be convinced might read an enlightening book by the late Samuel Butler, one of the most thoughtful and brilliant writers of the last century. The story is entitled "Erehwon," which suggests that it was meant to be "Nowhere" spelled backwards. The scene is laid back of the high mountains of New Zealand, where Butler seemed to have discovered a unique class of people: If a bank president had embezzled the funds of a bank, or if some one else committed something that civilized people call crime, such persons were not sent to jail or prison, but to a "straightener," who treated the unfortunate one daily for a suitable time, each day friends and relatives inquiring solicitously how the patient was getting along, displaying deep interest in his progress, and showing great pleasure and gratification when any one was cured. But if some one had a disease he was at once sent to a criminal court. Mr. Jones, we will say, is led into court charged with tuberculosis. The judge asks him what he has to say for himself, and he replies that he was born with a weak constitution, that he is poor and has been forced to work in inclement weather and unventilated surroundings, and so developed tuberculosis. Thereupon the judge, with the judge's zeal for justice, turns over the pages of his docket and says, "Mr. Jones, weren't you in this court a year ago for pneumonia?" The poor fellow replies "Yes—" he had been working in the rain and cold, and had not known that it would cause pneumonia. The judge promptly replied that ignorance was no excuse for crime. On further examination it was disclosed that he was once in court afflicted with a severe cold; it was therefore clear that he was an habitual criminal, and thereupon he was sent to prison for life.

I am not at all sure which kind of judge should be considered the more intelligent, and I am inclined to think that Samuel Butler had the same idea.

CHAPTER 40

WHY CAPITAL PUNISHMENT?

So long as men discuss crime and penalties they will discuss capital punishment. It is not easy to select the valid reasons for and against any sort of punishment. One who really seeks to know and understand goes over and over the question, and winds up at last by denying the validity of all punishment. Which means, of course, that society should not deliberately cause any one to suffer for any act that he commits. The difference between the one penalty and another depends entirely upon the reactions of the individual who fixes the penalties or discusses the subject.

It is almost universally believed that the death penalty is the most serious infliction that can be visited upon any individual. This is the reason people range on the opposite sides of the much-mooted topic. Those who are for it believe in this penalty because it is the worst fate that man can visit upon his fellow man. Those who are against are influenced by the same reason. No one is either for or against it on account of the effect on society, for it is out of the question to tell whether it increases the number of murders or lessens it. Even if this could be told, it would not settle the question. If so, more men would believe in some obvious form of physical torture like regular beatings or maimings, or starving or branding, or burning or boiling, or continuous torment of the victim up to the time of death.

There are various reasons why this cannot be settled. First, no one knows the effect of the different sorts of punishment toward preventing others from killing. Nor do they know which gives the most pain to the sufferer, or just how the pain administered upon one human being will affect others who know it, or whether men, women and children in general should be allowed to see the sufferings of the guilty or be compelled to see these victims while in agony, so that the spectacle of agony shall be expected to keep others from committing the same crime. Neither do they know whether visualizing and hearing of the effects of punishment of one deters others, or induces others. Or whether, even if it served to deter in this particular way, it might not render men, women and children callous to human distress.

A Chicago sheriff once had an unusual brainstorm: Instead of hiding the condemned, the execution, and the excutioner, he took the other course. He had the scaffold erected in the jail corridor so that the prisoners would be obliged to see and hear all that occurred at the righteous killing. Of course, the brainstorm sheriff assumed that the jail contained the future murderers of Chicago, and assumed that if they saw and heard all the grim act, they would never kill, if, indeed, they ever got out. But this noble experiment does not seem to have produced the intended effect.

The hanging or electrocuting of a human sacrifice can be witnessed by only a few, although nothing else would draw such audiences as this every-day viciousness. Nor are the pictures allowed to be shown in the movies, although this would bring the matter most vividly before the people. And if capital punishment deters, nothing else than witnessing the hangings and other executions could produce the result. No one has yet settled whether the event of execution should be exploited or advertised. If not made public, how can it deter others? If made public, what effect will it have on the born and unborn? Before one starts on a journey, he should know where he wants to go, else he may take the wrong road. Only one thing is certain about capital punishment or its effect, that it is administered for no reason but deep and fixed hatred of the individual and an abiding thirst for revenge.

Whether one is for or against capital punishment depends, in the last analysis, on what sort of person he is; whether he is sensitive and imaginative and emotional, or whether he is cold and stolid and self-centred. And what he is depends on his inherited structure and his environment. So far as I can remember, I got my first impression of capital punishment from my father when I was very young, probably not over seven or eight years old. He told me about a murder that was committed when he was a young man, which happened in the town adjoining the one where he lived. In those days the murderer was hanged outdoors in broad daylight, and every one was invited to see the act and all the grewsome details that went with it. It was an eager, boisterous and anxious assembly, each pushing and crowding to be in at the moment of the death. My father managed to get well in front where he could watch the spectacle; but, he told me, when he saw the rope adjusted around the man's neck and the black cap pulled over his head, he could stand no more. My father turned away his head and felt humiliated and ashamed for the rest of his life to think that he could have had that much of a hand in killing a fellow man.

In most of the countries of the world the death penalty has been reserved for murder, on the theory, I suppose, that it is the most terrible crime ever committed. How is it so terrible? Is it because a human being has been put to death? If so, execution is just as bad, and much more deliberate. Is it, then, that it is more evil to take life than to commit any other act? If it is because to kill is evil, it means that he has what the law terms a wicked and malignant heart; although, as a matter of fact, the heart is not involved. Should the culprit be hanged because he has a wicked heart? Then all people merit death upon the same logic, for when one hates or despises another he usually wishes the other were dead, and has a feeling of pleasure if he learns of the death. Probably very few people have lived long in this world without wishing that some person or persons would die.

The killer's psychology is not different from that of any other man. Indeed, in a large proportion of the cases the murderer had no malice toward the dead. Is it, then, a worse crime if there is no malice? What then becomes of the wicked and malicious heart, said to be the reason for the crime and for the punishment? Something else must be found as a reason for putting the offender to death. Is he to suffer death because he has so grossly violated some other person's right? There are many other ways of destroying peoples' lives, and it is done day by day, by the slanderer, the libeller, and the one who takes away another's means of livelihood, whether in or out of the protection of the law.

But capital punishment is not administered for murder alone. Even in the State of Illinois there are two offenses punishable by death: murder and kidnapping. The latter is a recent statute passed, like all other new penal laws, when such reason as man has was lost through hatred and fear. Really, this law was passed so that in case a kidnapper takes a child and holds it for ransom, and for some reason the distracted parents cannot or do not pay the ransom, the kidnapper will kill the child to prevent its giving evidence in court. In some States rape is also subject to the death penalty; this, too, is a direct inducement for a ravisher to kill as well as rape; if caught, he must die anyhow, so he is persuaded by the law to kill the evidence of his guilt.

Up to a hundred and twenty-five years ago England punished some two hundred offenses by death. Amongst these were: picking pockets, gypsies remaining in the kingdom one month, the unlawful hunting or killing of deer, stealing fish out of a pond, injuring Westminster Bridge or any other bridge. The early American colonists made twelve offenses punishable by death, among which were blaspheming, the hitting or striking of a parent by a child over sixteen years old, and witchcraft, a favorite crime for which our Puritan fathers provided the death penalty; all the preachers and most of the judges abhorred this offense. To quote Warden Lewis Lawes, of Sing Sing prison, "When they stopped killing witches, witches ceased to exist."

Why does a portion of the world still insist upon the death penalty for murder? Different people would give different reasons for this, but the real reason is that human beings enjoy the sufferings of others. The issue is always clouded by false statements, foolish inferences, and a wild appeal to the mob. Are there any facts to justify the belief that the death penalty lessens murder? Most of Europe has either abolished it by law or has practically ceased to use it. Italy abolished it for more than fifty years. When Mussolini came into power it was revived for political offenses. But Italy is in the hands of one man who no doubt thinks that his rule rests on arbitrary power. England has kept the death penalty on its books for many years but seldom uses it. England and Wales together, with some fifty million population, do not execute more than from fifteen to twenty people a year. Perhaps thirty or thirty-five are convicted and given the death penalty, but nearly half of these are reprieved in the Home Office; and in England a life term means not more than twenty years.

It has for years been the stock-in-trade of the haters to tell how much better the law is enforced in England than in the United States, and that this is the reason that there is less crime in Great Britain. But the statement is absurd and untrue. In proportion to the population, the United States executes four times as many as England and Wales, and this takes no account of the quasi-judicial killing by lynching of negroes in the South, and even in the North. So long as the hangers here could get by with the statements of the stern enforcement of the law in England they seemed to rest content; but when every one learned the truth they took up a new refrain: It was not that England punished individuals, but that their punishments were surer and quicker. The deterrent is not many punishments, but sure and quick ones, they now say.

No one knows much about why men violate the law, or why they do not. It is probable that the criminal statutes and the convictions have little to do with the conduct that we call crime. Human conduct is not controlled by statutes. It is true that of the people arrested a much larger proportion are convicted in England than here, but what does this prove? Scotland Yard seldom takes any one into custody except on thorough investigation and convincing proof. This is not brought about by the third degree. No officer could remain on the police force in that country if he resorted to the shameless beating and brutality that everywhere prevails in America. When the English police take one into custody he is pretty sure to be guilty. In America it is not uncommon to arrest five or ten, or even fifty, and subject them all to all sorts of indignities in order to find the one man. In the meantime, if the matter is at all sensational, the police are spurred on by continuous startling stories broadcast by the press, and the whole populace gleefully and righteously joins in the man hunt. I do not know how swift and sure is justice in the United States, or in any other land. In truth, I know little about the meaning of the word, and in this all men are alike. But I know this, that there is no country in the world, so far as I have investigated, where in any case that attracts attention a defendant is placed on trial so soon after the alleged offense as in our country. Professionals who criticise the courts in the interest of cruelty are given to pointing to cases that have been long waiting for trial. These delays sometimes happen before trial, sometimes after conviction and retrial. In almost every instance these delays are caused by the prosecution, when they do not dare dismiss the case for fear of criticism and know that they cannot convict.

Here in America it often happens that one is indicted one day and on the way to doom the next; and sometimes on the very same day. In the last few months we have been regaled with the quick responses of judges to public opinion. Really there is no reason for judges to intervene between the mob and the prisoner. They do not, in fact, intervene, but obey orders, and frequently are a part of the mob. These judges have been giving sentences running all the way from one year to one hundred and fifty years. It is only fair to note that in England the public press cannot comment on the facts, or alleged facts, of a criminal case until it is on trial, and then give only the barest report of the testimony. In this country, every detail, clue, surmise, and theory is given out every day until the public is as certain of the guilt of the defendant as the prohibitionist is of the sanctity of the Volstead Act.

When men recover from the obsession that it is only punishment and its dread that keep others from crime, they will be able to undertake the question of social order sanely and scientifically. They will accomplish real results without violating the safeguards of freedom, destroying liberty, and making a nightmare of life. There are more violations of law in America than in any European country; probably many more. What is the cause and what is the remedy? Is it bigger and better laws, or more and harder laws, or bigger and better prisons, or bigger and hotter frying-pans on which to sizzle the victims of luck and chance? Or, is it nothing of the sort?

All the European and Asiatic countries are made up of a homogeneous people. They live the same kind of lives, understand each other's speech, and, in the main, have the same religions, customs, habits, and ways of doing and thinking.

Their civilization is old, and they are not beset with strong ambitions. They have few fears and fewer hopes. America is new and big and ambitious and hopeful. Every one is looking forward to wealth to be got in some way, little matter how.

Every country in the world is represented in the various activities of this country; every creed and custom and manner of life, all hoping and expecting to get on. We have at least one race-question that is not seriously a factor anywhere else in the world, except in South Africa, and that is the negro problem. The Africans are the only people here who came without their own choice. They were brought here in slave ships, lived three hundred years in servitude, were then given what was called their freedom and turned out to shift for themselves.

I shall not discuss the negro question, as it is only a small part of the question now under examination. As might be known, the negroes have furnished inmates of prisons far beyond their proportion. They have also gone silently, unknown, unnumbered, and almost unwept to the gallows and to the electric chair. This is due to their inability to defend themselves, to their poverty, and to the deep prejudice that everywhere blocks their way.

The large immigrations from Europe have been of the poorest as a rule, and mainly the peasant class. They were optimistic, ambitious and active. It took them a long time to learn about our tastes, customs and methods. There are towns in our mining and manufacturing districts where more than thirty or forty languages are habitually spoken. Organizations like the Ku Klux Klan have done a great deal to create friction, prejudice and violence. A large proportion of our people are strangers and virtually aliens in their own new land. It takes a long time to become one-hundred-per-cent Americans and eligible for the D. A. R.'s and other superexclusive and patriotic societies.

In addition to all this, the Volstead Act has brought a reign of terror and oppression, outrage and assassination, to all classes of people; and this will not end until Volsteadism and all its kind are dead and done with.

Law violations come chiefly from our industrial centres. Our farmers make no trouble. They patiently submit to being sheared by all the fleece-gatherers that come their way. They live lonely lives and cannot be aroused into thinking or acting. Even the automobile and the radio cannot give them a good education or a broad outlook on life. Along the great farming section that stretches over the United States and Canada there is practically no variation in ways and habits from one to the other side of the line. In the larger cities it is somewhat different, for Montreal, Quebec, Toronto, Winnipeg and others are made up of a fairly homogeneous class that has little likeness to the general mixture in the United States. When our country is as old and as fixed in its separate groove as England, France, Germany, and China, we will be like them. It cannot be brought about by surer and sterner laws, but by age and its tempering, and that alone.

If State killings are what we need, we have more of these than any other land on earth, so far as I know. If it is laws that we need, we have them to spare, for no other land has spawned them out as we have. If the general opinion of the United States is reflected in court procedures, newspapers, and public gossip, the roughneck crimes are not the only ones in which we excel. It is universally known that all our municipal governments, most State groups, and all sorts of public boards are corrupt, and men almost invariably have grown rich and influential in "serving the people." From time to time it has been proven that the departments of the Federal government are the same. No one seems ever to consider these facts as having any bearing on crime. All we lack, say the Bromides, is more laws and worse ones, more enforcement and harsher methods, more terror and despair and confusion. To borrow from Pickwick: "Chops and Tomato Sauce."

No one can find any facts to prove that capital punishment has any effect toward preventing killing; no intelligent person disputes that we have more murders and more capital punishment than any European land. How about our own country? Some eight States have abolished capital punishment, and in these States the homicide rate is much lower than in the majority of the States of the Union. If I reasoned like the haters, I would say that this proves that capital punishment increases crime. But it does not even prove that. Most of the States where capital punishment is abolished are in the farming districts. In the South amongst the farmers the executions are more numerous than in any Northern State because of the situation and feeling between the white and black, and the impossibility of the colored man to ever get a fair consideration and chance. It will be long, long years before this situation can be overcome, and it will not be reached by legislation.

The list of evils that laws cannot cure would fill a larger volume than the number of evils that they try to cure. Some people glibly tell us that they would be in favor of abolishing the death penalty if men could be kept in prison for life. Most men who are sentenced to prison for life stay till the end of their days; but why should a man stay in prison for life, no matter what he has done? Nature has something to say about man's activities. Parents have children in their youth. They sail the oceans and explore the mines and go to war, and fight, and sometimes kill. They produce life and destroy it while young. When they are old they no longer populate the earth, or cut down forests, or work in mines, or go to war. No matter what they may have done in youth, when age comes they look for a snug harbor where they can doze their lives away.

I know one man who was sentenced to death when in his early teens who is now a helpless, tottering, garrulous old man.

He killed a little girl at fifteen, and yet the Commonwealth of Massachusetts still keeps him inside its prison walls. I once thought I would try to get him out. When it was discovered I was informed that it had been attempted before; that they put a cat in Jesse Pomeroy's cell, and he carved it to pieces while it was alive. I went to the warden with the story, to investigate; he told me that he had been warden there for more than twenty years, that he had often heard the tale and had asked other wardens and guards who had been there before his time, and the story was absolutely false and unfounded, without one scrap of evidence to support it. Then the warden added: "I have been here a long time. I will guarantee that you can put any animal, even a rat, in a convict's cell and he will pet it and treat it with the greatest kindness, he is so anxious to have its companionship."

If there ever was a reason for sending a man to prison, that reason no longer exists after he becomes old and harmless; or at any other time when it is fairly sure that he can live outside.

Death penalties have never been given because of any measure of the extent of guilt involved in the act, but simply because it was considered at the time and place the most serious of crimes. Nothing was so terrible as witchcraft, once upon a time, and this was because God said, in Exodus, "Thou shalt not suffer a witch to live." The victims of this commandment and the laws following have died in the most terrible ways. They have been torn limb from limb, boiled in oil, smothered, flogged to death; they have died by thumbscrews that slowly broke their bones; they have been drowned in water and burned by fire, all with the cocksureness of the judge who now pronounces doom for a human being whose mind he cannot understand and whose motive he could not possibly fathom.

Most people are familiar with the story in Exodus where the children of Israel, while journeying in the desert, found a man who had been picking up sticks on the Sabbath. He was brought to Moses and Aaron, and they were not satisfied what should be done in such a heinous offense, so it was referred to the Lord, and he decided that the man must surely be put to death; he must be stoned to death without the gate, which they forthwith proceeded to do.

Next to religious crimes, political crimes have always been accounted the most grievous and wicked and visited with the hardest penalties. This in spite of the fact that these victims are usually moved by the highest ideals, and ordinarily the future justifies the acts of rebels. Of course political crimes will always be punished strenuously. When a public benefactor generously chooses to rule a country, fixing his own salary, the hours of business, the amount of assistance he shall have, and what he may do, then the people should be very grateful and make his tenure safe, his work pleasant, yield him implicit obedience, and let him help himself.

The early Anglo-Saxons of England made their statutes very clear as to purpose. Here is a provision for habitual criminals:

"At the second time let there be no other bot if he be foul than that his hands be cut off, or his feet, or both, according as the deed may be, and if then he have wrought yet greater wrong then let his eyes be put out or his nose and ears and the upper lip be cut off, or let him be scalped so that punishment be inflicted and also that the soul be preserved."

I wonder why our present crusaders have not seen this statute?

Those who believed in the most cruel vengeance were still worried about the victim's soul. In the pronouncement of the death penalty now the judge adds: "May God have mercy on your soul." Probably this is true, because the judge does not know how to destroy the victim's soul himself and the law-makers, as a rule, consider this beyond their jurisdiction. However, with most punishments lawmakers and executioners do the best they can even to accomplish this end. When judges blithely and sonorously add to the sentence: "And may God have mercy on your soul," they have their fingers crossed.

The people of to-day deny that they punish from vengeance. They admit that they have indignation against the criminal, but their indignation is "righteous" indignation. The word "righteous" only confesses hypocrisy. Hatred is hatred. Prefixing the word "righteous" makes it in no way different. In punishment every effort is made all down the line to magnify the ferocity of the act and the moral delinquency of the condemned, so that the punishment will be fixed in hatred and anger and carried out in the same spirit. This carefully created emotion is called "righteous" indignation.

Are men kept from killing their fellows because they are afraid to kill? Every one who kills, excepting those who kill in the heat of passion, prepares a way of escape. The killer never intends to be caught, and often he is not. In the crimes of profound feeling and passion consequences are thrown to the wind and the certainty of the punishment of death does not prevent the act. If people are really kept from punishment through fear, then the more terrible the punishment provided the greater the fear. The old forms of torture should be brought back. These measures would have a tendency to scatter fear all over the place. The public has grown so soft that present methods no longer terrify. They forget the injunction of Nietzsche, "Be hard!" Our degenerate and effeminate lawmakers even seek to make death by the State as painless as possible, and thus take away most of the fear that is supposed to prevent the weak from committing crime.

If one should take the pains to ask a dozen men and women which they would prefer, life imprisonment or death, almost all of them would say that they preferred death. True, when the time came to die they might wish to live under almost any circumstances. But, as a theoretical proposition, without the imminence of death, almost all men and women prefer death to long imprisonment. There is certainly much less fear of death than of long imprisonment in the mind of one who is about to kill.

If hanging John Smith is to keep other people from murder, how is it to be accomplished? Plainly, it must be necessary that the public should know that John Smith is hanged. Both in England and America this was once made clear by hangings on a high hill in broad daylight, which were attended by thousands of people. These were abolished mainly because it was found that the spectacle, instead of preventing crime caused it, through suggestion. No country, however fierce and barbarous, would provide for public hangings to-day. This method of killing is not even contained in the Baumes laws. As a rule, the State kills people in the dark, with no one present except a few officials, a physician, who is not there to save life, and a minister, who is supposed to inform God to watch out for the victim's soul.

If men are to be kept from killing by fear, then all human beings of all ages, especially the young, should see what it means to die at the hands of the State. In this way the wicked impulse to go out and kill would visualize something of the wages of crime. These pictures are not shown because, in spite of the hatred and vengeance of the public, even the very common man still has some vague feeling that the young, especially, act from suggestion.

If the full details of executions could be vividly told; if men and women could visualize the horror coming from the fear and dread of this shameful and cruel death; if people could feel the agony of the days of waiting; if they could grasp every detail—all normal human beings would be so shocked to think of their part in the horrible deed as to get rid of the barbarism that inspires the desire to have some unfortunate killed by the State. The newspapers do much to bring this home to the average citizen. The trouble is that most men and women will not read them or permit the young to read the ghastly details. The weak or erotic who enjoy the story are sometimes induced by suggestion to repeat the crimes.

Another consideration that should have weight against killing by the State is the mistake often made in fixing just who is guilty. Every one knows the uncertainty in identifying those with whom one has little or no acquaintance. Almost every one has, one time or another, stepped up to some one in a restaurant or other public place only to discover that he had mistaken a stranger for some friend that he knew well. This sort of thing occurs almost daily on the streets; yet witnesses recognize, juries convict, judges sentence, and the executioner acts on the flimsiest identification. Especially in times of excitement and public outcry are mistakes often made. In these days it is seldom that men are acquitted. Any circumstance is enough to identify and convict and make the jury do their bit in stopping the crime wave.

It is well known that mistakes are made by courts and juries in ordinary matters. It is common for men to disparage the judgment of both. Few remarks about court proceedings are more common than, "I wouldn't trust a jury; I would rather have one or two judges pass upon the case." When a mistake is made and the wrong man is put to death it is always stoutly denied, and the only time it is admitted is when a man supposed to have been murdered turns up still alive after the execution has taken place. Warden Lewis Lawes, in his excellent book, "Life and Death in Sing Sing," states:

"Since 1189, when electrocution for murder was legally established in New York State, 431 men and 6 women have been committed to Sing Sing Prison for execution. Of these, 266, including 2 women, were electrocuted. Before the date set for electrocution, 2 died natural deaths, 3 committed suicide, 2 drowned while escaping, and 11 were pronounced insane and transferred to Dannemora State Hospital; 13 are now in the deathhouse, making a total of 297 who are dead, insane, or awaiting execution. The convictions of 54 men and 2 women were reversed by the Court of Appeals. Of these 31 were acquitted; 5 were reconvicted and executed; one was reconvicted and his sentence commuted to natural life; 14 were convicted of murder, second degree, and 1 is awaiting execution. The fact that 31 persons were acquitted and 19 others convicted in a lower degree after having been convicted of a capital crime causes one to wonder how many of the 261 who were executed might not have received new trials and been acquitted or convicted on a charge which did not exact the death penalty if they too had had money and friends to engage the most able legal counsel. . . . If juries and judges can err in one proved case, is it not possible that there may have been other errors which cannot now be corrected because the unfortunate man is dead? As a matter of fact, the juries and judges erred in 13 per cent of the original commitments for murder, first degree; and 51 per cent—more than half—of these persons were acquitted on retrial as not guilty. Is not the percentage of probable error entirely too high to warrant a penalty that is irrevocable? . . . The further assumption that the murderer is a dangerous criminal from whom society must be protected is flatly disproved by the figures, which show that 90 per cent of the men and women committed for murder, first degree, had no felony record. Nor is there a single instance in which a prisoner pardoned or specially commuted for murder, first degree, returned to Sing Sing because of a second homicide."

We all know the error of human judgments. It is easier for juries and judges to make mistakes in men on trial for murder than in any other affairs of life. The defendant is hated and hounded and despised. He is looked upon with obliquy and shame, and is almost always prosecuted by a skilled lawyer, and defended by some one not equal to the dangerous task. He is worried, harried, friendless, and in despair. Every word is construed against him, inference is made over-important. The dice are loaded from the start, and mistakes are many and common. No one can think of an irreparable verdict like death without shuddering at the contemplation of mistakes that can in no measure be repaired.

Quite apart from the rest, how far should society go in its wrath? The victim is not the only one injured. Where the punishment is death every member of the family, to the remotest generation, is injured by the shameful death of their kin. In the case of which my father told, I knew some of the third and fourth generations of relatives; it was often mentioned that an ancestor, or maternal uncle, or a distant relative, had been hanged.

Life is hard enough for most men and women without adding to the burdens and sorrows of a family who can neither outlive nor forget.

CHAPTER 41

A NEW HABIT

BEFORE I was of age I began speaking and debating. No doubt early environment was largely responsible for this. Before I was old enough to go to school at the academy I used to go up to the building every Friday night in the autumn and winter months. For several years, while I was in my later teens, the Literary Society met in the schoolhouse. My older brother Everett and my sister Mary were members of the organization, and before I was old enough to join I used to go to hear the essays and debates. It was some very pressing interference that caused me ever to miss one of these meetings. Our father always encouraged us to go, and sometimes he went along. As soon as possible I became a member and participated in the scholarly activities.

My interest in these exercises was stimulated by my father. The fact that he was a heretic always put him on the defensive, and we children felt that it was only right and natural and loyal to echo and champion his cause. Even in our little shop the neighbors heard vigorous discussions and found my father willing to meet all comers on the mysteries of life and death.

As a listening youth, my moral support was with my father. I never doubted that he was right, and the fact that most of the community was on the other side made me feel surer that his was the just cause. But in spite of the majority of the people being against his views, most of them respected him and his sincerity and recognized his learning and ability. Perhaps that early and exciting environment implanted a certain liking

for exchange of ideas and the evolving of whatever mentality
and personality that it thus brought about.

When I retired from the practice of law, I naturally could
not remain entirely idle. To be sure it was a relief to know
that I was not bound to do anything; still, loafing is not easy,
especially to one who has lived so actively for so long a time.
There seemed to be nothing that I could do but write and
speak. I had done some of both, during spare time, for many
years, but never considered myself an expert. I had written
some articles that had appeared in magazines, on subjects that
I was deeply interested in, and I had even written several
books that I could not say attracted any great attention, although two ran through several editions, and are still going
pretty well, due somewhat to the number of copies that I buy
and give away. The others did not do so well, but have some
readers. All my life I had made my living, and found considerable recreation in public speaking when I had the time to
spare; and in talking to courts and to juries I had practiced so
much and so long that I had learned to interest and hold an
audience, and there were many subjects that I very much enjoyed discussing.

Writing and speaking are two very different arts, of course.
In speaking, one easily has words to burn, as it were, and
slips in grammar, and repetition, are not so noticeable; indeed,
often the latter serves to strengthen and emphasize an important point. One can even make a poor start in a sentence and
with certain control and resourcefulness have it come out
passably well after all. Then, I never attempt speaking on any
subject that I am not thoroughly familiar with, and so know just
what I want to say. Political issues have always interested me,
and I have generally taken part in all important campaigns
since Grover Cleveland's first election.

In the last presidential campaign I was enthusiastically for
Governor Alfred Smith, and against prohibition, and spoke

nearly every night for six weeks before the election, and always in places of importance, and always had fine audiences, although I never thought that my favorite could win. In spite of the Wet and Dry issue and the many bigoted people who refused to vote for a Catholic, the main cause of Smith's defeat was the seeming prosperity which the Republicans have always worked to the limit. But all this time everybody was buying stocks; clerks, stenographers, errand-boys, men, women and children were growing rich. All of them gave wise tips to every one else. Any one with any sense should have realized that stocks were far too high, but the Republicans, with their money and luck, made the wage-earners believe that things would go higher still if Mr. Hoover was elected. When, a year after election of that magician, all stocks went down with a crash, and all sorts of business went to the bottom, too, the pikers, and even the professionals, did not know which way to turn. Now and then a wise Democrat would whisper to me confidentially, "Isn't Smith lucky that he didn't win?" This always made me tired; the Democrats are forever copying the Republicans because the Republicans have all the money; that is, a few of them have it. These knowing Democrats reminded me of my first vote for Grover Cleveland. Then, as always, the Republicans claimed that disaster and ruin would surely follow Democratic victory. We were told that unless Cleveland was defeated times would be hard. Well, Cleveland was elected and there was a substantial business reaction and considerable poverty, but I never knew a Republican to say that Blaine was lucky that he was not elected. They simply said that the hard times came because Cleveland got in, and they have said so ever since. As a matter of fact, it was a year from the time Hoover was elected until the panic, and in that year stocks went up as never before. On an average, the substantial stocks almost doubled in price in that one year after Hoover's election. And it should be remembered that the greatest financier since Hamilton, was Secretary of the Treasury Andrew Mellon.

If Smith had been elected there probably would have been a panic the day after his success, because the Republicans have made the people believe that Republicanism and prosperity are synonymous words; and indeed so they are with many Republicans. But it would not have been much of a panic. Stocks had just begun to soar highest when Hoover was elected.

I have been interested in every campaign from the time I cast my first vote. Never in my experience has a political candidate met all the issues of the campaign with the frankness and courage shown by Alfred E. Smith. While the defeat of Smith was overwhelming, it was not due to Smith, but resulted from a combination of causes that were overpowering.

It was unusual and most gratifying to see how many intelligent men and women recognized the straightforwardness of Smith and voted irrespective of party. The colleges and universities were an outstanding example of the truth of this statement. It seemed as though the teachers of these institutions voted almost unanimously for Smith. This, in spite of the fact that they had generally been aligned with the Republican party, and that there are few Catholic instructors in these institutions.

I cannot remember that I ever looked for a chance to talk. I am sure that neither directly nor indirectly did I ever challenge any one to debate, or seek to draw any one into debating. I have always been called on for much more than I wanted to do, or could do. For a great many years I spoke in various parts of the country without taking any compensation except expenses; and often, for some certain cause, where my interest and sympathy were strong and the urge was high and the treasury low, I have even paid the expenses myself. For the past forty years I have spoken in Chicago frequently and have never asked for money, and seldom received it.

From time to time, over a period of years, I debated at the Garrick Theatre on Sunday afternoons with George Burman Foster, a professor in the University of Chicago, and with Frederick Starr, also at the head of a department of the Chicago University, and others equally well known here and elsewhere. These debates were solely for the benefit of a free-thought organization that had a hard enough time to get along. I never accepted a penny for myself, but did insist that the others should always be paid a moderate amount.

I debated then as I do now, because of my interest in certain public questions. But since I have retired from business, and the demand upon my time and strength has grown from month to month, I lately have taken a fee for speaking and debating in connection with forums of various organizations, almost always outside Chicago. Especially has this come about since the panic, when I, in common with so many others, met marked losses and needed to do something to bridge the situation or else have to seriously cut down my living expenses, which in any event were never exorbitant. The reason for mentioning this is the numerous false reports about enormous amounts of money I have received in my life, including fees for addresses and debates. This would and should be no one's business, anyhow; there is no more reason that a public speaker should not be paid for his addresses than that a merchant should not be paid for his wares. All people seem anxious to live in this world, and it has been a long time since the ravens have been found feeding the prophets.

I would never undertake to instruct any one how to speak, but am besieged with requests to do so, as well as about how to become a lawyer of worth. The truth is that in this as well as in everything else, one needs individuality. People like to hear some one who is "different" even though they utterly disagree with what is said. And every one is "different" if he has ideas and has mastered a subject and learned to express himself well. I hope people have outlived oratory. Almost none of that is sincere. The structure, the pattern, the delivery are artificial.

When I was beginning to absorb and to act, all the young lawyers and speakers were aping Ingersoll's style. No one ever really spoke as he did; one could analyze Ingersoll's speeches if not imitate them; every sentence was rhythmical and in prose; as much so as the best of Keats or Robert Burns, or Housman in poetry. There was never so much as a word awry. There were the exact number of feet to fit the prose measure, and the subject. Evidently most of his speeches were accurately prepared; and, above all, he had something to say. I heard him twice, and with every one in the audience I was entranced. Along with the other aspiring lawyers I tried to adopt his style, and I think I succeeded fairly well, at that time, but it was not Ingersoll. Others tried, too, but most of them failed, so far as I knew. I have found a few who mastered his form of expression, but they lacked what Ingersoll never lacked, and that was something worth saying.

I took myself in hand. I made up my mind that I could not be Ingersoll and had no right to try, and did not want to try; that the best I could do was to be myself. For years, before juries, on the platform, in conversation, I have first of all tried to know what I was talking about, and then to make my statements clear and simple, and the sentences short. I am not at all sure that this is the best method for writing and speaking. The reader has time to consider, and go over the pages if he will; if he misses a word or does not understand one, or even an idea, he can look things up in the dictionary or encyclopædia. But the listener has but one chance, and that is as the information or opinion hastens along; so the words must not be too long, or too unfamiliar, nor spoken too rapidly for assimilation. Some grasp spoken matter quickly, and some need time to catch what they are not accustomed to hear. The speaker must aim to reach practically every person in his audience; therefore he must not speak too fast or use too many uncommon words.

My public talks have been mainly about politics, economics, labor, religion, prohibition, crime, and now and then on literary celebrities and what they have said and done. My debates have been on prohibition, religion, politics, and science. As a man's life consists largely of his ideas, I have felt free to present these questions as a part of myself and my life. Even this I have stated in my addresses and debates, so that my hearers would understand me and my attitudes from the start. Since I retired from the practice of law I have devoted more time than ever before to speaking and debating, but this activity will naturally decline, and already is waning, and probably nothing else will take its place.

In these debates, most of the speakers, whoever they were, have very nearly echoed each other's sentiments. This of course saved me from varying my arguments to any great extent. There is nothing new to say about prohibition; and little new about religion, except as scholars and excavation have added proof that the stories of the Old Testament did not come from Jews; and that every idea in both the Old and New Testaments had its origin long before the books, and that all of the events, and the stories, bedtime or other, were generally about something very different from the subjects they are ordinarily supposed to cover.

There is scarcely a city or town in the United States with a population of one hundred thousand or over where I have not spoken, excepting in Oklahoma. This discrimination was not due to any feeling I had against Oklahoma, or to any ban placed by them, but, somehow, it has never been along my line of travel. There are few towns of fifty thousand any place in the country where I have not spoken, and I have been in many of much smaller size. Most of the larger cities I have visited over and over again. In 1930 and 1931 I did more of this than ever before; I know of no reason for it but that I could lend myself to more engagements than when I had been otherwise occupied.

I spent a good deal of the winter of 1930 and 1931 in the South. I seem much like the Northern evangelists who are specially concerned over the souls of the Southern crackers in the winter time, but do not worry so much about them in the summer. During that season I visited most of the Southern States, in most of their large towns. On almost all occasions the audiences were large and decidedly responsive. In the debates there were generally a Rabbi and a Protestant and a Catholic. I alone represented the unrighteous, although I frequently had some consolation, and sometimes aid, from the Rabbi. One thing that especially impressed me was the eagerness with which all the religionists have seized upon the cryptic, imaginary, and more or less vapid assertions of Eddington and Jeans. No one doubts their learning and brilliancy in their special field, but that field is not religion. In that they stand like all the rest of us. Their claims carry no authority, but they are to be judged by their investigation of matter outside their realm, and on the consistency and reasonableness of their opinions.

It is more than strange that not one of these men has ever professed to believe that the Bible is an inspired book in the sense that it was given by God to man or that it is authentic upon the matters taught therein. Not one of them has announced any belief in personal immortality; true, they occasionally talk vaguely about spirit, without defining the word or attaching to it any such meaning as is taught by the orthodox. Neither of them would have been classed as a Christian forty-five years ago, or would be, now, by any orthodox believer. They do not claim to believe in individual consciousness after death nor an individual soul. They do not teach the resurrection of the body that all the Christian creeds assert as an article of faith. The statements of these men of their belief or unbelief in God and immortality would not so very long ago have sent them to the stake. The fact that orthodox Christians so eagerly grasp the vagrant straws floating by shows they are now content with the very smallest fragment of all that once they were positive was true.

Few men who are important in any community retain the old conception of the Bible, of a God, of hell, and their immortality, such as was once believed. Men have long been taught that they are immortal; that they are indestructible, and that the Bible is the direct word of God, and that miracles were once performed. It takes a long time for the world to abandon a fixed belief, with all the urge of the present and the past imploring its people to cling to faith.

CHAPTER 42

QUESTIONS WITHOUT ANSWERS

FEW debaters that I have ever met have had anything new to say about religion. Still fewer quibble a great deal about the meaning of the word "religion." I am well aware that it has been given all sorts of meanings by all sorts of men and all sorts of faiths. This is true because men have been loath to give up the word "religion" after they have lost faith in every idea that has so long been associated with creeds. To the great majority of the people of the Western world, religion is associated with gods and devils and angels, with heaven and hell, with life and death, either through the existence of a soul or the resurrection of the body, or both. If people wish to sense something of the change that has come over the world in religious beliefs they should remember that practically every Christian creed contains the words, "I believe in the resurrection of the body," and then ask themselves how many people that they know have faith in any such idea, which was specifically taught by St. Paul, and accepted by the Christian church.

But all of them talk of God as familiarly as though he lived in their apartment building, and they speak of the soul and spirit as if they knew what they were talking about. To seem to be very rational, they always expatiate on the wonders of the universe; the infinite number of stars, the grains of sand upon the shore, the greatness of man's intellect (without naming whose) and then, to cinch the audience and trap the agnostic, they ask, "Could all these produce themselves?" They implore the unbeliever please to explain how all this came to be; and after this, always meant to be startling and original thinking, they declare that it can be explained only by the existence of

God, who must have made it all. And they look down upon the agnostic, or atheist, or infidel, or whatever they call him, with scorn and pity; but always with more scorn than pity. Few of them seem to know that this argument was old two thousand years ago; that, in fact, so far as we can know, it may have always suggested itself to the mind of man. They ring in a few cryptic sentences from Eddington, Jeans, Millikan, and generally add that the best and biggest scientists now say that there is no such thing as matter.

I have just stopped to take a look at "The Stars in Their Courses," by Sir James Jeans, a fascinating little book, one of the latest discussions issued from the press. In it he gives the orthodox no ray of hope: The Earth was purely an accident, which may be over with soon; the old-time ideas of matter are changing; no one can tell how much more they will change; and no one knows very much about anything, and the little that is known is hardly worth knowing. All of which is probably true. Over and over he uses the word "matter" as it has always been used. I am inclined to think that no scientist disbelieves in matter, though we may revise, and no doubt have modified, some of the ideas that have been held concerning it.

I make no claim to being a physicist, although I have always been interested in physics. But whenever I go across a high trestle or a long span of steel and cement in Switzerland, or any other section of the Alps, and look down out of a car-window a thousand or more feet below, I am quite certain that I am sustained by something besides faith and by something that, whatever its form, has more substance than air or steam, or what we call a vacuum. I am quite prepared to believe that the sustaining substance has no such density as it appears to have; that, in fact, it is very porous; but, it holds up the train. I once asked the eminent physicist, A. Michelson, how large the earth would be if it could be compressed into a solid mass. He answered, "O—perhaps about the size of a marble."

I did not ask how large a marble; it really made very little difference. I presume solids are not so very solid; but, whatever it is that holds up a train over a chasm it is something that appears to have length, breadth, and thickness, and seems to be solid and hard, and keeps it from falling down into the depths below. If the scientists ever see fit to substitute some other word for "matter"—well, "it'll be all right with me." But I shall still trust the bridge and the chair I sit in.

None of these new discoveries seem to have any effect upon the seemingly important questions, "Is there a God?" and "if so, what is he like?" and "is a man alive when he is dead?" For any one interested in knowing just how religious are Mr. Jeans et al., he might do well to try and read his latest little book, "The Myterious Universe." I read it and found it decidedly illuminating, and some of it I understood.

It might be worth while to give a little attention to the old-time statement that there must be a God, for the universe could not make itself. When I am daringly asked if I can imagine the universe making itself I always frankly admit that I cannot imagine it; but still the question provokes some thought. If God made the universe, when did he make it? What did he make it of? Did he make it out of nothing? If so, can any one imagine something being made of nothing? It might be interesting to sit quietly down for a day or two, say, and try to imagine something being made of nothing. If you cannot imagine this, then was there matter before God made the universe? If so, did that matter always exist? Did it come before God came, or after, or at the same time? And suppose that God did not make matter out of nothing? Then the matter must have existed independently of God, and, if so, in what form did it then exist? It must have had some shape of which we can conceive.

Can one conceive matter when ready for the hand of God? It is difficult to imagine anything in some other form or manner than the way it now is. If one should conclude to think about these things before undertaking to talk about them, it might delay the conversation.

Then what about God? Did he exist in all eternity? Or, can you imagine all eternity? Assuming that you might imagine all eternity, how long would you need in which to imagine it? Is God something, or is he nothing? If he is non-existing, then can you imagine nothing that is something? If he is something, then did he always exist, or did he create himself? Did God who was already nothing make himself into something? If God is something, and existed from eternity, then is he not a part of the universe? And are not God and the universe the same thing? Did the same God who made this universe make all the infinite stars in the heavens, and did he make the sun and moon and stars for the inhabitants of the earth, or doesn't any one know anything about it? And if no one knows, or can know anything about it, why not say so? How can any one say that there is a God simply because he cannot imagine a universe creating itself? How do we know that the universe could not create itself as well as a God could make himself or herself, or itself? How does any one know that the universe could not exist without a cause? Does not the believer mean that he cannot understand or imagine how the universe could exist without a cause? If your senses prove to you that there is a universe, and your reason tells you that there must be a God who made it, or, that there must be a maker and you will call him a "God," then, do you stop asking questions? There certainly is one obvious question, so obvious that even a fundamentalist could not avoid thinking of it, and that is,—Where did God come from? The maker is surely bigger than his creation. If not, then the universe may have made God! Is it any more logical for you to tell me that the universe must have had a maker than for me to reply that, by the same logic, God must have had a maker?

Isn't it plain that an already serious question is complicated by bringing in a God? After all, when one is asked where the universe came from, isn't it a bit more modest and less foolish to answer, as I do, that I know nothing about it, rather than to assert that God made it, and, then, when asked where God came from, to suggest that God made himself "in the image of man"? The inhabitant of one of the tiniest of all the numberless planets! To the question of who made God, one might answer that some super-God made God; but this only calls for further questions about who, then, made the super-God, and —but one has to stop somewhere!

If there is a God, is he a being? Has he limitations in time and space?—or do you know anything about time and space? Has he length and breadth, thickness, or whatever dimensions metaphysics teach? I am in no way denying that there may be other dimensions, but I know nothing about them, either because I have not had the opportunity to devote to them, or because I am not able to understand them, or both. Is God a personal God? Of course the God of the Jews was a personal God. Very personal. If he is not personal, then does he pervade all space? Does he reach to every planet, and through The Milky Way, and out so far beyond, that The Milky Way would seem as though it were in your back-yard? Does he extend out into the Nebula M 31, which is so far off that it takes a hundred and forty million years for a ray of light to reach the earth, travelling all the time at the rate of 186,000 miles a second? Oh, pooh!—what does one know about it, anyhow, when he talks about God? Have you any conception of the being of whom you think you speak? Can one believe in a God without in some way forming an image of the entity of which he talks so much?

The response invariably hurled back has been standardized for years: does the doubter believe in electricity, in the telephone, and, now, in the radio? I may believe that electricity moves on a wire, by visualizing the wire and knowing that a force is sent across the wire. I have no conception of the force, but I do know how it behaves. I can form no image, because it is not a being, and not a subject for image. I do believe that a voice of some one whose voice I know speaks to me out of a box; I can form an image of the speaker, but what I hear are electric waves conducted along a certain path; I may have no conception of how the force is transferred; it is not a being, a thing, or object; it is not possessed of length, breadth, and thickness. The phenomenon of the voice coming out of the box can be explained and comprehended, but it cannot be visualized; there is nothing to imagine. It is not a form like a human being or any other being in which one may be asked to believe. The word "God" has come down through the ages as the name for a being who moves from place to place, who hears and sees and smells and feels, who has eyes and a nose; whom we address as "Our Father" because this word will the nearest express the attributes, the powers and purposes of this God to whom men are taught to pray. This God whom we ask to bring us what we need, to cure the sick, and heal the maimed, to defend the weak and vanquish the strong, whom men are urged to call upon in dire need, a real God whom the German asks to help kill Frenchmen and Englishmen, and whom the French and English besought to destroy Germans.

Since men have been taught to worship this being, man's God is endowed with all the characteristics of man; he loves and hates, he destroys and saves, he smiles, he curses, he is gentle, kind, compassionate, he is vengeful, cruel, and jealous. All his traits are human traits, all feelings and passions are human emotions. From the time man first talked of him, and besought him, and prayed to him, and hoped to go to him, so long as he must die, he has been visualized in human form, as one going up and down the earth not only destroying men in his hatred and wrath, but laying waste great cities and entire kingdoms, and fighting with other gods. Every one knows that through the ages this God has not been a force coming over a wire or a sound coming out of a box. To say that one can visualize a message or a wire or a voice coming through a radio is no sort of answer to the statement that one cannot believe in a being without forming a mental picture of the being. Before men pray in public with closed eyes and vacant stares, they must have a vision of the being to whom they speak, or else they are talking for the effect on the audience, which is probably the case.

Truth is, man has no conception of the origin of the universe. He has no scrap of evidence that it was ever made, or not made; except on the presumption that goes with the knowledge that it was here yesterday and last week and last year, and millions of years before. From this might be drawn the presumption that it has been here forever, but, it is only a presumption that cannot be proven. Not only is it not necessary for man to know everything, but it is impossible for him to know but the smallest fraction of what there must be to know. We gather knowledge by slow and patient labor, and there is little danger that we shall ever exhaust the unknown. No one should hesitate to admit that he does not know. Even the Christian world has gradually and markedly changed its idea of God. The flight of time and the growth of man have worn away some of the cruelty and barbarity of the Christian God. Probably few people of any sense or decent feeling would damn a race because an ancestor ate an apple when he was told that he should not. Such a God would be a devil, and could be worshipped only for fear. Neither could anything but a demon put a man to death for gathering sticks on Sunday, or drown all living things, or rain fire and brimstone on a city, or create a hell in which to torture human beings for all eternity. If I were afraid of the wrath of God, I should fear his vengeance more for believing that he is such a monster than I would because I insisted on thinking that he must have some of the commonplace virtues of men, and therefore could not have committed the deeds that his disciples charged him with.

Life cannot be reconciled with the idea that back of the universe is a Supreme Being, all merciful and kind, and that he takes any account of the human beings and other forms of life that exist upon the earth. Whichever way man may look upon the earth, he is oppressed with the suffering incident to life. It would almost seem as though the earth had been created with malignity and hatred. If we look at what we are pleased to call the lower animals, we behold a universal carnage. We speak of the seemingly peaceful woods, but we need only look beneath the surface to be horrified by the misery of that underworld. Hidden in the grass and watching for its prey is the crawling snake which swiftly darts upon the toad or mouse and gradually swallows it alive; the hapless animal is crushed by the jaws and covered with slime, to be slowly digested in furnishing a meal. The snake knows nothing about sin or pain inflicted upon another; he automatically grabs insects and mice and frogs to preserve his life. The spider carefully weaves his web to catch the unwary fly, winds him into the fatal net until paralyzed and helpless, then drinks his blood and leaves him an empty shell. The hawk swoops down and snatches a chicken and carries it to its nest to feed its young. The wolf pounces on the lamb and tears it to shreds. The cat watches at the hole of the mouse until the mouse cautiously comes out, then with seeming fiendish glee he plays with it until tired of the game, then crunches it to death in his jaws. The beasts of the jungle roam by day and night to find their prey; the lion is endowed with strength of limb and fang to destroy and devour almost any animal that it can surprise or overtake. There is no place in the woods or air or sea where all life is not a carnage of death in terror and agony. Each animal is a hunter, and in turn is hunted, by day and night. No landscape is so beautiful or day so balmy but the cry of suffering and sacrifice rends the air. When night settles down over the earth the slaughter is not abated. Some creatures see best at night, and the outcry of the dying and terrified is always on the wind. Almost all animals meet death by violence and through the most agonizing pain. With the whole animal creation there is nothing like a peaceful death. Nowhere in nature is there the slightest evidence of kindness, of consideration, or a feeling for the suffering and the weak, except in the narrow circle of brief family life.

Man furnishes no exception to the rule. He seems to add the treachery and deceit that the other animals in the main do not practice, to all the other cruelties that move his life. Man has made himself master of the animal world and he uses his power to serve only his own ends. Man, at least, kills helpless animals for the pleasure of killing, alone. He breeds horses and dogs, and fixes a gala day which is a society occasion when both men and women dress for the event, whereupon they turn loose a puny fox and set on its trail a pack of hounds trained for the chase. The noble men and women, riding at a mad pace, follow over hill and dale until, after hours of effort, the exhausted fox is unable longer to escape them, and with great glee they see it torn to pieces by the hounds.

Even intellectual men and presidents go to Africa for the purpose of hunting big game. They cannot run so fast as the deer and the giraffe, and they are no match for the lion, the panther, and the tiger. But they have invented a means whereby they can stand at a safe distance and kill them without giving them a chance of defense or escape. Man cares nothing for the pain of any animal when his pleasure is involved. He plans and spreads nets for the unwary creatures passing through the fields. He sets traps in whose sharp teeth the unsuspecting fur-bearing kinds are caught; and after prolonged sufferings they die, and he takes the pelts off the wild animals' carcasses and uses them to cover his own. He carefully raises herds of cattle, and at the allotted time takes the calf from its mother, cuts its throat for veal, and drinks the mother's milk. He builds great slaughter-houses in which to kill animals by the million, that he may use them for food. He raises sheep that he shears in the spring to weave into cloth to cover himself, and then, according to his desires, kills them and eats their flesh. He makes a shambles of the earth in order to satisfy his appetites and give him joy.

Nowhere in the universe is there evidence of charity, of kindness, of mercy toward beasts or amongst them, and still less consideration amongst men. Man is only a part of nature, and his conduct is not substantially different from that of all animal life. But for man himself there is little joy. Every child that is born upon the earth arrives through the agony of the mother. From childhood on, the life is full of pain and disappointment and sorrow. From beginning to end it is the prey of disease and misery; not a child is born that is not subject to disease. Parents, family, friends, and acquaintances, one after another die, and leave us bereft. The noble and the ignoble life meets the same fate. Nature knows nothing about right and wrong, good and evil, pleasure and pain; she simply acts. She creates a beautiful woman, and places a cancer on her cheek. She may create an idealist, and kill him with a germ. She creates a fine mind, and then burdens it with a deformed body. And she will create a fine body, apparently for no use whatever. She may destroy the most wonderful life when its work has just commenced. She may scatter tubercular germs broadcast throughout the world. She seemingly works with no method, plan or purpose. She knows no mercy nor goodness. Nothing is so cruel and abandoned as Nature. To call her tender or charitable is a travesty upon words and a stultification of intellect. No one can suggest these obvious facts without being told that he is not competent to judge Nature and the

God behind Nature. If we must not judge God as evil, then we cannot judge God as good. In all the other affairs of life, man never hesitates to classify and judge, but when it comes to passing on life, and the responsibility of life, he is told that it must be good, although the opinion beggars reason and intelligence and is a denial of both.

Emotionally, I shall no doubt act as others do to the last moment of my existence. With my last breath I shall probably try to draw another, but, intellectually, I am satisfied that life is a serious burden, which no thinking, humane person would wantonly inflict on some one else. The strange part of the professional optimist's creed lies in his assertion that if there is no future life then this experience is a martyrdom and a hideous sham.

CHAPTER 43

FUTURE LIFE

DIFFERENT theories have been advanced to show the origin of the belief in a future life. It very likely arose from dreams wherein the dead visit the living in their sleep. Every one has had this experience for himself. Often in my sleep I have had conversations with those who I knew were dead, yet they were so lifelike that I argued with myself whether the visit could possibly be real or not. Frequently the vision has remained with me in my first waking moments and it has taken an effort to satisfy myself that the incident was but a dream. It is not difficult to understand how primitive people could believe that they had conversed with the dead. All people are familiar with dreams. Not only are men subject to them, but the other animals as well. One who watches the sleeping dog often sees manifestations that the animal is hunting or running or playing. Dreams are fairly well understood by the biologist and the psychologist. At least, so much has been learned and written about them that it is not necessary to discuss the process here.

Then, too, it is easier to believe in life than in death. Life is the obvious thing for the living; absence of companions or acquaintances needs explanation. With the primitive man who misses his friend it is easy to think that he has wandered away. If the body still stays in the hut, it soon seems obvious that something important has happened that brings the inaction and the result that come with death. Thus arises the dual nature of man. One part has left his abode; the other remains until it must in some way be disposed of for the good of those who still live. But the part that has strayed away may return, so food is left at the door of the hut and is placed on the grave, in case of his homecoming.

So strong are dreams and visions that we often hear intelligent people argue with the greatest certainty that the dead come back, and are in constant communication with the living. In fact, a considerable body of people who call themselves Spiritualists are more or less organized in every country. These believe in the constant communication between those who live in the flesh and the souls of those who are dead and buried. The roll of membership has always shown a considerable number of men and women of marked ability.

The fact that there is a general belief in a future life is no evidence of its truth. Men have always harbored delusions of all kinds. Sometimes they abandon the ones held for other delusions, or give them up without providing for any substitutes.

In my early life I was much alarmed about my soul. Not that I ever feared that I should go to hell; I never believed in that sort of God. If I had I should have gone mad, as many others have done. I cannot recall that either my father or mother gave me any opinion about a future life. They certainly never sought to make any of us children believe either way. In the time and town where I was born, every one, so far as I knew, believed in a future life. Still, I observed when very young that none of them wanted to die. This in spite of the fact that they never tired of telling what a poor life this one is and how glorious the next would be. Almost every one in the country round went to church; although that fashion even there has gone into neglect and disuse to-day. Where I lived there were a great many ardent Spiritualists. This was not long after spiritualism was discovered, or invented, as the case may be, which occurred near Rochester, N. Y., in the middle of the last century. Two girls, the Fox sisters, seemingly exhibited new and strange powers and activities. Many men and women of eminence, including a considerable number of ministers, were carried away by the new-fangled and marvellous idea that the spirits of the deceased were able to communicate with those on earth. To be sure, it was not really new. The Bible is replete with such phenomena, as well as much other literature of the world; but it seemed new to the people of that day. A number of our neighbors accepted this fresh revelation. Each community soon developed its own mediums and their followers. Somehow I am satisfied that the converts came from people who had already virtually abandoned the old religion but still wanted to keep their souls. No living organism is willing to stop living.

In the hectic days after the Civil War many people embraced spiritualism, for the friends of dead soldiers were anxious to receive messages directly from the ones they loved. These they often seemed to get, though it was cryptic and not couched in good English, but, after all, as the medium contended, fairly good considering the means that had to be used to let the dead talk to their survivors.

My soul troubled me more then than now. My parents were growing old, or so it seemed to me then. When I visited my childhood home, long after, I found that the stone above my mother's grave related that she had died when only forty-seven years old; I am well-nigh thirty years older now than she was then, and I am still young. My mother seemed to me much older then than I seem to myself now. Often I went to seances and visited mediums, and this I continued to a much later date. In fact, I have visited them in most American cities of any importance, and many in Europe. I really have wanted to believe it all and therefore tried to, but in vain. I know that a considerable number of noted scientists have been and are Spiritualists. Every one knows of Sir Oliver Lodge, perhaps the greatest physicist in the world. Most educated people know of the famous naturalist, Alfred Russel Wallace, who discovered the law of evolution and reported it practically on the same day as Darwin announced the theory. Crookes, a well-known English scientist, and Flammarion, the French astronomer, and many other leaders in various fields, were and are supporters of spiritualism. But that a man is a scientist of attainments, and eminent in one field, does not make his opinion on any other subject more valuable than a shoemaker's; it would not be so good, in fact, on shoes.

After many years of examination and reading I am satisfied that spiritualistic manifestations are nine-tenths a fraud, and one-tenth unexplained phenomena; that the belief in this faith is about an equal mixture of credulity and the will to believe; there is no evidence of any value on which to base it. Spiritualists and other religionists have a weird idea of evidence. I have recently been examining a book on the "Evidence of Christianity" written by Simeon Greenleaf, who was a distinguished law lecturer in Harvard seventy-five or more years ago, the author of "Greenleaf on Evidence." He proceeds to proclaim principles such as the presumption of ownership going with long possession of land, and uses those principles that are rational in the affairs of life to prove that a man was born without a father, and that he walked on the water and rose from the dead. In a long life of varied activity I have discovered how easy it is to induce one to believe something that he wishes to believe. I am so sure of this, that if I am really anxious to have one believe something I spend most of my time in an effort to make him want to believe, and he will do the rest without any help from me.

It is not strange that men cling so tenaciously to the belief in immortality. In a large majority of the cases the belief is not a belief, but, in reality, a hope. Few ever investigate the evidence; they are afraid to face the question. Any one who even speaks of it as questionable meets the reception of the heralder of bad news. Almost every one who enters any discussion of it remarks that if there is no future existence then life is not worth while. It is amazing what confidence they feel that the being who made this life which is a failure would do any better with another. Most people instinctively feel that God couldn't do worse; and yet we are constantly told how much worse he can do and probably will do for most of the people of the earth.

If there is one single scrap of proof that we are alive after we are dead, why is not that scrap given to the world? Certainly under all the rules of logic, the one who assumes that an apparently dead person is still alive should be able to produce substantial proof. Not only is there no evidence of immortality, but the facts show it is utterly impossible for us there should be a life beyond this earth.

The word "immortality" must infer that the I or the you persists after we go down into the grave and our bodies are mixed with the elements; that memory, too, must be carried on; if memory does not persist there is no immortality; unless I know and can remember my life upon the earth, then there can be no connection between a future life and the present one. I will in that event be made over new. This can be no consolation to me now, because the new person will be some one else.

If I have a soul where did I get it? I know that my mother had some ten thousand cells that under certain conditions would produce a human being. To accomplish that, a cell needs must be fertilized by a spermatozoon from the body of my father; the ordinary male has some billion of these germs that could fertilize a cell; by some circumstance, fortuitous or otherwise, a certain cell and a certain spermatozoon met, a process of growth, change, and development resulted, and that finally became me. The other cells that were not fertilized and the spermatozoa that were not utilized in fertilization produced no human being. Neither the cell nor the sperm contained a soul; if so, then I must have some ten thousand brother-and-sister souls somewhere in the universe left unattached on my mother's side, and some billion more on my father's side; instead of my parents having eight children, they must be responsible for ten thousand billion. This is entirely too impossible and too long a chance for any one to hope for, no matter how strong his desire may be.

If I have a soul, then when did it start? It was not in the cell nor the spermatozoon. Could two substances without a soul produce a soul? If so, we have no knowledge of it, and no one pretends to know a thing about it. When the cell and the sperm come in contact the cell soon divides, then each of those new cells divides, and so on, until there are millions of cells, and finally a child is completed and born. Before life, and all through life, cells develop and increase and die by the millions, until finally through disease or old age or accident the remaining cells fall apart and decay. Did each of these cells through life and into death contain individual cells that will sometime meet as other human beings in a mythological place called Heaven, or in another place called Hell?

Of course the whole idea is shocking to any sort of reasoning process. The cells fall apart, and the man is buried in the grave, and in time mixes with the elements; he becomes a part of the grass, the trees, and all sorts of plants and animals, which in turn live and die and are mingled with all the varieties of life that still persist. Assuming that the individual has a soul, what becomes of it? Does any one ever dare to think of such a possibility? No; each one accepts the idea because he wishes to have a soul, but he never really seeks to know. Suppose that you were suddenly told that on the first day of next month you are going to Timbuctoo, that you must stay there for a year, and that you are to go alone, what do you imagine you would do? You no doubt would turn to the maps, or go to the railroad offices and steamship lines and try to find out how one would make the journey, and what sort of a place it is where you are to spend such a long time away from your familiar associates and old habits and accustomed environment, and what you would really occupy yourself with in the new place. Any person with any sense would make that much effort, at least.

But suppose that you were told that on a certain day you were to go to Paradise City, that you were never coming back, that you must stay there through all eternity, and that you were going to leave your body here, assuming that you were a reasonable human being, what would you do? First, you would try to find out where Paradise City is, what sort of transportation you would take, what kind of people were there, and, if you were not to take your body, just what you would take, and just what the place is like; and, would you stay on the ground, or would you live like a chipmunk, or a mole, or roost in trees, or float about in the air? Did any one who tries to believe in the idea ever ask himself these questions? If the departing one is going to Paradise City, and that spot is not on this earth, then where is it? All the other planets of the solar system are far away; the nearest one is millions of miles from here. The moon has no atmosphere and is wrapped in the icy clutch of eternal frigidity in which no life, as we know it, could possibly exist. The other stars of the universe are thousands of light years from the earth; of course, no human mind can imagine how a soul could travel the infinite distance of time and space. If the journey is to be made, then after the first twenty or thirty miles the rest of the millions of miles is such a frigid stretch that even the imagination can form no conception of its iciness; suppose Heaven is in the Milky Way, the home of countless planets, many of them of enormous size; a distance so great that it is not spoken of in miles; instead of miles, mathematicians find out how long it would take light travelling at the rate of one hundred and eighty-six thousand miles a second to reach the Milky Way; some of these stars are so far away that it takes more than a million years for their rays to reach the earth. With nothing to take, and no means of travelling, and nowhere to go except through endless millions of miles of space, it is evident that in order to believe one must first take leave of one's senses and refuse to even try to think.

I once heard a ten-year-old girl cogitating over the death of some one that had dreaded death but tried to be comforted with the belief that she would live again. The child said, "Father, if God is going to let her come back to life sometime, why did he make her die awhile first, and then have to go to the trouble of bringing her back to life, when she didn't want to die? Why didn't he just let her go on living right along?" That is a question that might well disturb any theologian who ever lived. Death is the common lot. But why death, if we are to continue living? If there is no death, what reason can there be for putting a human being in the ground, letting his flesh and bones decay, and sending his soul adrift up in the Milky Way, or somewhere else in infinite space? Why was he not born there? The reason is that the men who wrote the stone tablets long ago did not know that there is a Milky Way; they never got beyond a firmament above the earth whither men and women went up and down a ladder.

If there is any proof that man can get, why should not those who hold that proof reveal to the rest of us what it is? The reason they do not is because they cannot form even a conception, much less furnish a fact. None can know this better than those who profess to believe. The truth is, no one really believes in immortality. Belief must mean something more than desire or hope. Nothing in life that ever befell man is so important as life beyond the grave. Every one knows that earthly life is very short. They know that it is filled with disappointments, that to live is to suffer in body and mind. Most people are haunted by fear; if perchance they have friends, these die and leave them bereft. For a short time they live, fighting poverty, grieving over the loss of those they love, and most of all dreading for themselves the great destroyer of all delusions and illusions of life, Death. If man still lives when he is dead, why should he not want to understand all about it? Why should he put his fingers in his ears and run away when the subject is even broached? He would rather cherish the yearning and the faint glimmer of hope than to seek to find out. No one knows another, or himself, except by the physical structure and its manifestations.

There is no evidence of mind or personality existing outside of or apart from a physical form. Every one knows of the infinite number of deaths and dissolutions, and they also know that, so far as any scrap of evidence is concerned, individual death means the end of the individual life. They know that a dead body weighs no more and no less than a living one. They know that in dissolution nothing has "passed on" or off. A substance that once had life ceases to function, and at once decay begins. Those who say that there is no proof on either side of the question of immortality know better, if they ever dare to think. As well say that one may put a lump of coal into a grate and see it dissolve in flame and heat and ashes and say that there is no proof that the lump of coal is gone. We know that it has been changed to heat and smoke and ashes before our very eyes. We know that the lump of coal is gone; it has been reduced to its elements and can come back no more. We know that the same process goes on with a dead body; and of the billions that have been born and have lived and died there has never yet been a single exception to that rule. Every one, sooner or later, sits beside the bed of a beloved one and sees his life ebb away never to return, and still men say that there is no proof that death is death. I know no parallel in human presumption like this denial of the most evident and important fact that confronts mankind. Most of us would be willing to accept the slightest proof; but man hopes and prays and beseeches, but not a single sign comes out of the infiinte silence and the night.

By every method of reasoning we all know that each individual had a beginning. We likewise know just when and where and how. Can any one imagine an eternity with one end cut off? We know that we had a beginning; by all logic, as well as by the obvious facts, we know that we must likewise have an end; and as to the end, also, we know how and when it shall come. But we are solemnly assured that our consciousness, which we call life, and our memory, which strings its beads together, constitute our soul.

What are consciousness and memory? I have no remembrance of the months when I lay in my mother's womb, nor, to go farther back, when I was carried about in the shape of germs and sperms in the plasm that runs back through the generations that lived and died before I was conceived, probably back to the ooze and slime from which life came. I have no remembrance of the first few months after I was born. I know that I lay blinking and winking at the sun, crying and laughing without knowing the reason why, or even knowing that I was I; neither do I remember when I was an infant in my mother's arms, when I commenced creeping on the floor, when I put together certain sounds which my mother through love and imagination translated into words and meanings. So far as I am concerned, my awareness developed with my body. The early incidents that must have strongly appealed to my consciousness as a little child are all forgotten. I am sure of no recollections back of the district school.

I know that as I grow older my consciousness will begin to fail. I am inclined to think that it has already begun to slip but has not yet reached the toboggan. I know that my memory is not so alert as it once was, and nowhere so tenacious nor so quick. I am quite convinced that the tissues are hardening and the impressions that are now made on the brain are nowhere near so deep as in my plastic youth, when I was laying up all sorts of information to be used later in life to help me with living. I am quite sure that from now on every impression made on me will be slighter and last a shorter time, and if I shall have the great satisfaction sought by all men and women of living to the time of senility, I shall live in a perfectly vegetative existence with about the same consciousness that I had as I lay waiting in my mother's womb. Strange it is that all men who declare so loudly that they know there is a future life prefer senility to heaven. At least they are content to wait.

Often we hear the statement made that Nature never placed in man a desire that she did not gratify. This foolish remark is repeated and chorused by human parrots, as other birds learn other things without knowing the meaning of what they say. Few of the desires of my life have been gratified, and the same is true of most men. Every one who pauses a moment to think about it realizes how silly is this remark. Our yearnings and wishes far outrun our realizations. It is most likely that we desire things the more deeply because we cannot get them. But no man desires another life. That is the last thing he wants. His desire is to hold fast to the one that he has. He lives, and so he wants to live. But this is not peculiar to man; every other living creature on the earth shuns death and desires to live. Every tree and plant reaches out for life and uses every effort to go on living. Will all the other animals and plants take on immortality? Schopenhauer called this desire to keep on "the will to live." I think a better designation would be "the momentum of a going concern." Everything that is set in motion keeps going for a stretch of time after the power is turned off. If the desire to live proved anything it means that there is no future life, so we hang tenaciously to the life we have.

Men and women who profess Christianity die by thousands every day. No matter how fatal the disease, how great the agony, how sure they are of heaven, they will travel the world over and be cut to pieces by inches so that they can stay in this vale of tears a few days longer, when they might be singing hosannahs and enjoying all the pleasures of the blest. If any one knew of, or even had a strong belief in, a heaven of peace and comfort and joy they would be more anxious to go there. No one ever witnesses a group of children with tickets for the circus tarrying long outside the big tent when they know that the show is going on.

Every scientist knows that the individual begins to die when he begins to live. In youth and early maturity, when life is virile, when the emotions are strong and the love of living is at its height, life overcomes death and the excess adds to the size and strength of the structure. But there comes a time at life's meridian when the powers are fairly equal, and then the decline sets in; the old tissues die faster than the new ones are supplied, lost tissues are never fully replaced, strength begins to wane, and with it tenacity of power and memory; and finally life is gone.

Man's body is a home for disease; in fact, he is a travelling boarding-house for microbes. In youth his strength and vitality are enough to overcome them; in old age, for lack of other food, these parasites devour their home; and the boarders and the house go down together. This may not be a pleasant simile, but it is true. An optimist may be "a cheerful idiot," but he is at least an idiot and is proud of it. Probably he is right, but some of us cannot help knowing what we know.

Man is not only the home of microbes, but of all sorts of vain and weird delusions. How does he come to think himself so important? Man really assumes that the entire universe was made for him; that while it is run by God it is still run for man. God is just a sort of caterer whose business it is to find out what men want and then supply these wants. I remember John Roach Straton telling how God saved his life by coming down from heaven and opening his automobile door so that the reverend gentleman could get out and avoid an accident. He regarded it as nothing strange or incongruous that God should act as his chauffeur at that exact instant. The story would have seemed more reasonable if God had kept him alive awhile longer after having taken the trouble to save his life.

From where does man get the idea of his importance? He got it from Genesis, of course, which told of the creation of the earth, first, for Adam and Eve, and for the rest of mankind after that. The sun was of minor significance, made only to light the day for man, and the moon, of still less value, was for lighting the night. The stars were scarcely worth mentioning. "The stars he made also," we are told. Stars were just ornaments, sticking up in the firmament close to the earth. This is the only mention of the stars in the story of creation, excepting as they are alluded to in comparing the numbers of certain Jewish tribes "watching the stars," and one star is reported to have led three camels across the desert and to have stopped and stood still directly over a stable where Jesus was born. Is it easy to imagine a star coming down and halting over a stable in Galilee, when one pauses to remember that all stars are infinitely larger and hotter than the earth itself? It must come very close, of course, in order to point out the stable, or the village, or the planet, in fact. Yet there are full-grown men and women who have gone to school and have read and studied who profess to believe this childhood fairytale.

Every one knows that the conception of the earth as given in Genesis once filled the whole horizon of the intellectual universe. Whatever else existed was only for lighting the earth, adorning the heavens and pleasing our artistic and æsthetic sense, and that all the trimmings in the heavens were very close to the earth; so close that Jacob, in his vision, beheld the angels descending and ascending on a ladder, the only means of communication between heaven and earth known to the Jews at that time.

The conception of immortality, so far as the Western world is concerned, came from the ignorance of two thousand years ago. A primitive tribe of nomads believed that the whole universe was made for them. Small wonder that they could not believe that they should die and be no more. The universe had been specially created for them, this was their abode, and their only neighbors were God and the angels, and Satan, who was also specially brought into existence for them.

If man would exercise such little imagination as he has, and would contemplate all the life of the universe, human and animal and plant, he would have to admit that every form of life comes and goes in the same way. If he could feel the eternity through which all have lived and died, the eternity back of us, and the eternity still to come, then, in spite of how selfish, self-centred and superficial he is, might he not at least doubt that he and he alone of all created and uncreated things is worthy and eligible for immortality? He might even understand that whatever his deserts he might not get them, and therefore he should make the most of what he has. Not a single syllable can be said for the immortality of man that cannot be said for every other animal that ever roamed the plains and fields and woods, for every fish that lives in the sea, or ever lived in the sea, for the birds that soar above the earth and every creeping thing that grovels upon it;—yes, and for every microbe that boards alike upon the lords of the earth and the beggars that they turn from their doors. The whole idea is too illogical, absurd and impossible to find lodgment in any healthy brain.

But still men not only steadfastly refuse to think on this subject, but they openly proclaim that it is best to believe even if it is not true. It may be that a lie is more consoling than the truth, but it is a very dangerous doctrine. Who are the ones that are to choose the lies to be insisted upon and the truths that are to be denied? On the whole, the truth conserves and lengthens and adds to happiness. Most of the best things that have come to men are the result of discovering facts, of earnestly seeking and finding truths. Then, too, it is altogether possible that those who feel so sure that they can tell what is best for men to believe may be entirely wrong.

There is an interest in every organism to preserve what it has, especially its life. With this is the desire to keep its dreams and hopes and faith. But while every being may cherish what it has, still, if for any reason he casts it off, he soon ceases to mourn, and even forgets what he so reluctantly threw aside. I have questioned many people who have given up immortality whether it causes them pain because they no longer believe in a future life. Invariably they have answered "No," that they had lost all desire they once had for immortality. For myself, I frankly confess that I at one time tried very hard to hold to what I really felt was a delusion. I tried to because I could not bear parting forever with family and friends. When I met the question fairly and was convinced that it was a delusion and an empty dream I no longer worried, and was thoroughly reconciled to the fact. I am inclined to think that when once the race realizes that this world is the only world it will ever know, it will accept this conclusion without pain or regret. No one lives who is not unhappy as well as happy; let him look for a moment at the other side. Suppose we felt that the organism that each knows as "I" must live forever; through endless eons it must endure suffering, disappointments, and bitter cares; that there would be no chance to rest; no soothing, kindly Nirvana in which there is no thought, no pain, no joy, no dread—would not the prospect drive one to madness and despair?

The truth is that death, even as it has been distorted by religious teachings, is not man's first concern. It is the immediate things in life that bring trouble and worry and care; it is the next month's rent, the bill for food, the doctor, the lawyer, and the other heralds of misfortune. Man's first concern is the immediate disaster that he cannot dodge.

When we abandon the thought of immortality we at least have cast out fear. We gain a certain dignity and self-respect. We regard our fellow-travellers as companions in the pleasures and tribulations of life. We feel an interest in them, knowing that we are all moved by common impulses and touched by mutual understanding. We gain kinship with the world. Our neighbors and friends and we ourselves are travelling the same route to a common doom. No one can feel this universal relationship wthout being gentler, kindlier, and more humane toward all the infinite forms of beings that live with us, and must die with us.

CHAPTER 44

DELUSION OF DESIGN AND PURPOSE

SELDOM do the believers in mysticism fail to talk about the evidence of purpose and design shown in the universe itself. This idea runs back at least one hundred and five years, to Paley's "Natural Theology." There was a time when this book was a part of the regular course in all schools of higher learning, which then included theology; but the book is now more likely to be found in museums.

Paley points out that if a man travelling over the heath should find a watch and commence examining it he would soon discover in the watch itself abundant evidence of purpose and design. He would observe the wheels that fit into each other and turn the hour hand and the minute hand, the crystal made to fit over the face, etc., etc.

What the hypothetical man would observe and conclude would depend on the man. Most men that we know would think that the watch showed a design to accomplish a certain purpose, and therefore must have had a maker. They would reach that conclusion because they are familiar with tools and their use by man. But, suppose the watch had been picked up by a bushman or some other savage or an ape? None of them would draw an inference, for the article would be new to them. Supposing, instead of a man, a coyote or wolf came upon the watch, turned it over and examined it, would the animal read or sense any design? Most assuredly not. Suppose the civilized man should pick up an unfamiliar object, a stone, or a piece of quartz; he might view it and examine it, but it would never enter his head that it was designed, and yet on close inspection and careful study the stone or quartz is just as marvellous as the watch.

Paley passes from the watch to the human structure and shows how the mouth and teeth are adjusted to prepare the food for man's digestion, and how his stomach is formed to digest it; how the eye and ear were made to carry sensations to the brain, etc. Many of the clergy say the same thing to-day, in spite of the fact that the organs of man were never made for any such purpose. In fact, man never was made. He was evolved from the lowest form of life. His ancestors in the sea slowly threw its jellylike structure around something that nourished it and absorbed it. Slowly through ages of continued development and change and mutations the present man was evolved, and with him the more perfect and adaptable and specialized structure, with which he sees and hears and takes his food, and digests it and assimilates it to his structure. The stomach was not made first, and then food created for its use. The food came first, and certain forms of life slowly developed an organ that would absorb food to be utilized in the process of growth. By degrees, through the survival of the construction most fitted for life, the stomach and digestive apparatus for men and other animals gradually grew and unfolded in endless time.

To discover that certain forms and formations are adjusted for certain action has nothing to do with design. None of these developments are perfect, or anywhere near so. All of them, including the eye, are botchwork that any good mechanic would be ashamed to make. All of them need constant readjustment, are always out of order, and are entirely too complicated for dependable work. They are not made for any purpose; they simply grew out of needs and adaptations; in other words, they happened. Just as God must have happened, if he exists at all.

Turning from Paley and his wornout watch to the universe

and the physical world in general, is there any more evidence here? First, the "design and order" sharks ought to tell what they mean by their terms, and how they find out what they think they understand. To say that a certain scheme or process shows order or system, one must have some norm or pattern by which to determine whether the matter concerned shows any design or order. We have a norm, a pattern, and that is the universe itself, from which we fashion our ideas. We have observed this universe and its operation and we call it order. To say that the universe is patterned on order is to say that the universe is patterned on the universe. It can mean nothing else.

The earth revolves around the sun in a long curve not far from a circle. Does that show order? Let us suppose that instead of going in a circle it formed a rectangle. Would this not have been accepted as order? Suppose it were a triangle, or any other figure. Suppose it took a toothlike course, would that, then, be considered order? As a matter of fact, the earth does not go regularly in the same path around the sun; it is drawn out into the universe with the whole solar system, and never travels the same course twice. The solar system really has an isolated place in space. The sun furnishes light and heat to nine different planets, of which the earth is one of the smallest and most insignificant. The earth has one satellite, the moon. Saturn and Jupiter have eight moons each, and, besides that, Saturn has a ring that looks very beautiful from here, running all around the planet. We do know that all the planets of the solar system, and the sun as well, are made of the same stuff. It is most likely that every moving thing in the universe has the same constituents as the earth. What is the plan that gave Jupiter eight moons, while only one was lavished upon the earth, supposed to be the special masterpiece of the Almighty, and for whose benefit all the hosts of the heavens were made? Jupiter is three hundred and seventeen times the weight of the earth, and it takes four years for it to go around the sun. Perhaps the universe was made for inhabitants that will one day live on Jupiter.

It is senseless to talk about order and system and design in the universe. Sir James Jeans' book, published in 1931, "The Stars in Their Course," tells us his theory of the origin of our solar system, which is of more interest to us than the Milky Way. The theory of Jeans, and most of the other astronomers, is that there was a time when all the planets of the solar system were a part of the sun, and that some wandering star in its course across the heavens entered the sphere of the sun and dragged after it the planets and moons that make up the solar system by the power of gravitation. This is the planetismal theory, postulated by Professors Chamberlain and Moulton, of the University of Chicago. These mighty chunks of matter drawn from the sun rushed on through space at a terrific speed, and each was caught by gravitation and revolved around the sun. Their distance from the sun depended largely upon their size before gravitation held them in its grasp.

There is nothing in the solar system that could be called design and order. It came from a catastrophe of whose immensity no one could even dream. Religionists have pointed to the ability of an astronomer to fix the time of an eclipse as evidence of system. There are only a few heavenly bodies involved in an eclipse of the sun or moon, from the standpoint of the earth. The motions and positions of all these bodies are well known, and from this the passage of another heavenly planet or the moon between the earth and the sun can be easily determined. It matters not whether the date of an eclipse is far-off or near-by, the method is the same. To an astronomer the computation is as simple as the question propounded to the first-grade pupil: "If John had three apples and James gave him two more, how many apples would John then have?"

We know that gravitation caught the various planets at a certain point as they sped across space, and that these accidents of colliding bodies are very rare; the reason is that regardless of what seems to be the distance between the stars, they are so far apart that it is almost impossible for them ever to meet. To quote from Jeans': "For the most part, each voyage is in splendid isolation, like a ship on the ocean. In a scale model in which the stars are ships, the average ship will be well over a million miles from its neighbor."

Still, catastrophes have occurred and do occur. Our solar system was probably born from one. The moon was thrown from the earth by some pull of gravitation. The heavens are replete with dark planets, and parts of planets, and meteors hurrying through space. Now and then one drops onto the earth, and is preserved in some park or museum; so that in various parts of the world numerous specimens exist. If there was any purpose in the creation of the universe, or any part of it, what was it? Would any mortal dare to guess?

Our solar system is one of the smallest of the endless systems of which we have any knowledge. Our earth is eight thousand miles in diameter. The star, Betelgeuse, is so large that it would fill all the space occupied in the heavens in the whole orbit made by the earth going around the sun. There are many stars known to be much larger than Betelgeuse. The diameter of this sun is thirty-seven thousand times that of our little earth, for which all the universe is supposed to have been made, and whose inhabitants are endowed with everlasting life.

When the telescope is turned toward the heavens we learn another story. Leaving the sparsely settled section of eternity in which we live forever, and going out into the real main universe, we find worlds on worlds, systems upon systems, and nebula after nebula. No one can possibly imagine the dimensions of endless space. The great Nebula M. 31 in Andromeda is so far away from the earth that it takes light nine hundred thousand millions of years to reach our planet. The nebula itself is so vast that it takes fifty thousand years for light to cross it.

To make it still more simple I have taken the pains to figure the distance of this nebula from our important planet, called the earth, which boasts of a diameter of eight thousand miles. This nebula is 5,279,126,400,000,000,000 miles away from us, if my computations are right. I would not positively guarantee the correctness of the answer, but I think it is all right, although I did it by hand. I have gone over the figures three times, and got a different result each time, so I think the answer can be pretty well depended upon. I cannot help feeling sorry for the residents of Nebula M. 31 in Andromeda, when I think what a great deprivation they must suffer through living so far away from our glorious planet, which Mark Twain named "the wart," but which theology has placed at the centre of the universe and as the sole concern of gods and men.

What lies beyond Andromeda? No one can answer that question. And still there is every reason to believe that other worlds and systems and nebulæ reach out into stellar space, without end. It is obvious that no one can form a conception of the extent of space or the infinite number of suns and planets with which the limitless sky is strewn. No one can vision a beginning or an end. If it were possible for any fertile mind to imagine a conception of the end of space, then we should wonder what lies beyond that limit. We cannot attain the slightest comprehension of the extent of our pigmy solar system, much less any of the greater ones. The planet which is the farthest from our sun is Pluto, one of the smallest in our system. The diameter of Pluto's orbit around the sun is only about 7,360,-000,000 miles. This may be taken as the extent of our solar system. This can be compared with the distance to the nebula in Andromeda, which I hesitate to record again, showing the trifling importance of our whole solar system in so much of the universe as we can scan.

When the new telescope is completed and mounted on the

top of Mount Wilson, it is hoped that we can produce figures of distance that are real figures.

Among the endless number of stars that whirl in the fastnesses of illimitable space, how many millions of billions of planets are likely to be in existence? How many of these may possibly have as much special and historical importance as the tiny globe to which we so frantically cling? To find that number, go and count the grains of sand on all the coasts of all the waters of the earth, and then think of the catastrophe that would result to the coasts if one grain were shattered or lost.

In spite of the countless numbers of bodies moving about in limitless space, and the distances between them so great that they seldom clash, still they do sometimes clash. What is our solar system in comparison with the great nebula out there in the beginning, or end, or middle stretch of real space? Compared with that part of the heavens the density of the stellar population of our solar system is like the prairies of Kansas compared with the city of New York. Can anything be inferred about the origin or arrangement of all this, so far as man can tell, except that it is the outcome of the merest, wildest chance?

But let us try to clear the cobwebs from our brains, and the dizziness from our stomachs, and come back to earth, as it were. Let us talk of something where we can deal with what at least approaches facts. Does the earth show design, and order, and system, and purpose? Again, it would be well for the designers to tell what the scheme really is. If the plan is so clear as to justify the belief in a master designer, then it must be plain that the believers should be able to give the world some idea of the purpose of it all. Knowing winks and Delphic utterances and cryptic insinuations are not enough. Was the earth ever designed for the home of man? Sir James Jeans, in his admirable book on astronomy, shows us in no uncertain way that it evidently was not; that the human race has made the most of a bad environment and a most unfortunate habitation. Strange that the high-priests of superstition should so convulsively clutch Jeans and Eddington; neither one believes in a future life of the individual; neither one believes in the God of the theologians; neither believes in a special revelation, although Jeans does manage to say that Venus is the planet that the religionists thought was the star that led the camels over the desert to the stable where Jesus was born. Is this science or religion?—this bit of hearsay.

Even had this planet been meant for life, it plainly was not meant for human life. Three-fourths of the surface is covered with water, which would show that if it was ever designed for life it was designed for fishes and not for men. But what about the dry land? Two-thirds of this is not fitted for human beings. Both the polar zones are too cold for the abode of man. The equatorial regions are too hot. Vast deserts are spread out in various sections, and impassable and invincible mountain ranges make human habitation and the production of food impossible over immense areas. The earth is small enough, to begin with; the great seas, the wide useless stretches of land and the hostile climates have shrunk the livable portion almost to the vanishing point, and it is continually shrinking day by day. The human race is here because it is here, and it clings to the soil because there is nowhere else to go.

Even a human being of very limited capacity could think of countless days in which the earth could be improved as the home of man, and from the earliest time the race has been using all sorts of efforts and resources to make it more suitable for its abode. Admitting that the earth is a fit place for life, and certainly every place in the universe where life exists is fitted for life, then what sort of life was this planet designed to support? There are some millions of different species of animals on this earth, and one-half of these are insects. In numbers, and perhaps in other ways, man is in a great minority. If the land of the earth was made for life, it seems as if it was intended for insect life, which can exist almost anywhere. If no other available place can be found they can live by the million on man, and inside of him. They generally succeed in destroying his life, and, if they have a chance, wind up by eating his body.

Aside from the insects, all sorts of life infest the earth and sea and air. In large portions of the earth man can make no headway against the rank growths of jungles and the teeming millions of animals that are seeking his death. He may escape the larger and most important of these only to be imperilled and probably eaten by the microbes, which seem instinctively to have their own idea of the worth and purpose of man's existence. If it were of any importance, we might view man from the standpoint of the microbe and consider his utility as the microbe's "meal-ticket." Can any one find any reason for claiming that the earth was meant for man, any more than for any other form of life that is spawned from land and sea and air?

But, how well is the earth itself adapted to human life? Even in the best parts of this world, speaking from the standpoint of man, one-fourth of the time it is too cold and another fourth of the seasons it is too hot, leaving little time for the comfort and pleasure of the worthiest product of the universe, or, that small fraction of it that we have some limited knowledge about.

Passing up the manifold difficulties that confront man and his brief life and career upon this mundane sphere, let us look at the world itself. It is a very wobbly place. Every year, upon the surface of this globe, and in the seas that cover such a major part of it, there are ten thousand earthquakes, ranging from light shocks to the total destruction of large areas of territory and the annihilation of great numbers of human lives. Were these, too, designed? Then, there is no such meaning as is usually applied to the word "design." What "design" was there in the earthquake that destroyed Lisbon in 1755? The entire city was blotted out, together with the destruction of thirty thousand to forty thousand human beings. This earthquake occurred on a Sunday which was also a saint's day, and a large number were killed in a cathedral, which was also destroyed. And yet people talk about design and purpose and order and system as though they knew the meaning of the words.

Let us look at the earth as it exists to-day. It is not the same earth that came into some sort of separate existence millions of years ago. It has not only experienced vast and comparatively sudden changes, like the throwing up of mountain ranges in the cooling and contracting processes, but other changes not so sudden and acute have worked their way through ages of time, and changes are still going on all the time all over the earth. New lands keep rising, others sinking away. Volcanoes are sending out millions of tons of matter each year, new islands are rising above the surface of the sea, while other islands are lowered beneath the waves. Continents are divided by internal forces and the ruthless powers of the sea.

Great Britain was cut off from the mainland not so very long ago, according to geological time. The shores of America and Africa were once connected, as seems evident from looking at the maps, and countless other geological shiftings have happened all over the surface and inside the earth, so that the world was no more made as it is now than was man created as we find him to-day. The destruction of the island of Martinique, the Mont Pelée disaster, the earthquake of San Francisco, are all within the memory of many now living. Active volcanoes are continuously pouring solid matter into the waters and slowly or rapidly building up new land where once was only sea.

The various archipelagoes are instances of this formation of fairly recent times. The Allegheny Mountains were once thirty thousand feet high. The crevices of their rocks have been penetrated by rain, split by frost and ice, pulverized by friction, and every minute are moving off toward the Gulf of Mexico. This range of mountains, which once reached an altitude of thirty thousand feet at the highest point, now has its highest peak but six thousand feet above the sea. These mountains have been worn down day after day, and the Ohio and Tennessee and Mississippi Rivers, carrying off the sediment, are building up the delta on the Louisiana coast. The earth and its seas were never made; they are in constant flux, moved by cold and heat and rain, and with no design or purpose that can be fathomed by the wit of man.

The delta of the Nile has through the long ages been carried down in mud and sand and silt from two thousand miles away and deposited in the open sea; and this is also called design by those who look for things they wish to find.

Nature brings hordes of insects that settle over the land and destroy the farmers' crops. Who are the objects of the glorious design: the farmers who so patiently and laboriously raise the crops or the grasshoppers that devour them? It must be the insects, because the farmers hold prayer meetings and implore their God to kill the bugs, but the pests go on with their deadly work unmolested. Man prates glibly about design, but Nature furnishes not a single example or fact as proof. Perhaps the microbe who bores a hole into the vitals of man and brings him down to his death may believe in a Providence and a design. How else could he live so royally on the vitals of one of the lords of creation?

All that we know is that we were born on this little grain of sand we call the earth. We know that it is one of the smallest bits of matter that floats in the great shoreless sea of space, and we have every reason to believe that it is as inconsequential in every other respect. On board the same craft, sailing the same seas, are all sorts of living things, fighting each other, and us, that each may survive. Most of these specimens are living on the carcasses of the dead. The strongest instinct of most of our crew is to stay here and live. The strongest in intellect and prowess live the longest. Nature, in all her manifestations, is at war with life, and sooner or later will doubtless have her way. No one can give a reason for any or all of the manifestations which we call life. We are like a body of shipwrecked sailors clutching to a raft and desperately engaged in holding on.

Men have built faith from hopes. They have struggled and fought in despair. They have frantically clung to life because of the will to live. The best that we can do is to be kindly and helpful toward our friends and fellow passengers who are clinging to the same speck of dirt while we are drifting side by side to our common doom.

CHAPTER 45

THE LAW AS IT IS

In the summer of 1931 I had the opportunity to carry out an idea that had been in the back of my head for years—I wanted to help prepare a "movie" giving the main proofs of evolution, so far as it could be presented on the screen. I called in Doctor H. M. Parshley, an excellent zoologist associated with Smith College, to help carry out the plan, which resulted in a picture that illustrates the process of evolution; but—whether it will prove to be a success I cannot say; for the present it is well received and favorably reviewed and well attended. Perhaps, however, the general theatre-going crowd is not sufficiently interested in anything solely educational to give it an outstanding vogue. But it may help, at that, until people catch up, or something better is provided.

I have one further ambition that I may accomplish—I would like to produce a screen-picture showing the cause of crime and the treatment that probably would remove it from the world—but I cannot expect too much of the short time that is left of my life, and perhaps this dream is among the ones that will not come true.

For the past two or three years I have been only waiting. The time is too short for making any extensive plans. Anyhow, my strength is not equal to sustained exertion. It would not be possible for me to do the things that I once did. So, like others, I am giving a large part of what is left to reminiscences and dreams.

I cannot appraise myself, and will scarcely try. Sometimes I think that I have occupied too much space in the public eye; and that it is due to no merit or demerit of my own, but purely to chance. Then again, I think that whatever I have done is due to a degree of ability that I cannot estimate or understand. As a lawyer I cannot appraise myself. I know only one way that this can be tested, and that is by results. Under this test I believe that few lawyers have accomplished more in court than I have. Most of my criminal cases have been very difficult. This does not mean that my clients have been guilty or bad. In my vocabulary there is no such word as "guilt" and no such thing as moral wrong. Believing that the law of cause and effect reaches through every part of the universe—believing that men and women do what was set down for them to do and what was indestructibly woven through the whole warp and woof of life, I come to but one conclusion—no one deserves either praise or blame. In my defense of men and women I have sought to bring courts and juries to understand the philosophy which I think is largely responsible for what success I have had. Often my clients did not do the things with which they were charged; sometimes they did do them, and then I tried to make courts and juries understand the reasons why.

Various newspapers and magazines have stated how many murder cases I have tried, and that I never had a client executed. These stories have been exaggerated as to the number, which I do not know myself. Most of these trials have been long drawn out. Twice, at least, I have spent two years in a single case. I have been much in court for nearly half a century, and have tried many cases in many different States. It is true that I have never had a client executed in any case where I was employed and participated in the trial. I did undertake to save the life of a poor demented imbecile who killed the first Carter Harrison while he was mayor of Chicago, and I did not succeed; but he had been tried and sentenced and the case had been affirmed by the Supreme Court, when, with two fine lawyers, S. S. Gregory and James Harlan, I ventured to save him on an inquest of sanity, and we failed. Every one believes now, and most people believed then, that he was insane and idiotic; but he had killed a mayor, as another crazy man had killed President James A. Garfield, and was promptly hanged for the deed; but the execution of Guiteau, who was plainly insane, did not prevent another lunatic from killing President McKinley. In all these cases the people of course wanted the killer put to death, and the voice of the people is the voice of their God.

Prendergast, the slayer of Carter Harrison, was not the only one put to death when I had sought to help after there had been a trial and a conviction. For many years I tried to prevent all hangings in the State, and occasionally would snatch a brand from the burning. But I never had a client hanged when I undertook the trial of his case, and I never shall, for I would not dare to take another chance. Through it all, I have never picked my cases, but have taken what came along, so far as I could. I know that I have been unusually successful in winning them; whether I am an able lawyer or not I do not know or care; to be simply an able lawyer means no more than it would to be able to lift the strongest weight—like Sandow.

The lawyers who work for corporations as a rule deal in technicalities and fine-spun theories of law. They weave their webs as skilfully as spiders setting their nets for flies. As a rule they are called into cases of financial importance to find some point on which to base a defense. They have good minds and remarkable powers of concentration, but all that can be said is that through chance and training they have drifted into this sort of work; it requires no better brain than is necessary in some other kinds of law work, and probably not so good a mind as in certain fields of scientific work.

I never liked technicalities. I believe that few cases are ever won that way; I preferred to take the outstanding facts and do the best I could with what was obvious to all. This was my way, and I have almost invariably accomplished what I set out to do by this method; but I am not sure that it was the best way; I only know that it was my way.

The practice of one kind of law requires no more brains than the practice of another, and there are other realms of intellectual life that demand greater brain power and higher concentration than any branch of law. If I were to begin my life again, and had a chance to choose, I would adopt scientific research and make a specialty of some division of that form of learning, which has always interested me more than any other field of study.

The trying of cases in courts calls for an acute intelligence, the capacity for instantaneous thought and for deciding what to do in the twinkling of an eye. Delay often means defeat; one must strike while the iron is hot. The situation demands perfect self-possession; no matter how apprehensive one may be internally, he must remain as calm and unruffled externally as a placid pool. Seldom have I quarrelled with attorneys on the other side, with courts, or with hostile witnesses; when sure that the testimony of such a witness could not be modified, I rarely was curious or unduly inquisitive, but left it as it was. A jury watches every movement of a lawyer, and the verdict depends to a considerable extent on what the jury thinks of him. The jurymen do not like to see a lawyer browbeat a witness or quarrel with the court, unless it is plain that the judge is wrong. They do not have much confidence in a lawyer if he asks them to believe strange or preposterous things. This is not complimentary to their mentality; most of the men in the panel have some sense, plenty of charity and understanding, and often have made mistakes themselves; in short, they generally are human, and, after all, if a jury wants to save the client they can find a good reason why they should, and will.

The problem is to bring about a situation where court and jury want a lawyer's client to win.

Of course I have wandered far afield in my profession. I have interwoven it with other activities. I have always leaned strongly toward science and longed to give myself over to its study. I know something of astronomy and geology; I know a good deal of biology and psychology; that is, I would know a good deal of psychology if there was much to know. In that department of science I have spent a great deal of time and labor, and no one can make much of a success of any subject unless he knows a good deal about man himself. He may, it is true, make a dry argument on a drier point of law, emphasizing the importance of the letter over the spirit, but he can seldom travel far.

The practice of law has always appealed to the spectacular in life. It has been the gateway to politics and public life, while science furnishes some sort of a key to the mysteries of the universe. A sight of a courtroom in full action does not compare with a view of the heavens on a clear night, or the revelations of a microscope when turned in a certain direction, and focussed just right. The future is with science and not with the law. Very rapidly the business of the lawyer is being absorbed by other lines which save both time and money and get easier and surer and better results.

In my opinion, lawyers have always had too much to do with public affairs. Legislative bodies are filled with them. Their debates are long and prosaic; they never take a direct line when another can be found. Business men and physicians and scientists are much more practical; no business could be conducted on the lines of a court hearing. Lawyers work as though eternity is at their disposal and time would stand still to listen to their palaver.

Not only have I been interested in science, but I have liked to study sociology, philosophy and religion. I have found much in

Little Louis Epstine

By CLARENCE S. DARROW

Author of "Resist Not Evil," Etc.

HIS story is about little Louis Epstine, aged nine years. As might be guessed, Louis was a Jew. But there are different kinds of Jews. There are Jews who live on Grand Boulevard, and Jews who live on Maxwell Street. For the most part, the Jews on Grand Boulevard own wholesale clothing stores, and, for the most part, the Jews on Maxwell Street work in the stores. Louis Epstine lived on Maxwell Street. When this tale began, he had only one hand. How he lost the other is a matter quite outside of this story. It seems as if he was run over by a beer wagon when he was a baby. His nurse—or, no, it was an older sister, just past five—left him for a moment alone on the street, and the wagon came along. But he had long since forgotten all about this, if indeed he ever knew.

When Louis Epstine was nine years old, he went to a Jewish charity school. This was kept up by the wealthy Jews, who wished to do something for the poor. The fathers and mothers and brothers and sisters of the little fellows worked for the men who paid for the charity school. The patrons of the school never asked why their employees had to use the charity school. People do not get rich by asking foolish questions of this sort.

Louis was not the only child in the family. His mother had five more besides him, and they all lived together in two large rooms back of a bakery. They had lived a whole year without moving. The rent was five dollars a month. Louis had plenty of playmates when he was a child, for Maxwell Street is

© 1903 by the Pilgrim Magazine Co., Ltd.

she worked, what poor clothes she had, how she never went to a circus or killed a rat in the gutter, or had any kind of fun; how she got up every morning and fixed his breakfast before he was out of bed; and how she washed the dishes after he had gone to sleep. He felt very tenderly toward her. It was really more pity than love. And then he remembered a string of great red glass beads that he had seen hanging in the department store on the corner where he sold his papers, and which were marked forty-eight cents, and he thought how happy his mother would be if he could buy this string of beads. He was only a boy, and did not know why the beads were not as valuable as a string of pearls, and perhaps they were. So in his foolish, boyish mind he conceived the thought of saving enough money to buy the beads and giving them to his mother at Christmas time. He kept out a penny or two each day and carefully hid it away until he had thirty-five cents that no one but himself knew anything about. Every morning when he took his stand before the great store he looked in through the polished window to see that the beads were still hanging in their place. As Christmas time drew on, he always looked with quaking heart, for he felt almost sure that some rich lady would buy them before he had saved enough.

The eighteenth of December came around. The day can easily be remembered, because it was so very cold. This morning was far the coldest of the winter, and all through the night Louis had kept waking up because there were not enough quilts on the bed. In the morning he was ready to get up

and go after his papers before the usual time. His mother urged him not to go, telling him it was too cold, but Louis would not hear to this; it was only a week till Christmas time, and, besides, if it was cold he could sell more papers, for some of the other boys would stay away. So his mother got him a cup of coffee and a big slice of black bread with some yellow stock yards' butter—not a bad breakfast for a poor child in the Ghetto. In fact, somehow he had been getting pretty well fed this fall and winter. He still had the memory of a nice turkey that the alderman had sent them on Thanksgiving, and there was a rumor in the ward that this year another one would be sent on Christmas. Some of the boys said that the alderman wanted to be assessor in the spring. Louis did not know what this was. He had never even seen an assessor, but then he had never seen a king.

Well, on this morning, after breakfast, Louis' mother bundled him up the best she could. His shoes were not very good. He had bought them "second hand," or whatever it is with shoes. And they were really not mates, but neither were his feet exactly, for that matter. One shoe had a hole on the side and was ripped down the back, but otherwise was pretty good. The other was worn through in one place on the bottom and his old stocking stuck out at the toe. Both of them were pretty large, but his mother had always told him that large shoes wore the best and would wear the longest

Little Louis Epstine.

A magazine story by Clarence Darrow published in *The Pilgrim*, December, 1903.

all of these that was useful in court. Literature, also, has always held out its fascinations. I like a good book on any subject; but as a rule lawyers are not great readers; nor do they produce much literature; now and then a lawyer does write a good book, but it is rather seldom, and generally such a lawyer has abandoned law for literature; ordinarily, lawyers feel that literature should be avoided because it is too imaginative and absorbing.

I have given a considerable share of time to public addresses, and have put some of my ideas into magazine and other articles, and have even written a few books, one or two of which seem to be considered fairly good; at least they are so considered by me. One of my books is on crime, placing this question on a scientific and philosophical basis. Enrico Ferri, the great Italian criminologist, who recently died, strongly endorsed it in a work of his own on the subject. But although my book is thoroughly scientific, so far as we have gone with the problem, it has attracted little notice. What the public wants in the way of books on crime is detective stories that appeal to the passions. The public has so long been taught to hate and judge that it seems hopeless to try to teach any sane and humane ideas of conduct and reasoning. And yet, if a lawyer really knows something of science and life and reactions, and is able to express it simply, he can get a great deal of responsive understanding from jurors. Most of them have done things not exactly right, and of course all of them have wanted to; when their imagination is reached they can feel for the other fellow.

I would feel better about my work if I could see that any advance had been made in law since I was admitted to the bar, more than fifty years ago; in science and mechanics the world has been made over new, and on the purely intellectual side of life we have discovered new ways of thinking. Even in religion there is an entirely modified and broader attitude. The practice of medicine and surgery has changed almost as much since I was born as the ideas of witchcraft and sorcery in comparison with the Middle Ages. The whole material world has been made over, but the law and its administration have stood like adamant, defying time and eternity and all the intellectual and ethereal changes of our day and age.

CHAPTER 46

SLOWING DOWN

Since my return from Europe, in the spring of 1930, my activities, or rather my inactivities, have undergone a radical change, I have not been in court except on some formal matter that needed no concentrated application. I had definitely abandoned the practice of law. While nominally I have had an office, and my name and number in the telephone directory, I have not been inside the place more than two or three times in as many years.

It is strange how soon and completely one may change his daily scheme of living, and how rapidly the old fades away into the past. Time was when, save for temporary absence, I went down town to my office in the morning as regularly as a cow goes in and out of the barn at certain times of the day. Going down town in the morning and coming back at night grows so automatic that one scarcely recollects the trip from time to time. After changing in my way of life, it came to be a burden to go at all; in contemplation of going, the twenty-minute trip seemed like a hundred miles on the train, and the well-known faces at the office soon became so alien to my life that it meant an effort to go in and reopen the old associations in the scene and setting that had so lately been a part of my very self.

In spite of the hold of habit, man is a very adjustable animal. Not only do I seldom go down into the heart of the city, but I rarely go out of the neighborhood where I live, except for some specific and necessary reason. I can board a train and cross the continent, and crisscross it, without feeling any trouble or fatigue, and, as a matter of fact, I do travel a great deal; but that has become a habit, now, and therefore requires no readjustment; I have a definite purpose, and it does not affect my mind or feelings as a strange step or an inconvenience. I have lived for twenty-three years in the same apartment, and do not like to move. Indeed, I rarely go out except for a short walk. My son Paul and his wife and three daughters live a block away, and often I go to see them, or some of them come to my home; it is surprising how strong the tendrils bind one to those they love and to habitual haunts. An automobile ride in the evening or a game of cards or just a visit with my son and his family at the end of the day has grown all-sufficient for my social needs, and it is an effort to do more than that. Luckily, my eyesight serves me well, and here are books in every room, so I do not need to be lonely, and I am not.

I still enjoy a lecture, or a debate, if I participate, and cannot feel that I am failing, but perhaps I am. I shall never know that I slip until I slide, and mayhap I will not know it then.

My chief burden is my daily mail. I do get letters that I like to read, but along with them come many, many others that are a tax upon my time and strength, and there are others that leave me sad. Scarcely a day passes without word from some unfortunate within prison walls, or one confronted with some such danger. In one day, last week, I received five from different penal institutions in America. These, added to the customary appeals from poverty-stricken people everywhere, make any day dark. After reading a few of these letters one is scarcely inspired to feel optimistic about life or to rave about a kind and merciful Providence in charge of the destinies of us all.

How foolish and bromidic people can be. And how they drivel of getting what one deserves, and how love begets love, and good gets its sure reward. I cannot go about the country opening jail doors, I wish I could. Sometimes I write a letter in reply to some victim of fate, saying how helpless I am and how impossible it is to do anything toward mercy and understanding in a crazy world, but even this does not help my state of mind. The way of the world is all very, very weird; there are ten thousand seeking to get people into trouble to one who may try to get them out. Then I am told that people are so very bad. Yes, I know—but what people?

But I must leave this theme, for I do not want to write another book; and there are enough of the public now who think there must be something the matter with me, feeling as I do about these matters. These people are right if we grant their own assumption that they are sane. Then there is the daily lot of letters from cranks—just plain cranks, who do not know that they are that way, any more than the rest of us realize just what we are, or what others think we are. Countless persons send me their efforts at literature—manuscripts large and small; books that have never been honored with the attention of any editor, and never will be; and poems and plays, and skeleton forms of all kinds of writing—articles, essays, stories, on every conceivable subject, asking for my endorsement, a preface, in advance, or later, a review, often wanting me to place their work with publishers or to pay for private publishing and circulating, and even proposing that they hope I will finance them through an indefinite term of development of their talents, naming cities where they prefer to live. One such optimist sent his appeal air-mail, possibly thinking thereby to hasten on a first contribution. Seldom do any of them enclose return postage for their prized productions, that sometimes arrive insured, with requests to safely send them back. I am regarded as the chief support of our branch postoffice. Why these trusting strangers should send these things to me and depend on my judgment of them, and expect me to find publishers for them, I cannot imagine. If I knew that much about the business I would know how to write things myself that the publishers would not repeatedly return. I know only one way to tell whether the others write what is worth while, and that is by seeing if their ideas tally with mine; generally they do, or the authors would not send their stuff to me, but I have neither the time nor energy for the writing of prefaces, and so their prospective audience does not get an inkling of what not to read.

Of course I get a great number of letters asking me to take all kinds of cases—forlorn, impossible cases, foolish, ridiculous cases, murder cases, pathetic, haunting cases; letters from people who have been sold out by their lawyers and are searching for a chance to be sold out again. Often there are heirs to vast estates, offering to divide their millions with me whenever I will win their suits. Trinity Church, in New York City, is one of the stand-by cases. Thirty-five years ago, while in the East, I received a telegram from a Chicago lawyer-friend of mine, asking me to come to New York posthaste to go into an important case with him, which proved to be another effort to get the Trinity Church property delivered to the rightful heirs. I urged him gently but firmly to come home with me and forget it, but he would not leave. The members of the family who were his clients were the direct heirs, and not only had wicked men conspired to steal from them, but God was using this stolen property for a church and burying-ground. I told my friend that I did not care to look into the title; assuming that his claim was right, he would not live long enough even to make a start. But my advice was of no avail. He took a room in the home of one of the heirs, and never came back to Chicago. Twenty-five years later he died in that house in New York, and was not even buried in Trinity churchyard.

I get letters about other estates well known to most lawyers and shunned by all; letters about patent rights where some cruel lawyer has been "bought off," and concerning heartless creditors about to foreclose mortgages; and my advice is sought, and costs and personal expenses in pursuing such cases besides. What can I do? I am sorry for most of them; perhaps all of them have my pity. But, then, I have to be sorry for myself, as well.

There are the boys who wish to become lawyers, and want me to tell them how, and ask to be allowed to work their way for nothing in my offices, and especially to let them know just how I got my start and made my way into regular practice. And these, and an endless procession of school children want my autograph to add to their collections, and some of these and many others ask for my photograph, as they have the habit of doing with most of those who are at all in the public eye, I suspect.

For those who seek to learn how to cross the threshold of life I feel sorry, but I cannot tell; the only way to go is to stumble on as every one has always done. I know that the troubles of the young lie very deep; they have no experience and background to balance and temper their energies and emotions, their hope and dope. And then, as Olive Schreiner said, "Ambition is so common, and genius so rare."

Letters asking for money for various causes and purposes could not possibly be listed, but I cannot help them, although I know how much they need it, for it is all that I can do to take care of myself. Very lately one came which gave me a point in financing, a subject that I have never known much about myself. This letter related that in various ways the writer had drifted into debt to a large number of people, amounting to nearly ten thousand dollars, and that his creditors were annoying him; he wanted me to give him the total to pay them off so he could owe it all in one place to one person, in which way he could handle it easier. Perhaps the scheme was a really good one, but somehow it did not happen to appeal to me.

But the greatest crop of letters that come, in season and out, in a steady stream, are from those who are anxious to save my soul. As a rule they come from kindly, well-meaning people who feel it their duty to rescue me from my impending doom. They write me long, long letters, and original prayers, and some of them set hours of the morning or evening when I am to know that their entreaties to heaven in my behalf are going on the year around, and they quote passages and chapters from the Bible without end, and expect me to reply at length to each and every suggestion and assertion.

I get religious books and tracts, pamphlets, and brand-new Bibles and Testaments, and church literature, more than I find time to unwrap and dispose of. They all state that they are doing it for my "own good." But why bother so about me? If God is supposed to see and know all, and determine how things are to be, surely they might let him look after me along with the rest; and they hardly can think that they know better what should be done in my case, or that anything is not observed without their calling attention to it, or properly managed without their praying to have it looked after according to their wishes.

Occasionally a letter is abusive, as though I am doing the writer a personal wrong, and even insulting him, because I do not hold his views about religious matters. It is impossible for me to see his standpoint, or understand how such natures get pleasure out of trying to make me unhappy, or frighten me into their way of thinking. I sometimes try to guess what sort of looking person will take the time and trouble to write such a letter and spend two cents to get it into my hands; for often that class send their words of wisdom in some way that requires my signature to show that I got it, or at least put their names and addresses on the envelopes to make sure in that way. Many of these speak for themselves even before the envelopes are broken, and others are never read beyond the first few lines, for they all express themselves in the same vein, and generally ask me to be sure to read what they have to say to the end.

But mixed in with all the stereotyped and strange messages that come, often I find letters from friends, old and new, who have more or less fine sentiments and congenial thoughts; letters that make one remember that there is scattered through life a degree of sympathy and understanding and that the world is kindly and warm and humane and loving, in spots; letters such as any one finds time to read and that make one feel better all day without exactly knowing why, like the stimulant that cuddled itself against one's heart in the good old days when a person took a glass of wine or brandy for his stomach's sake.

Every few days I get some letter or other from a friend asking why they never see me any more, whether they have in some way offended me, and hoping they may clear up the mistake, if so be. I then have to answer, "No—nothing like that has happened; I am always glad to see my loyal and devoted companions, of course," and that I am only letting go of things in general. Nature treats all her children as she does the fields and forests; in the late autumn, as the cold blasts are coming on, she strips us for the ordeal that is waiting. Our steps grow slower, our efforts briefer, our journeys shorter; our ambitions are not so irresistible, and our hopes no longer wear wings. "Of course I shall go to see you soon," I say, "and will have you over to our house. We have been intending to call you up, but, there are some things that we must get done first, and, I think we will stay at home to-day, but—" from where I sit, ah—the bed looks mighty comfortable, and I think I will take another nap, so I go on—" soon, though, we surely shall get together." And I mean it, too, but, next day the big armchair in the front room lures me back to its depths, and by and by I gaze out of the window down over the treetops of the park; the walk winds through the green velvety grass on to-

ward the lake so blue and beautiful; I think I have done
enough for this morning; I think I will slip back and take another nap; I really do not feel like going anywhere else to-day.
Perhaps to-morrow—or the day after—I shall go and visit my
friends—perhaps!

CHAPTER 47

TOWARD THE END OF THE TRAIL

THIS story has stretched itself to a preposterous length. I hope no one will feel that I have used more type than was needed to record the outstanding affairs of any life. I have no exaggerated idea of the value of my own existence, or even of those close to me, to warrant so much as I have written. How many of the billions of the people who have lived upon this earth have left a record of their names in books, or manuscripts, or on carved stones, that could last a year after they were safely dead? None of the silent workers of the world, whose life and blood and toil are really responsible for what man is pleased to call the civilization of the world, have spoken so loudly or cried so hard as to be heard beyond the home of the neighbor who lived next door. What we call Time rolls on its course, and in the twinkling of an eye turns the puppets into oblivion regardless of how wildly they shout that the multitude may know that they are here.

It is not from any magnified conceit about myself that so much paper and ink has been squandered to relate this story. But when an old man sits down to tell what he has seen and felt, and maybe done, and what he thinks he thought, he rambles on and on as though the world were listening to his voice. But the book is long enough; in fact, much too long; and I shall bring it to a close. This I must do though it seems easier to ramble on than it does to stop.

This is the first autobiography that I have ever written. Strangely enough, as it draws to a close, it gives me the feeling of an obituary carved on a marble stone. And yet, I cannot realize that I am old, and that the sun has so quickly passed from the morning over the meridan, and is already rapidly sinking behind the clouds. Where can the long day have gone? It has been only a short time since I started on the road with all the world before me, and immeasurable time ahead for the journey I was to take; and now the pilgrimage is almost over and the day is nearly done.

What strange phantoms fill the mind of man! As a child, the world was unexplored and endless days and years were waiting for my eager feet. And now, where are those days that seemed to stretch out and away to eternity? What a difference between the length of the way when first one stands expectant with his life before him, and when nearing the end he dreamily looks back over the now-familiar path.

When I was a boy I used to drive a horse. I sometimes went beyond my home town, and the road seemed very long. But I noticed that it shortened every time I went that way again. I suppose it was because I grew so familiar with the objects along the highway that the route no longer seemed an interminable expedition, but a succession of short jaunts marked off by certain houses, and trees, and crossroads that I learned to look for as I went by.

Then, too, as I started out in the morning of life the path seemed long and alive with venture. Now, as I look backward, from this end, I behold a far-reaching chain of well-beaten by-paths, and marble stones along the way. How endless the unexplored road appeared to be and how very short the foot-worn trail seems now! There are so many other ways for measuring distance besides in miles. It is really meted out in emotions and sensations. All of the unknown looms larger and more enticing because we do not see the end, or know what objects we shall find along the way.

Just back of our house in Kinsman was a forest—oh, so large!—when I went through it as a child. But later on, after I had many a time raced around and played amongst the trees until I knew them, every one, it was so shrivelled that I could see clear through it without taking a single step.

When I was young, I used to look into the blanched faces of the old and observe their tottering, uncertain steps, and try to imagine the long, long journey they had come; it seemed that it must have been an infinite distance utterly beyond perception. The path had no personal relation to me. I could not penetrate the far-off time and space that stretched between myself and them. It was so far away that the old had no kinship or connection with me and my little range. If perchance now and then my attention would be called to the fact that all the sons of men had gone down that road, and that some day I, too, should be near the end, it brought no fear or worry, or realization of the fact, that now seems so true, and near, and grim.

And yet even now I can gaze placidly down the road without fear or special sorrow, or real regret. If once more I were starting along the way and could have the benefit of knowing in advance all that I have found out, no doubt I would constantly and widely vary the course that I followed in my blind and wanton years. But no child can begin the journey with the knowledge and experience of age. Wisdom cannot come from listening to the old, or reading what they say, but from life alone. And then, wisdom for the old is not wisdom for the young. If one could know in advance what would befall the day he would not be so joyous over the glorious sun rising in the east and bathing all the world with rich tints of rose and gold. The beauty of the earth sparkling with jewels on every leaf and stem and flower and blade nodding in the morning glow would be scorched by the consciousness of the coming midday heat. Whether Nature has a plan for deliberately luring youth cheerfully along the path, all unconscious of the end, or whether neither age nor youth can visualize reality, is not worth while to decide.

When a child, I was told that life, as I saw it unrolling to my intoxicated eyes, was not life at all, but only a beguiling dream; that the awakening would come on apace, and the dream would fade away. Whether the travelled road, as I look back, is a myth, I cannot tell and do not care. I only know that youth is youth and age is age, and the vision through which man views the world must hold a philosophy in keeping with his years. In that event, as he nears the end, he can look back upon the past without reproach or regret over what cannot be changed.

The zest of life fades away with the lengthening of the journey; else the aged would tear themselves to fragments in defying rocks and thorns in their mad quest for more. In youth, the earth seems none too large for us to encircle with our ambition and strength and love of life. But in age, a trip from the bedroom to the dining room, and thence on to the living room, is often far enough; then the imagination pictures a jaunt back to the cozy bedroom as most satisfying and restful to the exhausted emotions and the worn-out frame.

As the spirit and imagination of the youth look forward, so the feelings and tastes of the old turn to the past with its indolence and ease. To the youth, there is no life but the future, dangling with promises before his eager sight. Even in middle age one scarcely notes the waning emotions and the lessening zeal; not until he has journeyed far is he conscious of the approaching end, and even then he still finds enjoyment in reveries, remembrances, and the fairyland of dreams.

From what we have experienced as we blundered along our little path, we confidently and foolishly prate to the young of pitfalls to be avoided, just ahead. If the aged can get a belated emotion from freely offering advice, the youth can afford to pause and listen for the moment to his well-meant cautioning, but he need not act on the warning words. The young cannot live the life that is urged by the old. They speak a language that he has not yet learned. Time enough to heed the foolish croakings when he, too, is old and can no longer understand the young.

For either old or young nothing is so vain as regret, for at every crossing along the way each one has taken the road that seemed the best. All are led by feelings and desires that inevitably fix the goal. Neither could possibly foretell whether some other turning might result for better or for worse. One road may be easier or harder, another may be brighter or darker, but both roads, and all roads, lead to futility and oblivion. When one stands at the close of life he can make little use of what is left, so he naturally reviews the bygone years to find where he made mistakes; most likely he imagines that he might have done better for himself and others, and thus falls into moralizing about wasted opportunities and lost advantages. He forgets that the young listen only to the call of Nature waiting to lead them over the rose-strewn path awaiting their impatient feet.

Youth is the actor, age is the preacher. Youth says "Yes," and age says "No." It is perhaps as impossible to reconcile youth and age as it is to harmonize life and death. To the young their elders are old fogies who are always in the way. Experience can come only from one's own life. No one can live any other life, or really understand any other. He cannot even understand his own. No doubt Methuselah mourned over the shortcomings of the young who had lived but a few of his nine hundred and sixty odd years. But years do not necessarily develop wisdom; and there is no question as to whether waning faculties and tissues can be most reliable, for time inevitably causes decaying intellect, failing emotions, dulling sensations, and, withal, a wary and overcautious attitude to life in general. The opinions of the old are of no value to the young; they are out-of-date notions of conditions that are gone forever.

The apostle, two thousand years ago, had a saner view of life. He sang that when he was a child, he understood as a child, spoke as a child, felt as a child, but now he had put off childish things. He was doubtless right in characterizing his youth, but probably wrong in appraising himself in his old age. There is that "second childhood" which lacks the virility and dauntlessness of youth, whose pratings are no wiser than the sanguine prattle of the immature. The old often conclude their lamentations with the declaration that they wonder what the world is coming to. The fallacy in the reasoning is in ignoring the fact that the young will eventually be old, and it is forgotten that when the young shall have grown old they will no longer be the young.

Whether Nature has any purpose or not, man, like all the rest of animal life, is born puny and weak and helpless and without knowledge or understanding. He persists through childhood, youth, manhood, and old age. If he is spared through so long a time he goes out of existence as helpless and thoughtless as he came. If it had been consistent with Nature and life the child would have been born old. He would have entered the world with the experiences and the emotions that now come with maturity and years. His daring would be tempered with caution, his hopes checked by fears, his ambitions clouded with what the world calls wisdom, and the radiance of the morning and the noonday of his life dimmed by the twilight and obscured by the dark. We can conceive of no law of Nature that could make the young like unto the old, or make them both young and old; that would make the venturesome prudent, the curious sophisticated, and, in short, the living dead.

Whether the young could live without the old may not be clear, but it is reasonably certain that the old could not live without the young. For age to find fault with youth may be likened to the decaying tree in the forest that beholds with contempt the young sprout just pushing itself up through the mould; the dying oak may once have been the strongest and most virile of the forest; it seems to have forgotten that once upon a time it was a sapling insistent with growing life, crowding aside everything standing in its way; an ambitious sprig, reaching out its little roots for nourishment for itself. If the decaying tree had consciousness and imagination it should rather welcome the young shoot that will one day help preserve the forest, which in the eyes of Nature is much more important than any individual tree.

The young indulge in activities that seem useless to the old. Age forgets that physical exercise is an end in itself. The old man may go to the post-office for his letters and slowly walk back home. He has lost that quality that makes the youth run swiftly to the post-office for the joy of running back. It may be true that all exercise is only a means to the end; but, the mail is the desired end for the one, and the tingling of the blood for the other.

Every youth is a Columbus landing on an unexplored continent where all is mysterious and strange. He is not content to be told about the beasts and birds, the jungles and the woods. The dreams, fulfilments or failures, aspirations and experiments, thrills and tragedies that others have seen and heard and felt he wants to taste and test for himself.

Often it seems strange that of the infinite patterns that have been presented by Nature seemingly for our choice we did not select some other scheme. But no act was induced by choice; each one was the result of what went before, and if we look at life in its entirety we understand that we could have gone no other way.

In spite of all philosophy we are prone to feel regret over things beyond recall; but, alas, we go over the road once, and for all, and the best that we can do is to place a few markings along the way to help point the path for those who follow close behind.

When I was young I was taught all about the meaning of life, its high purposes, its snares and rewards and goals. Since then I have read many books teeming with "Beware" signs and rules and all sorts of formulas for "Good Thinking" and "Right Living," and have even tried to follow some of the promising advice, but often have drifted into what seemed easier ways and more alluring paths. The ideal road recommended seemed always rough and hard and uninviting, with but the vaguest promises of something better beyond. So, like the rest, I took the road that seemed to lead straight to pleasures close at hand. Thus I have blundered on my way, and have snatched as much enjoyment as possible from the stingy fates. I have tasted the hardness of the imaginary rewards along the blood-stained road of the pilgrims who follow the narrow and lonely way, and I have feasted with those who bring soothing and pleasant compensations to soften life. But even so, I would not undertake to prescribe which route to risk; but, whichever way one wanders, and whatever befalls, it does not last long enough to really matter a great deal.

Life is not easy. It is neither pain nor pleasure. We live, while our brief span lasts, quite regardless of joys or sorrows. We hurry along the highway before us because of deep yearnings and innate urges which we automatically obey. Whichever way we turn, the same doubts and difficulties plague us, the same appetites, habits, and visions beguile us, and we do not even choose whether to go on or to give up the game.

But if planning were possible, what would be the use? No one can penetrate into the future but a little way; at the beginning he cannot even guess what the end will be, and no revelation comes as he moves on; each day must be sufficient unto itself. The mariner who steers his ship across the sea does not fasten the rudder so that he will sail straight ahead; the best he can do is to change his course according to time and tide and wave and wind, keeping in view only the general direction and the journey's end.

As I write these pages I am close to seventy-five years of age. I realize that however the situation may seem to change from day to day, the destination is but a little way beyond. Am I satisfied with the trip and the results attained? To this I must answer "Yes" and "No," for as I journeyed along I could see ahead such a very short way through the mist and fog; if life could be lived backwards, and one could begin with the knowledge and experiences of years, it might be possible to do better;

but, on the other hand, in that case one might not even start! It is only the hope that the way will be smoother and the landscape more attractive that leads us on and on, until the night steals down and obscures the view.

I feel certain that the chief factor that determines whether life is worth the while to the individual is the nature of each human structure. Men do not really live in the present; they live in the past and in the future, and this is due to the peculiar organism that we did not create or choose, and whether one is satisfied with the past and hopeful of the future does not depend on accomplishments but on illusions and emotions.

Life and the enjoyment of existence is not woven from grim realities but is built on the hope that to-morrow will be less irksome than to-day. For it is modified with the everlasting insistence that over and above all is a purpose and a guiding hand that is beneficent and kind, and would not leave a hair unnumbered or let a sparrow fall unnoticed to the ground. Those who cherish such hallucinations forget that the all-loving power is inflicting tuberculosis, cancer, famine and pestilence on the trusting, simple sons of men. Few people try to think. Most of them deliberately chloroform themselves, lest a random thought might find lodgment in their brains. But with cocksureness they glibly advise others how to live and what to do. These all-knowing ones are forever prating of duty. Duty to what, and to whom, and why? Every one who looks at life with calm compassion and comprehension must admit the weakness of man, the terrible obstacles in his way, the severity of Nature, the infinite capacities of human beings for pain and misery. If he frees himself to some extent from the common ills and evils that surround mankind, he is torn and troubled with sorrow for his less-fortunate fellow beings. All about him are prisons and asylums and almshouses filled with the victims of misfortune. Others, equally the product of forces of Nature, are in hospitals, ill or maimed or mangled or dying.

Most men and women are haunted by poverty, and all are

helpless in the clutch of a relentless fate. The imaginative man pities the deaf, the dumb, the infirm, the poor, and even the defenseless animals who suffer untold agony without relief. If he wants to escape suffering with the world he must harden his sensibilities and close his ears and shut his eyes.

The outstanding fact that cannot be dodged by thoughtful men is the futility of it all. It is the consciousness of this, and the dread of total annihilation that has caused men to create the hope of another life, wherein mistakes and maladjustments of this life are to be somehow compensated by some form of eternal bliss. It is extraordinary that they can expect such belated favors of the same power that has made the lot of all conscious beings so hard to bear in the only world that we have ever known.

Every sentient thing draws back at the approach of death; this is instinctive, and goes with the will to live. I do not relish the prospect of parting with life, because I do not like to give up those that I love, and I have lived so long that I have formed the habit of living, and the process of giving up a fixed habit is never easy. But while I cherish no hope, or even desire, for another consciousness and another life, neither do I fear or especially dislike the idea of approaching Nirvana, which at least brings rest and peace. I have found that no one wants another life; we all want to go on living, which is quite a different matter.

I have always felt sympathy for all living things, and have done the best I could to make easier the lot of those wayfarers whom I have met on my journey through the world. I have judged none, and therefore condemned none. I believe that I have excused all who are forced to live awhile upon the earth. I am satisfied that they have done their best with what they had.

At seventy-five, I am not sure of how much or how little I have really accomplished, if anything, for the fellow beings of my day that live as my neighbors for a time and then are seen no more. I am reminded of what Simon is reported to have said when Jesus came to his boat in the early morning, "Master, we have toiled all night, and taken nothing."

It is possible that no life is of much value, and that every death is little loss to a world that seems bent on its way, utterly heedless of all the lessons of the past.

If I have been charitable in my judgments of my fellow man; if I have tried to help him as best I could; if I have done my utmost to truly understand him, I know why I have taken this course—I could not help it. I could have had no comfort or peace of mind if I had acted any other way. I have been interested in the study of man, and the motives that move and control his life. I have rejoiced with him, and have grieved with him; I have followed my instincts and feelings and sought to rescue the suffering when I could. But I know that I have done it more or less involuntarily as a part of my being, without choice, and without stopping to weigh which were most deserving or worth saving. If I had paused, I should probably still be wondering and doing nothing. I claim no credit, and I want no praise.

When I was a boy I used to wonder what the old could find to make it worth while to stay alive. I no longer marvel, for I know. True, I am old, and I can almost see the end, but I still live. The sun greets me in the morning with its warmth and cheer. The air is bracing, and the jaunt from the bedroom to the dining room is new each day, and as twilight comes on the bed seems alluring and grateful to the exhausted emotions and the weary brain. It is pleasant to awaken in the morning, and most agreeable to go to sleep at night; then some fancies and illusions still possess my mind. I am quite satisfied that many more days will come and go; if I were once more a child, worn out with a hard day's play, I would lie down with the same sense of more days to come. I have no idea just how many more days will find me here still greeting the friendly sun, but neither did I know when I was ten years old.

I know that the mortuary tables give a longer expectation of life at ten years than at seventy-five, but what of that? Is not a minute as large a fraction of eternity as a thousand years?

Each day is lived for itself, and even now I have my joys. To-night my friend, William Holly, is coming to dine and spend the evening in my home. He is wise, and kindly, and dear to me. I am sure that we shall have a most companionable evening together, discussing the ignorance and inhumanity of the world, the men that we admire and approve, and those whom we disagree with and dislike. And then, I am sure that my son Paul will come to-night, and I am always happy when he enters the room, for in his life of forty-seven years he has never given me an unkind word or shown any unfriendly conduct to regret; and he may bring his family along to gladden the evening hours. He now has three daughters, Jessie, Mary, and Blanche, and as they live but a block away we see each other often and they are a pleasant consolation in my closing years. Then there is my sister Jennie, the youngest in our family, who is a teacher, and my brother Herman, next youngest, who is a proofreader in Chicago. These two are the only ones left besides myself of our large brood, but there are nieces and nephews and other relatives and intimates. Often we have a roomful gathered around us, and we read aloud from the crowded shelves of my library, or from some of the many newer publications that steadily creep in, despite my resolutions to be content with what I have. Strange, that however our emotions wane and our bodies fail to respond, still the tendrils that attach us to those we love are ever green.

I know that when the guests are gone, Mrs. Darrow will fold back the bed and prop the pillows below my overhead light with tender, loving care, and I shall grow deliciously drowsy over the pages of a book from the stack on the round marble table-top at my side, and I shall drift off into dreams without fear or regret, and most likely awaken again to welcome another day, and whatever simple joys it may unfold.

Still, even old men have more extensive visions, and all my hopes are not limited by the day or night. I may go to Europe again in the spring, if the stock market recovers and I have enough left that I dare to spend. It looks as though something might be done; the newspapers say that the President is to appoint another commission to find out the cause of the trouble, and prescribe the remedy, and I am sure that after their report prosperity will be just around the corner.

I would like to go to Europe just once more. I would like to cross Trafalgar Square with its hundreds of pigeons being fed by the tourists, for the natives are too poor these times to share their crumbs with their pets; I would like to saunter over the Thames to the Parliament Building and to awaken in the Metropole Hotel, where I have stayed so many times during the past thirty-odd years, and hear *Big Ben* boom out the early hours, calling London to be mindful of the flight of time.

I would like to again visit Montreaux and view the magnificent Alps across the lovely Lac Léman, from the immense windows and the large balcony of the Hotel Beau Rivage, looking out upon the tremendous snow-banked Dents du Midis exactly opposite, like a keystone at the arch of the lake with its steep, sloping, colorful sides; and far away, beyond and above the rest looms Mont Blanc, placid, majestic and unconscious of fleeting time as it has always been. I would like to sit sunning myself in that rare atmosphere, lazily wondering how long the Alps have been there, and how long that beautiful blue lake has reflected the white-capped peaks upon its glassy bosom, and how long, perchance, the scene will continue, when I can see it no more.

And I would like to go to the Riviera again. I would like to sit and gaze once more over the magic Mediterranean, that is so entwined with the history, art and civilization of all the world, and very particularly with the day-dreams of my childhood inspired by my father's reverence for the historic sea.

Yes, I certainly should go to the Mediterranean once more and idle along its wondrous curves and capes, and drink its blue beauty with my eyes and senses and reveries and memories. I think I can stand the trip, for modern travel is very easy. The distance across the ocean is less than the length of a week. I shall be very careful of myself through the winter ahead so that I shall have the strength to go in the spring. And the spring will come soon, of course, with its warmth and life and brightness, better than any other tonic that I can take. Yes, I may go again, and once more I may see the beloved Mediterranean, ... I may, ... I may . . . .

THE MASSIE TRIAL

THE MASSIE TRIAL

It had been four years since I closed my office door and definitely withdrew from the practice of law. I was satisfied that fifty-one years of active court life was enough; in fact, too much. I was not sure that I needed a rest, but, like the pupils at school who grow weary and fretful when the warm days come on, I decided to pack my books, close the door, and go away. No longer would I get up when the whistle blew and hurry off from home because some one was about to sound a signal. So now I would no longer awaken in the morning, scramble into my clothes, manage to eat my breakfast, and get down to my office early enough to be in court at ten o'clock. I knew that if I was there on time, the judge would be late, but if perchance I did not get into court on the dot, there was the judge, sitting on the bench, painfully showing that he was annoyed because I had kept him waiting, while the county was paying the bill; this, of course, called for a rebuke, but that grew milder and gentler as the years wore on.

But still, I no longer wanted to feel obliged to be somewhere at nine o'clock, or ten o'clock, or any other o'clock, so I retired for good and all—this time. I had tried several times before to bid "Farewell" to my workaday world, but, reading, visiting, motoring, and even moonshining, grow monotonous at times; and even though there is nothing to do, one is bound to awaken in the morning from force of habit. It mattered not how hard I tried to go back to sleep, and how strongly I reminded myself that now I could luxuriate in my morning nap as long as ever I liked, I was wide-awake and unable to lose myself again.

The old involuntarily take on the habits of the young and

grow drowsy as daylight wanes, and this leads to awakening early in the morning, the very time of day when I once was so eager to doze along. So, altogether, loafing is not so ideal as it seemed to one who was anxious to welcome it as a dear dream come true. Four years of freedom from work, seemingly doing as I pleased, gradually grew monotonous and dreary. I was tired of resting.

So, when I was aroused from my seclusion and urged to go to Honolulu to defend Mrs. Fortescue and Lieutenant Massie, I wondered if I could stand the trip, and I was not certain that I could bear the daily routine, beginning in court early each day, and watching and catching all that goes on in a trial; I was not even sure that my mind would click with its old-time vigor.

I communicated my doubts and fears and misgivings to the friends and the relatives of my prospective clients. They decided to take a chance; one venture more or less to a sorely perplexed man or woman in the intricate meshes of the law does not mean so much as to one who is free from trouble.

Many times I have been asked why I went to Honolulu. I was not sure then, and am not sure now. I had never been to that part of the Pacific; I had heard of and read about its unusual charm, and longed to sometime see it, but whenever I could go so far away, for so long a time, I found myself embarking for Europe instead, feeling that I would get more and see more there for the time and money that would be required. I had never doubted the beauty and worth of the Hawaiian Islands, but rather thought of them as a fair illustration of a story I had heard, that was credited to Samuel Johnson, who was asked if a certain natural wonder was worth seeing, to which he replied that it was "worth seeing, but not worth going to see."

But the more I thought of those islands in the Pacific that I had so long wanted to see, and the more I investigated the strange and puzzling case, the more I felt that I had better go. I had read the press reports and I knew that the elements connected with it were absent from most criminal cases. To any one having in mind a composite picture of a criminal, as most men see him, such a picture would be as far from resembling my clients as anything could be. All of them were as high-minded, honest, kindly, and sympathetic as it is possible to find. It was obvious that there was no sordid or common motive back of the weird tragedy that time and fate had woven around their lives. It was a study in psychology beyond any question, and such cases have always interested me.

From the first, like most persons with imagination, as I read the accounts of the tragedy I wanted these people to win. Then, too, the so-called "depression" had swept away practically all the savings that I thought I had for keeping me comfortable to the end, and I needed the fee. This was not at all large, but it was sufficient. I do not know the relative importance of these motives, but I know that these reasons, and others, took me to Honolulu.

After two and a half days of travel overland and five across the ocean, Mrs. Darrow and I landed in Honolulu. Too many writers have ably described that Eden for me to undertake it here, beyond admitting that it is the only place I ever visited that turned out better than I expected. We were escorted to the hotel, and immediately I began the investigation of the case. By nighttime I had seen all my clients and most of the witnesses and given interviews to all the local and mainland reporters.

Before going into the case I had made it clear that this would not be a question of race, but of causes and motives. To my surprise, I felt better after the first day's activities than at any time since my retirement. At least it seemed so, to my delight. The next morning I went into court and asked for a week's time for preparation. This was promptly granted.

I found that a great deal of preliminary work had been done before my arrival. Mr. George Stanley Leisure, a young lawyer of New York City, accompanied me from Chicago; he proved to be a careful student and was of great assistance in the case. We grew to be close friends as the trial went on. At San Francisco we were joined by Lieutenant L. H. C. Johnson, a law graduate from Berkeley, who had given up the profession when the war came on, and joined the navy instead. He brought with him to the boat a full statement of most of the witnesses and persons involved, so that by the time we reached Honolulu we were all quite familiar with the case, and had about determined our course. As we docked, we were met by Mr. Montgomery E. Winn, who had thoroughly briefed the case as to the law and the facts, and who rendered most important services in the trial.

However much one may read of Hawaii, the stranger is apt to think of these islands as a foreign and uncivilized territory; to most people in all ages the words foreign and uncivilized mean much the same thing. But, aside from the greater number of brown people that one notices, there is no striking difference between the residents of Hawaii and ourselves.

Every case has difficulties peculiar to itself. There is scarcely anything of more importance in the fate of the defendants than the setting and surrounding of the drama. Hawaii was entirely new to me, and I made the island and its people a matter of first consideration. The story of the tragedy for which my clients were indicted has been widely published, and in various forms has been spread broadcast over the world. Despite all this, there was little chance to be deceived regarding the facts. Still many conflicting versions have been sent around the earth.

Thomas H. Massie, at the time of the trial, was a young man about twenty-seven years old. He was born in Kentucky, and had managed, by industry and the self-denial of his parents, to take a course of training which, with preparatory studies, required six years of hard work and close application. This qualified him for the position of a lieutenancy in the navy. After his graduation at Annapolis he married Thalia Fortescue, who was four or five years his junior. Mrs. Massie's family were old-time and well-known residents of Washington. Lieutenant Massie chose the submarine service, and was sent to Honolulu, where the United States has a large naval base known as Pearl Harbor. Here the Massies had lived for about two years when the now-famous tragedy attracted the attention of the world.

Lieutenant Massie is a kindly, sympathetic, human young man, generally liked by all who come in contact with him. I have seldom had a client for whom I formed a stronger affection. Mrs. Massie is a clever, unassuming, attractive young woman. She was but little interested in the usual round of social festivities that are common in army and navy headquarters when a country is at peace. She had a taste for books, made few close associates, had no special liking for card games, dancing, teas, and the activities that necessarily make up a large part of army and navy life when time hangs heavy on their hands.

One evening in the early winter, Lieutenant and Mrs. Massie went with some friends to a well-known inn. This was a restaurant of good repute, patronized largely by army and navy officers and their families and friends, and tourists who frequent and enjoy the social amenities of life.

Honolulu is, of course, a part of the United States, so prohibition prevails there just as it does on the mainland. When I say that it is observed the same there as here I mean it literally; so, at the party there was some drinking, no doubt, although no disorder, nor anything that could possibly be called unusual since the passing of the Volstead Act. So far as the evidence reveals, no one was intoxicated, but possibly some of them had drunk all they needed. Sometime around midnight, Mrs. Massie left the restaurant alone, unobserved; the evening was warm, rather stifling in the inn, so, Mrs. Massie went out to get some fresh air, as she had often done before. She had not been drinking; in fact, she seldom drank at all, and only moderately at any time, because she really does not care for intoxicating liquor. She had been present on other similar occasions, and, when she no longer cared for the gaiety, had gone home alone, so that her disappearance would not cause any special concern.

Mrs. Massie strolled along the brightly lighted street, and turned off into another road that led toward her home, a street frequented by many others, and one used by officers and their families when they got on and off the street cars in that vicinity. As Mrs. Massie walked along this street an automobile drove up behind her and stopped, and the occupants forced her into the car, taking hold of her roughly and pushing her in as she protested and tried to resist. Quickly she was driven away. None of the occupants were Americans. One was a Hawaiian and the others were of mixed blood. All of them were well known to the police, and were what in refined sections like Chicago and New York are called "gangsters."

It is my purpose here to sketch the story without elaboration or undue detail. My clients have heard it often enough, and then, too, the case against the assailants has not been entirely disposed of at this writing, although it has been tried once. None of these defendants lived in that part of Honolulu, but they had been visiting a road house or dance hall that Mrs. Massie had passed on her way to the point where she was waylaid. After taking her into their car, they drove her to a lonely spot, and, against every effort she could make, took her out of the car, broke her jaw in two places, and ravished her. Then they pointed her toward the main road, and drove away. Almost immediately after she reached the main thoroughfare a man and his wife overtook her, assisted her into their machine, and took her to her home.

When Lieutenant Massie found that his wife had left the inn and had not returned, he set out to find her. He telephoned to his house, but got no answer. With one of his friends he drove to one or two residences, occupied by friends, but she had not been seen or heard from, so he telephoned to his home. This time Mrs. Massie answered, evidently in great distress. Lieutenant Massie hastened home, and found his wife in a sad state of agitation and agony. He at once sent for a physician, and later she was taken to a hospital, and for weeks was under constant care and treatment.

The five accused men were soon put under arrest, and four of them were positively identified by Mrs. Massie. It was afterwards proven that all of them were present in that part of the town that night. One of these men owned the car in which Mrs. Massie was taken away; the number on this car was noted before she was hurried into the car, and was the number identified by the city clerk.

The conduct of certain policemen in charge of the case was soon under suspicion. Several of these officers at once took the side of the men who assaulted Mrs. Massie. This called for an investigation of the police department, and the chief and a number of other important members were dismissed, and the whole force reorganized.

After the assault many strange stories were circulated about the situation. These were often conflicting, and always sensational, and most of them highly improbable if not impossible. Some of these were sent to the mainland, and reproduced with all sorts of variations. The only basis upon which these rested was that Mrs. Massie had gone alone from the inn. No one who knew her had ever criticised her conduct, or had the slightest reason for suspicion about her.

Mrs. Massie was able positively to identify four of her assailants, yet the fact that the jury who tried them disagreed gave some color to suspicion, although in the trial no attack was made on Mrs. Massie's story or her character.

I have never had many acquaintances among the officers of the army and navy. So far as I have known them, I have always found them personally agreeable, but their views generally are not like mine. Still, I have so often differed with the ideas of most of my friends and associates that the opinions of people very seldom disturb me, however we may disagree. I have observed that in every community where soldiers and sailors and their officers are stationed a considerable percentage of the population are more or less hostile to them. I am sure that this was so in Honolulu, though I could hardly understand why any one should have that feeling. But I know that human beings are not easily solved, and are nowhere near so forthright as the other animals that inhabit the earth.

Oahu, the island upon which Honolulu is situated, has not more than one hundred and fifty thousand people; so, of course every one knows every one else, and small-town stuff is naturally rife.

Colonel and Mrs. Granville Fortescue, the parents of Mrs. Massie, have lived for many years in Washington, D. C., where they are well known and thoroughly respected. The news of the attack on Mrs. Massie reached them at their summer home on Long Island. Immediately Mrs. Fortescue started on her five-thousand-mile trip to Honolulu. Mrs. Fortescue is an attractive woman of intelligence and force of character, and on her arrival in Honolulu she at once undertook her daughter's cause. Like the others close to Mrs. Massie, she was shocked at the jury's disagreement, in spite of ample evidence, in the trial of the assailants, and this disagreement increased the number of idle and silly stories that passed from tongue to tongue. Now and then some of these were published in newspapers and magazines. Was there no way to vindicate Mrs. Massie's good name? Lawyers are aware that rarely is any one convicted in a criminal case after a disagreement of a jury. The Massies were advised by their lawyers that it would be almost hopeless to get a conviction unless one or more of the accused would confess. So, one night, a number of people, who evidently sympathized with the Massies, kidnapped one of the defendants and, as reported, obtained a confession. A photograph of the man's bare back showed bruises, plainly indicating that he had been through the third degree. The Massies' lawyers advised that the photograph would bar using any confession thus gained. The situation was growing more serious, and something must be done.

It is not easy for well-disposed men and women deliberately to kill human beings. Then, too, Lieutenant Massie is a gentle, kindly man who would find it hard to kill outside of his profession, and probably not easy then. Also the discipline of soldiers and sailors is very strict. They are thoroughly taught not to take human life except under the rules of war, and not to violate the law. All this may seem illogical and absurd, but, so is life. Mrs. Fortescue and Lieutenant Massie construed their lawyers' statement concerning the condition of the mutilated defendant who had confessed as at least a hint as to how a confession should have, or might have been obtained. Anyhow, they at once began to consider how to get a confession from one of the other defendants without leaving any trace of force that would make it incompetent evidence.

The leader of Mrs. Massie's assailants, Joseph Kahahawai, was a Hawaiian. He was naturally strong, and a trained athlete. He had been conspicuous in football, baseball, boxing, and in all sorts of sports. Kahahawai had been released on bail, awaiting another trial under the law as then administered in Hawaii; while out on bail the defendant was required to report in court every morning about nine o'clock; so Lieutenant Massie and Mrs. Fortescue planned to pick up Joseph Kahahawai at the courthouse and take him to Mrs. Fortescue's cottage, about two miles away, on a certain morning after he had reported. His size and strength and prowess were so great that it was decided to have some one else along to assist in case it should be necessary. So two non-commissioned sailors, Jones and Lord, were taken into the scheme. Both these men were strong and fearless and loyal, and, like all the sailors, devoted to Thomas H. Massie.

Mrs. Fortescue prepared a paper in the form of a subpœna, addressed to Kahahawai, commanding him to appear forthwith before the high sheriff of the island of Oahu. They arrived at the courthouse in two motors, one driven by Mrs. Fortescue and the other by Lieutenant Massie, who was slightly disguised. One of the sailors handed Kahahawai the subpœna, stating that Sheriff Ross wished to see him at once, and they hurried him into the machine and drove away.

Mrs. Fortescue had rented a cottage on her arrival in Honolulu; it was located in an attractive spot on a well-settled street. Two other houses were within twenty-five or thirty feet of her home. It took but a short time to reach the place, and they drove directly to the garage back of the house, from where Kahahawai was quickly urged in through the back door and told to sit down in the front room. Massie took a chair in front of Kahahawai. Lieutenant Massie stated in few words why they were there; that they wanted him to give a signed confession, telling the truth, and to do it at once. During this time Massie held his revolver directly in front of Kahahawai.

In the trial no one who was in the cottage testified but Massie. He told the jury of his emotions when the man who had ravished his wife sat there in front of him, how it recalled all the anxiety and trouble he and his wife had lived through for two or three months, and that he proposed to have the matter settled now. At first Kahahawai denied having had anything to do with the affair; but Massie grew insistent and threatening, and thereupon Kahahawai said: "Yeah, we done it——"

Massie testified that neither he nor the others had any intention of killing Kahahawai when they took him to the house, but, when he heard the man in front of him admit that he had ravished his wife, he was overcome with emotion, and he must have shot involuntarily, as he remembered no more. The neighbors in both adjoining houses heard the shot; only one bullet was fired. Of course, so far as the legal guilt of each and every one connected with the transaction was concerned, it mattered not who fired the shot, or whether Massie or any one else intended to kill. All four were in an agreement to commit a felony; perhaps the taking of Kahahawai to the home of Mrs. Fortescue, and certainly the use of firearms to intimidate and threaten was a felonious act, and each was responsible for the conduct of all. However great the provocation, and whatever the moral responsibility, there was no question about the law. Even though Thomas Massie shot accidentally, or while his mind was a blank, each was responsible because the killing occurred after the illegal combination was formed.

I am satisfied that there was no intention to kill on the part of any of the defendants, and I believe that most people who heard or followed the case were likewise convinced. There was evidently no preparation for any such dire result.

The bullet went through the lungs and large artery, and the lungs almost immediately filled with blood. Kahahawai lived but a few moments, and there was no struggle of any kind in the house. The body was taken to the bathroom and washed, and they hurriedly considered what could be done; one thing was plain: it must be taken away, and soon. So they wrapped the dead man in a sheet from one of the beds, took a piece of tarpaulin found in the garage, left there by a former tenant, and placed this over the sheet; Kahahawai was then carried out and put into the car, which was driven by Mrs. Fortescue, when the officers overtook it and halted its occupants, rapidly heading toward the high land that bordered the sea. Mrs. Fortescue was in the front seat and Lieutenant Massie was sitting at her side. Lord was in the back seat; Jones had stayed behind to clear up and set things in order in the house.

Where the three in the car were really going I suppose they hardly knew; they were hastening from the scene of the tragedy; they were obeying an instinct that all men follow. Their fast driving had attracted the attention of the police, and word had already gone out from headquarters to watch for and pursue the car.

Near the top of the slope of Diamond Head, a huge prominence jutting out into the sea, they were stopped and taken into custody, and conducted back to police headquarters. All the defendants were placed in the keeping of the United States Government at the Naval Reserve, within the gates of Pearl Harbor, about ten miles from the city.

Of course, all the attorneys for the prosecution, and those for the defense, as well as the judge, knew that legally my clients were guilty of murder. Yet, on the island, and across the seas, and around the earth, men and women were hoping and praying and working for the release and vindication of the defendants. As in similar cases, every one was talking about "the unwritten law." While this could not be found in the statutes, it was indelibly written in the feelings and thoughts of people in general. Which would triumph, the written or the unwritten law, depended upon many things which in this case demanded the most careful consideration.

First, what was the feeling in Honolulu? The island of Oahu, on which this city is located, holds most of the population of the Hawaiian group of islands. Oahu is the third largest in area, Hawaii being three or four times as large; it was the excellent harbor facilities at Honolulu that were first of all responsible for the number of people who settled there. The island of Oahu has about one hundred and fifty thousand inhabitants, and of these probably one hundred and thirty thousand are in Honolulu; of this population, at least nine-tenths could be classed as dark people: Hawaiian, Japanese, Portuguese, Chinese, Filipinos, Porto Ricans, and those who are a mixture of these and other races, and also the different races whose blood is blended with the whites.

The Hawaiians, who settled these islands, are called the natives, and, by some historians, are said to have been superior to any other races known. This claim may or may not be exactly true, but certainly they must have been one of the superior races of men; as near as can be determined, they were a large, symmetrical people, intelligent, good-natured and fine-featured. There are probably not more than two thousand pure Hawaiians on the islands to-day. The first influx of the white man brought them syphilis, which decimated the islands; the survivors were mingled with the whites, and at this time the Hawaiians and their mixtures are more numerous than any other blends. Next in importance are the Japanese; these are prolific and thrifty. The others are substantially in the order given, and no one is counted white unless of "pure" stock. This assumes that we know the meaning of the words "pure" and "white," neither of which really exists anywhere in the world. If one goes back far enough to count, the so-called "pure" whites are not more than one-tenth of the entire population of Oahu. The "long thin line" is growing shorter and thinner and darker every day.

The Hawaiian Islands have good schools, and all classes are accepted alike, and are equally admitted to all public places, and in most private homes. So far as I know, the Hawaiian Islands, especially Oahu, is the most obvious melting-pot in the world. What about "race prejudice"? I found none. Certainly none among the whites against the brown people. Many of the best-known and most intelligent whites have married members of other races in the South Seas. It is not safe to express prejudice against any race whatsoever in the islands; one may suppose a man to be "pure" white, but he may be blended with something else, or some of his relatives, or his best friends, are almost sure to be of mixed blood.

I trust my figures as to races, proportions, and so forth, will not be taken too seriously. I have not had time and opportunity for making sure, but my statements are near the truth, and in effect are truth, if not literal truth, and they are not carelessly made.

If there is no prejudice on the part of the white people against the brown, how about the attitude of the brown toward the white? This is a very different matter, which I was bound to consider in the trial of the case. Not so long ago the Hawaiians owned all the islands; now they have practically none of the land; most of it is owned by the whites. How did they get it? I don't know. Probably the way we got the United States from the Indians. The white men know more than their brown brothers, for they know that the meaning of life is to get all the property there is. The whites are not bad; they are just made that way. Are the brown people smart enough to understand this? I would say, "Rather!"

A clever Hawaiian princess is quoted as saying that the white man came to Hawaii, and urged the simple natives to turn their eyes upward to God. They did as they were bid, but when they looked down to earth again their land was gone. The other brown people, the new-comers, have accumulated little property, as yet, but the Japanese and the Chinese are rapidly getting on, and they do not really love the white man, either. All these brown folk feel toward the white man of the islands about as the American Indian feels toward our generation. Even though the white planters meant to be fair, they are sure to be more or less judged by results, and in Hawaii the whites have been successful beyond their fondest dreams.

I came to know more of the Hawaiians than of the other brown people, although I met a number of Japanese and Chinese, and they seemed not much different from other people; but I am sure that no other residents of the islands are better liked than the Hawaiians. They are kindly, cheerful, accommodating, and trustworthy, as a class. The Hawaiians are the politicians of the islands. They seem to hold most of the offices, and are obliging and prompt in the service of the public. At that, there are Hawaiians who are gangsters and hoodlums, but it is unreasonable and unfair to charge any land or any class with the derelictions of individuals.

It was unfortunate that all the men who assaulted Mrs. Massie were brown. This only meant that all men are more apt to associate with their own kind than with others. To be sure, it had to be admitted that the race question was a disturbing factor in the case. I have never felt any bias against any people on account of color or race, and I did not have then, and do not now have any race feeling growing out of the Fortescue-Massie case.

No lawyer on either side raised the question of color or race, and I knew it would have been fatal to our side to let anything of that sort creep in. I was morally certain that the majority of the jury would be brown men. I knew that the white men had no prejudice against the brown ones, nevertheless the brown men were prejudiced against the white. I was quite sure that had I been a brown man, and a native living under the circumstances that they met in Hawaii, I should have felt as our Indians do about the "pale-faces" who now own the land over which their ancestors reigned so long.

Nothing was more important to the case than picking a jury, and in this task we used all possible care. In spite of the fact that many more brown men were called than white men, when we finally accepted the panel it was made up of six white and six brown jurors—though, later on, we learned that two of the white men had Hawaiian wives. Nearly all of the nationalities to be found on the island were represented. Most of the men in the jury box were intelligent; for scholarship and native ability they would compare very favorably with a jury gathered in the United States.

The grand jury that returned the indictment against the defendants in this case were mostly white men, and for a long time they refused to find a bill against the defendants. Finally the judge took the matter into his own hands and ordered the grand jury to return the bill, but even then they refused to indict for first-degree murder, and made the charge murder in the second degree.

Throughout the islands the feeling amongst the brown people against the defendants was strong. The slain man was a Hawaiian, and, though none too popular in life, a host of his friends rallied to his funeral, the largest ever assembled in Honolulu, excepting that of a prince or princess once upon a time. That Kahahawai had been in prison and was generally known as a hoodlum seemed to be forgotten by his followers, and their feelings were strengthened by the circumstances of the strange tragedy surrounding his death. With the complexion of the jury, and the intense sentiment for the deceased, the situation seemed none too good. The cruel assault against Mrs. Massie seemed lost sight of in the spotlight which created a sort of halo around the head of Kahahawai.

Both sides seemed to have the utmost confidence in Judge Charles S. Davis. He was born in New England, and brought to Honolulu by his father when a young boy. His father practised law there for many years, and was long regarded as one of the leaders of the Bar. Judge Davis was educated in California, and himself was a prominent figure in Honolulu after admission to the Bar. Every one in the islands had full faith in his ability and integrity, and he was a man of broad and humane tendencies. This in no way prevented his instructing the jury in no uncertain terms, and with sufficient frequency, that no conceivable provocation could justify taking the law into one's own hands. Also, his instructions left no doubt that each member of a conspiracy was responsible for all the acts of every other member, and that even if Lieutenant Massie was insane when he fired the shot, it could in no way excuse him or any one associated with him if the conspiracy to commit a felony was formed before he became insane.

The attorneys for the State offered no direct evidence of the tragedy at the Fortescue cottage. They did present evidence, circumstantial and direct, to prove the taking of Kahahawai from the front of the courthouse door. They showed who hired the automobiles, and who was present when the deceased was taken; they produced the pretended subpœna that was handed to Kahahawai before he entered the car, and proved that Mrs. Fortescue had prepared it. They proved that a shot was fired in the house, and that some blood was still on the floor. They proved the wild flight of the car carrying the dead man, the capture of the passengers, and their subsequent statements. The circumstantial evidence was so strong that it was necessary for the defense to put in full evidence as to the carrying away of Kahahawai and the way he was killed in the house, and to admit the connection of all the defendants with the tragedy.

The whole case was dramatic and intensely interesting, if not haunting. The courtroom was jammed with anxious listeners, day after day, many waiting outside all night so they would be sure to get in when the case opened in the morning. The Honolulu papers carried a full stenographic report of the case, and the daily press on the mainland gave almost as full an account.

The judge held, no doubt correctly, that the defense had no right to introduce evidence to prove the assault on Mrs. Massie. This, on the theory that, no matter what the provocation might be, no one had the right to take the law into his own hands. But we were permitted to prove whatever Lieutenant Massie knew about it, and everything that he had been told by his wife or any one else regarding the assault; this permitted the wife to tell in court every detail as related by her to her husband, and also allowed the physicians to repeat to the jury all the reports made to Massie concerning the condition of his wife. In this way, the jury heard the whole story of the assault on Mrs. Massie.

The main interest of the trial was the testimony of Lieutenant Massie and that of his wife. As I recall it now, each of these witnesses was on the stand for two days. The stories were so intense and tragic that people left the courtroom completely overwhelmed, and many of them in tears.

At one point of the cross-examination, a paper was handed to Mrs. Massie for identification. She was asked if the paper bore her signature. All of Mrs. Massie's counsel knew what the document was. Several months before the assault, or the trial of the assailants, she had taken a course at the University of Honolulu; in this course the students were asked to psychoanalyze themselves in writing. Mrs. Massie prepared her story and gave it to the professor. She answered the questions honestly and clearly. The students had been told that the communications were to be treated in absolute confidence. I never knew, or asked, what was on that paper. We never expected to meet it in court.

Mrs. Massie read the paper in her hand, and in answer to the question told the attorney general that it was a privileged communication, at the same time proceeding to tear it to ribbons and then to little bits so that it could not possibly be put together. The action caused a profound sensation in the courtroom. Neither lawyers nor judge said anything whatever; they seemed too dazed to utter a sound. Mrs. Massie walked away from the witness-chair to where her husband sat at the side of

the other defendants, slipped her arm about his neck and wept
aloud on his shoulder most pitifully. Many others in the courtroom had to resort to their handkerchiefs. Every one seemed
to be on her side; they felt that it was an outrage that a matter
of this nature should be dragged forth in court, and all admired and approved her courage in tearing up the paper beyond further use. Personally, I did not consider it of special
importance one way or another; I certainly did not feel that it
hurt our case.

I have listened to a great many witnesses in courts. I cannot
recall any whose testimony was more impressive than that of
Lieutenant Thomas H. Massie and his wife, Thalia. The realization of the torture they had been compelled to endure,
through no fault of their own, could not but make a profound
impression among the islanders and the mainland public as
well. I am sure their release was due to this more than anything else. From the nature of the case, there was nothing we
could do but bring home to people, so far as possible, the inherent rightness of our clients, and the human element and
action in it all.

Mrs. Massie was not a party to the trial. It was simply a
question of what a husband and mother were justified in doing
under the circumstances of the case. It was a contest over the
question of whether it was a duty of one to obey the dead
letter of the law, or the living emotions upon which all life
rests. I have heard few people seriously say that they would
not have done the same thing in either situation as husband
or mother. Whatever the husband's feelings, they are not so
interwoven with living as the mother's. All animal life depends alike upon the instincts of the mother, and automatically
she forgets herself in protecting the life of the offspring. The
emotion is not wholly love; it is biological. The life of the
mother cannot be considered as against the child, among humans any more than in other species. It is true that men have

provided by statute that the unborn child may be sacrificed to save the mother, but this is a human statute, and has nothing to do with the deep instincts that preserve the species.

This principle did not apply to the two sailors, of course; these two young men acted from a sense of loyalty and devotion, and their names were scarcely mentioned in the case. I felt certain that no jury would convict them if they acquitted the others.

Seldom have I known a case where there was less conflict in the evidence. There really was nothing to be denied. The law was on the side of the State; life, and all the human qualities that preserve it, was with us. All we could do was to dramatize it as best we could. In this we had a great advantage: it was a gripping story, not only in Honolulu, but in the United States, whose press sent over many representatives. The story lent itself to publicity, touching, as it did, the deepest emotions and questions; and on all sides one heard how individuals and groups felt, and what *they* would have done. Really, people are much alike when one gets beneath the crust.

It is safe to say that when the case went to the jury every one expected an acquittal, and looked for it soon; the reporters who followed the proceedings, word for word, felt confident that the jury could not but acquit.

But Judge Davis had told the jury in a dozen different ways that they must not be human; the law allowed them to think, but did not permit them to feel, in spite of the fact that they were born to feel. No one expects the law to be human, but it must be logical though the heavens fall, and all the earth with it.

The case had been submitted to the jury. The afternoon wore on, and no verdict, although rumors were humming as to how the matter stood. Every one declared that the majority of the jurors were for the defense. In fact, either seven or eight of them were, at first; but, they were shut in and locked up for the night without agreeing on a verdict. Nearly two days drifted away, people more and more awaiting an acquittal.

At last we went to the courthouse to receive the verdict; but it was not an acquittal. The jury returned a verdict of manslaughter, with a recommendation for leniency. We could hardly believe that we had heard aright! Mrs. Massie shook with sobs. Lieutenant Massie tried to console her. Mrs. Fortescue sat bolt upright, her face as unemotional as Fate itself. She seemed not to think or feel, but she was doing both; but the jury and the spectators must not detect it, and they did not.

I arose and asked that the jury be polled. I have done this and heard it done, for more than fifty years. I have not yet found one juryman who did not answer that it was and is now his verdict. Of all the senseless acts of men, none is so useless as polling a jury. Afterwards, the different members began to assure us that they were sorry for the verdict, but could not help themselves; they had to follow the instructions of the court. This, too, I had heard before. That alibi was old when Moses crossed the Red Sea, or where the Red Sea was; at least, it was old then if they had jury trials in those days, which they did not, when Moses was around.

The two sailor boys asked if it meant that they were all going to prison. I replied that it looked that way just then. Then we all began preparing alibis, as lawyers always do. I indicated that I was the only one who needed an alibi, as they had let me try the case practically alone. We finally agreed that the judge was to blame. This is always a first-rate alibi: the judge should not have instructed them so much on the side of the State; judges should talk awhile on our side, and then on the other. Then we wondered how he came to do as he did, for we all agreed that he was a good fellow, and would have acted the same as our clients did under similar circumstances. Then we sighed, and modified it, and said that anyhow he would have acted the same way if he had not been a judge.

But, soon we calmed down, and realized that the problem to determine was what to do about it. There were several turns we might take. We could appeal to another court. This one can always do, and then be beaten again. It was also suggested that we wait awhile, until we heard from the public. We heard right away. The whole world seemed up in arms: what?— send men and women to prison just because they violated a law?—when every one knew that any one would have done as these people did, if they had the courage.

We waited a day; we waited two days. The jurors began openly explaining how they did not want to do it; they had been with our side from the start, but the judge's instructions did the mischief. The third day, the attorney general came to see me; the prosecution did not like the verdict; he said the governor could help us out if he wanted to, which we admitted would be fine. After several conferences it was arranged that the governor should pardon our clients. Then, it was said, he would commute the sentence to one hour in the office of the high sheriff. I had seen the high sheriff and thought he was all right—for a sheriff. What was the difference, I asked, between a pardon and a commutation? Well, the governor wanted a commutation. I pointed out that there was quite a difference, but, anyhow, we were pretty well satisfied, either way.

To be sure, we knew that our clients might be deprived of their citizenship; but, none of them had ever voted, anyhow; three of them lived on the high seas, where no one votes, and the other was a woman who lived in Washington, D. C., and so was disqualified. We knew that if ever we wanted a pardon we would get it, as we have, in the case of Lieutenant Massie. At any rate, no one went to prison, and no one paid a fine.

This commutation was exercised by Governor Judd of Hawaii. The Governor of Hawaii is appointed by the President of the United States. I had not met the governor until we talked about the pardon or commutation. He seemed to be a very fine fellow, but, all governors seem that way. All the same, he took a heavy load off my mind at that particular time, although I am certain that it was not the governor but the public that was responsible for the commutation of the sentence. I do not believe it would have been granted at the time save for the almost universal demand from America, and the general sentiment all over the world.

I feel that I know why and how the jury found the verdict. A jury of white men would have acquitted. This in no way prejudices me against the brown section of Hawaii; they feel that the white men get everything but a few offices. This feeling does not originate from any dissatisfaction about special individuals, as a rule, but comes from the obvious fact that the whites have most of the land and money; the brown men just think it isn't fair; and so do I. Like them, I do not know what can be done about it, now; probably nothing at all. Our clients were white, and a white jury no doubt would have acquitted them almost without argument; and I think it should have been done so. At that, I believe that the brown members wanted to be fair; there were Chinamen in the jury box, and Japanese, and Hawaiian and mixed bloods; it was not easy to guess what they were thinking about, if anything at all. Obviously, they do not think as we do, about our side of a situation. And it must be remembered that the judge instructed them so positively that it left little leeway. They were given three verdicts to choose from: murder in the second degree, or manslaughter, or not guilty. They returned a verdict of manslaughter, and of their own accord agreed to add a clause asking the court to be lenient.

To show that all the brown men did not view the case in the same light, I must state that the last man to consent to the verdict was a man whose wife is a Hawaiian, and who is himself half Hawaiian, and I must add that the other half of him is Scotch. This latter may account for his staunch effort to stick to his own convictions. I was informed, but cannot state it as a fact, that every one of the jurors asked Governor Judd to commute the sentence.

The governor was very kind and considerate, after commuting the sentences. He told us that he had a business appointment and had to leave, but that we might as well stay in his office until the high sheriff was ready to take us down to Pearl Harbor, the naval headquarters. Although I had expected some such sequel, it was with a sense of great relief that I returned to the Alexander Young Hotel; and my clients went back to their quarters.

There was nothing left of the case excepting to advise Mrs. Massie what to do regarding the further prosecution of her assailants. Mr. Massie and his associates were given a leave of absence to rest from their strenuous life and recent experiences, and then, with other marines, were ordered to report at a base on the mainland.

If the prosecution of the assault case was to go on, Mrs. Massie must remain in Honolulu alone for an indefinite period. She longed to come back home after the trying ordeals there. Some of her friends urged her to stay and fight it out to the end. Without the least hesitation, I advised her to come home with us when we left the island; she had been forced to tell her painful story twice in court, the second time to all the world that cared to listen, an experience that no twenty-year-old girl could go through without horror. In the first prosecution of the assailants the jury had disagreed owing to the corruption in the police force, which had since been remedied. Still, the harm had been done, and no one could expect the testimony to be much different from the first. Then, since the first trial, the killing had occurred, and the defendants were freed; I knew it would be futile to go over it all again. I did not think that Mrs. Massie should or could go through the strain again. I thought that for the good of my clients, and the peace of the island that I had learned to love, even the memory of it all should be forgotten as soon as possible. I was sure the State wanted no further trouble and would be glad to get rid of the case if Mrs. Massie did not stay. My opinion, which was supported by the other lawyers in the case, prevailed; and we all sailed away together.

I had been asked by the attorney general if I would come into the case with him and his associates to help prosecute the assailants of Mrs. Massie, for which I was offered a fee; but I explained that I never had prosecuted any one, and it was too late for me to begin now.

I felt, as we went away, that we were leaving the island more peaceful and happy than I had found it, for which I was very glad. I left without any feeling of enmity toward any person there, and I hope that those whom I met, at least, held none toward me.

It is quite possible that discerning readers may guess that I like Hawaii, particularly Honolulu, and Oahu, on which that beautiful city is built. I admit that I do. I have missed few opportunities to see the world. The beauty-spots of Europe are almost as familiar to me as those of my own land; but from the morning when I opened my eyes to see Diamond Head towering from the soft South Seas, standing guard, with its huge light at its pinnacle, over this picturesque place, to the afternoon when I slowly floated away, watching Diamond Head fade from my sight, lost in the mist, I loved Honolulu and the island that it adorns.

I realize that many things enter into one's likes and dislikes of people and places, and I am aware that everything somehow seemed to conspire to impress me with the beauty and charm of this land; somehow, I have never seen such a gem as Oahu, rising from the mighty ocean that rolls over the coral reefs, to wash the shores of that fairyland. Her gentle mountains, her tropical forestry, her warm, hospitable people, and the perfume of flowers in varieties unlike anything I have found anywhere else will be among my most lasting and pleasing memories.

How kind and friendly people were! I dare not attempt to speak of them individually, for it is not easy to say that one impressed me more than another; but some portraits are indelibly etched upon my brain, and some pictures will reappear and delight me to the last of my days. I would like very much to go back, to see and enjoy it all once more, as it is. And I should like to find it still more enchanting in that Nature specially fitted this magic spot to help work out the old problem of race with its loves, its hatreds, its hopes and fears. It seems fit that the Hawaiian Islands, basking in the great sea between the oldest and newest civilizations of the world, might one day lead the union of the diverse races of man. I would like to believe that this favored land might prove to be the place where the only claim to aristocracy would be the devotion to justice and truth and a real fellowship on earth.

Perhaps I am only dreaming about Honolulu. But whether asleep or awake, I trust I may see it all again. I would so much like to go and visit once more a genial and wise physician whose inviting home nestles in a wooded garden, with a roomy front porch facing the Pacific only a few steps away; he was always glad to see me, and sometimes I stole away from the stress and strain of court and contention to rest and talk, and even listen, about the endless problems that have ever been too deep and complicated for the minds of men. From there, I would like to gaze again upon those wonderful waters that have come almost a third of the distance around the earth to greet and charm me. I would like once more to watch the rows upon rows of waves as they dash into foam and iridescent colors over the coral reefs that protect the shore.

I would like once more to lounge in those beguiling easy-chairs on the broad veranda on the shore of that benign isle, and bathe in the silver spray and hear the siren song of those soft, caressing waves at my very feet, as they elusively come and go.

I hope I shall see Honolulu again, its palms, its Pali and Diamond Head, its flowers and friends—and if I weary of too much beauty and joy, I may steal, once more, to the shelter of that veranda beside the sea for a still longer siesta in the shade of the cocoanut trees, close my eyes to all else, rest my mind from thinking, let the lull of the salt breeze soothe my senses, and mayhap sweetly dream that I am softly sailing out over the languorous Pacific, midst showers of "liquid sunshine"— surrounded by daylight and moonlight rainbows—never to come back again.

APPENDIX

JOHN P. ALTGELD

In the great flood of human life that is spawned upon the earth, it is not often that a man is born. The friend and comrade that we mourn to-day was formed of that infinitely rare mixture that now and then at long, long intervals combines to make a man. John P. Altgeld was one of the rarest souls who ever lived and died. His was a humble birth, a fearless life and a dramatic, fitting death. We who knew him, we who loved him, we who rallied to his many hopeless calls, we who dared to praise him while his heart still beat, cannot yet feel that we shall never hear his voice again.

John P. Altgeld was a soldier tried and true; not a soldier clad in uniform, decked with spangles and led by fife and drum in the mad intoxication of the battle-field; such soldiers have not been rare upon the earth in any land or age. John P. Altgeld was a soldier in the everlasting struggle of the human race for liberty and justice on the earth. From the first awakening of his young mind until the last relentless summons came, he was a soldier who had no rest or furlough, who was ever on the field in the forefront of the deadliest and most hopeless fight, whom none but death could muster out. Liberty, the relentless goddess, had turned her fateful smile on John P. Altgeld's face when he was but a child, and to this first, fond love he was faithful unto death.

Liberty is the most jealous and exacting mistress that can beguile the brain and soul of man. She will have nothing from him who will not give her all. She knows that his pretended love serves but to betray. But when once the fierce heat of her quenchless, lustrous eyes has burned into the victim's heart, he will know no other smile but hers. Liberty will have none but the great devoted souls, and by her glorious visions, her lavish promises, her boundless hopes, her infinitely witching charms, she lures her victims over hard and stony ways, by desolate and dangerous paths, through misery, obloquy and want to a martyr's cruel death. To-day we pay our last sad homage to the most devoted lover, the most abject slave, the fondest, wildest, dreamiest victim that ever gave his life to liberty's immortal cause.

In the history of the country where he lived and died, the life and works of our devoted dead will one day shine in words of everlasting light. When the bitter feelings of the hour have passed away, when the mad and poisonous fever of commercialism shall have run its course, when conscience and honor and justice and liberty shall once more ascend the throne from which the shameless, brazen goddess of power and wealth have driven her away; then this man we knew and loved will find his rightful place in the minds and hearts of the cruel, unwilling world he served. No purer patriot ever lived than the friend we lay at rest to-day. His love of country was not paraded in the public marts, or bartered in the stalls for gold; his patriotism was of that pure ideal mold that placed the love of man above the love of self.

John P. Altgeld was always and at all times a lover of his fellow man. Those who reviled him have tried to teach the world that he was bitter and relentless, that he hated more than loved. We who knew the man, we who had clasped his hand and heard his voice and looked into his smiling face; we who knew his life of kindness, of charity, of infinite pity to the outcast and the weak; we who knew his human heart, could never be deceived. A truer, greater, gentler, kindlier soul has never lived and died; and the fierce bitterness and hatred that sought to destroy this great, grand soul had but one cause—the fact that he really loved his fellow man.

As a youth our dead chieftain risked his life for the cause of the black man, whom he always loved. As a lawyer he was wise and learned; impatient with the forms and machinery which courts and legislators and lawyers have woven to strangle justice through expense and ceremony and delay; as a judge he found a legal way to do what seemed right to him, and if he could not find a legal way, he found a way. As a Governor of a great State, he ruled wisely and well. Elected by the greatest personal triumph of any Governor ever chosen by the State, he fearlessly and knowingly bared his devoted head to the fiercest, most vindictive criticism ever heaped upon a public man, because he loved justice and dared to do the right.

In the days now past, John P. Altgeld, our loving chief, in scorn and derision was called John Pardon Altgeld by those who would destroy his power. We who stand to-day around his bier and mourn the brave and loving friend are glad to adopt this name. If, in the infinite economy of nature, there shall be another land where crooked paths shall be made straight, where heaven's justice shall review the judgments of the earth—if there shall be a great, wise, humane judge, before whom the sons of men shall come, we can hope for nothing better for ourselves than to pass into that infinite presence as the comrades and friends of John Pardon Altgeld, who opened the prison doors and set the captive free.

Even admirers have seldom understood the real character of this great human man. These were sometimes wont to feel that the fierce bitterness of the world that assailed him fell on deaf ears and an unresponsive soul. They did not know the man, and they do not feel the subtleties of human life. It was not a callous heart that so often led him to brave the most violent and malicious hate; it was not a callous heart, it was a devoted soul. He so loved justice and truth and liberty and righteousness that all the terrors that the earth could hold were less than the condemnation of his own conscience for an act that was cowardly or mean.

John P. Altgeld, like many of the earth's great souls, was a solitary man. Life to him was serious and earnest—an endless tragedy. The earth was a great hospital of sick, wounded and suffering, and he a devoted surgeon, who had no right to waste one moment's time and whose duty was to cure them all. While he loved his friends, he yet could work without them, he could live without them, he could bid them one by one good-bye, when their courage failed to follow where he led; and he could go alone, out into the silent night, and, looking upward at the changeless stars, could find communion there.

My dear, dead friend, long and well have we known you, devotedly have we followed you, implicitly have we trusted you, fondly have we loved you. Beside your bier we now must say farewell. The heartless call has come, and we must stagger on the best we can alone. In the darkest hours we will look in vain for your loved form, we will listen hopelessly for your devoted, fearless voice. But, though we lay you in the grave and hide you from the sight of man, your brave words will speak for the poor, the oppressed, the captive and the weak; and your devoted life inspire countless souls to do and dare in the holy cause for which you lived and died.

INDEX